PERCEIVING, SENSING, AND KNOWING

TOPICS IN PHILOSOPHY

PERCEIVING, SENSING, AND KNOWING

A BOOK OF READINGS
FROM TWENTIETH-CENTURY SOURCES
IN THE PHILOSOPHY OF PERCEPTION

EDITED, WITH AN INTRODUCTION BY
ROBERT J. SWARTZ

UNIVERSITY OF CALIFORNIA PRESS
Berkeley   Los Angeles   London

#4737887

University of California Press, Ltd.
London, England

ISBN: 0-520-02986-0
Library of Congress Catalog Card Number: 75-3778
Copyright © 1965 by Robert J. Swartz

Printed in the United States of America

2 3 4 5 6 7 8 9

ACKNOWLEDGMENTS

Acknowledgment is gratefully made to the following publishers, editors, and authors for permission to include previously published material:

To the Aristotelian Society (A. A. Kassman, Honorary Secretary and Editor) for the following essays from the *Proceedings of the Aristotelian Society:* "The Myth of Sense-Data," by W. H. F. Barnes (XLV, 1944–45); "Some Judgments of Perception," by G. E. Moore (XIX, 1918–19); "Seeing and Seeing As," by G. N. A. Vesey (LVI, 1955–56), and "Seeing," by G. J. Warnock (LV, 1954–55); and for the following from the *Supplementary Volume:* "The Causal Theory of Perception," by H. P. Grice (XXXV, 1961), and "Is There a Problem About Sense-Data?" by G. A. Paul (XV, 1936).

To the Directors of *The Journal of Philosophy,* Professors Chisholm and Firth, and Mrs. C. I. Lewis, for "The Problem of Empiricism" (XLV, 1948) and "'Appear,' 'Take,' and 'Evident'" (LIII, 1956), both by Roderick M. Chisholm; "Ultimate Evidence," by Roderick Firth (LIII, 1956), and "Professor Chisholm and Empiricism," by C. I. Lewis (XLV, 1948).

To the editor of *Mind* and the authors for "Empirical Propositions and Hypothetical Statements," by Sir Isaiah Berlin (LIX, 1950); "Sense-Data and the Percept Theory," by Roderick Firth (LVIII, 1949, LIX, 1950), and "The Problem of Perception," by A. M. Quinton (LXIV, 1955).

To the editor of *Philosophy* and the author for "Some Elementary Reflexions on Sense-Perception" by C. D. Broad (Vol. 27, 1952).

To George Allen & Unwin Ltd., London, and The Macmillan Company, New York, for "Visual Sense-Data," by G. E. Moore, reprinted from *British Philosophy in the Mid-Century,* C. A. Mace, ed., Copyright 1957 by George Allen & Unwin Ltd., and "Sensation," by Gilbert Ryle, reprinted from *Contemporary British Philosophy, Third Series,* H. D. Lewis, ed., first published 1956.

To Routledge & Kegan Paul Ltd., London, and Hillary House Publishers Ltd., New York, and the author, for an excerpt from *Scientific Thought,* by C. D. Broad, first published in 1923.

To Prentice-Hall, Inc., Englewood Cliffs, New Jersey, for "The Theory of Appearing," by Roderick M. Chisholm, reprinted from *Philosophical Analysis,* Max Black, ed., Copyright © 1963. First published in 1950.

To The Open Court Publishing Company, LaSalle, Illinois, for Chapter VIII, Book II of *An Analysis of Knowledge and Valuation,* by C. I. Lewis, first published 1946.

To Methuen & Co. Ltd., London, for "The Causal Theory," reprinted from *Perception,* by H. H. Price, first published in 1932.

CONTENTS

IV. PERCEPTION AND
EMPIRICAL KNOWLEDGE

CONTRIBUTORS

WINSTON H. F. BARNES (1909—   ) formerly taught at the universities of Durham and Edinburgh, and was the Sir Samuel Hall Professor of Philosophy at the University of Manchester until 1973. He is author of *The Philosophical Predicament.*

SIR ISAIAH BERLIN (1909—   ) has taught at Harvard University, Bryn Mawr College, Oxford University, and the City University of New York. He is presently President of Wolfson College, Oxford, and President of the British Academy. His publications include *Historical Inevitability, Two Concepts of Liberty, The Hedgehog and The Fox, Karl Marx, The Age of Enlightenment, and Fathers and Children.*

CHARLIE DUNBAR BROAD (1887—1971) was a Fellow of Trinity College, Cambridge, and Professor Emeritus of Moral Philosophy at Cambridge. His chief publications are *Perception, Physics, and Reality; Scientific Thought; The Mind and Its Place in Nature; An Examination of McTaggart's Philosophy;* and *Five Types of Ethical Theory.*

RODERICK M. CHISHOLM (1916—   ) is Elton Professor of Natural Theology at Brown University. His books include *Perceiving: A Philosophical Study, Realism and the Background of Phenomenology,* and *Theory of Knowledge.*

RODERICK FIRTH (1916—   ) has taught at the College of William and Mary and at Swarthmore College and is now Alford Professor of Natural Religion and Civil Polity at Harvard University.

H. P. GRICE (1913—   ) was a fellow of St. John's College, Oxford, and is presently Professor of Philosophy at the University of California at Berkeley.

CLARENCE IRVING LEWIS (1883—1964) was the Edgar Pierce Professor of Philosophy at Harvard University. His principal works are *Mind and the World Order, A Survey of Symbolic Logic, Symbolic Logic* (with C. H. Langford), *An Analysis of Knowledge and Valuation,* and *The Ground and Nature of the Right.*

GEORGE EDWARD MOORE (1873—1958) was Professor of Philosophy at Cambridge and a Fellow of Trinity College. His publications include *Principia Ethica, Ethics, Philosophical Studies, Some Main Problems of Philosophy, Philosophical Papers,* and *Commonplace Book.*

GEORGE A. PAUL (1912—1962) was a Fellow of University College, Oxford.

HENRY HABBERLEY PRICE (1899—   ) is Wynkeham Professor Emeritus of Logic at Oxford and a Fellow Emeritus of New College. His books include *Perception, Hume's Theory of the External World, Thinking and Experience, Belief,* and *Essays in the Philosophy of Religion.*

ANTHONY M. QUINTON (1926—   ) is a Fellow of New College, Oxford.

GILBERT RYLE (1900—   ) is Waynflete Professor of Metaphysical Philosophy Emeritus at Oxford and Honorary Fellow at Magdalen and Queen's Colleges, Oxford. He is author of *The Concept of Mind, Dilemmas,* and *Plato's Progress.* He was also editor of *Mind* from 1947-71.

GODFREY N. A. VESEY (1923—   ) was Lecturer at King's College, University of London, and is presently a Professor of Philosophy at the British Open University. He is author of *The Embodied Mind* and *Body and Mind.*

GEOFFREY J. WARNOCK (1923—   ) was a fellow of Magdalen College, Oxford, and is presently the Principal of Hertford College, Oxford. His publications include *Berkeley, English Philosophy since 1900, Contemporary Moral Philosophy,* and *The Object of Morality.*

INTRODUCTION

This is a collection of philosophical works concerned with perception and its role in the acquisition of knowledge. The selections included have been chosen to reflect the predominant attitudes of English-speaking philosophers in this century toward the traditional problems of perception.

To most of us, in our ordinary day-to-day frame of mind, perception is hardly problematic. We are all intimately acquainted with the experiences of seeing, hearing, feeling, smelling, and tasting, and we accept certain basic facts about these experiences as indisputable. Though we are generally ignorant of the physiological processes that result in perception, we feel that there can be no question that we perceive things and events in the external world, and that, in most ordinary circumstances, our senses can be trusted to reveal the external world to us in the way it is. But philosophers, for the most part, have found these dictates of common sense not as obviously true as we assume. Some have felt that they are simply mistaken—that we are confused about perception; while others who have felt that they could be established have usually required a substantial amount of philosophical theory to do so. But even if they are obviously true, there is still the matter of filling in their details. Just what does the perception of things, as we experience it, involve? And what guarantees the reliability of the senses? Most of the issues in the philosophy of perception arise out of different attempts to answer these questions.

The problems about perception that are discussed in this volume have their roots in a tradition of thinking about the senses, their functioning, and their trustworthiness that is an offspring of postrenaissance philosophy. I would like to comment on this tradition to help set the points of view expressed here in context and perspective.

It is incontestable that sense-perception plays a crucial role in the natural sciences. It serves as the sole means through which we can gather information about the world around us. Knowledge of general laws is posterior, in the empirical sciences, to knowledge of particular instances, and for the latter the evidence of the senses is required. If the natural sciences have promise of advancing human knowledge, this promise must be rooted in a trust in the veracity of the senses. But mere faith in the senses is not enough. It must be shown that observation, accommodated to circumstance and condition, can lead to reasonable and true judgments. This is, of course, a problem not only about scientific judgments, but also about many of our everyday commonsense beliefs; but it was the early development of the sciences that provided the impetus for the rethinking of matters connected with perception and knowledge. The result was a strong current of philosophical thought about the rational foundations of empirical knowledge and a fundamental approach to perception that, in large part, is peculiar to and has permeated western philosophy since the seventeenth century.

The first mature expressions of this approach appear in the philosophies of Descartes and the British Empiricists, Locke, Berkeley, and Hume. Their reflections about perception and knowledge typically begin with questions about the reliability of the senses. We all claim to know things about objects and events in the external world through the use of the senses. But do we really know these things? For a belief to be knowledge it must not only be true, but rationally justified; yet isn't the evidence we have for our empirical beliefs at any given time compatible with their falsity? Couldn't they all be mistaken? And, in fact, does what the senses provide us justify us even in the slightest in believing what we do about the external world? Skeptical challenges of this sort were, of course, not new in philosophy, and the seventeenth- and eighteenth-century thinkers who were faced with them took them in the usual way: as challenges to show what rational basis empirical beliefs have. To meet these they undertook both the more ambitious program of showing that we could achieve certainty with respect to these beliefs, and the less ambitious one of showing that there are good, though perhaps not perfect, grounds for them. It is in the way that they dealt with this fundamental epistemological problem about the justification of our empirical beliefs—a way dictated largely by their views on perception—that these modern philosophers differ from their predecessors.

How can beliefs about the external world gain rational assurance? Seventeenth- and eighteenth-century thinkers, on the whole, had the same views about this class of beliefs that many twentieth-century thinkers have. The rational assurance any one of these beliefs has for some individual (if it has any at all) can be derived neither from some intrinsic feature of the proposition believed, nor from its immediate acceptance in perceptual situations, but rather must come from its relations, by valid principles of inference, to other rationally acceptable beliefs. Propositions about external things are contingent, not necessary, but what was crucial for these early philosophers was the belief that, in contrast to statements like "I am in pain," they are not capable of immediate and noninferential justification. Put in these terms, the basic epistemological problem they attempted to solve was whether there was any information that a person had available to him, or any other beliefs that he had, that did, or at least could, lend credibility to his beliefs about the external world. The most promising circumstance for the existence of such support is in perception, so the first thing asked was whether there is anything provided us in perception that can lend rational assurance to the beliefs we form about the external world. This was usually construed as a question about the nature of the "evidence of the senses"—whether what we *do* form these beliefs on the basis of does lend credibility to them—though sometimes it was taken as a question about the possibility of *providing* a rational basis for our empirical beliefs.

There are many ways of trying to answer these questions, but most of them proved to be unsatisfactory to seventeenth- and eighteenth-century epistemologists. For example, one might want to appeal to other beliefs of the same kind in support of some particular belief about the external world that is called in question. But the standard reply to this was that these other beliefs could be challenged in the same way. Perhaps a more natural answer would be to appeal to the fact that we do perceive certain things. "Of course we know things about material objects and events in the external world because these are what we see, hear, feel, taste, and smell." But this type of answer is unsatisfactory also: the same kinds of skeptical doubts can be raised about it. To get the process of rational justification started at all it was thought that what must be found is something in perception that is immediately and *noninferentially* credible; and this usually meant that it had to be immune from doubt, something of which we could be absolutely certain. Once this is found there remains a question as to whether our beliefs about the external world can be based on it in a way that insures that *they* are rationally warranted. For example, it is not sufficient to show that we *actually form* our beliefs on this information, or that we can; rather, it must be shown that these beliefs can be *rationally derived* from this information—a logical matter. But the first step to be taken is to inquire whether there is anything in perceptual situations that is immune from doubt.

This was usually approached by considering how things appear to us, as opposed to the way they really are. We seem incapable of error, or at least doubt, about the former, whereas we do not about the latter. For example, we may entertain doubts about the truth of our judgments about the *real* colors and shapes of material objects, but it seems impossible to be in doubt about the colors and shapes that objects appear to be, the textures they appear to have, etc. But are these apparent colors (etc.)—the basic contents of our perceptual experience—qualities of things that exist in the external world? If they are then we can be certain of something, at least, about the external world in perception.

The usual answer to this question was that they are not. Many reasons, sometimes quite complex ones, were offered in support of this, but the most famous of the arguments of seventeenth- and eighteenth-century philosophers is one that many twentieth-century philosophers rely on as well: the argument from illusion. It involves a consideration of deceptive perceptual phenomena—illusions, hallucinations, and the like—and, in general, the disparities that can exist between the way things appear and the way they are. Things that exist in the external world can appear different to different people, or to the same person, under dissimilar conditions, even though the objects do not change at all. If apparent qualities were qualities of external objects, then these objects would have contradictory qualities at the same time. But this is impossible. How, then, can these qualities be qualities of external objects? Furthermore, how can the objects themselves be part of the content of our perceptual experiences? Couldn't what is really present to our minds in perception exist even though there were no external world at all? Surely in a dream or hallucination we can have the same kind of experience—one identical in content—that we have now, when reading this page. Hence, our perceptual beliefs and judgments about things and their qualities in the external world go beyond the content of the experience of perceiving itself. This explains why these beliefs are not self-justifying—why they require inferential support if they are to be credible.

But what are the contents of perceptual experience? What ontological status should we assign to them? What we are supposed to be incapable of error about in perception is the existence of certain kinds of *qualities*—called "sensible qualities." These were thought to exist only when we are aware of them and some philosophers felt that they serve to differentiate perceiving from other psychological processes, as well as the different senses from one another. The colors we are aware of when we see things are essential to the experience of seeing and, as such, do not exist in the external world. But what are these sensible qualities qualities of? What is the object of sense-experience if not a material thing? Numerous answers have been suggested. Some have spoken as if nothing but particular instances of the sensible qualities themselves are present in sense-experience; others have maintained that sensible qualities are qualities that belong to the state of mind of sense-experience itself, the *manner* with which we have these experiences. But by far the most popular answer has been that they are qualities belonging to a special kind of object, variously called a sense-impression, a sensation, or an idea. This object of sense-experience does not exist in the external world but is supposed to enter into, and depend for its existence on our consciousness whenever we see, hear, feel, taste, or smell things. It is this view that is most often cited by contemporary sense-datum theorists as the main predecessor of their position (though not all twentieth-century philosophers who utilize the sense-datum *terminology* have committed themselves to such an act-object analysis of sense-experience). Finally, most philosophers have suggested that our relation to these contents is a cognitive relation. Having a sense-experience entails *knowing* its content. Perception was considered to involve the presence of a mental state divorced in its content from the external world, of which we are immediately and noninferentially cognizant whenever it occurs.

The point of this theory—though it is sometimes stated in a very misleading way—is *not* that it is a mistake to think we perceive things in the external world. Sometimes the British Empiricists seem to be claiming this—that it is *false* to say that we perceive material objects. Rather, the point is a more subtle one. It is that the perception of things in the external world is not what we tend to think it is—a *direct* apprehension of a sort that provides at least some beliefs about the external world with immediate justification *independent* of their relations to other beliefs. The idea that is being combatted is that perception is a confrontation of man with the external world in which he can simply read off the character of what he perceives directly. What is argued is that the perception of things is a much more complex phenomenon than we ordinarily suppose: it involves a basic experience whose content is distinct from anything in the external world, but which is related to the external world in certain definite ways. To make this distinction clearer some philosophers have employed a different terminology in speaking of sense-experience from the terminology they employ when they speak of perception—for example, Berkeley often states his view by claiming that it is a mistake to think that we *immediately perceive* things in the external world, and he often goes out of the way to tell his readers that in saying this he does not want to deny that what we *perceive* are the familiar objects we think we are perceiving, the chairs and tables about us. Many contemporary philosophers who share this view make the point by saying that what is being offered in this theory of perception is an *analysis* of the perception of things, *not* a theory that implies that we do not perceive things in the external world. Contemporary sense-datum theorists, for example, maintain that sense-data are the objects of sensing, not of perceiving. The objects of perceiving are still thought to be the things in the external world we claim to see, feel, etc. Sensing a sense-datum is a necessary, though not a sufficient, condition for perceiving things.

Once perception is conceived in this way, the basic problem about empirical knowledge that we began with requires rephrasing in something like the following way: Is the relation between the contents of sense-experience and the external world such that it allows us validly to infer from one to the other? Our beliefs about the external world are based on our sense-experiences, but go beyond them; and this was usually taken to mean that they were *inferred* from our immediate knowledge of the content of sense-experience. But whether or not this view about the *genesis* of our empirical beliefs is correct, the question remains whether empirical beliefs *can be validly inferred* from our knowledge of the contents of our sense-experiences. To decide whether such an inference is a valid one, it is first necessary to find out the relation between sense-experience and the objects of perceptual judgments, the things and events in the external world we claim to know about on the basis of sense-experience.

Traditional philosophers have taken two main positions about sense-experience and material objects: the causal theory and phenomenalism. The causal theory is a view closely allied to the scientific conception of material objects, and many feel it is the most natural position to adopt once the traditional theory of perception is accepted. It is that material objects are things which exist apart from sense-experiences, but which *causally determine* the content of these experiences. The classical statement of this view is found in Locke's representative theory, though there are many subtly different versions of it. Phenomenalism is usually associated with J. S. Mill and the nineteenth-century positivist Mach, though an earlier version of it can be found in the writings of Berkeley. In Berkeley's works phenomenalism was adopted to remedy what he thought were irremediable defects in Locke's causal theory, and to explain how knowledge of external things is possible. It is primarily the view that material things are *nothing but* bundles of actual and possible sense-impressions or sensations—"permanent possibilities of sensation," as Mill put it.

Both theories dictate different conceptions of the nature of the inference from sense-experience to external things. On the causal theory it was usually thought that beliefs about the external world could be supported by a straightforward causal inference in which the existence of sense-experiences of certain kinds provides good inductive grounds for certain of these beliefs. The standard empiricist critique of the causal theory—stated very forcefully in Berkeley and Hume—is that knowledge of the contents of sense-experiences cannot provide good inductive grounds for believing propositions about external objects, and that, in fact, the theory leads to skepticism. There can be no basis *in experience* for this type of inference, since material things are thought to exist beyond experience. Furthermore, if one attempts to secure the legitimacy of the inference by adding further premises, as Descartes attempted to do, one will be forced to add premises that are not rationally justified. Hence, if empirical knowledge is to be shown to be possible, one must adopt some other position about sense-experience and material things that is in accord with the facts and that will allow rational support to be conferred on beliefs about material objects by our knowledge of our sense-experiences. The alternative position usually adopted was, of course, phenomenalism. One of the main concerns of more recent causal theorists has been to formulate the causal theory in such a way as to avoid this type of criticism, although some philosophers have been more inclined to reject the strict empiricist principles on which the objection is based.

If one accepts phenomenalism, then beliefs about the external world, to be rationally founded, must also be based on inferences from occurrent sense-experiences; but these inferences are construed as inferences to other possible sense-experiences, are usually considered probabilistic in character, and their validity is conceived to depend on premises about the regular association of sense-experiences in the past. If the predicted experiences actually occur then, supposedly, further verification of the belief is obtained, and its probability increases. In this century the more subtle details of phenomenalism have been worked out, and though there have been a number of different versions of this view, they all share common ancestors in the theories of some of the earlier empiricists.

On most traditional and contemporary versions of these theories, even though the structure of the inference required to justify beliefs about the external world is construed in various ways, it is still maintained that ultimate appeal to knowledge of actual sense-experiences is necessary for the justification of these beliefs. Those who feel that this inference can be valid when based *only* on knowledge of present and past sense-experience (the latter obtained via memory experiences) subscribe to one of the dogmas of both traditional and contemporary *empiricism,* although there has been some disagreement among traditional empiricists as to whether such an inference, founded solely on premises about sense-experience, can ever assure the certainty of beliefs about external objects. Most contemporary empiricists accept a probabilistic account of empirical knowledge. There have, of course, been some non-empiricists who subscribe to the thesis that it is necessary to appeal to knowledge of sense-experiences to justify beliefs about the external world, but who have felt that further *nonempirical* premises are required to make the inference rationally acceptable; and there have been philosophers who accept the theory of perception that I have outlined, but who adopt the skeptical position that there can be *no rational ground* for believing propositions about external objects on the basis of sense-experience, even though we (irrationally) do form these beliefs in this way. Descartes and Hume, respectively, are notable examples of philosophers who hold these positions.

Most of the early modern philosophers who have dealt with perception and knowledge have held that the *foundation* of our empirical beliefs lies in knowledge of the contents of sense-experience, in the sense that these beliefs are *actually formed* on the basis of, or *inferred* from, this immediate knowledge; but only some of them have held the view that this inference is *rationally* founded, and not all who do hold such a view have maintained that it is rational on the basis of sense-experience alone. But all these positions are set within the framework of the theory of perception that I have described above. The fundamental problem that arises about the justification of empirical beliefs is formulated in the terminology of this theory: Is the connection between *sense-experience* and the external world such that one can *validly infer* from one to the other? It is clear that the theses that perceiving involves sense-experience, and that we have a privileged epistemological position with respect to this type of experience, have been the cornerstones of one of the strongest traditions of modern epistemology.

This tradition has been carried on in this century, though there have been many differences of opinion and subtle modifications of it among its adherents. But there has also been a rather marked reaction to it by a wide variety of philosophers of different persuasions. Most notable are the criticisms offered by many post-World War II Oxford philosophers who have attacked not only the fundamental conception of knowledge as a structure based on sense-experience, but also the idea that perceiving involves sense-experience. The latter sort of criticism has usually been directed at the predominant interpretation of the traditional thesis in the twentieth century—sense-datum theory—and it is in the controversy about sense-data that one finds perhaps the most detailed work that has been done in the philosophical study of perceptual consciousness. This interplay between traditional and dissident elements has created a dialectic that I have tried to reproduce in the pages of this anthology. Wherever possible, I have joined traditional treatments of topics in the philosophy of perception with criticisms or contrasting views. I have arranged the material to reflect what seems to me to be the natural divisions of the area: Part I includes comprehensive discussions of the nature of perceiving and the objects of perception, as well as studies of particular types of perception; Part II contains material representative of the sense-datum controversy and, in general, focuses on problems about the conscious experience of perceiving, especially when construed as sense-experience; Part III deals with phenomenalism and the causal theory, as they have been developed, defended, and criticized recently; and Part IV includes works on problems about the way in which empirical knowledge is based on the evidence of the senses, especially in connection with the traditional thesis that sense-experience is the *rational foundation* of empirical knowledge. In each one of these areas major contributions to the philosophy of perception have been made in this century, and I have tried to present some of these in the following pages.

Robert J. Swartz

University of Illinois
September, 1964

I. PERCEPTION AND THE OBJECTS OF PERCEPTION

SOME JUDGMENTS OF PERCEPTION

G. E. MOORE

I want to raise some childishly simple questions as to what we are doing when we make judgments of a certain kind, which we all do in fact exceedingly commonly make. The kind of judgments I mean are those which we make when, with regard to something which we are seeing, we judge such things as "That is an inkstand," "That is a tablecloth," "That is a door," etc., etc.; or when, with regard to something which we are feeling with our hands, we judge such things as "This is cloth," "This is a finger," "This is a coin," etc., etc.

It is scarcely possible, I think, to exaggerate the frequency with which we make such judgments as these, nor yet the certainty with which we are able to make vast numbers of them. Any man, who is not blind, can, at almost any moment of his waking life, except when he is in the dark, make a large number of judgments of the first kind, with the greatest certainty. He has only to look about him, if he is indoors, to judge with regard to various things which he is seeing, such things as "That is a window," "That is a chair," "This is a book"; or, if he is out-of-doors, such things as "That is a house," "That is a motor-car," "That is a man," or "That is a stone," "That is a tree," "That is a cloud." And all of us, who are not blind, do in fact constantly make such judgments, even if, as a rule, we only make them as parts of more complicated judgments. What I mean is that, when we make such judgments as "Hullo! that clock has stopped," or "This chair is more comfortable than that one," or "That man looks like a foreigner," judgments of the simpler kind with which I am concerned are, so far as I can see, actually a part of what we are judging. In judging "That clock has stopped," part of what I am actually judging is, so far as I can see, "That is a clock"; and similarly if I judge "That tree is taller than this one," my judgment actually contains the two simpler judgments "That is a tree," and "This is a tree." Perhaps most judgments which we make, of the kind I mean, are, in this way, only parts of more complicated judgments: I do not know whether this is so or not. But in any case there can be no doubt that we make them exceedingly commonly. And even a blind man, or a man in the dark, can and does, very frequently, make judgments of the second kind—judgments about things which he is feeling with his hands. All of us, for instance, at almost any moment of our waking life, whether we are in the dark or not, have only to feel certain parts of our own bodies or of our clothes, in order to make, with great certainty, such judgments as "This is a finger," "This is a nose," "This is cloth." And similarly I have only to feel in my pockets to judge, with regard to objects which I meet with there, such things as "This is a coin," "This is a pencil," "This is a pipe."

Judgments of this kind would, I think, commonly, and rightly, be taken to be judgments, the truth of which involves the existence of material things or physical objects. If I am right in judging that this is an inkstand, it follows that there is at least one inkstand in the Universe; and if there is an inkstand in the Universe, it follows that there is in it at least one material thing or physical object. This may, of course, be disputed. Berkeley, if I understand him rightly, was clearly of opinion that there was no inconsistency in maintaining that there were in the Universe thousands of inkstands and trees and stones and stars, and that yet there was in it no such thing as matter. And perhaps the definition of matter, which he adopted, was such that there really was no inconsistency in maintaining this. Perhaps, similarly, other philosophers have sometimes adopted definitions of the expressions "material things" and "physical objects," which were such that all the judgments of this kind that we make might quite well be true, without its being true that there are in the Universe any material things whatever. Perhaps, even, there may be some justification for adopting definitions of those terms which would yield the surprising result that we may, with perfect consistency, maintain that the world is full of minerals and vegetables and animals, of all sorts of different kinds, and that yet there is not to be found in it a single material thing. I do not know whether there is or is not any utility in using the terms "material thing" or "physical object" in such a sense as this. But, whether there is or not, I cannot help thinking that there is ample justification for using them in another sense—a sense in which from the proposition that there are in the Universe such things as inkstands or fingers or clouds, it strictly follows that there are in it at least as many material things, and in which, therefore, we can *not* consistently maintain the existence of inkstands, fingers, and clouds, while denying that of material things. The kinds of judgment which I have mentioned, and thousands of others which might easily be mentioned, are obviously all of the same sort in one very important respect—a respect in which, for instance, such judgments as "This is an emotion," "This is a judgment," "This is a colour," are *not* of the same sort as they are. And it seems to me that we are certainly using the term "material thing" in *a* correct and useful way, if we express this important common property which they have, by saying that of each of them the same can truly be said as was said of the judgment "That is an inkstand": that, just as from the proposition "There is an inkstand" it follows that there is at least one material thing, so from the proposition "There is a tablecloth," it follows that there is at least one material thing; and similarly in all the other cases. We can certainly use the expression "Things *such as* inkstands, tablecloths, fingers, clouds, stars, etc.," to mean things such as these in a certain very important respect, which we all understand, though we may not be able to define it. And the term "material thing" certainly is and can be correctly used to mean simply things such as these in that respect—whatever it may be. Some term is certainly required to mean merely things such as these in that important respect; and, so far as I can see, there is no term which can be naturally used in this sense except the term "material things" and its equivalents. Thus understood, the term "material thing" certainly does stand for an important notion, which requires a name.

And, if we agree to use the term in this sense, then it is obvious that no more can be necessary for the truth of the assertion that there are material things, than is necessary for the truth of judgments of the kind with which I propose to deal. But no more can be necessary for the truth of these judgments than is actually asserted in or logically implied by them. And if we approach the question what is necessary for the truth of the assertion that there are material things, by asking what it is that we actually assert when we make such judgments as these, certain reasons for doubting how much is necessary are, I think, brought out much more clearly, than if we approach the question in any other way. Many philosophers have told us a very great deal as to what they suppose to be involved in the existence of material things; and some, at least, among them seem to have meant by "material things" such things as inkstands, fingers and clouds. But I can think of only one type of view as to the constitution of material things, which is such that it is tolerably clear what answer those who hold it would give to the simple question: What is it that I am judging, when I judge, as I now do, that that is an inkstand? The type of view I mean is that to which the view that Mill suggests, when he explains what he means by saying that Matter is a Permanent Possibility of Sensation, and also the view or views which Mr. Russell seems to suggest in his "Our Knowledge of the External World," seem to belong. In the case of views of this kind, it is, I think, tolerably clear what answer those who hold them would give to *all* the questions I want to raise about judgments of the kind I have described. But it does not seem to me at all certain that any view of this type is true; and certainly many philosophers have held and do hold that all views of this type are false. But, in the case of those who do hold them to be false, I do not know, in any single case, what answer would be given to *all* the questions which I want to raise. In the case of philosophers, who do not accept any view of the Mill-Russell type, none, so far as I know, has made it clear what answer he would give to *all* my questions: some have made it clear what answer they would give to *some* of them; but many, I think, have not even made it clear what answer they would give to any. Perhaps there is some simple and satisfactory answer, which has escaped me, that such philosophers could give to all my questions; but I cannot help thinking that assumptions as to the nature of material things have too often been made, without its even occurring to those who made them to ask, what, if they were true, we could be judging when we make such judgments as these; and that, if this question had been asked, it would have become evident that those assumptions were far less certain than they appeared to be.

I do not know that there is any excuse whatever for calling *all* judgments of the kind I mean "judgments of perception." All of them are, of course, judgments *about* things which we are at the moment perceiving, since, by definition, they are judgments about things which we are seeing or feeling with our hands; and all of them are, no doubt, also *based upon* something which we perceive about the thing in question. But the mere fact that a judgment is both about a thing which I am perceiving, and also based upon something which I perceive about that thing, does not seem to be a sufficient reason for calling it a judgment of perception; and I do not know that there is any other reason than this for calling *all* judgments of the kind I mean judgments of perception. I do not want therefore, to assert that *all* of them are so. But it seems to me quite plain that enormous numbers of them are so, in a perfectly legitimate sense. This judgment, which I now make, to the effect that *that* is a door, seems to me quite plainly to be a judgment of perception, in the simple sense that I make it because I do, in fact, see that that *is* a door, and assert in it no more than what I see; and what I see I, of course, perceive. In every case in which I judge, with regard to something which I am seeing or feeling with my hands, that it is a so-and-so, simply because I do perceive, by sight or touch, that it is in fact a thing of that kind, we can, I think, fairly say that the judgment in question is a judgment of perception. And enormous numbers of judgments of the kind I mean are, quite plainly, judgments of perception in this sense. They are not *all*, for the simple reason that some of them are mistaken. I may, for instance, judge, with regard to an animal which I see at a distance, that it is a sheep, when in fact it is a pig. And here my judgment is certainly not due to the fact that I see it to be a sheep; since I cannot possibly see a thing to be a sheep, unless it is one. It, therefore, is *not* a judgment of perception in this sense. And moreover, even where such a judgment is true, it may not always be a judgment of perception, for the reason that, whereas I only see the thing in question, the kind of thing which I judge it to be is of such a nature, that it is impossible for any one, by sight alone, to perceive anything to be of that kind. How to draw the line between judgments of this kind, which are judgments of perception, and those which are not, I do not know. That is to say, I do not know what conditions must be fulfilled in order that I may be truly said to be *perceiving,* by sight or touch, such things as that that is a door, this is a finger, and not *merely* inferring them. Some people may no doubt think that it is very unphilosophical in me to say that we *ever* can perceive such things as these. But it seems to me that we do, in ordinary life, constantly talk of *seeing* such things, and that, when we do so, we are neither using language incorrectly, nor making any mistake about the facts—supposing something to occur which never does in fact occur. The truth seems to me to be that we are using the term "perceive" in a way which is both perfectly correct and expresses a kind of thing which constantly does occur, only that some philosophers have not recognised that this is a correct usage of the term and have not been able to define it. I am not, therefore, afraid to say that I do now perceive that that is a door, and that that is a finger. Only, of course, when I say that I do, I do not mean to assert that part of what I "perceive," when I "perceive" these things, may not be something which, in an important sense, is known to me only by inference. It would be very rash to assert that "perception," in this sense of the word, entirely excludes inference. All that seems to me certain is that there is an important and useful sense of the word "perception," which is such that the amount and kind of inference, if inference there be, which is involved in my present perception, that that is a door, is no bar to the truth of the assertion that I do perceive that it is one. Vast numbers, then, of the kind of judgments with which I propose to deal seem to me to be, in an important and legitimate sense, judgments of perception; although I am not prepared to define, any further than I have done, what that sense is. And though it is true that the questions which I shall raise apply just as much to those of them which are not judgments of perception as to those which are, it is, of course, also true that they apply just as much to those which are as to those which are not; so that I shall be really dealing with a large and important class among judgments of perception.

It is true that, if certain views which, if I understand them rightly, some philosophers have seriously entertained, were true ones, it would be quite impossible that any of them should be judgments of perception. For some philosophers seem to me to have denied that we ever do in fact know such things as these, and others not only that we ever know them but also that they are ever true. And, if, in fact, I never do know such a thing, or if it is never true, it will, of course, follow that I never perceive such a thing; since I certainly cannot, in this sense, perceive anything whatever, unless I both know it and it is true. But it seems to me a sufficient refutation of such views as these, simply to point to cases in which we do know such things. This, after all, you know, really is a finger: there is no doubt about it: I know it, and you all know it. And I think we may safely challenge any philosopher to bring forward any argument in favour either of the proposition that we do not know it, or of the proposition that it is not true, which does not, at some point, rest upon some premiss which is, beyond comparison, less certain than is the proposition which it is designed to attack. The questions whether we do ever know such things as these, and whether there are any material things, seem to me, therefore, to be questions which there is no need to take seriously: they are questions which it is quite easy to answer, with certainty, in the affirmative. What does, I think, need to be taken seriously, and what is really dubious, is not the question whether this is a finger, or whether I know that it is, but the question *what*, in certain respects, I am knowing, when I know that it is. And this is the question to which I will now address myself.

To begin with there is one thing which seems to me to be very certain indeed about such judgments. It is unfortunately a thing which I do not know how properly to express. There seem to me to be objections to every way of expressing it which I can think of. But I hope I may be able to make my meaning clear, in spite of the inadequacy of my expression. The thing I mean is a thing which may to some people seem so obvious as to be scarcely worth saying. But I cannot help thinking that it is not always clearly recognised, and even that some philosophers, to judge from what they say, might perhaps dispute it. It seems to me to be an assumption which is silently made in many treatments of the subject, and, as I say, it seems to me to be very certain indeed. But I think it is at all events worth while to try to make the assumption explicit, in case it should be disputed. If it really is not true, then the other questions to which I shall go on, and which seem to me really dubious and difficult, do not, I think, arise at all.

I will try to express this fundamental assumption, which seems to me so very certain, by saying it is the assumption that, in all cases in which I make a judgment of this sort, I have no difficulty whatever in picking out a thing, which is, quite plainly, in a sense in which nothing else is, *the* thing about which I am making my judgment; and that yet, though this thing is *the* thing about which I am judging, I am, quite certainly, *not,* in general, judging with regard to it, that *it* is a thing of that kind for which the term, which seems to express the predicate of my judgment, is a name. Thus, when I judge, as now, that That is an inkstand, I have no difficulty whatever in picking out, from what, if you like, you can call my total field of presentation at the moment, an object, which is undoubtedly, in a sense in which nothing else is, *the* object about which I am making this judgment; and yet it seems to me quite certain that of *this* object I am not judging that it is a whole inkstand. And similarly when I judge, with regard to something which I am feeling in my pocket, "This is a coin," I have no difficulty in picking out, from my field of presentation, an object, which is undoubtedly *the* object with which my judgment is concerned; and yet I am certainly not judging with regard to this object that it is a whole coin. I say that *always,* when I make such a judgment, I can pick out *the* one, among the objects presented to me at the time, about which I am making it; but I have only said that *in general* I am not judging with regard to this object that it is a thing of the kind, for which the term, which seems to express the predicate of my judgment, is a name. And I have limited my second proposition in this way, because there are cases, in which it does not, at first sight, seem quite so certain that I am not doing this, as in the two instances I have just given. When, for instance, I judge with regard to something, which I am seeing, "This is a soap-bubble," or "This is a drop of water," or even when I judge "This is a spot of ink," it may not seem quite so plain, that I may not be judging, with regard to the very object presented to me that it is, itself, a whole soap-bubble, a whole drop of water, or a whole spot of ink, as it always is, in the case of an inkstand, or a coin, that I never take the presented object, about which I am judging, to be a whole inkstand, or a whole coin. The sort of reason why I say this will, of course, be obvious to any one, and it is obviously of a childish order. But I cannot say that it seems to me quite obvious that in such a case I am not judging of the presented object that it is a whole drop of water, in the way in which it does seem to be obvious that I am not judging of *this* presented object that it is an inkstand. That is why I limit myself to saying that, *in general,* when I judge "that is a so-and-so" I am not judging with regard to the presented object, about which my judgment is, that *it* is a thing of the kind in question. As much as this seems to me to be a thing which any child can see. Nobody will suppose, for a moment, that when he judges such things as "This is a sofa," or "This is a tree," he is judging, with regard to the presented object, about which his judgment plainly is, that it is a whole sofa or a whole tree: he can, at most, suppose that he is judging it to be a part of the surface of a sofa or a part of the surface of a tree. And certainly in the case of most judgments of this kind which we make, whether in the case of all or not, this is plainly the case: we are not judging, with regard to the presented object about which our judgment plainly is, that it is a thing of the kind, for which the term which appears to express the predicate of our judgment, is a name. And that this should be true of *most* judgments of this kind, whether of all or not, is quite sufficient for my purpose.

This much, then, seems to me to be very certain indeed. But I will try to make clearer exactly what I mean by it, by mentioning a ground, on which I imagine it might perhaps be disputed.

The object of which I have spoken as *the* object, about which, in each particular case, such a judgment as this always is a judgment, is, of course, always an object of the kind which some philosophers would call a sensation, and others would call a sense-datum. Whether all philosophers, when they talk of sensations, mean to include among them such objects as these, I do not know. Some, who have given a great deal of attention to the subject, and for whom I have a great respect, talk of sensations in such a way, that I cannot be sure what they are talking about at all or whether there are such things. But many, I think, undoubtedly do mean to include such subjects as these. No doubt, in general, when they call them sensations, they mean to attribute to them properties, which it seems to me extremely doubtful whether they possess. And perhaps even those who call them sense-data, may, in part, be attributing to them properties which it may be doubtful whether they possess. If we want to define a sensation or a sense-datum, in a manner which will leave it not open to doubt what sort of things we are talking of, and that there are such things, I do not know that we can do it better than by saying that sense-data are the sort of things, *about* which such judgments as these always seem to be made— the sort of things which seem to be the real or ultimate subjects of all such judgments. Such a way of defining how the term "sense-datum" is used, may not seem very satisfactory; but I am inclined to think it may be as satisfactory as any which can be found. And it is certainly calculated to obviate some misunderstandings which may arise; since everybody can see, I think, what the thing is which I am describing as *the* thing about which he is making his judgment, when he judges "That is an inkstand," and that there is such a thing, even if he does not agree that this description applies to it.

I can, in fact, imagine that some of those who would call this thing a sensation would deny that my judgment is *about* it at all. It would sometimes be spoken of as the sensation which mediates my perception of this inkstand, in this instance. And I can imagine that some of those who would so speak of it might be inclined to say that when I judge "This is an inkstand," my judgment is about this inkstand which I perceive, and not, in any sense at all, about the sensation which mediates my perception of it. They may perhaps imagine that the sensation mediates my perception of the inkstand only in the sense that it brings the inkstand before my mind in such a way that, once it is before my mind, I can make a judgment about it, which is *not* a judgment about the mediating sensation at all; and that such a judgment is the one I am actually expressing when I say "This is an inkstand." Such a view, if it is held, seems to me to be quite certainly false, and is what I have intended to deny. And perhaps I can put most clearly the reason why it seems to me false, by saying that, if (which may be doubted) there is anything which is this inkstand, that thing is certainly not given to me independently of this sense-datum, in such a sense that I can possibly make a judgment about it which is *not* a judgment about this sense-datum. I am not, of course, denying that I do perceive this inkstand, and that my judgment is, in a sense, a judgment about it. Both these things seem to me to be quite obviously true. I am only maintaining that my judgment is *also,* in another sense, a judgment about this sense-datum which mediates my perception of the inkstand. Those who say that this sense-datum does mediate my perception of the inkstand, would, of course, admit that my perception of the inkstand is, in a sense, dependent upon the sense-datum; that it is dependent is implied in the mere statement that it is mediated by it. But it might be maintained that it is dependent on it only in the sense in which, when the idea of one object is called up in my mind, through association, by the idea of another, the idea which is called up is dependent on the idea which calls it up. What I wish to maintain, and what seems to me to be quite certainly true, is that my perception of this inkstand is dependent on this sense-datum, in a quite different and far more intimate sense than this. It is dependent on it in the sense that, if there is anything which is this inkstand, then, in perceiving that thing, I am knowing it *only* as *the* thing which stands in a certain relation to this sense-datum. When the idea of one object is called up in my mind by the idea of another, I do not know the second object *only* as *the* thing which has a certain relation to the first: on the contrary, I can make a judgment about the second object, which is not a judgment about the first. And similarly in the case of two sense-data which are presented to me simultaneously, I do not know the one *only* as the thing which has a certain relation to the other. But in the case of this sense-datum and this inkstand the case seems to me to be plainly quite different. If there be a thing which is this inkstand at all, it is certainly *only* known to me as *the* thing which stands in a certain relation to this sense-datum. It is not given to me, in the sense in which this sense-datum is given. If there be such a thing at all, it is quite certainly only known to me by description, in the sense in which Mr. Russell uses that phrase; and the description by which it is known is that of being *the* thing which stands to this sense-datum in a certain relation. That is to say, when I make such a judgment as "This inkstand is a good big one"; what I am really judging is: "There is a thing which stands to *this* in a certain relation, and which is an inkstand, and that thing is a good big one"— where *"this"* stands for this presented object. I am referring to or identifying the thing which is this inkstand, if there be such a thing at all, only as the thing which stands to this sense-datum in a certain relation; and hence my judgment, though in one sense it may be said to be a judgment about the inkstand, is quite certainly also, in another sense, a judgment about this sense-datum. This seems to me so clear, that I wonder how anyone can deny it; and perhaps nobody would. But I cannot help thinking that it is not clear to everybody, partly because, so far as I can make out, nobody before Mr. Russell had pointed out the extreme difference there is between a judgment about a thing known only by description to the individual who makes the judgment, and a judgment about a thing not known to him only in this way; and partly because so many people seem still utterly to have failed to understand what the distinction is which he expresses in this way. I will try to make the point clear, in a slightly different way. Suppose I am seeing two coins, lying side by side, and am not perceiving them in any other way except by sight. It will be plain to everybody, I think, that, when I identify the one as "This one" and the other as "That one," I identify them only by reference to the two visual presented objects, which correspond respectively to the one and to the other. But what may not, I think, be realised, is that the sense in which I identify them by reference to the corresponding sense-data, is one which involves that every judgment which I make about the one is a judgment about the sense-datum which corresponds to it, and every judgment I make about the other, a judgment about the sense-datum which corresponds to *it:* I simply cannot make a judgment about either, which is not a judgment about the corresponding sense-datum. But if the two coins were given to me, in the sense in which the two sense-data are, this would certainly not be the case. I can identify and distinguish the two sense-data *directly,* this as this one, and that as that one: I do not need to identify either as *the* thing which has this relation to this other thing. But I certainly cannot thus directly identify the two coins. I have not four things presented to me (1) *this* sense-datum, (2) *that* sense-datum, (3) *this* coin, and (4) *that* coin, but two only—*this* sense-datum and *that* sense-datum. When, therefore, I judge "*This* is a coin," my judgment is certainly a judgment about the one sense-datum, and when I judge "And *that* is also a coin," it is certainly a judgment about the other. Only, in spite of what my language might seem to imply, I am certainly not judging either of the one sense-datum that it is a whole coin, nor yet of the other that it is one.

This, then, seems to me fundamentally certain about judgments of this kind. Whenever we make such a judgment we can easily pick out an object (whether we call it a sensation or a sense-datum or not), which is, in an easily intelligible sense, *the* object which is the real or ultimate subject of our judgment; and yet, in many cases at all events, what we are judging with regard to this object is certainly not that it is an object of the kind, for which the term which appears to express the predicate of our judgment, is a name.

But if this be so, what is it that I am judging, in all such cases, about the presented object, which is the real or ultimate subject of my judgment? It is at this point that we come to questions which seem to me to be really uncertain and difficult to answer.

To begin with, there is one answer which is naturally suggested by the reason I have given for saying that, in this case, it is quite obvious that I am not judging, with regard to this presented object, that *it* is an inkstand, whereas it is not in the same way, quite obvious that, in making such a judgment as "This is a soap-bubble" or "This is a drop of water," I may not be judging, of the object about which my judgment is, that that very object really is a soap-bubble or a drop of water. The reason I gave is that it is quite obvious that I do not take this presented object to be a *whole* inkstand: that, at most, I only take it to be part of the surface of an inkstand. And this reason naturally suggests that the true answer to our question may be that what I am judging of the presented object is just that it is a part of the surface of an inkstand. This answer seems to me to be obviously on quite a different level from the suggestion that I am judging it really to be an inkstand. It is not childishly obvious that I am not judging it to be part of the surface of an inkstand, as it is that I am not judging it to be an inkstand—a whole one.

On this view, when I say such things as "That is an inkstand," "That is a door," "This is a coin," these expressions would really only be a loose way of saying "That is part of the surface of an inkstand," "That is part of the surface of a door," "This is part of the surface of a coin." And there would, I think, plainly be nothing surprising in the fact that we should use language thus loosely. What, at first sight, appears to be a paradox, namely that, whereas I appear to be asserting of a given thing that it is of a certain kind, I am not really asserting of the thing in question that it is of that kind at all, would be susceptible of an easy explanation. And moreover, if this view were true, it would offer an excellent illustration of the difference between a thing known only by description and a thing not so known, and would show how entirely free from mystery that distinction is. On this view, when I judge "That inkstand is a good big one" I shall in effect be judging: "There is one and only one inkstand of which *this* is part of the surface, and the inkstand of which this is true is a good big one." It would be quite clear that the part of the surface of the inkstand was given to me in a sense in which the whole was not, just as it is in fact clear that I do now *"see"* this part of the surface of this inkstand, in a sense in which

I do *not* "see" the whole; and that my judgment, while it is, in fact, *about* both the whole inkstand, and also *about* one particular part of its surface, is *about* them in two entirely different senses.

This view is one, which it is, at first sight, I think, very natural to suppose to be true. But before giving the reasons, why, nevertheless, it seems to me extremely doubtful, I think it is desirable to try to explain more precisely what I mean by it. The word "part" is one which is often used extremely vaguely in philosophy; and I can imagine that some people would be willing to assent to the proposition that this sense-datum really is, in some sense or other, a "part" of this inkstand, and that what I am judging with regard to it, when I judge "This is an inkstand," is, in effect, "This is an inkstand, of which *this* is a part," who would be far from allowing that this can possibly be what I am judging, when once they understand what the sense is in which I am here using the word "part." What this sense is, I am quite unable to define; but I hope I may be able to make my meaning sufficiently clear, by giving instances of things which are undoubtedly "parts" of other things in the sense in question. There is, it seems to me, a sense of the word "part," in which we all constantly use the word with perfect precision, and which, therefore, we all understand very well, however little we may be able to define it. It is the sense in which the trunk of any tree is undoubtedly a part of that tree; in which this finger of mine is undoubtedly a part of my hand, and my hand a part of my body. This is a sense in which every part of a material thing or physical object is itself a material thing or physical object; and it is, so far as I can see, the only proper sense in which a material thing can be said to have parts. The view which I wish to discuss is the view that I am judging this presented object to be a part of an inkstand, in this sense. And the nature of the view can perhaps be brought out more clearly, by mentioning one important corollary which would follow from it. I am, of course, at this moment, seeing many parts of the surface of this inkstand. But all these parts, except one, are, in fact, themselves parts of that one. That one is the one of which we should naturally speak as "*the* part of the surface that I am now seeing" or as "*this* part of the surface of this inkstand." There is only one part of the surface of this inkstand, which does thus contain, as parts, all the other parts that I am now seeing. And, if it were true that I am judging this presented object to be a part of the surface of an inkstand at all, in the sense I mean, it would follow that this presented object must, if my judgment "This is an inkstand" be true (as it certainly is), be identical with this part, which contains all the other parts which I am seeing: since there is plainly no other part with which it could possibly be identified. That is to say, if I am really judging of this presented object that it is part of the surface of an inkstand, in the sense I mean, it must be the case that everything which is true of what I should call "this part of the surface of this inkstand" is, in fact, true of this presented object.

This view, therefore, that what we are judging of the ultimate subject of our judgment, when we judge "This is a so-and-so," is, in general, merely that the subject in question is a *part* of a thing of the kind in question, can, I think, be most clearly discussed, by asking whether, in this case, this presented object can really be identical with this part of the surface of this inkstand. If it can't, then most certainly I am not judging of it that it is a part of the surface of an inkstand at all. For my judgment, whatever it is, is true. And yet, if this presented object is not identical with this part of the surface of this inkstand, it certainly is not a part of an inkstand at all; since there is no other part, either of this inkstand or of any other, with which it could possibly be supposed to be identical.

Can we, then, hold that this sense-datum really is identical with this part of the surface of this inkstand? That everything which is true of the one is true of the other?

An enormous number of very familiar arguments have been used by various philosophers, which, if they were sound, would show that we can not. Some of these arguments seem to me to be quite clearly not sound—all, for instance, which rest either on the assumption that this sense-datum can only exist so long as it is perceived, or on the assumption that it can only exist so long as it is perceived *by me*. Of others I suspect that they may have some force, though I am quite unable to see that they have any. Such, for instance, are all those which assume either that this sense-datum is a sensation or feeling of mine, in a sense which includes the assertion that it is dependent on my mind in the very same sense in which my perception of it obviously is so; or that it is causally dependent on my body in the sense in which my perception of it admittedly is so. But others do seem to me to have great force. I will, however, confine myself to trying to state one, which seems to me to have as much as any. It will be found that this one involves an assumption, which does seem to me to have great force, but which yet seems to me to be doubtful. So far as I know, all good arguments against the view that this sense-datum really is identical with this part of the surface of the inkstand, do involve this same assumption, and have no more force than it has. But in this, of course, I may be wrong. Perhaps some one will be able to point out an argument, which is obviously quite independent of it, and which yet has force.

The argument I mean involves considerations which are exceedingly familiar, so familiar that I am afraid every one may be sick of hearing them alluded to. But, in spite of this fact, it seems to me not quite easy to put it quite precisely, in a way which will distinguish it clearly from other arguments involving the same familiar considerations, but which do not seem to me to be equally cogent. I want, therefore, to try to put it with a degree of precision, which will prevent irrelevant objections from being made to it—objections which would, I think, be relevant against some of these other arguments, but are not, I think, relevant against it.

The fact is that we all, exceedingly commonly, when, at each of two times, separated by a longer or shorter interval, we see a part of the surface of a material thing, in the sense in which I am now seeing this part of the surface of this inkstand, or when at one time we see such a surface and at another perceive one by touch, make, on the second occasion, the judgment "*This* part of a surface is the *same* part of the surface of the same thing, as that which I was seeing (or perceiving by touch) just now." How commonly we all do this can scarcely be exaggerated. I look at this inkstand, and then I look again, and on the second occasion I judge "This part of the surface of this inkstand is the same as, or at least contains a part which is the same as a part of, the part of its surface which I was seeing just now." Or I look at this finger and then I touch it, and I judge, on the second occasion, "This part of the surface of this finger is the same as one of those I was seeing just now." We all thus constantly identify a part of a surface of a material thing which we are perceiving at one time with a part which we *were* perceiving at another.

Now, when we do this—when we judge "This is the *same* part of the same thing as I was seeing or touching just now," we, of course, do not mean to exclude the possibility that the part in question may have changed during the interval; that it is really different, on the second occasion, either in shape or size or quality, or in all three, from what it was on the first. That is to say, the sense of sameness which we are here concerned with is one which clearly does not exclude change. We may even be prepared to assert, on general grounds, in all such cases, that the surface in question certainly must have changed. But nevertheless there is a great difference in one respect, between two kinds of such cases, both of which occur exceedingly commonly. If I watch somebody blowing air into a child's balloon, it constantly happens, at certain stages in the process, that I judge with regard to the part of the surface which I am seeing at that stage, not only that it *is* larger than it was at an earlier stage, but that it is *perceptibly* larger. Or, if I pull the face of an india-rubber doll, I may judge at a certain stage in the process that the patch of red colour on its cheek not only is different in shape from what it was at the beginning, but is *perceptibly* so: it may, for instance, be a perceptibly flatter ellipse than it was to start with. Or, if I watch a person blushing, I may judge at a certain stage that a certain part of the surface of his face not only is different in colour from what it was, when I saw it before he began to blush, but is *perceptibly* so—perceptibly redder. In enormous numbers of cases we do thus judge of a surface seen at a given time that it is thus *perceptibly* different in size, or in shape, or in colour, from what it was when we saw it before. But cases are at least equally numerous in which, though we might, on general grounds be prepared to assert that it *must* have changed in some respect, we should not be prepared to assert that it had, in any respect whatever, changed *perceptibly*. Of this part of this surface of this inkstand, for instance, I am certainly not prepared to assert that it is now perceptibly different in any respect from what it was when I saw it just now. And similar cases are so numerous that I need not give further instances. We can, therefore, divide cases, in which we judge, of a part of a surface which we are seeing, "This is the same part of the surface of the same material thing as the one I saw just now," into cases where we should also judge "But it is perceptibly different from what it was then," and cases in which, even though we might assert "It *must* be different," we are certainly not prepared to assert that it is *perceptibly* so.

But now let us consider the cases in which we are not prepared to assert that the surface in question has changed perceptibly. The strange fact, from which the argument I mean is drawn, is that, in a very large number of such cases, it seems as if it were unmistakably true that the presented object, about which we are making our judgment when we talk of "This surface" at the later time, *is* perceptibly different, from that about which we are making it when we talk of the surface I saw just now. If, at the later time, I am at a sufficiently greater distance from the surface, the presented object which corresponds to it at the time seems to be perceptibly smaller, than the one which corresponded to it before. If I am looking at it from a sufficiently oblique angle, the later presented object often seems to be perceptibly different in shape—a perceptibly flatter ellipse, for instance. If I am looking at it, with blue spectacles on, when formerly I had none, the later presented object seems to be perceptibly different in colour from the earlier one. If I am perceiving it by touch alone, whereas formerly I was perceiving it by sight alone, the later presented object seems to be perceptibly different from the earlier, in respect of the fact that it is not coloured at all, whereas the earlier was, and that, on the other hand, it has certain tactual qualities, which the earlier had not got. All this seems to be as plain as it can be, and yet it makes absolutely no difference to the fact that of the surface in question we are *not* prepared to judge that it is perceptibly different from what it was. Sometimes, of course, where there seems to be no doubt that the later presented object is perceptibly different from the earlier, we may not notice that it is so. But even where we do notice the apparent difference, we do still continue to judge of the surface in question: This surface is not, so far as I can tell with certainty by perception, in any way different from what it was when I saw it or touched it just now; I am *not* prepared to assert that it has changed perceptibly. It seems, therefore, to be absolutely impossible that the surface seen at the later time should be identical with the object presented then, and the surface seen at the earlier identical with the object presented then, for the simple reason that, whereas with regard to the later seen surface I am not prepared to judge that it is in any way perceptibly different from that seen earlier, it seems that with regard to the later sense-datum I cannot fail to judge that it *is* perceptibly different from the earlier one: the fact that they are perceptibly different simply stares me in the face. It seems, in short, that when, in such a case, I judge: "This surface is not, so far as I can tell, perceptibly different from the one I saw just now," I cannot possibly be judging of the presented object "*This* is not, so far as I can tell, perceptibly different from that object which was presented to me just now," for the simple rea-

son that I *can* tell, as certainly, almost, as I can tell anything, that it is perceptibly different.

That is the argument, as well as I can put it, for saying
that this presented object is *not* identical with this part of
the surface of this inkstand; and that, therefore, when I
judge "This is part of the surface of an inkstand," I am
not judging of this presented object, which nevertheless is
the ultimate subject of my judgment, that *it* is part of the
surface of an inkstand. And this argument does seem to
me to be a very powerful one.

But nevertheless it does not seem to me to be quite conclusive, because it rests on an assumption, which, though
it seems to me to have great force, does not seem to me
quite certain. The assumption I mean is the assumption
that, in such cases as those I have spoken of, the later presented object really is perceptibly different from the earlier.
This assumption has, if I am not mistaken, seemed to many
philosophers to be quite unquestionable; they have never
even thought of questioning it; and I own that it used to
be so with me. And I am still not sure that I may not be
talking sheer nonsense in suggesting that it can be questioned. But, if I am, I'm no longer able to see that I am.
What now seems to me to be possible is that the sense-
datum which corresponds to a tree, which I am seeing,
when I am a mile off, may not really be perceived to *be*
smaller than the one, which corresponds to the same tree,
when I see it from a distance of only a hundred yards,
but that it is only perceived to *seem* smaller; that the sense-
datum which corresponds to a penny, which I am seeing
obliquely, is not really perceived to *be* different in shape
from that which corresponded to the penny, when I was
straight in front of it, but is only perceived to *seem* different—that all that is perceived is that the one *seems* elliptical
and the other circular; that the sense-datum presented to
me when I have the blue spectacles on is not perceived to
be different in colour from the one presented to me when I
have not, but only to *seem* so; and finally that the sense-
datum presented when I touch this finger is not perceived
to *be* different in any way from that presented when I see

it, but only to *seem* so—that I do not perceive the one to be coloured and the other not to be so, but only that the one *seems* coloured and the other not. If such a view is to be possible, we shall have, of course, to maintain that the kind of experience which I have expressed by saying one *seems* different from the other—"*seems* circular," "*seems* blue," "*seems* coloured," and so on—involves an ultimate, not further analysable, kind of psychological relation, not to be identified either with that involved in being "perceived" to be so and so, or with that involved in being "judged" to be so and so; since a presented object might, in this sense, *seem* to be elliptical, *seem* to be blue, etc., when it is neither perceived to be so, nor judged to be so. But there seems to me to be no reason why there should not be such an ultimate relation. The great objection to such a view seems to me to be the difficulty of believing that I don't actually perceive this sense-datum to *be* red, for instance, and that other to *be* elliptical; that I only perceive, in many cases, that it *seems* so. I cannot, however, now persuade myself that it is quite clear that I do perceive it to *be* so. And, if I don't, then it seems really possible that this presented object really is identical with this part of the surface of this inkstand; since, when I judge, as in the cases supposed, that the surface in question is *not,* so far as I can tell, perceptibly different from what it was, I might really be judging of the two sense-data that they also were not, so far as I can tell, perceptibly different, the only difference between the two that *is* perceptible, being that the one *seems* to be of a certain size, shape or colour, and the other to be of a different and incompatible size, shape or colour. Of course, in those cases, as in that of the balloon being blown up, where I "perceive" that the surface has changed, *e.g.* in size, it would have to be admitted that I do perceive of the two sense-data not merely that they *seem* different in size, but that they *are* so. But I think it would be possible to maintain that the sense in which, in these cases, I "perceive" them to *be* different, is a different one from that in which, both in these and in the others, I perceive them to *seem* so.

Possibly in making this suggestion that sense-data, in cases where most philosophers have assumed unhesitatingly that they are *perceived* to be different, are only really perceived to *seem* different, I am, as I said, talking sheer nonsense, though I cannot, at the moment, see that I am. And possibly, even if this suggestion itself is not nonsense, even if it is true, there may be other fatal objections to the view that this presented object really is identical with this part of the surface of this inkstand. But what seems to me certain is that, unless this suggestion is true, then this presented object is certainly *not* identical with this part of the surface of this inkstand. And since it is doubtful whether it is not nonsense, and still more doubtful whether it is true, it must, I think, be admitted to be highly doubtful whether the two *are* identical. But, if they are not identical, then what I am judging with regard to this presented object, when I judge "This is an inkstand," is certainly *not* that it is itself part of the surface of an inkstand; and hence, it is worth while to inquire further, what, if I am not judging this, I *can* be judging with regard to it.

And here, I think, the first natural suggestion to make is that just as, when I talk of "this inkstand," what I seem really to mean is *"the* inkstand of which *this* is part of the surface," so that the inkstand is only known to me by description as the inkstand of which this material surface is part of the surface, so again when I talk of "this material surface," what I really mean is *"the* material surface to which *this* (presented object) has a certain relation," so that this surface is, in its turn, only known to me by description as *the* surface which has a certain relation to this presented object. If that were so, then what I should be judging of this presented object, when I judge "This is part of the surface of an inkstand," would be not that it is itself such a part, but that *the* thing which stands to it in a certain relation is such a part: in short, what I should be judging with regard to *it,* would be "There's one thing and one only which stands to *this* in *this* relation, and the thing which does so is part of the surface of an inkstand."

But if we are to adopt the view that something of this

sort is what we are judging, there occurs at once the pressing question: What on earth can the relation be with regard to which we are judging, that one and only one thing
stands in it to this presented object? And this is a question
to which, so far as I know, none of those philosophers, who
both hold (as many do) that this presented object is *not*
identical with this part of the surface of this inkstand, *and*
also that there really is something of which it could be
truly predicated that it is this part of the surface of this inkstand (that is to say, who reject all views of the Mill-Russell
type), have given anything like a clear answer. It does not
seem to have occurred to them that it requires an answer,
chiefly, I think, because it has not occurred to them to ask
what we can be judging when we make judgments of this
sort. There are only two answers, that I can think of, which
might be suggested with any plausibility.

Many philosophers, who take the view that the presented
objects about which we make these judgments are sensations of ours, and some even who do not, are in the habit
of talking of *"the* causes" of these objects as if we knew,
in the case of each, that it had one and only one cause;
and many of them seem to think that this part of the surface of this inkstand could be correctly described as *the*
cause of this presented object. They suggest, therefore, the
view that what I am judging in this case might be: "This
presented object has one and only one cause, and that cause
is part of the surface of an inkstand." It seems to me quite
obvious that *this* view, at all events, is utterly untenable. I
do not believe for a moment, nor does any one, and certainly therefore do not judge, that this presented object has
only one cause: I believe that it has a whole series of different causes. I do, in fact, believe that this part of the
surface of this inkstand is *one* among the causes of my
perception of this presented object: that seems to me to be
a very well established scientific proposition. And I am prepared to admit that there *may* be good reasons for thinking
that it is one among the causes of this presented object itself, though I cannot myself see that there are any. But
that it is the *only* cause of this presented object I certainly

do not believe, nor, I think, does anybody, and hence my judgment certainly cannot be *"The* cause of this is part of the surface of an inkstand." It might, no doubt, be possible to define some *kind* of causal relation, such that it might be plausibly held that it and it alone causes this presented object *in that particular way*. But any such definition would, so far as I can see, be necessarily very complicated. And, even when we have got it, it seems to me it would be highly improbable we could truly say that what we are judging in these cases is: "This presented object has one and only one cause, of this special kind." Still, I do not wish to deny that some such view may *possibly* be true.

The only other suggestion I can make is that there may be some ultimate, not further definable relation, which we might, for instance, call the relation of "being a manifestation of," such that we might conceivably be judging: "There is one and only one thing of which this presented object is a manifestation, and *that* thing is part of the surface of an inkstand." And here again, it seems to me just possible that this *may* be a true account of what we are judging; only I cannot find the slightest sign that I am in fact aware of any such relation.

Possibly other suggestions could be made as to what the relation is, with regard to which it could be plausibly supposed that in all cases, where we make these judgments, we are in fact judging of the presented object "There is one and only one thing which stands to this object in *this* relation." But it seems to me at least very doubtful whether there is any such relation at all; whether, therefore, our judgment really is of this form, and whether, therefore, this part of the surface of this inkstand really is known to me by description as *the* thing which stands in a certain relation to this presented object. But if it isn't, and if, also, we cannot take the view that what I am judging is that this presented object *itself* is a part of the surface of an inkstand, there would seem to be no possible alternative but that we must take some view of what I have called the Mill-Russell type. Views of this type, if I understand them rightly, are distinguished from those which I have hitherto considered, by the fact that, according to them, there is nothing whatever in the Universe of which it could truly be predicated that it is this part of the surface of this inkstand, or indeed that it is *a* part of the surface of an inkstand, or an inkstand, at all. They hold, in short, that though there are plenty of material things in the Universe, there is nothing in it of which it could truly be asserted that *it* is a material thing: that, though, when I assert "This is an inkstand," my assertion is true, and is such that it follows from it that there is in the Universe at least one inkstand, and, therefore, at least one material thing, yet it does not follow from it that there is anything which is a material thing. When I judge "This is an inkstand" I am judging this presented object to possess a certain property, which is such that, if there are things, which possess that property, there are inkstands and material things, but which is such that nothing which possesses it is itself a material thing; so that in judging that there are material things, we are really always judging of some *other* property, which is not that of being a material thing, that there are things which possess *it*. It seems to me quite possible, of course, that some view of this type is the true one. Indeed, this paper may be regarded, if you like, as an argument in favour of the proposition that some such view *must* be true. Certainly one of my main objects in writing it was to put as plainly as I can some grave difficulties which seem to me to stand in the way of any other view; in the hope that some of those, who reject all views of the Mill-Russell type, may explain clearly which of the alternatives I have suggested they would adopt, or whether, perhaps, some other which has not occurred to me. It does not seem to me to be always sufficiently realised how difficult it is to find *any* answer to my question "What are we judging in these cases?" to which there are not very grave objections, unless we adopt an answer of the Mill-Russell type. That an answer of this type *is* the true one, I am not myself, in spite of these objections, by any means convinced. The truth is I am completely puzzled as to what the true answer can be. At the present moment, I am rather inclined to favour the view that what I am judging of this presented object is that it is itself a part of the surface of an inkstand—that, therefore, it really is identical with this part of the surface of this inkstand, in spite of the fact that this involves the view that, where, hitherto, I have always supposed myself to be perceiving of two presented objects that they really were different, I was, in fact, only perceiving that they *seemed* to be different. But, as I have said, it seems to me quite possible that this view is, as I have hitherto supposed, sheer nonsense; and, in any case, there are, no doubt, other serious objections to the view that this presented object is this part of the surface of this inkstand.

SOME ELEMENTARY REFLEXIONS
ON SENSE-PERCEPTION[1]

C. D. Broad

Sense-perception is a hackneyed topic, and I must therefore begin by craving your indulgence. I was moved to make it the subject of this evening's lecture by the fact that I have lately been reading the book in which the most important of the late Professor Prichard's scattered writings on Sense-perception have been collected by Sir W. D. Ross. Like everything that Prichard wrote, these essays are extremely acute, transparently honest, and admirably thorough. I shall not attempt here either to expound or to criticize Prichard, but he may be taken to be hovering, perhaps somewhat disapprovingly, in the background during the lecture.

"Sense-perception" is a technical term (and, I hasten to add, none the worse for that) used by philosophers and psychologists to cover the experiences which we describe in daily life as "seeing," "hearing," "touching," "tasting," "smelling," and perhaps some others. For human beings the three most important species are seeing, hearing, and touching. I shall confine myself to these.

Many philosophers have tended to concentrate on *seeing,* and to treat hearing and touching in a rather perfunctory way. That is a mistake. It is very rash to assume that what holds for seeing can be transferred without supplement, omission, or modification to hearing or to touch-

[1] Iyer Lecture, delivered before the Royal Institute of Philosophy, at University Hall, W.C.1, on Friday, 8th June, 1951.

ing. Seeing is, as we shall find, in some ways a very peculiar form of sense-perception.

I want to begin by considering the three main forms of sense-perception from what I will call a "purely phenomenological point of view." By this I mean that I shall try to describe them as they appear to any unsophisticated percipient, and as they inevitably *go on appearing* even to sophisticated percipients whose knowledge of the physical and physiological processes involved assures them that the appearances are largely misleading.

Sentences which begin with the phrase "I see" or "I am seeing" continue with a word or phrase by which the speaker intends to denote or to describe something which he claims to be seeing, e.g., "a penny," "the Albert Memorial," "a blue cross on a yellow field," and so on. This latter word or phrase is generally a name for, or a description of, a *body* of some kind. But that is not so invariably. A person may say: "I see a red flash." Here what he claims to see is an *event* and not a thing.

It will be useful at once to compare and contrast this with *hearing*. It is about equally common to speak of hearing a *body* and of hearing a *sound*. Thus, e.g., one can say: "I hear Big Ben" and "I hear a series of booming noises." Now in this case even the plainest of plain men would admit, with very little pressure, that when he says "I am hearing Big Ben" this is short for what would be more fully expressed by saying "I am hearing Big Ben *striking*." With very little more pressure he would admit that all that he literally *hears* is a series of booming noises of a certain kind. He says that he hears Big Ben striking, because he believes or takes for granted that these sounds *emanate from* a certain bell as a result of a certain rhythmic process going on in it. In general I think that common-sense would readily accept the following translation of such sentences as "I am hearing so-and-so," where "so-and-so" is a name or a description of a body. Such sentences, it would agree, are equivalent to: "I am hearing such and such a *noise,* and I take it to be coming from the *body* so-and-so."

I do not think that it makes any essential difference to

the above analysis whether what is heard is a discontinuous series of sounds, e.g., the tolling of a bell, or a long continuous sound, e.g., the roar of a waterfall. The continuous roar, like the discontinuous series of clangs, is taken to *emanate from* a certain body, as a result of a continuous physical process, instead of a discontinuous series of physical events, in it.

Now common-sense will not accept any such analysis of the sentence: "I am seeing the Albert Memorial." If you press a plain man with questions, you will easily get him to admit that all that he literally *sees* at any one moment is a *limited part* of the *outer surface* of a certain body. He will say that he *knows* that this must be continued and completed by areas which he is not at present seeing, so as to form the outside of a body, whether solid or hollow. And he will say that he *believes or takes for granted* or even *"knows"* that that body answers to the description of the Albert Memorial. But he will not admit that what he really sees is either a very quick sequence of colour-events or a continuous colour-process analogous to the continuous roar of a waterfall. Nor will he admit that the only sense in which he can be said to see a body is that he takes for granted that these colour-events or this continuous colour-process *emanate from* a certain body. This would plainly be a complete misdescription of the experience which one has when one says that one is seeing a body, as that experience appears to oneself at the time.

This may be reinforced by considering cases where a person *would* say that he is seeing, e.g., a red flash or a continuous glare, i.e. a colour-event or a colour-process. Suppose that on a dark night I were to see a series of flashes of a certain kind at regular intervals in a certain direction. I might well say: "That is the so-and-so lighthouse." But I should not say that I *see* the lighthouse. If anyone were to ask me explicitly, I should say: "No! I can't see *it;* I see only the flashes which I take to be made by the lamp in it."

There is the following important phenomenological difference between hearing a sound and seeing a flash. It would no doubt be quite usual to say "That flash *comes from* the lighthouse," just as we say "That sound *comes from* the clock." But there is this difference. The flash is literally seen as an occurrence of a certain colour within a *limited* region *remote from* the percipient's body. It may even be seen as having a definite shape and size, as, e.g., in the case of seeing a flash of fork-lightning. But the noise is not literally heard as the occurrence of a certain sound-quality within a limited region remote from the percipient's body. It certainly is not heard as having any shape or size. It seems to be heard as *coming to* one from a certain direction, and it seems to be thought of as pervading with various degrees of intensity the whole of an indefinitely large region surrounding the centre from which it emanates.

We may sum this up as follows. In its purely phenomenological aspect *seeing* is ostensibly *saltatory*. It seems to leap the spatial gap between the percipient's body and a remote region of space. Then, again, it is ostensibly *prehensive* of the surfaces of distant bodies as coloured and extended, and of external events as colour-occurrences *localized* in remote regions of space. In its purely phenomenological aspect *hearing* is ostensibly prehensive, not of bodies, but only of events or processes as occurrences of sound-qualities. It is not ostensibly saltatory, for these events or processes are not heard as localized in remote restricted regions of space. They are heard rather as emanating from remote centres and pervading with diminishing intensity the surrounding space.

Let us now compare and contrast seeing and hearing with *feeling*, still from the purely phenomenological standpoint. In the case of feeling we must first draw a distinction between what may be called its qualitative and its dynamical aspects. In the former it is more or less analogous to seeing and to hearing, but in the latter it is, so far as I can see, quite unique. When one has an experience which one would describe as "feeling a body," e.g., with one's hand, one feels it as rough or smooth, hard or soft, and so on. One also feels it as hot or cold. Both these features in the experience belong to its qualitative aspect, and we may distinguish them as "textural experiences" and "temperature-experiences." But closely bound up with the experience of feeling an external body is the experience of actively pushing or pulling it and making it move or stay still in spite of its varying degrees of resistance to one's efforts. This is an example of the dynamical aspect of the experience of feeling. Another example is the experience of trying and failing to move a resting body or to stop a moving one and failing because the resistance which it offers is too great. A third example is the experience of being forced to move in a certain direction by the thrust and pressure of a foreign body in spite of resisting to one's utmost. In these dynamic experiences one seems to oneself not merely to be prehending and exploring the surfaces of foreign bodies, as one seems to oneself to be doing in the case of sight. One seems also to be *interacting* with them, as one does not seem to oneself to be doing when one merely sees or hears them.

In the textural subdivision of its qualitative aspect the experience which we describe as "feeling a body" is much more closely akin to the experience which we describe as "seeing a body" than to any case of hearing. We never talk of feeling *events* or *processes* of roughness or smoothness or hardness or softness. In this respect feeling is ostensibly prehensive *only* of the *surface of bodies*. Just as we ostensibly see the surfaces of bodies, and see them as coloured in various ways, so we ostensibly feel them as rough or smooth, hard or soft. The difference here between sight and feeling is that the former is, and the latter is not, ostensibly saltatory. One can perceive a foreign body as rough or smooth, hard or soft, only when it is in contact with one's own body. It is a natural, if paradoxical, way of speaking to say that seeing seems to "bring one into direct *contact* with *remote* objects" and to reveal their shapes and colours, as feeling reveals the shapes and textures of objects which are literally in contact with one's skin.

When we consider temperature-experiences, however, we find that feeling provides an interesting intermediate case between hearing and seeing, in its phenomenological aspect. Suppose that one is in the neighbourhood of a fairly hot body, e.g., a radiator. Suppose that one gradually approaches it and finally touches it. While one is approaching it the feeling-experience is phenomenologically akin to the experience of hearing which one has when approaching a body which is emitting a continuous sound, e.g., a waterfall. The warmth, like the roaring, seems to pervade the region surrounding the body and to be present in steadily increasing intensity in regions close to it. But when one finally touches the body one has a temperature sensation (combined of course for the first time with textural sensations, and it may be with pain-sensations and dynamic experiences) which is phenomenologically akin to the visual experience which one would describe as seeing the coloured surface of a body. The hotness is now felt as spread out over a limited localized surface, just as the colour is all along seen to be. We say *both* that a body is hot and that it emits warmth; we say that it is red, but *not* that it emits redness; and we say that it emits a roaring, but *not* that it has the auditory quality of roaringness.

I will now leave the purely phenomenological description of the three main forms of human sense-perception, and begin to take into account what we know or believe about the physical processes involved in them. In the light of this knowledge or well-founded belief we can consider whether the phenomenological character of these experiences is or is not misleading as an indication of their epistemological character.

The first important fact that emerges is that, as regards its physical conditions, seeing is almost exactly analogous to hearing, although phenomenologically the two kinds of experience are so extremely unlike. From the physical standpoint seeing a body which is self-luminous, e.g., the sun or a glowing wire, is almost exactly like hearing the roar of a waterfall. From the phenomenological standpoint, as we have seen, the two experiences differ in kind. The former appears to the percipient as the prehension of the coloured surface of a remote definitely localized body, whilst the latter appears to him as the prehension of a process coming to him from a distant centre and pervading the intervening space.

The physical theory of sound fits in very easily with the phenomenological character of the experience of hearing. One can see or feel the clapper of a bell striking the inside of it, and can see or feel the surface throbbing. One can stamp one's foot at one end of a gallery and hear the echo appreciably later than the sound of the original stamping. So we have no difficulty in accepting the fact that one hears a sound when and only when a certain process, set up in the intervening air by the vibration of a distant body, reaches one's ears. But the physical theory of light conflicts sharply with the phenomenological character of the experience of seeing.

Nevertheless, the theory of geometrical optics and the later theory of physical optics are of course based on a systematic study of our experiences of seeing and feeling. Geometrical optics is based on correlating experiences of normal direct vision through a homogeneous medium with experiences of seeing in mirrors of various forms, of seeing through non-homogeneous media of various densities, and so on. Physical optics is based on a further correlation of all this with more recondite experiences of seeing, which can be had only by making astronomical observations or doing specially designed physical experiments.

Now as soon as one ceases to confine one's attention to completely standard cases of direct vision through a homogeneous medium, it becomes quite plain that seeing is radically different from what it appears *prima facie* to be. Before going into detail it will be as well to consider the logical principles involved.

Suppose that the experience which one should naturally describe as "seeing a body of a certain shape and colour at a certain place" really consists in or involves prehending a certain part of the surface of such a body at that place. Then it is *logically* impossible that that experience should have occurred when it did, unless there was at that time a body in that place, such that the part of its surface which was then facing one had the shape and the colour which one then saw. For that is part of what is *meant* by this account of the experience. It is important to notice that the mere fact that a transmissive process must take place in the intervening space and must affect one's eye, if the experience is to occur, is not by itself a conclusive objection. For this might be merely a causally necessary, but insufficient, condition for the occurrence of the experience. It is logically possible that this condition might be fulfilled and yet that the experience could not occur unless there were at that time a body of the required kind at the place in question. What would be fatal to the prehensive account of the experience would be if it could be shown that, provided one's eye is suitably affected, the experience may arise even though no such body is then occupying the place in question. Now there are empirical facts which make this practically certain.

Nothing more recondite than vision in a plane mirror is needed to justify this statement. Suppose one stands facing such a mirror and holds up one's *right* hand with the palm facing the mirror. Then one seems to see a hand, with the palm facing one, held up at a place some distance behind the surface of the mirror. Now we know very well that there is no such body in that place at the time. Moreover, what one seems to see presents the appearance which would be presented, *not* by one's right hand, but by one's *left* hand, if it were held up with the palm facing one at the place behind the mirror where one seems to see a hand. Yet here, just as much as in the most normal case of direct vision through a homogeneous medium, one seems to oneself to be prehending a part of the coloured surface of a certain body in a certain region of space remote from that occupied by one's head and eyes. This unavoidable appearance is *here* certainly misleading. No doubt it would be possible in theory to admit this, and yet to maintain that in the one case of direct vision through a homogeneous medium one really is (as one appears to oneself to be in *all* cases) prehending a part of the coloured surface of a remote foreign body. But, in view of the continuity between the most normal and the most abnormal cases of seeing, such a doctrine would be utterly unplausible and could be defended only by the most desperate special pleading.

The conclusion that the phenomenological character of the experience of seeing is a radically misleading guide to its epistemological character is strongly reinforced when we take into account the empirical facts which lie at the basis of the statement that light has a finite velocity. Suppose that on a certain occasion a person has an experience which he would naturally describe by saying that he sees a certain star in a certain direction. There is overwhelming evidence that he would be having precisely the same kind of experience on that occasion even if the star had ceased to exist for many years or had long ago moved into a quite different position relative to his body. That is to say, at the time when a sane waking person has an experience, which inevitably appears to him to be a prehension of a certain remote coloured body as now lying in a certain direction relative to his own, there may be nothing answering even remotely to the description of such a body anywhere in that direction. Therefore the phenomenological character of the experience is completely misleading as to its epistemological character.

Let us next consider the epistemological character of experiences of feeling. If we confine our attention to the waking experiences of sane persons in normal health, there is, so far as I know, little specific ground for doubting that touch is, as it appears to be, prehensive of the surfaces of foreign bodies in contact with one's own. The only direct counter-evidence that I know of is the experience of seeming to feel *two* bodies in contact with one's skin at a place where one's own sight and the sight and touch of others testify to the presence of only one. Such experiences are by no means common; for my own part I have seldom managed to get the experience of "feeling double." As regards the dynamical aspect of feeling, I do not know of any case of a sane waking person having an experience which he would naturally describe as pushing or pulling or being pushed or pulled by a foreign body, when there is good reason to hold that no such interaction is taking place. No doubt, if we take into account the dreams of sane persons in normal health and the experiences of madmen and of persons in delirium, the case is altered. In any dream the dreamer may seem to himself to be touching foreign bodies which feel rough or smooth, hot or cold. And in nightmares he may seem to himself to be struggling desperately to free himself from the weight or the grip of a foreign body. So it must be admitted that experiences, which are phenomenologically indistinguishable from waking experiences in which we say that we are feeling and interacting with a foreign body, can and do occur when the experient is not in fact prehending by touch or interacting with any such body.

I pass now from the physical to the anatomical and physiological conditions of our experiences of seeing, hearing, and feeling. There seems to be overwhelming evidence for the following statement. Even when a person's eyes or ears or skin are stimulated by the appropriate physical stimulus, he does not have any corresponding experience of seeing or hearing or feeling unless and until a certain internal change is transmitted from the stimulated sense-organ to a certain part of his brain and sets up some kind of disturbance there.

Now we can begin by making the same remark about this fact as we have already made about the fact that seeing or hearing do not occur unless and until a physical process of transmission has taken place in the medium between the foreign body and the eye or ear. The physiological and anatomical facts just stated do not suffice to prove that seeing, hearing, and feeling are not, as they inevitably appear to the experient to be, prehensions of external things or events and of certain of their intrinsic qualities. It might be that these processes in the sensory nerves and the brain are a causally necessary, but insufficient, condition for the occurrence of such experiences. It is logically possible that this condition might be fulfilled, and yet that one would not have an experience which one would naturally describe as seeing or hearing or feeling an external object of a certain kind in a certain place unless there were at the time an external object answering to one's description at the place in question. What would be fatal to the prehensive account of these experiences would be if it could be shown that, provided a certain area of one's brain were suitably affected, such an experience might occur even though no such object were then occupying the place in question. Now the visual, auditory, and tactual experiences which occur in dreaming and in waking hallucination seem to make this practically certain.

There is a logical point which should be emphasized here. Suppose it could be shown that the occurrence of a certain disturbance in a certain part of a person's brain at a certain time is the immediate *sufficient* condition of his then having an experience which he would naturally describe as seeing or hearing or feeling a foreign object of a certain kind in a certain place. Then it would follow at once that the actual presence of such an object in that place at that time *cannot* be a *necessary* condition of the occurrence of the experience. From this it would follow at once that the experience *cannot* be, as it appears to be to the person who has it, a prehension of the object in question. In that case the utmost that could be alleged is that the presence of such an object in the place in question at a somewhat *earlier* date is an indispensable *causal ancestor* of that disturbance in the brain which is the immediate sufficient condition of the occurrence of the experience.

Now I do not wish to commit myself to the sweeping assertion that the occurrence of a certain kind of disturbance in a certain part of a person's brain is the immediate *sufficient* condition, as distinct from an immediate necessary condition, of his having an experience which he would naturally describe as seeing, hearing, or feeling a certain kind of foreign object in a certain place. Therefore I cannot use the knock-down argument which I have outlined above. But that is not really needed in order to refute the prehensive account of such experiences. All that is needed is to show that a person can have experiences, which he would naturally describe as seeing or hearing or feeling a foreign object at a certain place, at a time when there is in fact no such object at that place. For this purpose it is enough to adduce the visual, tactual, and auditory experiences which occur in dreaming and in waking hallucination, and the visual experiences of "seeing" a mirror-image or a distant star which no longer exists.

It would, no doubt, be theoretically possible to admit the conclusion about dreams and waking hallucinations, and yet to maintain that a sane waking man, in his *tactual* experiences at any rate, really is prehending a part of the intrinsically hot or cold, rough or smooth, surface of a foreign body in contact with his skin. But anyone who does so is committed to the following paradox. He has to hold that the tactual experiences of dreams and hallucinations, on the one hand, and those of normal waking life, on the other, are utterly different in their epistemological character, in spite of being exactly alike in their phenomenological character. There is one respect, and one only, in which his position is less paradoxical than that of a person who should maintain that direct vision through a homogeneous medium is prehensive of remote foreign objects, whilst admitting that vision in a mirror or through a non-homogeneous medium cannot be so. There is a continuous series of intermediate cases between the most normal and the queerest instances of seeing by sane waking men. But there is no such series of intermediate cases between dreaming or waking hallucination, on the one hand, and normal waking sense-perception, on the other.

There is one other point which should be mentioned before leaving the present part of our topic. It might be alleged with considerable plausibility that a person could not have dreams or waking hallucinations unless and until he had had a good deal of normal waking sense-perception. It might further be remarked that we do in fact distinguish between our dreams and waking hallucinations, on the one hand, and our normal waking sense-perceptions, on the other. Now I think that some people would be inclined to hold that these observations undermine the argument from the occurrence of dreams and waking hallucinations to the non-prehensive character of normal waking sense-perceptions. Such a contention is, I think, mistaken.

The argument which is alleged to be undermined comes simply to this. There are certain experiences, viz., dreams and waking hallucinations, which exactly resemble normal waking sense-perceptions in all their phenomenological characteristics (including that of being ostensibly prehensive of foreign bodies and external physical events), but which are certainly not in fact prehensions of any such objects. It seems most unlikely that experiences which exactly resemble these in all their phenomenological characteristics, as do normal waking sense-perceptions, should be fundamentally unlike them in their epistemological character.

Now the mere fact that to have had normal waking sense-perceptions is a necessary causal precondition for having dreams and waking hallucinations does not entail or even make probable that the former differ fundamentally in their epistemological character from the latter. So this alleged fact is irrelevant to the validity of the argument and to the truth of its conclusion.

The fact that we do manage to distinguish between our dreams and waking hallucinations on the one hand, and our normal waking sense-perceptions on the other, might seem at first sight to be relevant in the following way. It might seem to be incompatible with the premiss that dreams and hallucinations exactly resemble normal waking sense-perceptions in all their phenomenological characteristics. That, however, is a mistake. We do not distinguish the two kinds of experience by noting dissimilarities in their *phenomenological* character. We do so by considering the *inter-relations* of experiences with the earlier and later experiences of the same person and the contemporary experiences of others.

On the whole, then, I see nothing for it but to draw the following conclusion. Our waking experiences of seeing, hearing, and touching are not, as they appear to us to be, prehensions of foreign bodies and physical events and of certain of their intrinsic qualities.

We are now in a position to consider the notion of "sense-data" or "sensa," which played so great a part in the philosophy of sense-perception in the first thirty years of this century and has been so heavily belaboured since then. It seems to me that the best way to approach the question is the following. For such reasons as I have given above, most philosophers have felt obliged to deny that experiences of seeing, hearing, or feeling are prehensions of foreign bodies and physical events, and to deny that they even contain prehensions of such entities as constituents. To that extent they felt obliged to hold that the phenomenological character of such experiences is a misleading guide to their epistemological character. But many of them saw no reason to think that the phenomenological character of these experiences is so radically misleading as it would be if they were not *prehensions of anything* and did not even contain as constituents *prehensions of anything*. They therefore assumed without question that these experiences really are, as they appear to be to those who have them, *prehensions of particulars of some kind*, though not of the surfaces of bodies or of physical events. And they assumed without question that the qualities, such as redness, squeakiness, hotness, etc., which we *seem* to ourselves to prehend on the surfaces of bodies or in physical events, really do belong to, and are prehended in, these non-physical particulars.

We can now give a description of the technical term "sensum" or "sense-datum." We give this name to that particular which a person *really is* prehending in any experience in which he *appears to himself* to be prehending a physical event or a part of the surface of a body. We give it on the double assumption (i) that he *is* prehending a particular of some kind, and (ii) that he is *not* prehending a physical event or a part of the surface of a body. If this account of the meaning of the term be accepted, one thing at least is certain. The use of it presupposes a positive doctrine, viz., that experiences of seeing, feeling, and hearing do consist in or involve *prehending* a particular of *some kind*, which has, and is prehended as having, a certain intrinsic quality, e.g., redness or hotness or squeakiness.

Unless this assumption is true there is nothing answering to the above description of a "sensum" or "sense-datum." So the question arises whether there is any reason to doubt this assumption.

In order to deal with this we must now consider more carefully a notion which I have so far left undiscussed, viz., that of prehending a particular. I have intended to use this phrase as equivalent to one which was introduced many years ago by Earl Russell, viz., "being *acquainted with* a particular." I prefer this terminology to Russell's for the following purely linguistic reason. An essential feature of any experience which Russell would describe as "being acquainted with a certain particular" is that the latter presents itself to the experient as having a certain quality, e.g., as red, as hot, as squeaky, etc. Now it is linguistically awkward to say that a person is "acquainted with a certain particular as red." But it is not unnatural to say that a person "prehends a certain particular as red." I use the expression "*S* prehends *x* as red" as precisely equivalent to the phrase "*x* sensibly presents itself to *S* as red."

The meaning of these phrases cannot be defined, it can only be exemplified. One thing that is certain is that to prehend *x* as red is utterly different from *judging* that it is red or *knowing* that it is red. In the dark and with my eyes shut I can judge that my doctor's gown is red, and in one sense of "know" I may be said to know that it is red. But in such conditions I am not prehending anything as red, or, what is precisely equivalent, nothing is being sensibly presented to me as red. Consider, again, the case of a cat or a dog, which has eyes very much like ours, but presumably lacks general concepts and therefore cannot literally know or judge that a certain predicate belongs to a certain subject. It may have, and very likely does have, experiences which would be described by saying that certain particulars sensibly present themselves to it as red or as hot or as squeaky.

It is generally taken to be meaningless to suggest that a particular which was not in fact red could sensibly present itself as red, or, what is equivalent, could be prehended as red. Suppose that a creature, which has appropriate general concepts and is capable of making judgments and knowing facts, prehends a certain particular as red. Then, it would commonly be said, this experience suffices to enable him to *know* the fact that it is red. Whether he does or does not *actually* contemplate this fact at the time depends on various contingent circumstances. These remarks about prehending are perfectly general; they would apply equally if we substituted for "red," which I have merely taken as an example, such words as "hot," "squeaky," etc.

I do not think it is worth while to spend much time over the question whether prehending could properly be described as a form of *knowing*. If we use "know" in such a way that what is known must be a *fact*, it is certain that prehending would not be a form of knowing. For, if we prehend anything, it is *particulars*. But the word "know" is often used as principal verb in a sentence in which the grammatical object is not a subordinate clause of the form "that *S* is *P*," but is the name or description of a particular. I should say, e.g., "I knew McTaggart, but I did not know Sidgwick." In many languages these two senses of "know" are expressed by different words, e.g., in German by *wissen* and *kennen*. There is therefore nothing in the usage of the word "know" to rule out the suggestion that prehending might properly be described as a form of "knowing," in the sense of "kenning" though not in that of "witting." A more substantial point is this. Even if prehending could not be properly described as a form of knowing, in either of these senses, it is conceived, as we have seen, to be most intimately bound up with the possibility of knowing certain facts about the particulars prehended.

I will now try to say what I think is involved in asserting that certain experiences are prehensions of particulars of some kind as having certain intrinsic qualities. (1) The phrase "being a prehension of" is taken to denote a certain *relation* which holds between *experiences* of certain kinds and *particulars* of certain kinds." Examples of such experiences are visual, tactual, and auditory sensations. (2) The particulars in question are such that adjectives like "red," "hot," "squeaky," etc. (used in the *non-dispositional* sense in which they occur in such sentences as "This *looks* red to me," "This *feels* hot to me," and so on), can be predicated of them. (3) If an experience *e* is a prehension of a particular *x*, it is *ipso facto* a prehension of *x* as having a certain quality *c;* and it is logically impossible that *x* should be prehended as having *c* unless it does in fact have *c*. (4) Corresponding to any such experience *e* there is *one and only one* such particular *x*, of which *e* is a prehension. This may therefore be described as *"the* particular of which *e* is a prehension." (5) It is *logically* possible that a particular, which was in fact prehended on a certain occasion by a certain person as having a certain quality, should have existed and had that quality at that time even though it had not been prehended either by him or by anyone else. (6) It is *logically* possible that there should be particulars which are never prehended by anyone, but are of the same kinds as those which are actually prehended. Thus, e.g., it is logically possible that there should be particulars which are squeaky, in the sense in which that word is used in the sentence "That sounds squeaky," but which are not prehended by anyone. (7) It is *logically* possible that a particular, which was in fact prehended on a certain occasion by a certain person, should then have been prehended by *another* person, either instead of or in addition to the one who actually prehended it.

It should be noted that in all these statements I have been careful to use the phrase *"logically* possible," i.e., not internally inconsistent nor inconsistent with any *a priori* truth. If we were to substitute for this the phrase *"causally* possible," i.e., not inconsistent with any actual law of nature, the case would be altered. Take, e.g., the case of a person who holds that auditory sensations are prehensions. He could consistently hold that it is *causally* impossible for there to be a squeak which is not prehended by anyone. He could consistently hold that it is *causally* impossible that the very same squeak which is prehended by one person should be prehended by any other. What he could not consistently hold is that these suggestions are *logically* impossible. I think that we ought, nevertheless, to realize that such a person would be asserting an extremely queer proposition. So far as I can see, he would have to assert that the conditions which are *causally necessary* to produce a squeaky particular are always *causally sufficient* to evoke in a certain *one* person an experience which is a prehension of that particular as squeaky. And he would have to add that they are also causally sufficient to ensure the *non-occurrence* of such an experience in *any other* person. The following would be a particular instance of this general proposition. It might be held that the occurrence of a certain event in a certain person's brain is causally necessary to *generate* a squeaky particular. It might be held that this event is also causally sufficient to evoke in that person's mind an experience which is a prehension of that particular as squeaky. And, finally, it might be held that the fact that this event happens in the brain of *that* person suffices to ensure that no such experience will be evoked in the mind of *any other* person. It should be noted that the evidence for the general proposition, or for this or any other specialization of it, would have to be empirical. It is not easy to see what adequate empirical evidence there could be.

It remains to consider, very briefly, the main grounds which might be alleged for doubting the prehensive account of visual, auditory, and tactual sensations, and therefore for doubting whether there is anything answering to the description of "sensa" or "sense-data."

(1) It seems just as plausible to hold that one is prehending something as coloured or as squeaky in the case of dreaming and imaging as in the case of normal waking sense-perception. Now on reflection it would appear to many persons to be, not merely causally impossible, but *absurd* to suppose that a visual or auditory image or the contents of a dream could exist except as contents of a certain one person's experience of imaging or dreaming on a certain one occasion. If that is true, it cannot be a correct account of the visual, tactual, or auditory experiences of imaging or dreaming to say that they consist in prehending certain particulars as red, as squeaky, as cold, and so on. But the only reason for accepting the prehensive account

of the visual, tactual, and auditory experiences of normal waking life was that in them one seems to oneself to be prehending *something* as red or as squeaky or as cold, etc., even though reflection shows us that these "somethings" cannot be bodies or physical events. Now, whatever we may say of imaging, there is no doubt that the visual, tactual, and auditory experiences of dreaming are indistinguishable in their phenomenological character from those of normal waking life. If, then, the former cannot be regarded as prehensions of particulars of *any kind,* and the latter cannot be regarded as prehensions of *bodies* or of *physical events* (which is what they seem *prima facie* to be), there seems to be little ground for regarding the latter as prehensions of *anything.*

(2) The line of argument just stated is of course not demonstrative, even if one accepts its premisses. But many persons would be inclined to use the following more radical argument. They would say that it seems evident to them on reflexion that words like "red," "hot," "squeaky," etc., in their primary *non-dispositional* sense, can occur significantly only in such sentences as "This *looks* red to me," "This *feels* hot to me," "This *sounds* squeaky to me," and so on. They would allege that whenever these words are used significantly in sentences such as "This *is* red," "This *is* hot," or "This *is* squeaky," they are used in a *dispositional* sense. Thus, it would be said, "This *is* red" is significant only if it is interpreted as "This *would* look red to any person of normal eyesight under certain standard conditions of vision." And the others are significant only if they are interpreted *mutatis mutandis* in a similar way. Now the prehensive analysis of visual, tactual, and auditory sensations presupposes that there are entities which *are* red or hot or squeaky, where these words are used in the non-dispositional sense in which they are used in such sentences as "This looks red to me" or "This feels hot to me" or "This sounds squeaky to me." For the prehensive analysis asserts that to have a visual or tactual or auditory sensation is to prehend a particular which *has* a certain colour-quality or temperature-quality or sound-quality. Having

such a sensation just consists in prehending a certain particular as having a certain quality, e.g., redness, which it does in fact have. Thus, if the premiss of this argument be accepted, the prehensive account of visual, tactual, and auditory sensations cannot be correct, and there can be nothing answering to the description of "sensa" or "sense-data" given earlier in this paper.

(3) A final consideration which might be urged against the prehensive analysis is this. The only ground for holding that visual, tactual, and auditory experiences are prehensions of particulars of *some* kind is the fact that they inevitably seem to us to be such while we are having them. But they seem to us, while we are having them, to be prehensions of *bodies* and *physical events*. Now it has to be admitted that this is a delusion. Once that is admitted can we safely go on holding that they are prehensions of *anything*? Is it really credible that, if they were prehensions of particulars, they could be completely misleading as to the nature of those particulars?

SEEING

G. J. WARNOCK

It is in some ways an unfortunate fact that many, perhaps most, of those philosophers who have written about perception have in fact been primarily interested in knowledge—in the principles of human knowledge, in our knowledge of the external world, in the foundations of empirical knowledge. It may be that the theory of knowledge presents more interesting problems than perception does, but in discussing them perception itself cannot be ignored, and ought not to be treated in too perfunctory a manner. In this paper I wish to call attention to some points about seeing which have not perhaps been sufficiently remarked. Indeed, in the discussions of perceiving, observing, sensing, apprehending and the rest, it appears that simple seeing has often been neglected.

In the actual employment of the verb "to see" there appears at first sight to be a mere chaos of constructions and indeed of categories. In the case of most transitive verbs there are fairly clear and fairly close restrictions on the types of expressions which can properly occur as their objects, or in the other constructions, if any, by which they can be followed. By contrast one is inclined to say[1] that

[1] I say only that one is *inclined* to say this, since it is not clearly a proper thing to say. One may say that, *e.g.*, I saw the colour of his tie, that the colour of his tie is a quality of his tie, and hence that I saw a quality; or that I saw the untidiness of his room, *i.e.*, the untidy state of his room, and hence that I saw a state. But the reverse argument that one may see a quality, that redness is a quality, and hence that one may see redness, seems to lead to an uncomfortable conclusion. Similarly, that one may see the relation between the windows and the door suggests that one may see a relation, but one does not

one may be said to see at least (1) things (not necessarily material objects); (2) events, happenings, performances; (3) qualities; (4) relations; (5) states or conditions; and (6) facts (including negative facts). One may further be said to see where things are, how things are done or how to do things, why things happen, and whether things are happening. The list is not exhaustive, but it seems to me to be already extensive enough to make it clear that the verb "to see" is in some way an oddity; we need to investigate its seeming grammatical and categorical sprawl. It will appear also that the implications of its uses are by no means simple.

I

1. Consider first the statement that I once saw Lloyd George. Now if we take Lloyd George to have been what Prichard used to call a body, this statement entails that on at least one occasion I saw a body. It is now relevant to consider one of the reasons for which Prichard, and others, used to maintain that such a statement "will not stand examination". It was urged that, if ever a body were "really seen", it would necessarily appear as it really was; there are however admittedly cases in which this is not so, and, by a rather indefinite appeal to some sort of "continuity", it was concluded that in no case is it really so. Similarly Broad has maintained (in *Philosophy*, Jan. 1952 [pp. 36–37, this volume. Ed.]) that "in view of the continuity between the most normal and the most abnormal cases of seeing", it is necessary to conclude that in no case at all is seeing really "prehensive of bodies", or of the surfaces of bodies; and it appears that this conclusion is taken to refute any ordinary claim to see a body, at least as that claim would be commonly understood.

wish to say that one sees, say, proximity. The rather bald expressions in the text should be interpreted in terms of the various constructions which we do employ, not as licensing constructions which we do not. The need for caution here was pointed out to me by Mr. H. P. Grice, to whom I am indebted also at many other points.

If I understand these arguments rightly, they turn on the point that, if A really prehends (or apprehends) X, it is impossible that X should appear to him as it is not; I am not sure whether it would have been asserted also, what is not the same thing, that it is impossible that A should take X to be what it is not. Broad appears to incline to this latter assertion, since he does not think it clearly mistaken to suggest that "prehending might properly be described as a form of 'knowing' "; but Prichard, at some apparent risk of inconsistency, maintains that we do habitually *mis*take the entities that we apprehend for bodies. However, we need not settle this point precisely; for it is in any case now possible to conclude that seeing is in fact neither prehending nor apprehending, nor is it commonly thought to be so. For, so far from its being impossible that, if I really saw Lloyd George, he should have appeared to me otherwise than he really was, perhaps impossible also that I should have been mistaken as to his identity or character, there is no need to deny that I saw Lloyd George even if every possible mistake[2] were actually made, or even if he appeared in the most un-natural guise.

Suppose for example, that I saw Lloyd George standing lost in meditation in Madame Tussaud's, and mistook him for a wax model of Winston Churchill; suppose, if you like, that he was actually pretending to be a wax model of Winston Churchill, and had disguised himself for the purpose; there would be in all this no reason at all to deny that I then saw Lloyd George. For to say that I saw Lloyd George does not entail either that I was then, or that I am now, able to describe his appearance correctly or even at all, that at the time I identified him correctly or even at all; it does not entail that he appeared to me to be Lloyd George, or that he appeared as Lloyd George normally did. Certainly if I now say that I saw Lloyd George, I do at least claim to have now, by whatever means and in spite of whatever disguises, identified as Lloyd George the person that

---

[2] This is, I fear, a rhetorical exaggeration. Mistakes exceeding a certain degree of wildness would justify the view that I was the victim of hallucination or in some other way in no fit state to see things.

I saw; but others might truly say of me, even though I would not say of myself, that I saw Lloyd George, even if I have not now, and had not then, any notion that it was Lloyd George that I saw. We may consider a more extreme case still. Suppose that, when I saw Lloyd George, I made no mistake only through making no judgment whatever, that I was not mis-led by appearances only because I was not led by appearances at all; suppose that I was an infant in arms. Even so, so long as there is reason to hold that I did, as we might say, "set eyes on" the man who was in fact Lloyd George, then there is reason to say that I saw him, even though I then neither made, nor could have made, any judgment at all, either right or wrong, about who or what it was that I saw.

2. I suspect that some philosophers have been mis-led in this matter by confining their attention to uses of the verb "to see" in the present tense and the first person singular. It has been rightly emphasized that the statement that one sees, say, a fox, is true only if there is a fox to be seen, and if what is seen is actually a fox. It follows from this that I would myself ordinarily say that I see a fox only if I not only believe with some reason, but believe that I know, that what I see is a fox. But the question whether I actually do see a fox is not the same question as whether I myself would say that I do. Not only might I falsely say that I do when I do not; others might truly say of me that I do, even though I would not say this or would actually deny it. If I say that I see a fox and am asked how I know that it is a fox, I cannot consistently say "I don't know—perhaps it isn't"; but if I say of someone else that he sees a fox and am asked how he knows that it is a fox, I may properly say "He doesn't know—he thinks it's a dog"—though of course I still imply that I know that it is a fox. Similarly with the past tense; if I now say that I saw a fox, although I thus purport to know now that it was a fox that I saw, I may quite properly deny that I knew this when I saw it. One who says that he sees purports to know; but one who does not know does not, for that reason, not see.

It is of course true that very often the best way to identify something, or to put one's self in a position to describe it correctly, is to see it, to have a look at it; it is however a mistake to suppose that seeing things essentially involves knowing, or getting to know, what they are, or what they are like, or even how they appear.

3. We must now consider some of the qualifications required by this rather bald conclusion. We need not go into the question whether it is necessary that one who is to be said to see should have eyes (though of course it is in any case a highly important fact that we do have eyes, that we have two of them, that they are as they are, and that they both point the same way); for without answering this question, we may say for a start that one who sees must have a field of vision, and that what he may rightly be said to see must be in it. Now what more than this ought we to say?

(*a*) The obvious point that one who sees must not only have his eyes open and in working order, but must also be conscious, is not quite so simple as it might seem. The infant of whom we say rightly that he saw Lloyd George doubtless set eyes on him in a normal, though non-adult, condition of consciousness; it is however clearly not necessary that the condition of consciousness should be normal. The taker of mescalin presumably sees what he looks at; but the open-eyed sleep-walker presumably does not; and there is room for many intermediate conditions. How far, then, may one deviate from normal conditions of consciousness without its for that reason being called in question whether one sees those things on which one's eyes are set? I do not know what can be said in general on this point, if anything can; it may be that only *ad hoc,* and probably sometimes rather arbitrary, decisions are possible for particular cases.

(*b*) It would, I imagine, be easily admitted, though some philosophers have seemed to deny, that the truth of the statement that Jones saw a fox is not impugned by Jones' mis-identification of what he saw, nor by his failing either to identify or mis-identify it, nor by his being mistaken as to its character or qualities. But, it might be said, not only must one who sees be conscious, he must in some way and degree be conscious *of* what he sees. If Jones sees a fox, he must at least be conscious of a—perhaps by him unidentified and unconsidered—*something* in his field of vision; if not, it must surely be absurd to say that he sees it.

Now let us widen the scope of this question by bringing in the notion of noticing. "Notice" appears to have at least two (relevant) uses; roughly, it means sometimes "to be struck by", sometimes "to pick out". Suppose that I am asked "Did you notice his tie?", in a context such that the question suggests that there was something noteworthy about it. Now I might be in no doubt that I did see his tie, but if I was not particularly struck by and perhaps cannot recall anything about it, I might answer the question in the words "No, not particularly". On the other hand, if asked "Did you see Lloyd George?" (*e.g.*, in the audience) I might reply that I did not, for the reason that I had not noticed him, picked him out in the crowd. It seems to me to follow from this that it scarcely makes sense to ask *in general* whether one who sees also notices. It is, I suppose, not inconceivable that a person should be of so enthusiastic or sensitively observant a nature that he noticed, was in some degree struck by, absolutely everything that he saw; but this is certainly not the common case, and indeed one might say that for most of us there is, about most of the things that we see, simply nothing to notice (particularly). It is even clearer that not every case of seeing is a case of picking something out; in this sense, when for instance one sees a large building from close at hand, one neither notices it nor fails to do so. Thus, when it is true that X saw Y, the question whether X noticed Y may not be in place at all; if it is in place, the answer may be Yes or No, depending on the sense in which the question is to be understood.

What then of "being conscious of"? Clearly there are some cases, and some senses, in which one may be said to see what one is not conscious of. One may, for instance, be quite unconscious of the dust on one's furniture, idiomatically "blind" to it, but one need not be said not to see it; one may indeed become unconscious of it precisely because one sees it so often. I think too that it would be intelligible to say that someone's attention was occupied so exclusively with, *e.g.*, what he was listening to, that he was quite unconscious of what he saw; perhaps also one may be said sometimes to remember seeing something that one was not conscious of at the time. But in absolutely ordinary cases the question is certainly obscure and perhaps unreal; if I report that Jones saw Lloyd George at a meeting yesterday, what could prompt you to ask me "Was Jones conscious of him?"? If Jones were an ambitious Liberal of the appropriate date, it might indeed be said of him that he was agreeably conscious of his leader's presence in the front row; but one is not in this sense conscious of all that one sees, nor indeed is it necessary that one should see what one is thus conscious of. I suspect that, if there is a sense of "being conscious of" so different from that of "noticing" that one is in general and always conscious of what one sees, it is such that it is to be simply analytic that what one sees one is conscious of; but whether there is any utility in such a sense seems to me doubtful. One might be inclined to sponsor such a use of "conscious of" in the hope of evading an apparent dilemma: if one abandons, as clearly one must abandon, the idea that one who sees must have actual knowledge of what is before his eyes, it may appear that seeing is in peril of becoming attenuated to the object's merely being before his eyes; it is however a mere physical fact that this is so, and it is rightly felt that seeing must amount to more than this. At this point, then, one may be inclined to say that one must be conscious of what one sees, thus bringing in more than the thing's merely being before one's eyes, yet less than one's having actual knowledge of it. This is, however, too obscure to be the solution of any difficulty, and should be regarded only as an incentive to the examination of particular cases. Certainly, if someone appears to be, and later sincerely asserts that he was, unconscious of something clearly before his eyes, there must always be a serious question whether he saw it; but such cases will differ, and we should not assume that in all it must be impossible so to explain his being unconscious of it as not necessarily to exclude saying also that he saw it.

(c) There is a variety of curious questions which might be raised about the thing seen, turning upon the question, where this is appropriate, *how much* of it must be seen for it to be true that simply the thing itself is seen. It used at one time to be urged that one never sees, at a given moment, the whole of any object at which one looks, and hence that one cannot be said simply to see it. This contention appears to overlook the seeing of, for example, rainbows. More seriously, it seems to confuse seeing only part of (the proper contrast with the whole of) an object, with seeing it only from one point of view—seeing only Lloyd George's left leg, for example, with seeing him only from the side. This is not unimportant, for whereas one might well hesitate to say that one had seen Lloyd George if one had seen, unfortunately, only his left leg, one would not so hesitate if one had seen him, naturally enough, only from one's place in the auditorium. It would be minute and tedious to elaborate this question very far; I would like to make only four general comments upon it. (i) It is clearly not in general necessary that one should see the whole of what one sees, even in cases where to speak thus is appropriate, for it to be simply true that one sees it. I have never seen the whole of Blenheim Palace, but there is no question that I have seen it. (ii) It is important to bear in mind the conditions in which particular types of things are customarily seen. We are accustomed to seeing people, for instance, partly covered by clothing, but do not feel inclined, since this is how we ordinarily see them, to complain that we see only part of them. Even if they were totally covered up, still, so long as what they were covered with was clothing or at least something commonly worn such as armour, we might say that we had seen them without qualification. The case would be altered if they were encased in boxes, particularly if these were quite rigid, and it is of course different also for objects which are not ordinarily covered at all. (iii) Some parts of some objects are more significant than others. One would be readier to say simply that one had seen Lloyd George, if one had seen only his face, than if one had seen only his feet. (iv) The question what it is proper to say will often depend also on the conversational context. For example, where the task is to find some object, it will not mislead to say that one sees it as soon as one has located it; but where the interest is in an object's appearance, inability to give an account of this might call for qualification of the claim to have seen it. Thus, if one were trying to locate the cricket pavilion on a very dark night, one might say that one saw it (implying "Now I know where it is") on seeing only a very small though recognizable part; but if one had seen only the top left-hand corner of a painting otherwise completely covered, to say simply that one had seen it (suggesting "I know what it looks like") would be improper. This is not of course to say that inability to describe an object's appearance is *always* a reason for qualifying the claim to have seen it.

So far, we have been considering the seeing of things, objects—not necessarily, of course, material objects. The case of seeing happenings, events, occurrences must be briefly dealt with, and in any case is similar in most respects, not quite in all. If, for example, I say truly that Smith saw the robbery committed, it does not follow that he then knew, or now knows, that that is what he saw happening, that any robbery was committed. He may have failed to realize, or perhaps not particularly noticed, what was going on; if so, he will not be a good witness to the event, but he still was a witness of it—he did see it happen. Again, one might properly say that the only witness of some occurrence was, unluckily, an infant, who had no idea what was going on and could not give any account of what he saw. The only important new point, I think, is this: one may not only fail to realize the nature of, or fail to notice, an event that occurs before one's eyes—it may be that the event occurs too quickly to be seen at all; so that even if warned and watching, and although the event does certainly occur before one, one cannot say that one sees it happen, or happening. It might reasonably be suggested, however, that there is an analogue to this in the case of an object which is in one's field of vision too briefly to be seen; in such a case it is clear that one simply does not see it; it is not a case of seeing but failing to notice. The conjuror sometimes eludes one's vigilance by diverting one's attention; but sometimes the quickness of the hand defeats the eye.

The argument so far can be summed up as follows. In any of the cases so far considered, we may take it that, if it is to be true that A saw X, then at least A must have set eyes on X, being conscious and with eyes in reasonable working order. It may in some cases be further required that A should have noticed X, picked X out; but this point does not arise in every case; and certainly it cannot be always required that A should have taken particular note of X. It may be that in some sense—which deserves more consideration than I have given it—it must be true that A was conscious of X; however, there is certainly *a* sense in which this is not necessary. It is in no case necessary that A should have identified X, or made a correct judgment of X's character or qualities, or even that he should have known how X appeared to him; on this last point, one might say vaguely that he always could have known this, but certainly he need not actually have done so.

It seems to me that these contentions have often been denied, perhaps inadvertently, and indeed that they must be denied in most attempts to exhibit seeing as consisting in, or even including, any sort of "apprehending" or "direct awareness"; for these latter expressions have commonly been defined by reference to what the percipient knows, in some cases "incorrigibly", to be true. One who sees, however, need not know anything at all.

II

1. The case is radically altered when we pass to the other constructions which I listed at the beginning. This is most obviously so in the case of (6), the seeing of facts; and this case can usefully be contrasted with those that we have just been considering. Suppose that I, who do not play chess, and a competent chess-player are watching together a game in progress. It is clear that, in the senses so far considered, he sees what I see, no more and no less; we both see the board, the pieces, the players, the movements made. But suppose that at a certain stage of the game my companion sees that White's bishop is dangerously exposed. Now although in a sense I still see what he sees, I certainly do not see this; and clearly the reason for saying that I do not see it is that I do not realize, and in my ignorance am not in a position to realize, that the piece in question is dangerously exposed. The facts that it is so, and that I have a good view of the game in which that is true, do not together add up to my seeing that it is so; for in this there would be essentially involved my noticing, realizing, getting to know that it is so. Nor, if I later learn how to play chess, can I say retrospectively that I saw that White's bishop was dangerously exposed; for I did not realize this at the time, and hence did not then see it.

One can say "I saw a fox but I did not know that it was one", or "He sees a fox but he does not know that it is one". By contrast one cannot say either "I saw that it was raining but I did not realize that it was", or "He sees that it is raining but he does not realize that it is".

2. Now of the other cases not yet considered I think one can say, not only that they share this feature, but also that they share it in virtue of being essentially variants of the same case. Consider a simple case of what we called, with hesitation, seeing a quality, for example seeing the colour

of Lloyd George's tie. It is clear that one could not rightly say that one saw the colour of his tie, if one did not get to know at the time what colour it was. At first sight this might seem anomalous. Why, one might ask, if I can rightly say that I saw the tie though I did not know what it was, can I not say that I saw the colour of the tie though I did not realize what it was? I imagine that the answer to this question—the question why we should speak in this way—would be that, unless I noticed the colour of his tie and hence knew what colour it was, there would be no point in making particular mention of the colour in saying what I saw. Similarly, there would be no point in asking the particular question "Did you see the colour of his tie?", if an affirmative answer to this question were compatible with the answerer's not knowing what colour it was. It is worth noticing that, if asked whether one could see, say, the shape of a building, it would be natural to reply in the words "No, I could not really *tell* from where I was standing". It would by contrast be plainly outrageous to reply "Yes, but I could not tell what shape it was".

Similar considerations apply to the seeing of relations, and states or conditions. To say "I thought he was a very tidy person until I saw the state of his room" is clearly to imply that I saw *that* his room was untidy; the point of making particular mention of the *state* of his room would be lost unless I meant to convey that I got to know what his room was like. Similarly, a newly immigrant Esquimaux taken on a tour of my garden might certainly be said to see my garden, but hardly the neglected condition of my garden; for his general ignorance of gardens would preclude him from realizing that it was, by comparison with other gardens, neglected. An expert who looks at the engine of a car might possibly see its condition at a glance, but I, though I see the same engine, do not see this. Again, suppose that an architect directs one's attention to the relation between the upper and lower windows of a façade; if one does not know what he has in mind, what exactly it is that he sees to be true of these windows, one would be guilty of some dishonesty if one claimed to see the relation in question. One might indeed say simply "No, I don't see it".

We may simplify the remaining cases by saying briefly: to see why the engine stopped is to see *that* it stopped for a particular reason; to see where the fault was is to see *that* it was in a particular place; to see how to cure it is to see *that* it could be cured in a particular way; to see whether there is petrol in the tank is to see *that* there is some (or is not). In effect, in all these instances alike it is the "see that . . ." construction which must be regarded as fundamental. It thus becomes important to examine this construction more closely. Perhaps it will be useful to consider the ways in which a claim to see that so-and-so might be attacked, since this should serve to bring out what it is that is claimed.

3. First, then, and very obviously, any such claim might be attacked by denying or questioning the fact alleged in the subordinate clause. If for instance I say "I had hoped to have a word with Jones, but I see that he isn't here", I would be conclusively shown to have been mistaken if it were shown that in fact Jones was present. One cannot claim or be said to see that *p*, if not-*p*, just as in such a case one cannot rightly claim or be said to know that *p;* and this is of course more than chance analogy.

Next, such a claim might be attacked on the ground that although what one claims to see to be the case is the case, yet one does not know that it is the case. Suppose that I say "I saw at once that he was seriously ill". It might be objected that I had not in fact realized this. "You did nothing about it for days; I don't believe you knew"; or that I lacked the necessary qualifications—"You're not a doctor; how could you have told that he was seriously ill?"; or that nobody could have known—"There weren't any particular symptoms at that time"; or again, that I ought not to speak so confidently—"You couldn't possibly have been sure". It is not in these cases disputed either that I saw him, or that he was ill; it is contended that, when I saw him, I did not or could not have *known,* and hence did not see, that he was ill.

Slightly different from this is the further objection that, although what one claims to see to be the case is the case, and although one may know that it is the case, still one does not *see* that it is the case. For example: "You knew he was ill from what the nurse told you; there weren't any visible symptoms". Similarly, if someone were to make the absurd remark "I see that the moon is 250,000 miles away" (and were to say this as if making a judgment of distance by eye, not reporting something that he had read), it would not be necessary to question either the fact or his knowledge of the fact; the absurdity would consist in the impossibility of discovering, or even estimating, just by looking, the distance away of such a distant object.

Thus the claim to see that p—mutatis mutandis for other tenses—appears to involve (i) that p is the case; (ii) that the claimant knows that p is the case; (iii) that there are in what he sees sufficient grounds for concluding that $p;$ and (iv) that he so concludes on those grounds.

4. It will be advisable to correct at once a possible wrong impression that might be conveyed by speaking, almost unavoidably, of "grounds" and "conclusions." We tend no doubt, and in general quite properly, to think of the grounds for a conclusion as being appreciably different from the conclusion, and of a conclusion as being drawn, reached, or arrived at, after at least some thought. In the discussion of seeing that p, however, all this may be inappropriate. The "ground" for saying, for instance, "I saw that he was mowing the lawn" may be simply that one saw him mowing the lawn; and in such a case that he was mowing the lawn would not be a "conclusion" drawn at length or with difficulty—nor, one might add, arrived at by inference. If the question be raised why in this case one should bother to say "I saw that he was mowing the lawn" at all, when one might have said simply "I saw him mowing the lawn", an important part of the answer would be that, however verbally alike, these constructions may have very different conversational points. Roughly, if what is of concern is what happened to the lawn, the former con-

struction is the more natural; if what is of concern is what he was doing, then the latter. There would often be hardly anything to choose between them, but this is not to say that there would never be any reason to pick one rather than the other.

Furthermore, in spite of the close verbal similarity between "I saw that he was mowing the lawn" and "I saw him mowing the lawn", there are important logical differences. Certainly neither sentence entails the other. For if he had a very strange sort of mowing machine I might see him mowing the lawn without seeing that that was what he was doing; and I might possibly, on seeing, say, cut grass flying into the air on the other side of a wall, be justified in saying that I saw that he was mowing the lawn, though it would scarcely be proper to say that I saw him mowing it.

Of course the "conclusion" *may* sometimes be quite remote from the "grounds". For example, on seeing chairs, tables, crockery, etc., being carried out into my neighbour's garden at about 4 p.m., I might say "I see that they're going to have tea in the garden". On seeing the flag at half-mast I might say "I see that someone has died". And there is also the rather special case of, for instance, seeing in the newspaper that income-tax is to be raised.

5. This last case raises a question of some interest. One can well imagine the protest being made "But you don't literally *see* that income-tax is to be raised". But why not? It might be said that all one literally sees is that the paper says so. But what if the paper is absolutely reliable, so that one can reasonably claim to know that what it says is true? Or again it might be said that all one literally sees are the *words* "Income tax is to be raised". But does one not literally see that those words are on the page? And if one sees this and knows what they mean, does one not see that a certain assertion is made, and hence—if the paper is known to be reliable—that something is the case? Or if the extreme position is taken that one literally sees only black marks on a white ground, one might ask why, if these marks are in fact printed words, it should be non-literal to say that one

sees the words. There is surely nothing non-literal in the statement that one sees, say, a drawing of Lloyd George, though this too may consist only of black marks on paper.

I believe that what this train of argument shows is, not perhaps that it either is or is not correct to say that one literally sees that income-tax is to be raised, but rather that the distinction here between literal and non-literal uses is less clear, or more arbitrary, than one might have supposed. No doubt it would be safe to say that such locutions as "seeing the solution", "seeing no hope", or "seeing prosperity ahead" are simply visual metaphors, that here there is no question of literal seeing. One might on the other hand be tempted to say that only visible objects can be literally seen. To say this, however, is not safe at all; for it appears to entail that *all* cases of "seeing that . . ." are cases only of metaphorical seeing; and this is too extreme. But if one accepts some such cases as cases of literal seeing, a series could be devised from these to the metaphorical cases a fair stretch of which would be indeterminate. To see Jones mowing his lawn gives so plain a reason for saying that he is mowing his lawn that one must surely concede that one literally sees that he is doing so; to see certain words in a newspaper gives a very different sort of reason for saying, for instance, that income-tax is to be raised; but there are other sorts of reasons from which it is not so different, and it is also a reason which a blind man could not have.

It is less important perhaps, to settle this question than to notice how this sort of doubt as to the propriety of saying "I see that . . ." differs from other sorts. It might be objected that, whatever sort of reason seeing certain words in a newspaper may give, it in no case gives a sufficiently good reason for saying that one sees that income-tax is to be raised. But to say this would be to object to the statement as being credulous, ill-founded, unwarranted, not as being non-literal. This is of course an entirely different objection, which would be rebutted, if at all, on quite different grounds; the dispute would concern, not linguistic propriety, but the strength of evidence.

My aim in this paper has been to call attention in the first instance to the wide variety of constructions in which the verb "to see" can occur, and then to clarify so far as possible the complex and confusing picture thus displayed at first sight. I have concentrated mainly on establishing one distinction, which can be briefly summed up as follows. If there is a sense, as there is, in which we speak of the ability to see as a physical capacity, in which to be able to see better than others is not to enjoy any superiority of wits, skill, talent, or experience, then there must be a sense in which seeing does not involve the acquired abilities to identify, recognize, name, describe, and so on. The recruit to the Observer Corps must learn how to identify aircraft, but he is already as well able to see them as he ever will be. By contrast, if only the comparatively expert is able to see why the engine stopped, what is wrong with the carburettor, how to put it right, and so on, then there must be as it were another sort of seeing in which the wits are essentially exercised, which requires experience or judgment, talent or skill. There is on either side of this broad division considerable complexity and some flexibility, distinctions which should certainly not be neglected; but I believe that those distinctions are neither so great nor so sharp as is the main distinction itself, nor so liable to generate confusion, if they are ignored, in philosophical argument about perception and knowledge.

I would like to append two final remarks. First, it is clear that much of what I have said of seeing could *not* be truly said of hearing or smelling, tasting or feeling. And second, it is a curious fact that, if I am right, the familiar philosophical distinction between sensing and observing does not fit the case of seeing at all; for though there are doubtless many cases in which seeing is a good deal more than sensing, there are many also in which it is much less than observing.

POSTSCRIPT, 1963

On re-reading this paper I observe that my closing summary of its thesis is confused. I speak there of "the ability to see" as a physical capacity. This is, I think, correct; a blind man may become "able to see" merely in virtue of a physical change, brought about perhaps by surgical operation. I go on, however, implicitly to identify the ability to see with the ability to see *things,* for example, airplanes; and this is surely a mistake. For, as for instance von Senden's collection of case-histories shows, some blind men who become able to see remain permanently unable to make any *use* of vision, and in some cases are even merely distressed and hampered by it; and in such cases it seems natural to say that, though now able to see, they never become able to see *things* at all. In my paper I distinguish "see" as followed by a "that"-clause, or other clauses, from "see" as followed by a name or substantive, a direct object; but I fail to distinguish from the latter, and at times confuse with it, "see" used intransitively, without any object at all.

I would still say that, for instance, "I saw Lloyd George" does not entail that I then recognized or identified any person as Lloyd George, any object as a person, or even any visual phenomenon as an object; but I would now say that, for it to be true that I saw Lloyd George, more is required than merely that I had and exercised, with Lloyd George before me, the ability to see. For it could not, I suspect, properly be said of me that I saw Lloyd George unless I had, besides the ability to see, at least some ability to pick out and identify objects, even if I did not, on that occasion, exercise this latter ability correctly or even at all. Thus—to refer back to section I.1. of my paper—the man who took the disguised and motionless Lloyd George for a wax model of Winston Churchill certainly, far astray though he was, did see Lloyd George; but the infant in arms—at least if it was a *very* young infant—perhaps did not. And again, in my closing section, while it may be true that "the recruit to the Observer Corps . . . is already as well able to see [aircraft] as he ever will be", though he cannot yet identify them, this ability which he has is not merely the ability to see.

G. J. W.

SEEING AND SEEING AS

G. N. A. Vesey

I

On looking at a thing sometimes we say "It's a torpedo, a lemon, an inkblot, solid, bent, green, etc.", and sometimes we say "It looks like a torpedo, like a lemon, like an inkblot, solid, bent, green, etc.". Sometimes we say of a person that he saw a torpedo, a lemon, an inkblot, and sometimes we say that he saw something as a torpedo, a lemon, an inkblot.

On what sort of occasions do we say "It looks like a torpedo" instead of "It's a torpedo"? Do we say "It looks like a torpedo" because the object in question does not look to us as it does when we unhesitatingly say "It's a torpedo"? But surely what we say when the object does not look as it does when we say "It's a torpedo" is either "It isn't a torpedo", or "It doesn't look like a torpedo".

It would seem that the object in question may look exactly as it does when, in other circumstances, we unhesitatingly say "It's a torpedo", and yet we may say, not "It's a torpedo", but "It looks like a torpedo". The implication is that the point of our saying "It looks like a torpedo" instead of "It's a torpedo" lies in the circumstances; not, so to speak, in the content, but in the context.

Under what circumstances, other than those in which we say "It's a torpedo", do we say "It looks like a torpedo"?

The answer, I submit, is that we say "It looks like a torpedo" when we have reason to believe that the object may not really be what it looks like. A reason to believe that an object which looked like a torpedo was not one would be that no one was at war. This would be a good reason if the object were observed out at sea, but not such a good one if it was seen on dry land.

A stick half in water looks bent to both the man who says "It's bent" and the man who says "It looks bent". But the man who says "It looks bent" thereby exhibits his sophistication in the matter of how an object's being half in water leads to his seeing it otherwise than as it is.

What an object looks like to somebody is what, on looking at it, that person would take it to be, if he had no reason to think otherwise. If he has a reason to think otherwise then he says, not "It is . . .", but "It looks . . .".

If a person has no reason to think that something is not what it looks like to him, can he, then, have no occasion to say "It looks . . ."? No; for sometimes we say such things as "He not only is a confidence-trickster, but what is more he looks like one". And we talk of people "seeing things for what they are". But even so, it is still the fact that a thing may look to somebody like something it is not which gives point to our remark. If confidence-tricksters always looked like confidence-tricksters our remark would not be understood.

II

Is the expression "It looks . . ." always used in the sense with which we have been concerned so far? On the face of it there would appear to be at least two other senses:

1. Sometimes a person says "It looks to me as if . . .", and sometimes "As I see it, . . .". For example, he may say "It looks to me as if there'll be no end to this inflation". He might as well have said "In my opinion . . ." or even "I think . . .". Contrast "It looks to me as if there'll be no end to this inflation" with "It looks like a torpedo". Whereas the former expresses the judgment that there'll

be no end to inflation, the latter does not express the judgment that the object seen is a torpedo. In saying "It looks like a torpedo" we report what would have been our evidence if, in the absence of reasons to think otherwise, we had judged it to be a torpedo.

The same sort of ambiguity is to be found in the expressions "It seems . . ." and "It appears . . .". The striation marks on an old cinematograph film present the appearance of rain. Yet it does not follow that it seems to the audience that it is raining. They are not taken in by the appearance of rain.

2. Sometimes we say of something, such as a formation of rocks or an inkblot, that it looks like, or that we see it as, say, an organist playing an organ. But in saying this usually we do not wish to suggest that the appearance of the object might mislead people into thinking that it really was an organist playing an organ, or a picture of one.

At one time the sort of toyshops which sold clockwork mice sold irregular-shaped pieces of dark-blue metal. Such an object looks like an inkblot, and the inkblot it looks like may look like an organist. But, in such a case, whereas somebody might ask for an ink-eraser, nobody, except as a joke, would ask who the organist was.

What else distinguishes this use of the expression 'looks like' from that considered first?

Someone might say "When we say of what we know very well to be rocks or inkblots that they look like organists playing organs, or lions and lambs, we are simply drawing attention to certain features, principally to do with the shape, which the object in question has in common with what we say it looks like". This answer is plausible until one reflects that we say of those 'reversible' or 'ambiguous' figures, beloved of the authors of introductory textbooks on psychology, that they look at one moment like one thing, at the next like another, in spite of there being no alteration in their shape. And it could hardly be maintained that the person who says of a reversible figure that it looks to him like a staircase is, in so saying, showing that he has reason to doubt whether the drawing actually is of a staircase.

Alternatively, it might be said that the person to whom a formation of rocks or an inkblot looks like an organist playing an organ is 'using his imagination'. What exactly does this mean? We talk of a person imagining he is the Chancellor of the Exchequer, or the inheritor of a vast fortune. Such a person pretends to himself that he is in the favoured state. Does the person who sees an inkblot as an organist pretend to himself that it is a picture of an organist? Does the person who sees a reversible figure as a staircase pretend to himself that it is a picture of one? He may well do so, but it does not seem essential to his seeing it thus.

If to say that the person who sees an inkblot as an organist is using his imagination is to mean that the psychological explanation of this is somehow different from that of his seeing it as an inkblot, then it would seem to be simply false. The reversible figures are in the psychological textbooks to bring out something about perception in general, namely that it is a function of the receiving organism as well as of the stimulus. It is not just a function of the stimulus when something is seen as 'meaningless' black and white marks, becoming also a function of the receptor when it is seen as, say, a vase. Perception is a function of both stimulus and receptor, throughout.

What might be meant when it is said that a person, who sees a formation of rocks or an inkblot as an organist playing an organ, is using his imagination, is this: Imagining is something we need not do. We can be content just to see the rocks as rocks, the inkblot as an inkblot. We don't have to 'go beyond' this, which is just as well since such going beyond is not directed to seeing things for what they are.

There are two points here, which, in reverse order, are:

(*a*) The person who says of an inkblot "It looks like an organist" is not doubtful as to whether it is a picture of an organist. If people said "Well, is it or isn't it?" all he could say was that they had misunderstood him. He does not doubt whether it is a picture of an organist. He knows perfectly well that it is not a picture of an organist but an inkblot. But his attention is not directed to seeing things for what they are.

(*b*) The person who says of an inkblot "It looks like an organist" can refrain from seeing inkblots as things, just as people can refrain from 'reading' the pattern of tea leaves left in cups.

I am not sure whether the second of these points is true. The reversibility of some of the drawings in the psychological textbooks depends on seeing first one part of the drawing as figure and the rest as ground, then the first part as ground and the rest as figure. To see the drawing for what it is, presumably we should have to see things otherwise than in terms of figure and ground. This may well be psychologically impossible, in which case it would not be true that we could refrain from 'going beyond' the marks on the paper. But at least such refraining would remain conceivable.

What is true, then, is that it makes sense to say that an inkblot does not, in the sense of 'looks like' in which to somebody it looks like an organist, look like anything to somebody else, who nevertheless sees it clearly.

In the other sense of 'looks like', however, it is hard to see what meaning could be given to talk of something not looking like anything. "I saw it, but I didn't see it as anything" seems to be self-contradictory, unless we choose to apply the expression 'not see it as anything' either (*a*) when what something is seen as is so indefinite as to be of negligible value in indicating what the object is, or (*b*) when what is seen is so strange as to defy description.

I will mark my non-acceptance of these meanings for 'not see it as anything' by saying "All seeing is seeing as".

III

"All seeing is seeing as." In other words, if a person sees something at all it must look like something to him, even if it only looks like 'somebody doing something'. The less definite one's perception the less chance of its being non-veridical, but also the less chance of its being useful.

Another way of expressing the point that all seeing is seeing as is to say that perceptions, like judgments, are either true or false. They are true when what the object looks like to somebody, that is, what on looking at it the person would take it to be if he had no reason to think otherwise, is what the object is; false otherwise.

It was said earlier that the point of our saying "It looks like . . ." as distinct from "It is . . ." lies in the context. It is tempting to imagine that the point lies, not in the context, but, somehow, in the content, that is, in the actual experience of seeing, itself. This temptation seems to be reinforced when it is said that perceptions, like judgments, are either true or false. It seems to be reinforced because the inference is drawn that if perceptions are like judgments in this respect, they must involve judgments. The assumption is that only judgments can be true or false.

In this manner, I think, are philosophers, like Dawes Hicks, led to say such things as: "I realise, of course, the awkwardness of saying, as many psychologists have felt themselves constrained to say, that judgment is involved from the outset in cognitive apprehension, that even the simplest cognitive state is in reality a state of judging. For unquestionably the term 'judgment', as ordinarily understood, expresses a highly reflective act, which depends for its exercise upon a definite recognition of the distinction between the subjective and the objective, such as no one supposes the primitive mind to be capable of. The difficulty here is, however, purely a verbal difficulty, and to throw it in the way is simply to obscure the issue".[1]

It is not perfectly clear what Dawes Hicks means by this.

We have already considered, by implication, one meaning which might be given to "All perception involves judging". It is, that I always judge things to be what they look like. With this meaning it is plainly false.

Dawes Hicks implies that it is not true of the judgment which is involved in 'even the simplest cognitive state' that it 'depends for its exercise upon a definitive recognition of the distinction between the subjective and the objective'. Presumably 'the subjective' is what a thing looks like, and 'the objective' what it is. What he says would seem to amount to the theory, which, I believe, is held by some philosophers today, that whenever something is seen as being of a certain sort, the idea that it is of that sort is 'entertained'. 'Entertaining a proposition' has been proposed by some philosophers as an element common to the analysis of both believing and disbelieving, that proposition. It is not always made clear whether or not the theory is one which we are supposed to test by introspection. If it were added that entertaining was the reverse of a highly reflective act, this would in effect rule out introspection as a test of the theory. Dawes Hicks implies that it is not true of the judgment that is involved in perception that it 'expresses a highly reflective act'.

With its modifications this theory, it seems to me, is quite safe from disproof. Disagreement between what the object looks like and what one judges it to be is not to the point. Introspection is not to the point. The trouble is that, at this stage, nothing seems to be to the point, except the power of one person to persuade another to extend his use of the word 'judgment' to cover cases he would not previously have used it to cover.

Perhaps the above theory of the role of judgment in perception is only adhered to because philosophers find

[1] G. Dawes Hicks. "Is There 'Knowledge by Acquaintance'?" *Arist. Soc. Supp.*, Vol. II, 1919.

repulsive the alternative theory and yet cannot bring themselves to renounce the dogma that only a judgment can be true or false.

The alternative theory is the theory that the judgment that is involved in perception is a judgment not about a material thing but about a non-material thing called a 'sense-datum'. Before considering this theory it will be as well to outline the problem to which it is thought by some to provide a solution, or, rather, for the solution of which it is thought to provide a language.

IV

Perceptions, like judgments, are either true or false. Many of our false perceptions we can correct by attending more closely to the object before us. But there are some, known as 'illusions', which persist despite all our efforts to see things as they are. Such false perceptions are thought of by unreflective people as tricks, oddities, exceptions to the rule, things to be explained away. 'The rule', here, is constituted by the vast majority of perceptions in which there is no disagreement between what people see things as, and what they believe, or find, them to be. These are the cases which provide no occasion for talking of what things look like, or what people see things as. And they provide no occasion for having to conceive of perception as something which occurs under such conditions as the state of the perceiver's nervous system. One might conclude from his lack of recognition of the dependence of his perceptions on the state of his nervous system, that the man in the street must think of himself, *qua* perceiver, as a disembodied spirit.

Some people see in the fact that perception occurs under conditions the necessity of concluding that we are not really aware of the material world.

A. C. Ewing, for example, writes (*Fundamental Questions of Philosophy* pp. 68–9): "Two different people looking at the same thing at the same time from different positions in space may see it differently, *e.g.* as having different shapes. But the same thing cannot really have two different shapes at the same time. Therefore they are not really seeing the same thing".

And Thomas Reid, in his *Essays on the Intellectual Powers of Man*,[2] considers the argument: "The table which we see, seems to diminish as we remove farther from it; but the real table, which exists independent of us, suffers no alteration. It was, therefore, nothing but its image which was presented to the mind". Reid's reply to this argument is as follows: "Let us suppose, for a moment, that it is the real table we see: Must not this real table seem to diminish as we remove farther from it? It is demonstrable that it must. How then can this apparent diminution be an argument that it is not the real table? When that which must happen to the real table, as we remove farther from it, does actually happen to the table we see, it is absurd to conclude from this that it is not the real table we see".

It is not only philosophers who consider that it follows from perception occurring under conditions that we are not really aware of the material world. A scientist[3] recently wrote: "Let us begin by considering how we get our information about the world from our senses: chiefly from sight, hearing, and touch. We know, for example, that when we see an object, the rays of light from the object enter the eye and are focused on the retina, where they cause sensitive cells to send messages or disturbances of an electrical nature along nerve fibres which go to the brain. These disturbances can be traced within the brain to regions which are known to deal with vision, and no doubt the nerve cells which they enter influence many others in the intricate layers of cells which form the cerebral cortex. There our present information comes to an end, although we are aware of the result. Out of the mes-

[2] Edited and abridged by A. D. Woozley, Macmillan, 1941, p. 145.
[3] J. A. V. Butler, "Pictures in the Mind", *Science News* 22, Penguin Books, 1951.

sages we make, and in some way are aware of, a 'picture' of the outside world.

We are so familiar with this picture that we take it to *be* the outside world. We say that we are 'looking' at the world, and primitive and simple people think that when they look out of their eyes and see what is before them, they are performing a positive act. There is no doubt that what we are aware of is a 'construct', made from the varied sensations which reach the brain; a picture which we make by selecting and emphasising some data and ignoring many others, a picture which in many ways is highly personal".

Philosophers are divided on the question of the relevance of psychological and physiological discoveries about perception to the propriety of our everyday language about what we perceive. The situation may be compared with that in which psychological theories about the causation of human behaviour are held by some, but not by others, to bear on the validity of the distinction between voluntary and involuntary actions. Philosophers who say that determinism and free-will are compatible usually defend their claim by 'analysing' voluntariness in terms of the tests we employ, when we are not philosophizing, to decide whether an action is voluntary. Philosophers who disagree with them reject this analysis as not giving the essential meaning of voluntariness, which, they say, is "such as to exclude from being voluntary any action which is causally determined". Similarly a philosopher who says that the psychology of perception is not relevant to the propriety of our everyday talk about what we perceive may analyse such a proposition as "Smith and Jones were seeing the same thing" in terms of the tests we employ, when we are not philosophizing, to decide whether the proposition is true. And a philosopher who disagrees with him will say "Ah, but the psychologists' discoveries show that when we say that Smith and Jones are seeing the same thing we are not using 'same' in its proper, strict, literal sense, but in a derived, loose or Pickwickian sense".

In neither case are the psychologists' discoveries felt to

make it impossible to use the language as it was used before: the tests that were applied can still be applied.[4] What is felt is that if the statements are to be true they must express no more than the results of the tests. They are no longer felt to be true in some sense, usually described as 'literal', 'strict', or 'real', in which, it is claimed, they were felt to be true before perception came to be thought of as occurring under such conditions as the state of the perceiver's nervous system.

V

The reasoning behind the sense-datum theory of perception would seem to be something like this:

(1) The problem arises from the fact that a material thing can look (feel, sound, etc.) like something it is not. This is because our alleged 'awareness' of material things is essentially 'under conditions'. Because it is under conditions, two different people looking at the same thing may see it differently, for example, one as a stick, the other as a snake. But what they are aware of cannot be both a stick and a snake. Therefore they are not really aware of the same thing.

(2) A material thing can look (feel, sound, etc.) like something it is not. That is, our perception of it can be mistaken. To make a mistake is to draw a false conclusion from given evidence. If there is not to be a vicious regress

---

[4] Berkeley, *Three Dialogues between Hylas and Philonous, in opposition to Sceptics and Atheists*, Third Dialogue. Philonous: If the term 'same' be taken in the vulgar acceptation, it is certain (and not at all repugnant to the principles I maintain) that different persons may perceive the same thing; or the same thing or idea exist in different minds. Words are of arbitrary imposition; and since men are used to apply the word 'same' where no distinction or variety is perceived, and I do not pretend to alter their perceptions, it follows, that as men have said before, 'several saw the same thing', so they may upon like occasions still continue to use the same phrase, without any deviation either from propriety of language or the truth of things. But if the term 'same' be used in the acceptation of philosophers, who pretend to an abstracted notion of identity, then. . . .

there must be some element in our alleged awareness of material things of which our awareness is such that mistakes are impossible, that is, of which we are aware otherwise than under conditions. Let us call this element the 'sense-datum', and our awareness of it 'immediate awareness'. The sense-datum is the evidence without which we could not draw a conclusion about the material world.

(3) Being something of which we are aware, the sense-datum is a thing, though not, of course, a material thing, since our awareness of it is not under conditions. To find out what is the sense in which two people can be perceptually aware of the same material thing we must discover what is the relationship between sense-data and material things.

'Real' or 'immediate' awareness, and its object, are defined in this theory in terms of the ideas (i) that, for perception to be veridical or non-veridical it must somehow involve a judgment, and (ii) that the evidence on the basis of which the judgment is made must be some thing of which we are aware in a manner otherwise than under conditions.

The expression 'that of which we are aware in a manner otherwise than under conditions' could be given meaning if we said that we were aware, in this manner, of, for example, the torpedo-like look of an object to us, or the staircase-like look of the reversible figure. With this meaning, all the conditions—not just those having to do with our position in space in relation to the object but also those having to do with our past experience, our present psychological 'set', and so on—under which we perceive material things, are allowed for in the 'object' of immediate awareness. They can be allowed for only because the 'object' is not a thing. It is not a thing,[5] and it is not a thought, and it is not a thought about a thing. And it is

[5] If the two different 'appearances' of a reversible figure were indeed things ('pictures') we could conceive of them projected out from our minds, on to a screen, side by side, and distinguishable. But the only images on a screen which could serve as projections of the two different 'appearances' would be identical.

only because it is none of these that it can constitute our experiential evidence for whatever may be our thoughts about the material world.

VI

But why cannot the object of immediate awareness be a thing, and yet be our evidence for whatever may be our thoughts about the material world?

To account for the fact that we often see a thing as, say, green, but not as any particular shade of green, or as triangular, but neither as scalene nor as equilateral, we refer to lack of 'attention'. It is no good just directing your gaze at something; to see it as having a determinate quality with respect to a certain determinable you must 'attend' to it with a view to ascertaining what that quality is.

The correlate, in psychological theory, of attention is 'interest' or 'set'. Some philosophers are inclined to deny that objects can be seen as, say, green but not any particular shade of green. They ask themselves, as an experiment, the question "Can I see this but not be aware of its precise colour?". They do not ask "Do we always notice what colour things are?". It would seem that the explanation of their answering the first question in the negative is that the very process of trying to answer it involves them in having a 'set' which they might otherwise not have had, namely the set which goes with their attending to colour.

An object, in virtue of being gazed at, in virtue of being before one's open eyes, is not evidence for any beliefs. It is my seeing an object as green, to do which I must to some degree attend to it, which may justify my believing it to be green.

If a sense-datum is a thing, then it cannot have only generic or indeterminate qualities; its qualities must be fully determinate. It cannot be just 'green', but must be some particular shade of green.

Suppose an object looks green to me. According to the theory with which we are concerned the analysis of this is into (a) my being immediately aware of a sense-datum of a certain determinate shade of green, say peacock green; and (b) my thinking that it is green. If the object looks peacock green, the first element in my perception remains the same, but the second becomes 'my thinking that it is peacock green'. My evidence—the sense-datum—is the same in both cases, but my thought is different. I might merely have noticed that it was coloured, but my evidential situation would be the same as if I had seen exactly what colour it was.

I conclude that, if we are immediately aware of the sense-datum, and if the sense-datum itself, in virtue of our being immediately aware of it, constitutes our evidence for whatever we think about it, then there can be no explanation for our thought about the sense-datum being whatever that thought is. There can be no explanation on the lines of the 'lack of attention' explanation of our not being perceptually aware of the fully determinate qualities of material things; for our awareness of the peacock green sense-datum, whether we think of it as peacock green, green, or merely coloured, is the same—immediate. And there can be no explanation on the lines of our being aware of a different object; for in each case it is the same, fully determinate sense-datum of which we are aware. So long as the sense-datum is a thing, and the awareness of it immediate, those facts of perception which we ordinarily account for by saying "He was not paying any attention to . . .", "His mind was elsewhere", and so on, on the one hand, and "His mind was fully on the . . .", "He was paying particular attention to . . ." on the other, simply cannot be accommodated in the language of sense-data and immediate awareness. But attention is a necessary condition of perceptual awareness. Hence, it seems to me, a solution to the problem of reconciling the notion of perception as occurring under conditions, with the 'common-sense' assumption that different people are frequently aware of the same thing, cannot be found by using the terms of the sense-datum language. Rather, it would seem, is a solution of the problem made impossible by so doing.

VII

A solution to the problem of reconciling the notion of perception as occurring under conditions, with the 'common-sense' assumption that different people are frequently aware of the same thing, is possible. It is possible if we are prepared (1) to renounce the dogma that only judgments can be true or false; (2) to extend our notion of what constitute the conditions under which awareness of the same thing by different people is possible. Ordinarily we do not regard the fact that different people are situated in different positions with respect to an object as entailing that they are not aware of the same object. We say, with A. E. Murphy[6], "To be sure, we gain our perceptual information about such objects through such expedients as looking at them, and what we thus see of them is the way they look (appear) under the conditions in which they can be observed. But how else would a human organism see a material object?".

What is required is that we should refuse to draw any distinction between such conditions of observation as position in space in relation to the object perceived and such conditions as the 'possession', by the perceiver, of an appropriate physiological apparatus. In so doing we may preserve the common-sense conception of the object of perception as a 'public object', even if we have to relinquish the idea that this public object has all the 'sensible' qualities (colour, smell, and so on) we perceive it as having.

[6] *The Philosophy of G. E. Moore*, 1942, p. 312.

VIII

My aim in this paper has been to combat the idea that in seeing an object as something, in recognising an object, there is necessarily involved a judgment, either about the object in question or about some other, non-material, object.

Whenever we see an object it looks like something, or looks to have some quality. But its looking thus is not to be identified with our judging it to be what it looks like. Nor is its looking thus to be identified with a judgment about some other thing, for in no 'thing' can we incorporate such conditions of observation as our attention to the features of an object.

In other words, the look of a thing is something phenomenal, not intellectual. But this is not to deny that experience and judgment are connected: for what an object looks like to a person is what he would judge that object to be if he had no reason to judge otherwise.

II. SENSING, SENSE-DATA, AND APPEARING

THE THEORY OF SENSA[1]

C. D. BROAD

The Notion of Sensible Appearance. I have now tried to point out what is the irreducible minimum of properties which ordinary people consider must be possessed by anything if it is to count as a piece of Matter. I have also pointed out, by anticipation, that the history of philosophy shows there to be a great difficulty in holding that there are any entities which fulfil all these conditions in a literal sense. Lastly, we have noticed that the question of the reality or unreality of Matter, thus defined, is not perfectly clear-cut, because of the practical certainty that many of our terms will have to be interpreted in a more or less Pickwickian manner, and the doubt whether it is worth while to go on using familiar phrases after their literal meaning has been departed from beyond a certain point. We must now consider what facts make it hard to believe that anything obeys all four conditions in at all a literal sense.

The difficulty arises because of the group of facts which we sum up by saying that it is necessary to distinguish between things as they are and things as they seem to us, or between physical reality and sensible appearance. Difficulties always arise when two sets of properties apparently belong to the same object, and yet are apparently incompatible with each other. Now the difficulty here is to rec-

[1] This selection consists of part of Chapter VII and the whole of Chapter VIII of *Scientific Thought.* I have titled the whole selection "The Theory of Sensa," whereas in *Scientific Thought* that is part of the title of Chapter VIII only; and I have omitted the author's lists of references at the end of each of these chapters. Otherwise, the material is as it appears in *Scientific Thought.* The changes have been made with the approval of Professor Broad. (Ed.)

oncile the supposed neutrality, persistence, and independence of a physical object with the obvious differences between its various sensible appearances to different observers at the same moment, and to the same observer at different moments between which it is held not to have undergone any physical change. We know, *e.g.*, that when we lay a penny down on a table and view it from different positions it generally looks more or less elliptical in shape. The eccentricity of these various appearances varies as we move about, and so does the direction of their major axes. Now we hold that the penny, at which we say that we were looking all the time, has not changed; and that it is round, and not elliptical, in shape. This is, of course, only one example out of millions. It would be easy to offer much wilder ones; but it is simple and obvious, and involves no complications about a transmitting medium; so we will start with it as a typical case to discuss.

Now there is nothing in the mere ellipticity or the mere variation, taken by itself, to worry us. The difficulty arises because of the incompatibility between the apparent shapes and the supposed real shape, and between the change in the appearances and the supposed constancy of the physical object. We need not at present ask *why* we believe that there is a single physical object with these characteristics, which appears to us in all these different ways. It is a fact that we do believe it. It is an equally certain fact that the penny does look different as we move about. The difficulty is to reconcile the different appearances with the supposed constancy of the penny, and the ellipticity of most of the appearances with the supposed roundness of the penny. It is probable that at first sight the reader will not see much difficulty in this. He will be inclined to say that we can explain these various visual appearances by the laws of perspective, and so on. This is not a relevant answer. It is quite true that we can *predict what particular appearance* an object will present to an observer, when we know the shape of the object and its position with respect to the observer. But this is not the question that is troubling us at present. Our question is as to the compatibility of these changing elliptical appearances, however they may be correlated with other facts in the world, with the supposed constancy and roundness of the physical object.

Now what I call *Sensible Appearance* is just a general name for such facts as I have been describing. It is important, here as always, to state the *facts* in a form to which everyone will agree, before attempting any particular *analysis* of them, with which it is certain that many people will violently disagree. The fundamental fact is that we constantly make such judgments as: "This *seems to me* elliptical, or red, or hot," as the case may be, and that about the truth of these judgments we do not feel the least doubt. We may, however, at the same time doubt or positively disbelieve that this *is* elliptical, or red, or hot. I may be perfectly certain at one and the same time that I have the peculiar experience expressed by the judgment: "This looks elliptical to me," and that in fact the object is not elliptical but is round.

I do not suppose that anyone, on reflection, will quarrel with this statement of fact. The next question is as to the right way to analyse such facts; and it is most important not to confuse the facts themselves with any particular theory as to how they ought to be analysed. We may start with a negative remark, which seems to me to be true, and is certainly of the utmost importance if it be true. Appearance is *not* merely mistaken *judgment* about physical objects. When I judge that a penny looks elliptical I am not mistakenly ascribing elliptical shape to what is in fact round. Sensible appearances *may* lead me to make a mistaken judgment about physical objects, but they *need* not, and, so far as we know, commonly do not. My certainty that the penny looks elliptical exists comfortably alongside of my conviction that it is round. But a mistaken judgment that the penny *is* elliptical would not continue to exist after I knew that the penny was really round. The plain fact is then that "looking elliptical to me" stands for a peculiar experience, which, whatever the right analysis of it may be, is not just a mistaken judgment about the shape of the penny.

Appearance then cannot be described as mistaken judgment about the properties of some physical object. How are we to describe it, and can we analyse it? Two different types of theory seem to be possible, which I will call respectively the *Multiple Relation Theory,* and the *Object Theory* of sensible appearance. The Multiple Relation Theory takes the view that "appearing to be so and so" is a unique kind of relation between an object, a mind, and a characteristic. (This is a rough statement, but it will suffice for the present.) On this type of theory to say that the penny looks elliptical to me is to say that a unique and not further analysable relation of "appearing" holds between the penny, my mind, and the general characteristic of ellipticity. The essential point for us to notice at present about theories of this kind is that they do not imply that we are aware of *anything* that *really is* elliptical when we have the experience which we express by saying that the penny looks elliptical to us. Theories of this type have been suggested lately by Professor Dawes Hicks and by Dr G. E. Moore. So far, they have not been worked out in any great detail, but they undoubtedly deserve careful attention.

Theories of the Object type are quite different. They do not involve a unique and unanalysable multiple relation of "appear*ing,*" but a peculiar kind of object—an "appear*ance.*" Such objects, it is held, actually *do have* the characteristics which the physical object *seems to have*. Thus the Object Theory analyses the statement that the penny looks to me elliptical into a statement which involves the actual existence of an elliptical object, which stands in a certain cognitive relation to me on the one hand, and in another relation, yet to be determined, to the round penny. This type of theory, though it has been much mixed up with irrelevant matter, and has never been clearly stated and worked out till our own day, is of respectable antiquity. The doctrine of "representative ideas" is the traditional and highly muddled form of it. It lies at the basis of such works as Russell's *Lowell Lectures on the External World*. In this book I shall deliberately confine myself to this type of theory, and shall try to state it clearly, and work it out in detail.

I propose now to state more fully the theory that appearances are a peculiar kind of objects, and to consider what sort of objects they must be. The reader will bear in mind throughout the whole of the long story which follows that there is a totally different view of sensible appearance, viz., the Multiple Relation Theory, and that this may quite possibly be true. In this book I shall leave it wholly aside. On the theory that we are now going to discuss, whenever a penny looks to me elliptical, what really happens is that I am aware of an object which is, in fact elliptical. This object is connected in some specially intimate way with the round physical penny, and for this reason is called an appearance *of* the penny. It really is elliptical, and for this reason the penny is said to look *elliptical*. We may generalise this theory of sensible appearance as follows: Whenever I truly judge that x appears to me to have the sensible quality q, what happens is that I am directly aware of a certain object y, which (a) really does have the quality q, and (b) stands in some peculiarly intimate relation, yet to be determined, to x. (At the present stage, for all that we know, y might sometimes be identical with x, or might be literally a part of x.) Such objects as y I am going to call *Sensa*. Thus, when I look at a penny from the side, what happens, on the present theory, is at least this: I have a sensation, whose object is an elliptical, brown sensum; and this sensum is related in some specially intimate way to a certain round physical object, viz., the penny.

Now I think it must at least be admitted that the sensum theory is highly plausible. When I look at a penny from the side I am certainly aware of *something;* and it is certainly plausible to hold that this something is elliptical in the same plain sense in which a suitably bent piece of wire, looked at from straight above, is elliptical. If, in fact, nothing elliptical is before my mind, it is very hard to understand why the penny should seem *elliptical* rather than of any other shape. I do not now regard this argument as absolutely conclusive, because I am inclined to think that the Multiple Relation theory can explain these facts also. But it is at least a good enough argument to make the sensum theory well worth further consideration.

Assuming that when I look at a penny from the side I am directly aware of something which is in fact elliptical, it is clear that this something cannot be identified with the penny, if the latter really has the characteristics that it is commonly supposed to have. The penny is supposed to be round, whilst the sensum is elliptical. Again, the penny is supposed to keep the same shape and size as we move about, whilst the sensa alter in shape and size. Now one and the same thing cannot, at the same time and in the same sense, be round and elliptical. Nor can one and the same thing at once change its shape and keep its shape unaltered, if "shape" be used in the same sense in both statements. Thus it is certain that, if there be sensa, they cannot in general be identified with the physical objects of which they are the appearances, if these literally have the properties commonly assigned to them. On the other hand, all that I ever come to know about physical objects and their qualities seems to be based upon the qualities of the sensa that I become aware of in sense-perception. If the visual sensa were not elliptical and did not vary in certain ways as I move about, I should not judge that I was seeing a round penny.

The distinction between sensum and physical object can perhaps be made still clearer by taking some wilder examples. Consider, *e.g.*, the case of looking at a stick which is half in water and half in air. We say that it looks bent. And we certainly do not mean by this that we mistakenly judge it to be bent; we generally make no such mistake. We are aware of an object which is very much like what we should be aware of if we were looking at a stick with a physical kink in it, immersed wholly in air. The most obvious analysis of the facts is that, when we judge that a straight stick *looks* bent, we are aware of an object which really *is* bent, and which is related in a peculiarly intimate way to the physically straight stick. The relation cannot be that of identity; since the same thing cannot at once be bent and straight, in the same sense of these words. If there be *nothing* with a kink in it before our minds at the moment, why should we think then of kinks at all, as we do when we say that the stick looks bent? No doubt we can quite well mistakenly *believe* a property to be present which is really absent, when we are dealing with something that is only known to us indirectly, like Julius Cæsar or the North Pole. But in our example we are dealing with a concrete visible object, which is bodily present to our senses; and it is very hard to understand how we could seem to ourselves to *see* the property of bentness exhibited in a concrete instance, if in fact *nothing* was present to our minds that possessed that property.

As I want to make the grounds for the sensum theory as clear as possible, I will take one more example. Scientists often assert that physical objects are not "really" red or hot. We are not at present concerned with the truth or falsehood of this strange opinion, but only with its application to our present problem. Let us suppose then, for the sake of argument, that it is true. When a scientist looks at a penny stamp or burns his mouth with a potato he has exactly the same sort of experience as men of baser clay, who know nothing of the scientific theories of light and heat. The visual experience seems to be adequately described by saying that each of them is aware of a red patch of approximately square shape. If such patches be not in fact red, and if people be not in fact aware of such patches, where could the notion of red or of any other colour have come from? The scientific theory of colour would have nothing to explain, unless people really are aware of patches under various circumstances which really do have different colours. The scientists would be in the position of Mr Munro's duchess, who congratulated herself that unbelief had become impossible, as the Liberal Theologians had left us nothing to disbelieve in. Thus we seem forced to the view that there are at least hot and coloured sensa; and, if we accept the scientific view that physical objects are neither hot nor coloured, it will follow that sensa cannot be identified with physical objects.

The reader may be inclined to say, "After all, these sensa are not real; they are mere appearances, so why trouble about them?" The answer is that you do not get rid of anything by labelling it "appearance." Appearances are as real in their own way as anything else. If an appearance were nothing at all, nothing would appear, and if nothing appeared, there would be nothing for scientific theories to account for. To put the matter in another way: Words like *real* and *reality* are ambiguous. A round penny and an elliptical visual sensum are not real in precisely the same sense. But both are real in the most general sense that a complete inventory of the universe must mention the one as much as the other. No doubt the kind of reality which is to be ascribed to appearances will vary with the particular type of theory as to the nature of sensible appearance that we adopt. On the present theory an appearance is a sensum, and a sensum is a particular existent, though it may be a short-lived one. On the Multiple Relation theory appearances have a very different type of reality. But *all* possible theories have to admit the reality, *in some sense*, of appearances; and therefore it is no objection to any particular theory that it ascribes a sort of reality to appearances.

I hope that I have now made fairly clear the grounds on which the sensum theory of sensible appearance has been put forward. Closely connected with it is a theory about the perception of physical objects, and we may sum up the whole view under discussion as follows: Under certain conditions I have states of mind called sensations. These sensations have objects, which are always concrete particular existents, like coloured or hot patches, noises, smells, etc. Such objects are called sensa. Sensa have properties, such as shape, size, hardness, colour, loudness, coldness, and so on. The existence of such sensa, and their presence to our minds in sensation, lead us to judge that a physical object exists and is present to our senses. To this physical object we ascribe various properties. These properties are not in general identical with those of the sensum which is before our minds at the moment. For instance, the *elliptical* sensum makes us believe in the existence of a *round* physical penny. Nevertheless, all the properties that we do ascribe to physical objects are based upon and correlated with the properties that actually characterise our sensa. The sensa that are connected with a physical object x in a certain specially intimate way are called the appearances of that object to those observers who sense these sensa. The properties which x is said to *appear to* have are the properties which those sensa that are $x's$ appearances *really do* have. Of course, the two properties may happen to be the same, *e.g.,* when I look straight down on a penny, both the physical object and the visual appearance are round. Generally, however, there is only a correlation between the two.

It follows from this theory that sensa cannot appear to have properties which they do not really have, though there is no reason why they should not have more properties than we do or can notice in them. This point perhaps needs a little more elaboration, since a good deal of nonsense has been talked by opponents of the sensum theory in this connexion. We must distinguish between failing to notice what is present in an object and "noticing" what is not present in an object. The former presents no special difficulty. There may well be in any object much which is too minute and obscure for us to recognise distinctly. Again, it is obvious that we may sense an object without necessarily being aware of all its relations even to another object that we sense at the same time. Still more certain is it that we may sense an object without being aware of all its relations to some other object which we are not sensing at the time. Consequently, there is no difficulty whatever in supposing that sensa may be much more differentiated than we think them to be, and that two sensa may really differ in quality when we think that they are exactly alike. Arguments such as Stumpf's render it practically certain that the latter possibility is in fact realised.

The real difficulty is when we seem to be directly aware

of some property in an object, and this property is not really present and is perhaps incompatible with others which are present. This is the kind of difficulty that the sensum theory is put forward to meet. We seem to recognise elliptical shape in the penny, when the penny really has the incompatible quality of roundness. The solution which the sensum theory offers is to "change the subject." *Something,* it admits, is elliptical, and something is round; but they are not the same something. What is round is the penny, what is elliptical is the sensum. Now, clearly, this would be no solution, if the same sort of difficulty were to break out in sensa themselves. In that case we should need to postulate appearances of appearances, and so on indefinitely.

We must hold, as regards positive sensible qualities which characterise a sensum as a whole and do not involve relations to other sensa, that a sensum is at least all that it appears to be. Now, so far as I know, there is no evidence to the contrary. Some people have thought that arguments like Stumpf's raised this difficulty; but that is simply a mistake. Stumpf's argument deals merely with the relation of qualitative likeness and difference between different sensa, and shows that we may think that two of them are exactly alike when there is really a slight qualitative or quantitative difference between them. This has no tendency to prove that we ever find a positive non-relational quality in a sensum, which is not really there.

Next, we must remember that attributes which involve a negative factor often have positive names. A man might quite well think, on inspecting one of his sensa, that it was exactly round and uniformly red. And he might well be mistaken. But then, "exactly round" means "with no variation of curvature," and "uniformly red" means "with no variation of shade from one part to another." Now universal negative judgments like these can never be guaranteed by mere inspection; and so, in such cases, the man is not "seeing properties that are not there" in the sense in which he would be doing so if a round sensum appeared to him to be elliptical. To sum up, it is no objection to the sensum theory that a sensum may seem to be *less* differentiated than it is; it would be a fatal objection if a sensum ever seemed *more* differentiated than it is; but we have no evidence that the latter ever happens.

Before going further we must remove a baseless prejudice which is sometimes felt against the sensum theory. It is often objected that we are not aware of sensa and their properties, as a rule, unless we specially look for them. It is a fact that it often needs a good deal of persuasion to make a man believe that, when he looks at a penny from the side, it seems elliptical to him. And I am afraid that very often, when he is persuaded, it is not by his own direct inspection (which is the only relevant evidence in such a matter), but by some absurd and irrelevant argument that the area of his retina affected by the light from the penny, is an oblique projection of a circle, and is therefore an ellipse. Accordingly, it is argued that we have no right to believe that such a man is directly sensing an object which is, in fact, elliptical. To this objection a partial answer has already been given, by implication. It is only when we are looking at a penny almost normally that any doubt is felt of the ellipticity of the sensum; and, in that case, the sensum is, in fact, very nearly round. Now we have seen that it is no objection to our theory that a sensum which is not quite round should be thought to be exactly round, though it would be an objection if an exactly round sensum seemed to be elliptical. The reason, of course, is that an ellipse, with its variable curvature, is a more differentiated figure than a circle, with its uniform curvature. There is no difficulty in the fact that we overlook minute differentiations that are really present in our sensa; difficulties would only arise if we seemed to notice distinctions that are not really present.

Apart, however, from this special answer, a more general reply can be made to the type of objection under discussion. The whole argument rests on a misunderstanding of the view about perception which the sensum theory holds. If the theory were that, in perceiving a penny, a man first becomes aware of a sensum, then notices that it is elliptical, and then infers from this fact and the laws of perspective that he is looking at a round physical object, the argument would be fatal to the theory. But this is quite obviously not what happens. Perceptual judgments are indeed *based upon* sensa and their properties to this extent, that if we were not aware of a sensum we should not now judge that any physical object is present to our senses, and that if this sensum had different properties we should ascribe different properties to the physical object. But the relation between the sensum and its properties, on the one hand, and the perceptual judgment about the physical object, on the other, is not that of *inference*. The best analogy that we can offer to the relation between our sensing of a sensum and our perceiving a physical object, is to be found in the case of reading a book in a familiar language. What interests us as a rule is the meaning of the printed words, and not the peculiarities of the print. We do not explicitly notice the latter, unless there be something markedly wrong with it, such as a letter upside down. Nevertheless, if there were no print we should cognise no meaning, and if the print were different in certain specific ways we should cognise a different meaning. We *can* attend to the print itself if we choose, as in proof-reading. In exactly the same way, we are not as a rule interested in sensa, as such, but only in what we think they can tell us about physical objects, which alone can help or hurt us. Sensa themselves "cut no ice." We therefore pass automatically from the sensum and its properties to judgments about the physical object and its properties. If it should happen that the sensum is queer, as when we see double, we notice the sensum, as we notice an inverted letter. And, even in normal cases, we generally can detect the properties of sensa, and contrast them with those which they are leading us to ascribe to the physical object, provided that we make a special effort of attention.

From what has just been said, it will not appear strange that, even though there be sensa, they should have been overlooked by most plain men and by many philosophers. Of course, everyone is constantly sensing them, and, in specially abnormal cases, has noted the difference between them and physical objects. But sensa have never been objects of special interest, and therefore have never been given a name in common speech. A result of this is that all words like "seeing," "hearing," etc., are ambiguous. They stand sometimes for acts of sensing, whose objects are of course sensa, and sometimes for acts of perceiving, whose objects are supposed to be bits of matter and their sensible qualities. This is especially clear about hearing. We talk of "hearing a noise" and of "hearing a bell." In the first case we mean that we are sensing an auditory sensum, with certain attributes of pitch, loudness, quality, etc. In the second case we mean that, in consequence of sensing such a sensum, we judge that a certain physical object exists and is present to our senses. Here the word "hearing" stands for an act of perceiving. Exactly the same remarks apply to sight. In one sense we see a penny; in a somewhat stricter sense we see only one side of the penny; in another sense we see only a brown elliptical sensum. The first two uses refer to acts of perceiving, the last to an act of sensing. It is best on the whole to confine words like "seeing" and "hearing" to acts of perceiving. This is, of course, their ordinary use. I shall therefore talk of seeing a penny, but not of seeing a brown elliptical sensum. I shall speak of the latter kind of cognition as "visually sensing," or merely as "sensing," when no misunderstanding is to be feared by dropping the adjective. This distinction will be found important when we come to deal with illusory perceptions.

I have now tried to clear up certain ambiguities in the sensum theory, and to remove certain mistaken objections which many folk feel against it. If it be admitted that there *may* be such things as sensa, and that the sensum theory at least provides a possible and even plausible way of analysing sensible appearance, we can pass to the question of the nature of sensa and their status in the universe. This splits into two questions, viz., (i) the relation of sensa to minds; and (ii) their relation to physical objects. Neither of these can be completely answered at the present stage, but we can say a good deal here that is relevant, and will be useful, about them.

(i) *Are Sensa in any way Mental?* Sensa have been supposed by many philosophers to be in some way mental. This opinion is based partly on sheer verbal confusions, and partly on genuine facts. The verbal confusion is that the word "sensation" has often been used ambiguously, and that, in one of its meanings, it does undoubtedly stand for something that is mental. When a man talks of a "sensation of red," he is sometimes referring to a red patch which he senses, sometimes to his act of sensing the patch, and sometimes to the whole complex state of affairs which, on the sensum theory, is analysable into (act of sensing)—directed on to—(red patch). In the second meaning, "sensation" is obviously mental; in the third it is undoubtedly a complex whole which involves a mental factor. In the first meaning it is by no means obvious or even plausible to say that a sensation is mental. I shall always use "sensation" in the third meaning. Now, as the same name is thus often used, both for the patch and for something which undoubtedly is mental, or is a complex, involving a mental factor, it is not surprising that some people should have been inclined to think that the red patch is itself mental. For is it not a "sensation"? And is not a sensation a mental state? This is, of course, mere verbal confusion, and need not trouble us further. But philosophers who have not fallen into this confusion between sensum, sensation, and act of sensing, have yet held that sensa are mental. The most important living holder of this view is Professor Stout (at any rate he held it at the time when he wrote the last edition of his *Manual of Psychology*).

Before we can profitably carry the discussion of this point further, we must clear up the various meanings which can be attached to the statement "*x* is mental." (1) The first distinction that we must draw is between being "a state of mind" and being "mind-dependent." It is commonly held (and I do not here propose to question it) that whatever is a state of mind is mind-dependent, *i.e.*, that it could not exist except as a constituent of *a* mind, and, in fact, that it could only exist as a constituent of *that particular* mind, whose state it is said to be. An example would be my belief that $2 + 2 = 4$ or my desire for my tea. But it seems perfectly possible that a term might be mind-dependent without being a state of anyone's mind. What would this mean? I think it would mean that such a term can only exist as a constituent of a *state of mind,* but that it is not itself a constituent of a *mind.* Take some admitted state of mind, such as my perception of my table. There is clearly an important sense which we can all recognise, even though none of us can define it, in which it is true to say that this perception is a constituent of my mind, whilst the table is not. I should say that there was also an important (though very different) sense in which it is true to say that the table is a constituent of my perception of it, so long as that perception lasts. It is thus quite common for a term to be a constituent of one of my states of mind without being a constituent (and therefore without being a state) of my mind. Now, if chairs are anything like what they are commonly supposed to be, they do not *only* exist as constituents of states of mind, since it is commonly believed that such things go on existing with little or no change of quality when we cease to perceive them. But, just as states of mind can only exist as constituents of minds, so there *might* be terms which can *only* exist as constituents of states of mind. Such terms would be mind-dependent without being states of mind. If Berkeley's famous saying that "the essence of a sensible object is to be perceived" be taken quite literally, it implies that such objects are mind-dependent, whilst it does not *imply* (though it is, of course, *consistent with*) the view that they are states of mind.

(2) Even when this distinction has been drawn, there is a possibility of confusion. We must distinguish a more and a less radical sense of "mind-dependence." The sense just discussed is the more radical, and may be termed "existential mind-dependence." A term that is existentially mind-dependent, though not a state of mind, can only exist as a constituent of a certain state of mind. But a term which was not existentially mind-dependent, might be to a certain extent "qualitatively mind-dependent." By this I mean that, although it can exist and have qualities when it is not a con-

stituent of any state of mind, it might acquire some new qualities or alter some of its old qualities on becoming a constituent of a state of mind. It is certain that everything that at some period in its history becomes a constituent of any state of mind thereby acquires at least one new quality, viz., that it is now cognised, or desired, or shunned, or so on, by that mind. And I do not see any reason in principle why these changes of relation should not produce changes in the non-relational qualities of the object. If wax melts when brought into the relation of proximity to a fire, I know no reason why some qualities of an object should not be added or modified when it comes into the relation of being sensed by a mind.

(3) Some psychologists, of whom Stout is one, draw a fundamental distinction between two sorts of states of mind. They divide them into acts and non-acts. And a state of mind which is not an act they call a *presentation*. I propose to state this distinction in a different way, for reasons which I will now explain. A little while ago I took my perception of my table as an undoubted example of a state of mind. And I said that there was no doubt that the table is a constituent of it. That is, I took the whole complex situation (my perceiving)—of—(table) as a state of mind. What Stout calls an "act" is "my perceiving." He calls this a "state of mind," I call it a "constituent of a state of mind." The table is not a constituent of the state of mind, in Stout's sense of the word, whilst it is a constituent of the state of mind, in my sense of the word. In my terminology the act may be described as the non-objective constituent in a state of mind whose other constituent is its object. An act is something which cannot exist by itself, but can only exist as a constituent in a complex, whose other constituent is its object. And it is, of course, the characteristically mental factor in such a complex, since the other constituent may (though it need not) be non-mental. My reason for calling the whole complex fact, and not the act itself, a state of mind, is the following: Practically everyone agrees that there are such things as states of mind. And practically everyone agrees that the phrase "my perception of the ta-

ble" describes something real. But people differ greatly as to the right analysis of this fact, and the notion of "act" is connected with one special mode of analysis which would not be accepted by everyone. It therefore seems better to give the name "state of mind" to the *fact* which everyone admits to exist, and not to a supposed constituent, which some people deny to be present in it.

It is quite easy to restate the distinction which Stout has in mind in terms of my phraseology. Some mental states can be analysed into an act directed on an object. These are non-presentational states of mind. Others cannot be analysed into act and object. These are presentations. A non-presentational state may contain a presentation as object. For instance, a feeling of toothache would be a presentation on Stout's view. For, according to him, it *is* mental and is *not* analysable into an act of sensing and a "toothachy" object; it is just a "toothachy" state of mind. Now, if I were to introspect my toothache, in order to describe it to my dentist, my introspection would be a non-presentational mental state whose object is a presentation; for it is a complex containing an act of introspecting directed on to a toothachy feeling. The perception of a chair would be an example of a non-presentational mental state, whose object is not a presentation, because not mental.

We are now in a better position to deal with the question: "Are sensa mental?" This might mean (1) Are they acts? (2) Are they states of mind analysable into act and object? (3) Are they presentations? (4) Are they existentially mind-dependent, though not states of mind? (5) Are they to some extent qualitatively mind-dependent, though not existentially mind-dependent?

No one has ever suggested that sensa are acts or that they are states of mind analysable into act and object. A red patch sensed by me when I look at a pillar-box is an example of a sensum. It is plausible to hold that the whole fact known as "my sensation of the red patch" is a state of mind, analysable into act of sensing and red patch sensed. But there would be no plausibility in holding that the red patch itself was an act, or that it was itself divisible into act and object. Thus, if sensa be states of mind at all, they must be presentations. Now, there are two very different views included under the statement that sensa are presentations. The first would deny the analysis of "my sensation of red patch" into act of sensing and red sensum. It would treat the whole thing as an unanalysable state of mind, and therefore as a presentation. This view would hold that there is no real distinction between sensa and sensations. It would say that "sensation of red patch" = "red patch sensed," and is a presentation.[2] The second view would admit that in my sensation of red we can distinguish my act of sensing and the red patch sensed; but it would hold that the red patch is itself a state of mind, and, being indivisible into act and object, is a presentation. I do not think that most philosophers have very clearly distinguished these two varieties of the presentational theory of sensa. Moreover, those philosophers who have accepted the analysis of sensations into acts of sensing and sensa, and have asserted that sensa are mental, have seldom clearly distinguished the alternatives that sensa are presentations and that sensa are mind-dependent without being states of mind. And lastly, the distinction between existential and qualitative mind-dependence has not always been clearly seen. So that there is a very pretty mess for us to wipe up as well as we can.

(1) *Are Sensations analysable into Act of Sensing and Sensum?* The most plausible argument against this analysis would seem to be the following: If we consider the various experiences called "sensations," we seem to be able to arrange them in an order, starting with those of sight, passing through those of taste and smell, and ending with bodily sensations, like headache. Now, as regards the top members of the series, the analysis into act of sensing and object sensed seems pretty clear. A sensation of red seems clearly to mean a state of mind with a red object, and not to mean a red state of mind.

If we now pass to the other end of the series the oppo-

---

[2] This seems to be Stout's view in the *Manual of Psychology,* but I may be misinterpreting him.

site seems to be true. It is by no means obvious that a sensation of headache involves an act of sensing and a "headachy" object; on the contrary, it seems on the whole more plausible to describe the whole experience as a "headachy" state of mind. In fact the distinction of act and object seems here to have vanished; and, as there is clearly *something* mental in feeling a headache, just as there is in sensing a red patch, it seems plausible to hold that a sensation of headache is an unanalysable mental fact, within which no distinction of act and object can be found.

Now this contrast between the top and the bottom members of the series would not greatly matter, were it not for the fact that the two kinds of sensation seem to melt insensibly into each other at the middle of the series. It is about equally plausible to analyse a sensation of a sweet taste into an act of sensing and a sweet sensum, or to treat it as an unanalysable mental fact, having no object, but possessing the property of sweetness. Common speech recognises these distinctions. We talk of a sensation of red, but never of a feeling of red or of a red feeling. On the other hand, we talk indifferently of a sensation of headache, a feeling of headache, a headachy sensation, and a headachy feeling. The English talk of a sensation of smell, whereas the Scots more usually speak of "feeling" a smell. Now sensations of smell are just on the borderline between the two kinds of sensation. The rule is that, when a sensuous experience seems clearly to involve act and object, it is called a sensation and never a feeling; when it is doubtful whether any such analysis can be applied, it is called indifferently a feeling or a sensation.

Now the fact that all these experiences are classed together as sensations, and that the two kinds melt into each other at the middle of the series, naturally tempts men to treat them all alike. If we do this, we must hold either (α) that it is a mistake to think that a sensation of red *can* be analysed into an act of sensing and a red sensum; or (β) that it is a mistake to think that a sensation of headache *cannot* be analysed into an act of sensing and a headachy sensum. The former alternative makes sensation and sensum fall together into a single peculiar state, even in the case of sight; and, since the experience as a whole certainly is mental, we have to say that a sensation of red = a red sensum = a feeling or presentation which is red. The second alternative is that which is taken by Realists, like Professors Laird and Alexander.

Now it is evident that, if you insist on treating all experiences which are called "sensations" in the same way, it is antecedently as reasonable to take the Laird-Alexander alternative as the Presentationist alternative. You might argue: "It is obvious that a sensation of red involves an act of sensing and a red sensum, so a sensation of headache must involve an act of sensing and a headachy sensum." Thus the mere fact that sensations can be arranged in a series, such as I have described, does not *specially* favour the presentationist view; since exactly the same type of argument, starting from the other end of the series, would lead to exactly the opposite conclusion. There are just two remarks that seem to me worth making at this point.

(a) I do not find either the realist or the presentationist view very satisfactory as a complete account of all the experiences which are called "sensations." But, if I were forced to take one alternative or the other, I should prefer the former. It seems to me much more certain that, in a sensation of red, I *can* distinguish the red patch and the act of sensing it, than that, in a sensation of headache, I *cannot* distinguish a headachy object and an act of sensing it. (b) I think, however, that there is no need to insist on the realist analysis of bodily feelings in order to deal with the question whether sensations be analysable into act of sensing and sensum. It seems to me that the simplest and least doubtful way of treating the whole question raised by the series of sensations is the following: The word "sensation," as commonly used, is defined, not by direct inspection, but by causation. We say that we are having a sensation, if our state of mind is the immediate response to the stimulation of a nerve. Now, since sensations are not defined psychologically through their intrinsic properties, but physiologically through their bodily antecedents, it is surely very likely that they may include two very different kinds of experience, one of which can and the other cannot be analysed into act of sensing and sensum. These might be called respectively "true sensations" and "bodily feelings." The mere fact that both are often *called* "sensations" is surely a very poor reason for insisting that the structure of both must be the same. It is true indeed that there are marginal cases of which it is very difficult to say into which class they fall. But this ought not to make us slur over the plain introspective difference between the top and the bottom members of the series. The top ones at least do seem quite clearly to involve acts of sensing and sensa on which these acts are directed. It does seem clear that, when I have a sensation of a red triangular patch, some things are true of the patch itself (*e.g.,* that it is red and triangular) which it is very difficult to believe to be true of my sensation of the red patch. If so, it seems necessary to hold that the sensation and the sensum are not identical; that the sensum is an objective constituent of the sensation; and that there is another constituent which is not objective and may be called "the act of sensing." Into the question whether this latter factor is capable of further analysis, and, if so, what the right analysis of it may be, it is fortunately not necessary to go for our present purposes.

I conclude, then, that some sensations at least are analysable into act of sensing and sensum, and therefore that we cannot argue that sensum = sensation = a presentation.

(2) *Are Sensa, though distinct from Sensations, themselves Presentations?* Though sensations are not presentations but contain objects, which are sensa, it is perfectly possible that these objects might themselves be presentations. To prove that sensa are presentations, it would be necessary to prove that they are states of mind. And this involves proving (*a*) that they are existentially mind-dependent, and (*b*) that they are constituents of minds and not merely of certain states of mind. Obviously it might be possible to prove the first, even if it were not possible to prove the second, of these propositions. I do not know of

any reasonably plausible argument to prove that sensa are not merely mind-dependent, but are also states of mind, once you accept the view that sensa must be distinguished from sensations. Indeed, the assertion would be open to the same kind of objection which we made to the view that sensa and sensations can be identified. On either view something is said to be a state of mind, though it possesses properties which it is very difficult to ascribe to states of mind. If a sensum be a state of mind, then there are states of mind which are literally red or round or hot or loud or triangular, and so on. I have no difficulty in believing that many states of mind *contain* such terms as objects, but I do find it very difficult to believe that any state of mind actually *is* a term of this sort. Yet the latter is implied by the statement that sensa are presentations, just as much as by the statement that sensations are presentations. In fact, the reasons which forced us to distinguish sensations from sensa, and to regard the latter as objects contained in the former, equally forbid us to treat sensa themselves as states of mind. This objection *may,* of course, be a mere prejudice; but it *is* worth while to point out that the view that sensa are presentations does logically imply the very paradoxical propositions that some states of mind are literally hot or red or round, for most philosophers who have held the view under discussion have successfully concealed this consequence from themselves and their readers. I shall therefore reject the view that sensa are states of mind, until someone produces much better reasons than anyone has yet done for believing such an extremely paradoxical proposition.

There are, however, quite plausible arguments to prove that sensa are existentially mind-dependent, though not states of mind. That is to say, that, although sensations are analysable into act and sensum, and the sensum must therefore be distinguished both from the sensation and from the act of sensing, which is the other factor in the sensation, yet these two factors are not capable of existing separately from each other. No act of sensing without some sensum on which it is directed, and no sensum without an act of sensing directed upon it. The arguments for this view are three: (*a*) The privacy and variability of sensa; (*b*) the analogy between sensa and bodily feelings; and (*c*) the analogy between sensa and so-called "mental images."

(*a*) We notice at once that sensa have some of the characteristics of physical objects and some of those of mental states. On the one hand, they are extended, and have shapes, sizes, colours, temperatures, etc. On the other hand, they do seem to be private to each observer; and this, it will be remembered, is one of the chief marks of the mental as distinct from the physical. It is at least doubtful whether two people, who say that they are perceiving the same object, are ever sensing the same sensum or even two precisely similar sensa. This does suggest that sensa are mental—at any rate in the sense of being mind-dependent.

If, however, we look more closely, we see that this conclusion does not necessarily follow. The facts are on the whole much better explained by supposing that the sensa which a man senses are partly dependent on the position, internal states, and structure of his body. Since no two men's bodies can be in precisely the same place at precisely the same time, it is not surprising that the sensa of the two men should differ. And, since the internal states and the minute structure of no two living bodies are exactly alike, it is still less surprising. Now this explanation not only accounts *as* well for most of the facts as the view that sensa are mind-dependent; it accounts a great deal better for some of the most striking of the facts. The orderly variation in the shapes of visual sensa, as we move about, is intelligible if we suppose that the sensa which we sense are partly conditioned by the positions of our bodies. The assumption that they depend on our minds gives no explanation whatever of such facts.

There is, however, a better form of this argument, which has, I think, been somewhat neglected by people who want to hold that sensa are *never* mind-dependent to any degree. It does seem to me undeniable that in certain cases, and to a certain extent, our past experiences and our present expectations affect the actual properties of the sensa that we sense, and do not merely affect the judgments about physical objects which we base upon sensa. We shall go into this point in some detail in a later chapter; at present I will just illustrate my meaning by two examples.

When I look at the "staircase figure," which is given in most psychology text-books as an instance of ambiguous figures, it seems to me that it actually looks sensibly different from time to time. Its sensible appearance changes "with a click," as I look at it, from that of a staircase to that of an overhanging cornice. This change tends to take place as I concentrate my mind on the idea of the one or on that of the other. Now, on the present analysis of sensible appearance, such a change as this involves an actual qualitative change in the sensum. So far is it from being a mere change in the judgments which I happen to base on one and the same sensum, that the direction of my thoughts changes first and is the condition of the change in the sensible appearance.

Again, when I turn my head, the visual sensa are not as a rule affected with any sensible movement. If, however, I put my glasses a little out of focus or look through a window made of irregularly thick glass, and then turn my head, the sensa do sensibly move. Whether they move or keep still seems to depend on my past experiences and my present expectations about physical objects. The whole psychology of vision is full of such cases, some of them of a highly complex kind.

Now, of course, these examples do not suggest for a moment that sensa are existentially mind-dependent, but they do strongly suggest that they are to some extent qualitatively mind-dependent. And it cannot be said here, as in the previous examples, that reference to the mind gives no help in explaining the facts. Here the boot is rather on the other foot. No doubt the facts just mentioned could *in theory* be accounted for by referring to the past history of the *body*, in addition to its present state and position. *I.e.*, we could talk learnedly about the traces left on our brains and nervous systems by the past experiences, and could say that they are among the conditions of our sensa. But this would not help us to explain any concrete characteristic of our sensa in any particular case. For the plain fact is, that we do often know what relevant experiences we or others have had, whilst we know nothing whatever in detail about traces in the brain and nervous system. So here a reference to *mental* conditions really does explain concrete facts, whilst a reference to *bodily* conditions does not. We shall have to return to this point at a much later stage.

(*b*) We have already noticed the arrangement of "sensations" in a scale from sensations of colour and sound to bodily feelings. We saw that this might be used as an argument to prove that even sensations of colour and sound are presentations, or equally as an argument to prove that even sensations of headache are divisible into act and object. Suppose we take the latter alternative, which, as I have said, seems to me to be the more plausible of the two, though I do not think that the facts compel us to adopt either. It is then possible to produce a fairly plausible argument for the view that sensa are existentially mind-dependent. The argument would run as follows: "Granted that a sensation of headache can be analysed into act of sensing and headachy sensum, it is surely obvious that the latter, from its very nature, could not exist without the former. An unfelt headache is surely a mere *Unding*. Now, if this be true of headachy sensa, does not the very continuity of the series of sensations on which you have been insisting make it likely to be true of red sensa, and indeed of all sensa? If so, sensa will be from their very nature existentially mind-dependent and incapable of existing save as objective constituents of sensations."

I think that this is quite a plausible argument, but I do not think it conclusive. Two questions could be asked about it. (*α*) Supposing it to be true that an unfelt headache is inconceivable, does the continuity of the series of experiences called "sensations," justify us in extending this conclusion to all sensa, and, in particular, to those of sight and hearing? Secondly (*β*), is it really true that an unfelt headache is inconceivable? (*α*) To the first question I answer that, as a matter of fact, I do not find the slightest intrinsic difficulty in conceiving the existence of unsensed red patches or unsensed noises, whilst I do find a considerable difficulty in conceiving the existence of unfelt headaches. I do not think that it is safe to reject this plain difference on the grounds of a mere argument from continuity.

(β) Moreover, I think I can see why it seems so difficult to conceive of the existence of unfelt headaches, and can see that this difficulty is not really conclusive. Our main interest in bodily feelings is that they are pleasant or painful; sensations of sight are, as a rule, intrinsically neutral, or nearly so. Now I am quite prepared to believe that an object has to be cognised by us in order to be pleasant or painful to us. For it seems to me that the pleasantness or painfulness of anything is (or, at any rate, depends upon) my recognising it and taking up a certain attitude of liking or disliking to it. It might, therefore, be perfectly true that an unfelt headache would not be *a pain,* just as an unmarried woman is not a wife. Since we are mainly interested in headaches as pains, we are inclined to think that an unfelt headache would be *nothing,* when the truth merely is that it would not be a *pain.* This would be comparable to the mistake which a fanatical admirer of matrimony would make if he ignored the existence of all spinsters because they were not wives. I, therefore, am not convinced that, if a feeling of headache be a genuine sensation and not a mere presentation, the headachy sensum which it contains could not exist unsensed. Still less could I extend this view to sight and sound sensa.

(c) The third argument for thinking that sensa are incapable of existing unsensed is founded on their resemblance to "mental images," whose very name implies that they are commonly supposed to be existentially mind-dependent, if not actually states of mind. The resemblances must be admitted, though in favourable cases there seems to be some intrinsic difference which it is easy to recognise but hard to describe. But it seems to me doubtful whether images are existentially mind-dependent. I do not see any very obvious reason why there should not be "unimaged" images. It is, of course, perfectly true that images are to a much greater extent qualitatively mind-dependent than are sensa. Most, if not all, of them depend on our past experiences; and many of them depend in part on our present volitions. Voluntary images do, no doubt, depend on our minds, in the sense that they would not be imaged here and now, if we did not *will* them. But exactly the same is true of many things, which no one would think of calling existentially mind-dependent. Most chemical reactions that take place in a laboratory would never have happened if someone had not deliberately mixed the reagents in a flask and heated the latter over a flame. No one supposes that this renders such reactions in any important sense mind-dependent. Thus the fact that some images are voluntary seems irrelevant to the present subject.

The other point, that all images that we can now image are in part determined in their characteristics by our past experiences, is more important. It must be counted along with the fact, already admitted, that many sensa are to some extent qualitatively mind-dependent. Here, as before, we can, if we like, substitute a reference to traces in our brains and nervous systems. But here, too, the doubt remains whether this kind of explanation is ultimately of much philosophic importance, in view of the fact that we often know directly what our relevant past experiences are, whilst the traces, etc., of the physiologist are purely hypothetical bodily correlates of these. Further treatment of this subject must be deferred till we face the problem of the part played by our own bodies in sensation and imagination.

I will now try to sum up the results of this rather long and complex discussion on the relation of sensa to minds and their states. The sensum theory is bound up with a special view as to the right analysis of the kind of fact which is described by such phrases as "my sensation of *x*." It holds that this is complex, and that within it there can be distinguished two factors—*x* itself, which is the sensum and is an object, and a subjective factor, which is

called the "act of sensing." The latter may, of course, be
capable of further analysis, such, *e.g.,* as Russell attempts
in his *Analysis of Mind;* or it may be (or contain) a peculiar unanalysable relation. Now, there is also a theory which
refuses to analyse "my sensation of *x*" in this way. It holds
that the whole thing is unanalysable into act and object.
On such a view the distinction between sensum and sensation vanishes; and the experience, which may be called
indifferently by either name, is a mental state of the kind
called *presentations.* This view is supported by reference
to bodily feelings, and by an argument from the continuity
between them and the higher sensations. As against this
we pointed out (*a*) that there is just as good reason to
use the argument from continuity in the opposite direction;
and (*b*) that very possibly, in spite of the continuity, there
is a real difference in nature between genuine sensations
and bodily feelings. In favour of the view that genuine
sensations are analysable into act and object, we pointed
out that there seems to be a plain difference between a
red patch sensed by me and the total fact described as
"my sensation of a red patch." And we suggested that
those who refuse to make this analysis are forced to the
very paradoxical conclusion that there are states of mind
which are literally red, round, hot, loud, etc.

The next point was this. Assuming that sensations are
analysable into act of sensing and sensum, we raised the
question whether sensa are states of mind, or, if not,
whether they are existentially mind-dependent. We agreed
that, if they are states of mind at all, they must be presentations. But we found no positive reason *for* thinking that
they are states of mind, and much the same reasons *against*
that view as led us to hold that sensations are analysable
into act and sensum.

We then discussed three more or less plausible arguments to show that sensa are existentially mind-dependent,
i.e., that they cannot exist except as objective constituents
of sensations. We saw no intrinsic reason why coloured
patches or noises should not be capable of existing unsensed. And we refused to be moved from this view by an

argument from continuity with bodily feelings. For we were far from sure whether bodily feelings really are analysable into act of sensing and sensum; and we suggested that, even if they be, it is by no means certain that their sensa could not exist unsensed. We tried to show why this was *thought* to be obvious, and to show that it is not really so.

The two remaining arguments seemed to us to show that sensa are partly dependent on the position, etc., of the *body*, but they did not have any tendency to show that they are *existentially* dependent on the *mind*. Still, some of the facts adduced did rather strongly suggest that sensa and, *a fortiori*, images, are to some extent *qualitatively* mind-dependent. We thought that this reference to the mind *might* be removed by extending the bodily conditions, so as to include physiological traces and dispositions. But, in view of the wholly hypothetical character of these, we were not prepared at this stage to deny that sensa and images might be to some extent qualitatively mind-dependent. And there we leave the matter, till we deal more fully with the part played by the human body in sense-perception.

We have seen that the whole question is highly complex, and that the arguments for the view that sensa are mental are by no means lacking in plausibility. We shall not therefore be tempted to think that everyone who has been persuaded by them must be either a knave or a fool. Some of those who call themselves *New Realists* have been too much inclined to take this attitude; and, on one reader at least, they have produced the impression of being rather offensively "at ease in Zion."

(ii) *How are Sensa related to Physical Objects?* We can now turn to the second question which we raised about sensa. The plain man does not clearly distinguish between physical objects and sensa, and therefore feels no particular difficulty about their mutual relations. We first come to recognise sensa as distinct from physical objects by reflecting on the fact of sensible appearance, and the contrast between it and the supposed properties of physical reality. But once the existence of sensa has been clearly recognised, the problem of their relation to the physical world becomes pressing. We all believe in a world of physical objects, and profess to have a great deal of detailed knowledge about it. Now this world of physical objects makes its existence and its detailed nature known to us by the sensible appearances which it presents to us. And, on the sensum theory, these appearances are sensa. Sensa are therefore in some way the *ratio cognoscendi* of the physical world, whilst the physical world is in some way the *ratio essendi* of sensa. Our problem therefore divides into an epistemological and an ontological one. The two problems are not ultimately independent, but it is useful to state them separately.

(1) How far is it true that our beliefs about the physical world depend on our sensa? Before we can answer this, we must draw some distinctions among our beliefs. First, there is our belief that there is a physical world of *some* kind. This, as we have seen, involves at least the belief that there are things which are relatively permanent, which combine many qualities, and which persist and interact at times when they are not appearing to our senses. These we may call *constitutive* properties of the physical world, since they are part of what we mean by "physical." Then there is the belief that these objects have spatial or quasi-spatial characteristics. This may almost be called constitutive, but it is a shade less fundamental than the first set of properties. Lastly, there are what might be called *empirical* beliefs about the physical world. These are beliefs about points of detail, *e.g.*, that some things are red, and that there is now a red fluted lamp-shade in my rooms.

Now I have already asserted that it is false psychologically to say that we, in fact, reach our perceptual judgments about the existence and properties of physical objects by a process of inference from our sensa and their properties. Further, it is false logically to suppose that the *existence* of a physical world in general could be inferred from the existence of our sensa, or from anything that we know about their intrinsic properties or their mutual relations. I suppose that the existence of sensa is a necessary condition, but it is certainly not a sufficient condition, of my belief in the existence of the physical world. If there were no sensible appearances to me, I suppose that I should not judge there to be any physical reality. But, on the other hand, there is nothing in my sensa to force me logically to the conclusion that there must be something beyond them, having the constitutive properties of physical objects. The belief that our sensa are appearances of something more permanent and complex than themselves seems to be primitive, and to arise inevitably in us with the sensing of the sensa. It is not reached by inference, and could not logically be justified by inference. On the other hand, there is no possibility of either refuting it logically, or of getting rid of it, or—so far as I can see—of co-ordinating the facts without it.

There are groupings among my own sensa and correlations between my sensa and those of others which fit in extremely well with the belief in a physical world of which all the sensa are so many appearances. It might be held that this at least forms the basis of a logical argument in inverse probability, to show that the belief in the physical world is highly probable. But the snag here is that all such arguments only serve to multiply the antecedent probability of a proposition, and, unless we have reason to suppose that this probability starts with a finite magnitude, they lead us nowhere. Now, although I do not know of any reason antecedently against the existence of a physical world, I also know of no antecedent reason for it. So its antecedent probability seems quite indeterminate, unless we are prepared to hold that the fact that everybody does in practice believe it, is a ground for ascribing a finite antecedent probability to it. It seems to me that the belief that there is a physical world is logically in much the same position as those assumptions about the constitution of the existent on which all inductive proofs of special laws of nature rest. If these assumptions start with a finite antecedent probability, their success justifies us in ascribing a high final probability to them. But do they have a finite antecedent probability? We can say of them, as of the belief in a physical world, that we all do believe them in practice, that there is no positive reason against them, and that we cannot get on without assuming them. But, having said so much, we shall do wisely to change the subject and talk about the weather.

We shall not then attempt to *prove* the existence of a world of entities having the constitutive properties of physical objects; for, if this can be done, I at any rate do not know how to do it. But we shall point out those facts about our sensa and their groupings which specially fit in with the view that sensa are various partial and fleeting appearances of relatively permanent and independent things. That is, we shall try to indicate those facts about our sensa which *would* give a high final probability to the belief in a physical world, *provided* it had a finite antecedent probability. This will be our main task in the next two chapters, which deal with the spatial and temporal characteristics of sensa and of physical objects and events. The first of these chapters will be concerned with the facts about our sensa which fit in with the view that they are appearances of objects which combine many properties, and which can be perceived by many different observers at the same time. The second will be concerned with the facts about our sensa which fit in with the view that they are relatively fleeting appearances of more permanent things and processes.

Now, assuming that there is a world of enduring and independent things, there is still room for wide differences of opinion as to the kind of whole that it forms, the way in which it is divided into parts, and the various empirical qualities which these parts possess. Common-sense and science are agreed that it is in some sense a spatial whole, whose parts have various shapes, sizes and positions, and are capable of moving about within the whole. This alleged spatial character of the physical world may be called "semi-constitutive"; for, as I have said, we hardly admit that a world of non-spatial entities would deserve to be called "physical," even though it were persistent, independent of us, and many-qualitied. Now, it is clear that all the spatial characteristics which we ascribe to the physical world are based, both in general outline and in detail, on the spatial characteristics of our sensa. Moreover, I think it can be rendered highly probable that, if there be a physical world at all, and our sensa be appearances of it, then that world is quasi-spatial. The importance and complexity of this subject seem to justify the length of the next chapter, in which I have treated it to the best of my ability.

When we come to the purely empirical qualities of the physical world there is a sharp difference of opinion between science and common-sense. The latter ascribes qualities, like colour, temperature, etc., to physical objects, whilst the former refuses to do so. In discussing this matter the partial dependence of sensa on what goes on inside the body of the observer becomes of great importance, and the concluding chapter has been devoted to this problem.

(2) This last question leads in the most natural way to the ontological problem as to the status of sensa in the existent world. There is a world of physical objects and a world of sensa. In some way the latter seems to be dependent on the former. But both are parts of the whole of existent reality. How are the two related? This is a problem which common-sense ignores, because it does not definitely distinguish between sensa and physical objects. Science also ignores it, because, although in theory it makes an equivalent distinction, it uses it simply as an excuse for ignoring sensa and concentrating on physical objects and processes. This is a perfectly legitimate procedure for the special purpose which natural science has in view, but it is not permissible to the philosopher. His whole business is to drag such skeletons from the cupboards in which it has been found convenient to shelve them, and to give them their right place in the whole scheme of things.

Now the epistemological and the ontological problems about sensa and their relations to physical objects are connected in the following way. Our primitive belief in the existence of a world of relatively permanent, independent, things is extremely vague. It is little more than a general scheme, in terms of which the actual groupings which we find among our sensa are stated. Even when we go a step further, and say that the spatial character and the special groupings of sensa practically force us to think of the physical word as a quasi-spatial whole, containing parts with fairly definite shapes, sizes, and positions, we still have only a very general, though much more definite scheme. Within this general quasi-spatial scheme all kinds of alternative specifications are possible. We are not tied down to any special view as to the number of its dimensions. Again, we are not tied down to any special view as to the "geometry" of it, when the number of its dimensions is settled. Lastly, we might put forward dozens of different theories as to the nature of physical objects, all compatible with the general scheme and with the special facts about our sensa and their groupings. It is this extreme variety of alternative theories, left open to us by the general concept of a physical world and the special facts about our sensa, which gives a legitimate hope for indefinite progress with the problem under discussion, provided the scientists and the patriots between them do not destroy civilisation, and with it all disinterested thinking. With traditional views about the nature of Space, Time, and Matter, it is extremely difficult to fit the world of sensa and the world of physical objects together into a coherent whole. But, once the immense number of possible alternatives within the scheme is grasped, the devising of theories of the physical object which shall give sensa a *locus standi* in the physical world will be a winter evening's pastime for symbolic logicians. This task we shall leave to those better fitted than ourselves to accomplish it; we shall be concerned rather with those facts about our sensa with which any theory of physical objects must deal.

The Critical Scientific Theory. I propose now to try to state clearly, in terms of the Sensum theory, what appears to be involved in the common scientific view of physical objects and their sensible appearances. As scientists never state their own position on this point clearly, it is necessary for us to do so for them. We can then see how far the view can be accepted, and how far its plausibility has depended on its modest obscurity.

Let us take the old example of a boy looking at a penny. He believes that it is quite literally round and just as literally brown. He believes that the brown (and, as he thinks, round) patch which he is sensing is quite literally a part (viz., the upper side) of the penny. And he believes that this, which he now sees, is the same as what he can feel if he puts out his hand. As he grows up he is probably told, on the authority of "science," that the penny is not "really" brown, though it is "really" round. The sort of reason which he is given for this startling statement is (so far as I can remember) that things appear to have different colours in different lights. If he should study heat and light, he will be told that the colour which he sees depends on vibrations which strike his eye, and that the temperature that he feels depends on molecular movements which are going on in the penny. He still thinks of the penny as literally round, and thinks now of all sorts of movements going on within its contour, and sending disturbances to his eye and his hand. But he no longer thinks of the penny as literally brown or cold. The brownness and coldness are thought to be *effects* which the processes in the penny produce by transmission. The round shape is "in" the penny; the brownness and coldness are not. They are *effects* which the penny produces "in" his eye or his hand or his brain or his mind. He still thinks that he literally senses the same round upper side of the penny, both with his eyes and with his hand, but he no longer thinks that there is a brown colour or a cold temperature literally spread over this round surface.

This, I think, is a fair account of what the average person with a scientific training believes on these matters; so far as anything so incoherent can be said to be believed by anyone. It is perfectly obvious that such a view as this cannot stand criticism. It is an inconsistent mixture of two utterly different theories of perception. As regards spatial attributes, it keeps to the naïvely realistic view of unsophisticated common-sense. According to it, the seen and felt shape is not an effect produced in us by something else. It is out there, whether we see it or feel it or not. Processes in it simply make us see it or feel it under suitable circumstances. But, as regards colour and temperature, the scientific theory takes quite a different view. It is a causal theory. The processes in the penny do not make us see a colour or feel a temperature which is already there to be seen or felt. They *produce* the colour or temperature "in us," to use a discretely vague phrase, which may cover our minds, our brains, and our special sense-organs.

Now this muddled mixture of theories is not consistent with itself or with the facts. It is inconsistent with itself for the following reason. When I look at a penny, the brown colour that I see is seen spread out over the round contour. Similarly with the cold temperature that I feel. We are asked to believe that there is brownness without shape "in me," and round shape without colour out there where the penny is, and yet that in some mysterious way, the shapeless brownness "in me" is projected into the round contour of the penny "out there." If this be not nonsense I do not know what nonsense is. We can all *say* this kind of thing, but can we attach any clear meaning to what we are saying?

Moreover, as Berkeley long ago pointed out, the theory only takes account of half the facts. Certainly colours vary with the illumination, the state of our eyes, and so on. But it only needs a little careful inspection to see that visible shapes also vary with changes in the medium, and with the position of the observer. If the former fact proves that colours and temperatures are not "in the object" but "in us," the latter should prove the same thing for visible shapes. It is impossible to reconcile the view that the penny is round, in the literal straightforward sense, with the view that, when we look at it, we literally sense visually the upper surface of it. For we sense all sorts of elliptical patches from various positions. It is clear that none of these can be *identical* with the round upper surface of the penny, and it is equally clear that they are not *parts* of it in the literal sense in which the King's head is a part of it.

If we want to be consistent then, we must treat visual shape in the same way as colour and temperature. What we sense visually is a sensum, and the shape and the brownness both belong to it. If anything be produced "in us" by an external object when we look at it, it is not just the colour, but is the whole patch with its colour and its shape. And, as we have seen, this patch cannot be regarded as being the upper surface of the external object, or as being literally a part of that surface. Nor can we any longer hold that what we sense by touch is literally identical with what we sense by sight, and that sight and touch merely reveal two different qualities of this one object. For what we sense tactually is round and of constant size. What we sense visually is not round, except when we are in that very special set of positions from which we are said to be "looking straight down on" the penny. And, even if we confine ourselves to this series of positions, the sizes of the various round patches which we sense are not the same for different positions in the series. It is therefore clear that the scientific view needs to be completely restated in terms of the sensum theory. And this is not easy, because the scientific theory assumed that we really were sensing the contour of the actual physical object out in space, and that our sensations were due to what was going on within that contour.

As we move about and continue, as we say, to "look at the same object," we are aware of a series of sensa, each having shape and colour, and all very much alike in these respects. But there are certain variations which we commonly overlook. These strike us in exaggerated cases, and can be noticed by careful inspection in all cases. Moreover, they are as a rule reversed when we retrace our steps. If we are going to attempt a causal theory of perception we must try to explain this conjunction of predominant agreement throughout the series with slight, regular, and reversible variations between its different members.

The explanation that naturally strikes us is that the series of sensa depends on two sets of conditions. One of these is relatively permanent, and accounts for the predominant agreement of the members of the series. The other is variable, and accounts for their minor variations.

Again, if we feel an object, such as a penny, and meanwhile look at it from various points of view, the series of predominantly similar, but slightly variant, visual sensa is correlated with an invariant tactual sensum. The shape of the latter is very much, but not exactly, like those of most of the former. It is exactly like that of the visual sensa which are sensed from a certain series of positions. As regards other qualities, there is complete difference between the visual and the tactual sensa. The former have colour, but no temperature or hardness; the latter have coldness and hardness, but no colour. Now we have to explain this predominant agreement, combined with minor differences, between the shapes of the many visual sensa and the shape of the one tactual sensum. And we have to remember that, as regards other sensible qualities, the difference is complete. Here, again, it seems natural to suppose that there is something common and relatively permanent, which accounts for the predominant agreement in shape between the visual and the tactual sensa, and something variable that accounts for their minor differences in shape. This other factor seems clearly to be connected with the position of the sense-organ. As the eye moves about, the shape of the visual sensa varies. The shape of the tactual sensum does not change: but then we cannot move the hand to a distance and continue to sense the tactual sensum at all, as we can change the place of the eye and still continue to see. We may further suppose that different factors are needed to determine such very different sensible qualities as colour and temperature; but it is reasonable to suppose that, whatever these factors may be, they are subject to some common condition which determines the very similar shape of both visual and tactual sensa.

Lastly, when we compare notes with other people who

say that they are looking at the same thing as we are, we find again a predominant agreement between their sensa and ours, combined with minor variations. It seems reasonable to suppose that there is a set of conditions, common to their sensa and ours, which accounts for the predominant agreement between the two. In addition, there must be variable factors, one specially connected with one observer and another with another observer. These are responsible for the minor variations. It seems, then, that we have good grounds for supposing that there are physical objects in the sense of conditions which (a) are common to us and to others; (b) are relatively permanent, and, at any rate, do not *ipso facto* change when we move about; and (c) determine in some way the attributes of our sensa, in conjunction with other conditions which do vary from person to person at the same time and for the same person at different times.

It might be asked at this point by a sceptical reader, "Why go outside the series of correlated sensa at all? Why not be content to take them as a fact? Why make them all depend on conditions outside the series of sensa itself?" As I have said, this is a step which everyone does take, but which no one can be logically compelled to take. At present we may say that what induces us to do this is the fact that we have reason to think that physical objects change and act on each other when we do not happen to be sensing any sensa from them. We can drop such series of sensa as I have been describing (*e.g.*, by turning our heads or going out of the room), and then by making suitable movements we can pick it up again either where we left it, or in a form that is obviously a later development of a course of change whose earlier stages we noticed before we turned away. It is facts of this kind which (rightly or wrongly) make us look beyond such series of correlated sensa to relatively permanent conditions, which lie outside the series and can develop on their own account when the series is interrupted.

Now these common and relatively permanent conditions might, for all that we have seen up to the present, be so utterly unlike the sensa that they condition that it would be misleading to call them physical objects. The question therefore at once arises: "Can we determine anything further about their properties, either with certainty or with reasonably high probability?" I do not think that we could determine anything further with certainty, but I do think that we might determine something further with high probability. It is, of course, perfectly true that a set of conditions—and, moreover, a set which is only one *part* of the total conditions—of a sensum, must not be *assumed* to resemble in its properties the sensum which it partially determines. On the other hand, it were equally unreasonable to assume that the two *cannot* resemble each other. There can be no inner contradiction in the qualities of shape and size, since *sensa,* at least, certainly have shape and size and certainly exist. If such qualities involved any kind of internal contradiction, no existent whatever could possess them. Hence it is perfectly legitimate to postulate hypothetically any amount of resemblance that we choose between sensa and the permanent part of their total conditions. If now we find that, by postulating certain qualities in these permanent conditions, we can account for the most striking facts about our sensa, and that without making this hypothesis we cannot do so, the hypothesis in question may reach a very high degree of probability.

Now we find that the visual sensa of a group which we ascribe to a single physical object are related projectively to each other and to the tactual sensum which we ascribe to the same object. If we regard their common permanent condition as having something analogous to shape, we can explain the shapes of the various sensa in the group as projections of the shape of their common permanent condition. If we refuse to attribute anything like shape to the permanent conditions, we cannot explain the variations in shape of the visual sensa as the observer moves into different positions. This does not, of course, *prove* that the common and relatively permanent conditions of a group of sensa do have shape, but it does render the hypothesis highly plausible. We have already seen that it is a legitimate one, that there is no reason why these common conditions should not have shape; we now see that it is also a plausible one, since with it we can, and without it we cannot, account for the variations in the shapes of the sensa of the group.

What about the so-called "secondary qualities," like colour and temperature? We know that Descartes, Locke, and the orthodox natural scentists, hold that we have no right to ascribe them literally to physical objects, whilst Berkeley and many other philosophers have argued that primaries and secondaries must stand or fall (and that they, in fact, fall) together. What is the truth about this matter? The first need is to state the doctrine of primary and secondary qualities in a clear and intelligible form. Unquestionably, colour and temperature belong to *our sensa,* at any rate, in the same literal way in which shape and size belong to them. What I am immediately aware of when I look at a penny stamp is as indubitably red as it is indubitably more or less square. Similarly, when I hold a round piece of ice in my hand, what I am aware of is as certainly cold as it is certainly round. Thus, to say that colours and temperatures are "unreal," or "do not really exist," is patently false, if this means that there is *nothing* in the Universe of which it is true to say: "This is literally red," or "This is literally cold." Such statements are true of many sensa, at any rate, and sensa are parts of the existing Universe.

The only substantial question is: "Do colours and temperatures ever literally belong to physical objects, or do they belong literally *only* to sensa?" What the scientist is trying in an extremely muddled way to do is to assert the *physical* reality of shapes and sizes, and to deny the *physical* reality of colours, temperatures, noises, etc. Now this view, when clearly stated, comes to the following: "Shapes and sizes belong to physical objects in the same literal way in which they belong to sensa, and from the shapes and sizes of sensa we can generally infer with reasonable certainty those of that physical object of which these sensa are appearances. Colours, temperatures, etc.,

belong literally to sensa, but they belong to physical objects only in a derivative and Pickwickian sense. There
must, of course, be *something* in the permanent conditions
of a group of sensa which wholly or partly determines
the colour or temperature of the latter. But this something
is not colour or temperature." We have seen what sort of
ground there is for the positive part of this view: is there
any good reason to believe the negative part of it?

It is sometimes thought that the physical theories of
light and heat positively *disprove* the common-sense view
that physical objects are literally coloured or hot. This is a
sheer logical blunder. The physical theory of light, *e.g.*,
asserts that, whenever we sense a red sensum, vibrations
of a certain period are striking our retina. This does not
prove that bodies which emit vibrations of that period are
not literally red, for it might well be that only bodies
which are literally red can emit just these vibrations. The
vibrations might simply be the means of stimulating us
to sense the red colour, which is literally in the body,
whether we happen to sense it or not. (I am quite certain
that this simple-minded theory cannot be made to fit the
extremely complicated facts; but it *is* compatible with the
fact that we only become aware of colours when vibrations
of a certain kind affect our eyes; and therefore *this fact*
does not, as is often supposed, refute the common-sense
view that bodies are literally coloured and that we actually
sense the colours which are on their surfaces.)

I think that the negative part of the scientific view does
express an important fact, but that it needs to be stated
in a much more guarded way. (1) It is *certain* that, if
physical objects possess shape and size at all, they must
have *some* other quality, related to shape and size in the
same general kind of way in which colour and temperature
are related to the shape and size of sensa. You cannot
have extension *et praeterea nihil;* you must have something that can be spread out and cover an area or fill a
volume. (2) There is no reason why these "extensible"
qualities, which *must* be present in physical objects, if
they be extended at all, should not actually be colour and

temperature. Since sensa certainly exist, and are certainly coloured, there can be no internal contradiction in the notion of an existent colour. (3) On the other hand, of course, the extensible qualities of physical objects *need* not be colour or temperature. So long as they are qualities that can cover areas and fill volumes, as colour and temperature do, they might differ from any quality that is ever present in our sensa. (4) Whilst we found that the assumption that the permanent conditions of groups of sensa have shape, and that they and our bodies have position, does help us to predict the shapes of various sensa in the group, we do not find that the ascription of colours or temperatures to these permanent conditions helps us to predict the colours or temperatures of the sensa in the group. It is found more profitable to correlate the colours and temperatures of sensa with the hypothetical movements of hypothetical parts of their permanent conditions. This does not prove, as has often been thought, that physical objects *cannot* literally have colours or temperatures. Of course, if the sensa that we sense cannot literally be parts of the surfaces of physical objects, it follows that the colours and temperatures of these sensa cannot literally *be identical with* the colours and temperatures of physical objects, even if the latter have such qualities. The facts under discussion do show that the hypothesis that physical objects literally have colours and temperatures, though legitimate enough, is not capable of empirical verification, and therefore cannot be asserted with any high probability.

The view which I have been trying to state may be called the *Critical Scientific Theory*. It is simply an attempt to formulate clearly, in terms of the Sensum Theory of sensible appearance, the view about the external world which has been at the back of the scientific mind since the time of Descartes and Locke. In its original form this view was a mass of inconsistencies, since it was naïvely realistic for our perception of shape, size, and position, and held a causal theory for our perception of colour, temperature, etc. This combination of theories proved to be inconsistent with the inextricable entanglement of the two kinds of qualities, which we actually find. Moreover, the naïvely realistic part of it proved untenable in face of the variations of visual shape and size, which are obvious when we view what is regarded as a single unchanged physical object from various positions.

Thus the only hope for the scientific view was to restate it in a completely causal form. A serious difficulty at once arose. The causal part of the old view presupposed the naïvely realistic part. When we were told that motions within a circular contour at a certain place in space caused sensations of colour and temperature "in us," we understood this, because we thought that we literally saw and felt this contour in this place. But, as soon as the theory is made *completely* causal, *both* spatial and non-spatial attributes belong primarily to the effect produced "in us" by something else. It then becomes difficult to see that we have any better right to regard this cause as literally endowed with shape, size, and position, than as literally endowed with colour and temperature. Yet the scientific theories about the causation of our sensations of colour, temperature, etc., are stated in terms which seem to lose all meaning unless the causes of these sensations literally have shapes, sizes, and positions. The Critical Scientific Theory, as stated by us, has been an attempt to meet these difficulties, to reformulate the distinction between primary and secondary qualities, and to estimate the amount of value which this distinction can justly claim.

I think that the Critical Scientific Theory is internally consistent, so far as it goes; but I certainly do not believe that it is ultimately satisfactory. In the first place, it continues to use a number of phrases whose meanings are no longer obvious when we have given up the notion that we literally sense parts of the surfaces of physical objects. It still talks of pennies being "round," of a number of different people at "the same time" and the same person at "different times" all perceiving "the same penny" from "different places." We must reinterpret all these phrases in terms of our sensa and their relations before we can hope to get a consistent theory. I shall try my hand at this very difficult job in the next three chapters.

Secondly, our theory uses the phrase that processes in external physical objects and our bodies "jointly produce in us" the sensa by which we become aware of them. The phrase in inverted commas covers a multitude of problems. Do physical processes create sensa out of nothing? Or do they just cause us to sense now one and now another selection out of a mass of already existing sensa? And, on either alternative, what is the status of sensa once they have come into existence? Do they just exist alongside of physical objects? Do they ever interact with each other or produce effects on the physical world? Or are they, in some Pickwickian sense, parts of physical objects? With some of these problems I shall try to deal in my last chapter.

VISUAL SENSE-DATA

G. E. MOORE

It seems to me quite plain that one of the commonest senses in which the word 'see' can be correctly used in English, perhaps the commonest of all, is that in which a particular person can be said, at a particular time, to be 'seeing' such objects as, e.g. a particular penny, a particular chair, a particular tree, a particular flower, or a particular horse, his own right hand, the moon, the planet Venus, etc. etc.—objects which I will call 'physical objects'. I have, indeed, once met a philosopher who told me I was making a great mistake in thinking that such objects are ever seen. But I think this philosopher was certainly wrong, and was thinking that the various correct uses of 'see' are limited in a way in which they are not in fact limited. I think there is no doubt whatever that the word 'see' can be correctly used in such a sense that, e.g. the words 'I have often seen pennies' or 'I have often seen the moon', when used by me and by many other people, are correct ways of expressing propositions which are true. I, personally, have in fact often seen pennies and often seen the moon, and so have many other people. But, nevertheless, I think there is a puzzle as to how the word 'see' is being used in this common usage.

There are two kinds of physical objects which we may at a particular moment be said to be 'seeing' in this common sense, viz. (1) objects which are transparent, like a drop of clear water or any ordinary glass tumbler or wineglass, and (2) objects which are opaque, like a penny or the moon. In the former case it seems possible that you may, in certain cases, see the whole object at once, both every part of its surface and its inside: it is, at all events, not clear that, in certain cases, you don't do this. But, in the case of opaque objects, it seems perfectly clear that you can be correctly said to be 'seeing' the object, in cases where (in another sense of 'see') you are *only seeing* one or several 'sides' of the opaque object, i.e. *some* part of its surface, but emphatically *not* all parts of its surface nor its inside. It seems, indeed, doubtful whether you can be correctly said to be seeing *it* unless you are seeing a *sufficiently* large part of its surface; and I am inclined to think that *how large* a part of its surface is 'sufficient' to entitle you to say you are seeing *it* is different in the case of different objects: e.g. it is quite plain that you can be correctly said to be seeing the moon when you *only see* the very thinnest crescent, whereas if you only saw such a small part of the surface of a penny, it would be doubtful if it could be correctly said that you were seeing that penny: you would be inclined to say that you did not see *it,* but only a small part of its rim. But where, for instance, you see the whole of the 'tail' side of a penny, but *don't* see the 'head' side, there is no doubt whatever that you can be correctly said to be seeing the penny. What is meant by 'seeing' the penny in such a case? There seems to me no doubt that, if you said to yourself, as you might, 'That is a penny', the demonstrative 'that' would be short for a phrase of the kind which Russell has called a 'definite description'; and, if you only said this to *yourself,* there would, of course, be no need for you to point at or touch anything, in order to show which object you were referring to, since you would be able to identify the object without any such gesture. The 'definite description' for which your 'that' would be short would be 'the object of which *this* is part of the surface'; and if 'know by description' were used in the way in which Russell uses it in *The Problems of Philosophy* (ch. v) you could be said to 'know' the penny 'only by description', although you can also correctly be said to be seeing the penny. I think, however, that this is an incorrect use of the word 'know'. We do not use the words 'See' or

'Perceive' in such a way that what you see or perceive is necessarily 'known' to you at all. Perhaps we might say that the penny in such a case is only 'seen by description'. But the important point is that, if in your 'That is a penny', the demonstrative 'that' is short for a definite description, then your proposition 'that is a penny' is a proposition which is 'about' or 'refers to' two objects at once, *not* only to one. This can be easily seen by looking at an example similar to what Russell gives as an example of a sentence which contains a definite description. Consider the sentence, 'The author of Waverley was a Scot.' It is undeniable that the proposition expressed by these English words says *something* about two objects, and not only about one. It says something *both* about the novel 'Waverley' *and* about its author. About the novel *Waverley* it says that it had one and only one author, and does *not* say that this novel was a Scot. But it does also say something not about the novel, but about its author; for it is of its author that it says he was a Scot.

But now, it is quite clear that, in the sentence, 'The author of *Waverley* was a Scot', the word 'Waverley' is also short for a description. It may be short, on different occasions, for a number of different descriptions. What do I mean by saying, as is true, that I possess a copy of *Waverley?* I might mean, and this is one of the simplest possible descriptions, 'I possess a copy of *the* book which was called *Waverley* by its author.' But, quite certainly, the novel *Waverley* is not being directly perceived by me now, though I am making a proposition about it. May it not be the case that, in our sentence 'the object of which *this* is part of the surface', the word 'this' is also short for a description? This seems to me to bring out the really puzzling question about the meaning of 'see' where the physical object which is seen is opaque; and there is a similar question where the physical object is perfectly transparent. I will only try to explain what the question seems to me to be in what is the simplest, but, also, I think, far the commonest case. The case in question is the case in which *both* (1) We are not seeing the physical object 'double', i.e. are not having what is often called a 'double image' of it, *and* (2) are not seeing two or more parts of the object's surface which are separated from one another by parts of its surface which we are not seeing, because they are hidden by intervening opaque objects. It is, I think, quite clear that you can correctly be said to 'see' a particular physical object in the common sense, even in cases where one or both of these conditions is (or are) not fulfilled; but I think far the commonest case is that in which both are fulfilled, and I propose to confine myself to that case.

What *is* the puzzle in the case of opaque objects seen under these conditions? It arises from the fact, which everybody knows, that, even where there is only one single part of an opaque object's surface which a man is seeing, and that part is large enough to entitle him to say correctly that he is seeing the object, yet the part of its surface in question may 'look' different to two different people who are both seeing that surface at the same time. For it seems to me quite plain that what is meant by saying that the same surface 'looks' different to two different people is that each is 'seeing', in a sense which I have called 'directly see', an entity which really *is* different from what the other is seeing. I have tried to explain what I mean by 'directly see' by saying that I use that expression to mean that sense of 'see' in which, if you look at, e.g. an electric light, then close your eyes and 'get', while your eyes are still closed, what is often called an 'after-image' of the light, you can be said to 'see' this after-image. It seems to me quite plain that 'see' can be correctly used in such a way that, in such a case, you do see the so-called 'after-image', although, in that case, you are certainly not seeing in the common sense any physical object whatever. And it also seems to me plain that, to say that, e.g. if I am wearing blue spectacles, a wall which is white but *not* bluish-white 'looks' bluish-white to me, is merely another way of saying that I am directly seeing an expanse which really is of a bluish-white colour, and which at the same time has to the surface which is not bluish-white a specific relation which, for the moment, I will call 'R'—a relation which entitles me to assert that, in directly seeing that bluish-white expanse, I am seeing the surface of the wall which is *not* bluish-white.

If I am *not* directly seeing a bluish-white expanse which *has* some such relation to a wall which is *not* bluish-white, how can I possibly know that that wall *is* looking bluish-white to me? It seems to me quite plain that I cannot 'see' in the common sense any physical object whatever without its 'looking' *somehow* to me, and, therefore, without my directly seeing some entity which has R to the object I am said to see, if the object is transparent and I am seeing the whole of it; and, if the object is opaque, under the conditions we are assuming, has R to the part of its surface which is the *only* part of its surface which I am seeing. And I think it is true that I so use the phrase 'visual sense-datum' that, from the fact that any entity is 'directly seen', in the sense explained, that entity *is* a visual sense-datum.

It is, I think, important to notice that it is only if 'looks' is used in one particular sense, that to say that a wall which is not bluish-white looks bluish-white to me involves the proposition that I am directly seeing a bluish-white expanse which has R to a surface that is not bluish-white. For there is another sense in which the word 'looks' is, I think, often used such that this consequence is *not* involved. What the two senses of 'looks' are can, I think, be very easily seen by considering the fact that if you see (in the common sense) two boats on the sea, one of which is quite near and the other at a considerable distance, you may be able to say with truth both (1) that the distant boat looks much smaller than the near one and (2) that the distant boat 'looks as if it were' much larger than the near one. Now, if 'looks' is used, as I think it sometimes is, to mean the same as what I have just expressed by 'looks as if it were', then proposition (2) could be expressed by 'The distant boat looks much larger than the near one', which would be inconsistent with proposition (1), unless 'looks' were being used in a different sense in expressing (2) from that in which it is used in expressing (1). But the two propositions are obviously *not* inconsistent with one another, hence 'looks', if it is used to express 'looks as if it were', must be used in a different sense from that in which it is used in (1). It is *only* if it is used as in (1) that it seems to me quite plain that the proposition that a physical surface looks bluish-white to me, entails that I am directly seeing an entity that *is* bluish-white.

Professor Ayer seems to have entirely misunderstood my view as to the relation of what I call a 'visual sense-datum' to such a proposition as is expressed by 'This is a penny'; for he asserts, twice over, that I take a visual sense-datum to be the *only* object about which we are making an assertion when we say 'This is a penny'.[1] I never, of course, held any view so silly. If I had, I should have been asserting that a visual sense-datum is what is being asserted to be a penny! He seems to have failed to understand that my view was that the demonstrative 'this', in such an expression, is short for a definite description, and that, therefore, in saying 'This is a penny' we are making a proposition about *two* objects, and *not* about one only, just as, when we say 'The author of *Waverley* was a Scot', we are making an assertion (but a different one) *both* about the novel *Waverley* and about its author. I do hold that, in making the assertion 'This is a penny', I am asserting *something* about a sense-datum, just as in 'The author of *Waverley* was a Scot', I am asserting *something* about the novel *Waverley*. But in both cases I am 'referring to' and 'denoting' (but in different senses) two different objects and not one only. It does not seem to have occurred to him that 'this', even when it 'refers to' an object which we are, in the common sense, 'seeing', may be short for a definite description; and that I was holding that in, 'This is a penny', it *is* short for a definite description, and, therefore, 'refers to' at least two objects, though in different senses. It is true I have said that, in such a case, a visual sense-datum is 'the real or ultimate subject' of our judgment,[2]

[1] *Philosophical Essays*, p. 78, note 3.
[2] *Philosophical Studies*, p. 236 [p. 14, this volume. Ed.].

which, of course, implies that it is *not* the *only* subject: but this expression is perhaps, nevertheless, misleading, and ought not to have been used. I used it because I was so impressed, as I still am, by the extreme difference between a 'this' which is short for a definite description and a 'this' which 'refers to' a visual sense-datum which is being directly perceived at the moment.

But I have to own that I now think I was mistaken in supposing that, in the case of 'seeing' an opaque·object, where in seeing it you are seeing only one visual sense-datum, the sense-datum can possibly be identical with that part of the opaque object's surface which you are seeing. I now think that it cannot possibly be identical with that part of the object's surface, i.e. that the relation which I have called 'R' above cannot possibly be the relation of identity. Until very recently I had thought that, though some of the arguments that purported to show that it cannot were strong, yet they were not conclusive, because I thought that, e.g. in the case where you directly see an 'after-image' with closed eyes, it was just possible that the after-image only looked to have certain colours and shape and size, and did not really have them. I made this suggestion in *Some Judgments of Perception,* but said there, several times, that it was perhaps nonsensical.[3] I well remember that, at the Aristotelian meeting at which I read that paper, Russell said that the suggestion certainly *was* nonsensical. I now feel sure that he was right; but, if so, then, when the same surface looks different at the same time to different people, the sense-datum which the one directly sees is certainly not identical with that which the other directly sees, and, therefore, they cannot both be identical with the surface which both are seeing. I was, therefore, certainly mistaken in supposing that, where an opaque object is seen, in the common sense, and only one sense-datum is directly seen in seeing it, the sense-datum in question is *always* identical with the part of the object's surface which is being seen. I was misled by the fact that it seems to me that you can always rightly say, in such a

[3] Ibid., pp. 245, 247, 252 [pp. 22, 24, 28, this volume. Ed.].

case, of a sense-datum which you are directly seeing, '*This* sense-datum *is* a part of the surface of a physical object.' I took it that the *is* always expresses identity, but it now seems to me that it certainly does not. But I still think that no philosopher, so far as I know, has explained clearly what the relation R is, where it is not identity.

THE MYTH OF SENSE-DATA

WINSTON H. F. BARNES

I

Our knowledge of the physical world is subject to many doubts and uncertainties but we commonly see no reason to doubt certain facts. We all agree, when we are out of the study, that we sometimes see tables and chairs, hear bells and clocks, taste liquids, smell cheeses, and feel the woollen vests that we wear next to our skin in winter. To put the matter generally, we agree that we perceive physical objects, physical objects being such things as tables, chairs and cheeses, and perceiving being a generic word which comprehends the specific activities of seeing, hearing, tasting, smelling, and feeling. These activities are invariably directed upon an object or objects; and this fact distinguishes them from other activities of ours—if that be the right word—such as feeling pained or feeling tired, which go on entirely within ourselves. We take it for granted that by means of the former activities we become aware of the existence, and acquainted with the qualities, of physical objects, and we further regard the kind of acquaintance which we acquire in this way as a basis for the far reaching and systematic knowledge of the physical world as a whole, which is embodied in the natural sciences.

Let us call experiences such as seeing a table, hearing a bell, etc., perceptual experiences; and the statements which assert the existence of such experiences perceptual statements. Many philosophers have cast doubt upon the claims made by such perceptual statements. They have produced arguments to show that we never perceive physical objects, and that we are in fact subject to a constant delusion on this score. As these arguments are by no means easily refuted and are such as any intelligent person interested in the matter will sooner or later come to think of, they are well worth considering. Moreover, certain modern philosophers claim to show by these arguments not only that we do not perceive physical objects but that what we do perceive is a different sort of thing altogether, which they call a sense-datum. They are obliged to invent a new term for it because no one had previously noticed that there were such things. This theory is obviously important because it not only claims to settle the doubts which we cannot help feeling when we reflect on our perceptual experience, but it makes the astonishing claim that we have all failed to notice a quite peculiar kind of entity, or at least have constantly made mistakes about its nature. I hope to show that the sense-datum theory is beset by internal difficulties; that it is not necessitated by the doubts we have about our perceptual experience; and finally that the doubts which are caused in us by a little reflection are allayed by further reflection.

The arguments which philosophers such as Professors Russell, Broad and Price use to demonstrate that we perceive not physical objects but sense-data, are many and various, and no good purpose would be served by stating them all, even if that were possible. Undoubtedly, however, these arguments do cause us to doubt whether we are acquainted with physical objects when we think we are; and, these doubts demand to be resolved in one way or another. If there is such a thing as a problem of perception, it must consist in reviewing the doubts which arise in our minds in this way. I shall select for brief statement three typical arguments so as to make clear the difficulties which are thought to justify the negative conclusion that we do not perceive physical objects and the positive conclusion that we perceive sense-data. There are two *caveats* to be registered. First, in compressing the arguments into a small compass I cannot hope to do full justice to the arguments, many and various, used by the sense-datum philosophers. I must leave it to the reader to decide whether I represent their general line of argument correctly or not. More than this I cannot hope to do; nor do I think more is necessary. Secondly, I should not be in the least surprised to be told that I already have misrepresented some of these philosophers by stating as one of their contentions that we do not perceive physical objects. Some of them would maintain that in some peculiar, or Pickwickian sense, to use Professor Moore's term, we do perceive physical objects. However, as, on their view, we do not perceive physical objects in the sense in which we think we perceive them, and we do perceive sense-data in precisely this sense, the misrepresentation is purely verbal and should mislead no one.[1]

I now proceed to state the three arguments. They are all taken from visual experience, and they all pose in one way or another what we may call the "appearance-reality" problem of perception.

(1) A penny appears circular to an observer directly above it, but elliptical to an observer a few paces away. It cannot *be* both elliptical and circular at one and the same time. There is no good reason for supposing that the penny reveals its real shape to an observer in one position rather than to an observer in any other position. The

[1] The sense in which, on the sensum theory, we perceive objects, is described as *direct perception* or *direct apprehension* by the exponents of the theory to distinguish it from the perception or apprehension of physical objects which the theory as sometimes expounded allows to be possible. (*The Philosophy of G. E. Moore*, pp. 629, 640–643.) This distinction is usually drawn by those philosophers who accept the position taken up by the philosophy of analysis that there are many statements such as 'I see the table,' 'I hear the bell,' which are certainly true, although the analysis of them requires careful thought; and at the same time are convinced by arguments which claim to show that we cannot in fact see the table in the ordinary sense of the word see. I can see no really important difference, however, between the two statements: (1) I see only sense-data in the sense in which I have been accustomed to think I see physical objects, and my relation to the physical object is not that of seeing but that of R. (2) I see only sense-data in the sense in which I have been accustomed to think I see physical objects, but I do see physical objects in the sense that I have a relation R to them.

elliptical appearance and the circular appearance cannot be identified with the penny or any parts of it, but they are entities of some kind. It is things of this sort which are called sense-data.

(2) The stick which looks straight in the air looks angularly bent when in water. There are good reasons for thinking that no such change of shape takes place in the stick. Yet there *is* something straight in the one case and something bent in the other, and there is no good reason for supposing either is less or more of an existent than the other. The straight-stick appearance and the bent-stick appearance are sense-data.

(3) There may seem to be things in a place when in fact there are no such things there, as illustrated by the mirages which appear in the desert and the highly coloured rodents which appear to habitual drunkards. Not unrelated to this type of experience is the one in which we see double. If an eyeball is pressed by the forefinger while one is looking at a candle flame, two flames are seen. Although it would be possible to say that one of the flames is the actual object and the other is something else, to be called a sense-datum, it seems even more evident here than in the previous instances that there is no good reason for distinguishing between the two in this way.

In all these cases there is a suggestion that what we see in certain cases cannot be a physical object or the surface of a physical object, but is some kind of non-physical entity. It is non-physical entities of this kind which are called sense-data. The argument goes even further by urging that, if in some cases we see non-material things, it is possible and indeed likely, that we do so in all cases. This plausible suggestion is accepted by certain sense-datum theorists such as Professor Broad and is extended to cover all forms of perceiving. With the acceptance of this suggestion we reach the basic position taken by one form of the sense-datum theory, viz., we perceive only sense-data, and consequently have no direct acquaintance through our senses with physical objects.

It is clear that, on this view, the term "sense-datum" has

as part of its connotation, the not being a physical body.[2] As everything I experience is a sense-datum, the sense-experience of a table, for example, differs not at all, in itself, from an hallucination or an illusion. These latter again seem to differ only in degree from the images we have while we are day dreaming, or those we have while dreaming in the proper sense, or again from the after-images, or as they are more properly called, the after-sensations which sometimes follow our visual sensations. All these appearances would be regarded by certain philosophers as in principle of the same kind. This position is paradoxical to common-sense which regards perceptual experience as giving first-hand acquaintance with physical objects, and hallucinations and illusions as failing precisely in this respect. The common-sense ground for the distinction however is removed by the sense-datum theorist, and if in fact he does believe in physical objects, he has to substitute a new ground of a far more subtle and elaborate nature. In some cases he may prefer to get along altogether without physical objects, and may even urge that if we once give up the common-sense ground of distinction as untenable there is no other ground for believing in them.[3] Such questions as these, however, are domestic problems of sense-datum theorists and need not detain us, as we are intent on coming to grips with the basis of the theory itself. It is important to note, however, that once the sense-datum theory is developed in the form stated above, it follows that, even if physical objects exist, they are never present in perceptual experience; and it becomes an open question whether they have any existence at all.

[2] "In the common usage, some characteristic which entailed 'not a physical reality' was put into the connotation of 'sense-datum'; 'sense-datum' was so used that it would be a contradiction to say of any object that it was *both a physical reality and also* a 'sense-datum'." (*The Philosophy of G. E. Moore*, p. 634.)

[3] As Dr. Luce does, in his "Immaterialism." (Annual Philosophical Lecture, British Academy, 1944.)

II

I shall consider later whether the arguments for the existence of sense-data in the sense indicated are valid. First, however, I want to state three considerations regarding the sense-datum itself. The first is of a very general nature and calculated to make us wonder whether a theory which departs so radically from common sense can be true; the second points out what extraordinary existents sense-data would be if there were such things; the third is directed to show that the kind of difficulty the theory was carefully framed to meet tends to break out anew within the theory.[4]

(1) The general consideration concerning the sensum theory is as follows: If the theory is true, then in all our perceptual experience sensa are interposed between us and the physical world, whereas it is one of our most strongly held beliefs that in perception we are face to face with the physical world. I do not wish to suggest that no attempt can be made to answer this obvious objection. The sensum theory can and does urge that in a Pickwickian sense of the term *perceive* we do perceive physical objects, i.e., we perceive sensa which are related in certain ways to physical objects. Nevertheless there is no doubt that, when presented with this type of explanation, we are apt to feel that we have been given a very inferior substitute in exchange for the direct acquaintance with physical objects

[4] As the form of sense-datum theory now to be considered is that which has been most clearly worked out by Prof. Broad, I propose to substitute for the word *sense-datum* in this section the word *sensum* which Prof. Broad himself uses in its place. We shall see later that what Prof. Moore and others have to say about sense-data makes it advisable to have different words for the two theories, distinguished as follows: *sense-datum*, the immediate object in perception which may or may not be identical with a part of a physical object; *sensum*, the immediate object in perception, taken to be non-physical. Prof. Price, whose views are very like those of Prof. Broad, speaks of sense-data, but would, if he had accepted this rule for the use of the two words, have spoken of sensa.

which we have been called upon to surrender. We receive
in no different spirit the other attempted rejoinder that
physical objects *are* sensa, or more elegantly, are logical
constructions out of sensa, and that whether we "talk"
physical objects or sensa is a purely linguistic affair. I shall
say nothing of this rejoinder now, as I shall have occasion
to discuss it later when I come to examine Mr. Ayer's view
that the sense-datum theory is not a theory at all, but
merely a new and better way of speaking of what we all
believe.

Not only do we feel that sensa are an inadequate substitute for the physical objects which we claim to be confronted with in perception, but they seem to be embarrass-
ingly numerous. Every appearance, however evanescent and
fleeting, can claim to be an existent. As ordinary men, we
contrast the intermittent character of our perceptual experience, broken as it is by sleep, lack of attention and
change of place, with the permanent or relatively permanent and continuing status of physical objects. The
changing facets of our perceptual experience we distribute
carefully, crediting some to the physical world and disown-
ing others as apparent only. The sensum theory credits
all alike to reality, since it considers each and every one
to be an individual entity. It is from this beginning that
the wilder excesses of realism took their origin, in which
not only reality but mind-independence was credited lav-
ishly to almost anything that could be named, until the
world began to take on the appearance of a great museum
in which a few of the contents were real operative beings
but the vast majority were exhibits only, ready to be produced on the appropriate occasion, but possessed of no
other ground of existence.

I am not inclined to over-estimate the effect that a general consideration of this kind can be expected to have,
but it is not lightly to be dismissed. There are philosophers
to whom a single departure from the norms of common
sense acts only as a stimulus to further more exciting
philosophical adventures in the realms of speculation, but
I confess that, for my part, I regard such a departure

rather as a danger signal, warning that it would be wise to consider whether the steps which have led to this departure are as secure as they appear to be.

It is one thing to assert of a theory, however, that it presents us with a large number of existents which seem unnecessary and which, if they existed, would make it difficult to justify our acquaintance with physical objects; it is quite another to show that the existents are not merely unnecessary but are open to grave objections. This is the second point to which we must now turn.

(2) There are two reasons for considering sensa to be very objectionable existents.

(i) In the first place, unlike physical objects they do not always obey the Law of Excluded Middle. If I contemplate an object at some distance, it often happens that I am uncertain whether it is circular or polygonal. It is necessary for me to approach closer before I can determine the matter with certainty. On the sensum theory, the mode in which the object appeared to me at first is a sensum, and every sensum *is* what it appears to be. Now this sensum appears neither circular nor non-circular. Therefore it is neither circular nor non-circular. Let us be quite clear on this point. It is not that I do not know whether it is circular or non-circular, though in fact it must be one or the other. It really is neither one nor the other. This kind of experience is more common than one is perhaps inclined to believe at first. When an optician asks you to read those minute letters inscribed at the bottom of his chart, there comes a time when you are compelled to say "I am not sure whether it is an M or an N," because the shape you see is sufficiently indeterminate for you to think it may be either. Of course, some eminent philosophers have thought that reality did not obey the Law of Excluded Middle, but it would be surprising to find Professor Broad in their company.

It is tempting to urge that we *must* know the shape of the sensum because an artist can sit down and draw something which reproduces the shape. A little reflection, however, will show that what the artist does is to draw something which, having a certain definite shape, will appear at a certain distance to be as indeterminate in shape as the object itself appeared. In other words, what the artist does is the same in principle as what a joiner might do by building another object like the first one which would give rise to the same sort of appearance as the first one. So far as I can see, all so-called sensa, i.e., colours, sounds, smells, etc., are indeterminate in this way, though under favourable conditions the range of indeterminacy is so limited that it is, for practical purposes, not of any importance.

(ii) The second reason for considering sense-data to be objectionable existents, though closely connected with the former is less formidable; but is worth mentioning because it leads up to a number of very interesting considerations. It is a necessary consequence of the fact that a sense-datum *is* what it appears to be that there is no possibility of making further discoveries about its nature. It is always possible to get to know more and more about a particular existent, such as an apple or a squirrel, and, so far as we can tell, this process need never come to an end. There is no progress to be made in our knowledge of any particular sensum. This contention may seem to go too far in view of the revelations which philosophers claim to have about sensa. It can, however, be justified. Our knowledge of things is increased either by observation or by experiment. Experiment, as a means of gaining knowledge of sensa, is clearly ruled out, since it is obvious that any movement on my part or interference with the conditions will only cause one sensum to be replaced by another. It does, however, seem as though I might increase my knowledge of a particular sensum by observing it more closely than I had done. Rather, we must say, "by observing it more closely than I am doing," for clearly, my closer observation can only yield me more knowledge if it follows uninterruptedly upon my first. It will not do for me to come back at 5 p.m. to a closer study of the sensum which my table presented at 3 p.m. Can I gain more knowledge by continuing to observe it at 3 p.m.? I think we must say that I cannot. If we were to maintain that this was possible, and that something in the sensum previously unobserved might by observation be brought to light, we should need some criterion for making certain that it was the same sensum which we were observing at a later date as at an earlier date. *But no observation or experiment can yield a criterion.* The sensum theorists offer us little help on this point. The only thing is to fall back on the principle that a sensum is what it appears to be. If we interpret this as meaning it is all that it appears to be *and nothing more,*[5] then the possibility of learning anything about a sensum is cut away at once, for the very good reason that we know all there is to know about it by simply having it. It is, I think, a very odd fact, if true, that there are existents such that their being known at all entails their being completely known.

(3) I come now to the third consideration. The sensum theory was devised to overcome the difficulty that we sometimes seem to be directly aware of some property in an object even though this property is not really present and is incompatible with others which are present. Sensa really have those properties which objects only appear to have. The chief convenience of the theory in fact is that it provides a home for every quality, real or apparent, which is experienced, and it does so by attributing to every such quality the status of a particular existent. If sensa could appear to have properties which they do not really have, the sensum theory would be bankrupt. It seems to me quite impossible to prove that sensa can appear to have properties which they do not possess. Nevertheless, the attempt is so interesting and throws so much light on the theory that I propose to undertake it.

Prof. Broad states: "It follows from this theory that sensa cannot appear to have properties which they do not really have, though there is no reason why they should not have more properties than we do or can notice in them,"[6]; again: "Sensa may be much more differentiated than we

---

[5] We shall see later that there are difficulties about other interpretations.

[6] *Scientific Thought,* p. 244 [p. 93, this volume. Ed.].

think them to be"[7] and "a sensum is at least all that it appears to be."[8] He also says: "Each sensum is a particular having those sensible qualities and that sensible form which it seems on careful inspection to have."[9]

Let us see why it is impossible to prove that a sensum can appear to be what it is not. Suppose that I am looking at a distant object and report: "I can see a circular pinkish patch." Looking more carefully I say later: "It is not pink, it is white with red spots." What are we to say if we hold the sensum theory? There seem to be several possible answers. We may say: (i) The sensum appeared pink but it is really white with red spots, or (ii) the sensum underwent a change, or (iii) there were two different sensa, or (iv) the sensum is white with red spots but I failed to differentiate it properly until I inspected it carefully. The sensum theorist will not choose (i), because he would then be faced with the appearance-reality problem breaking out again in sensa which were invoked especially to lay this spectre. He would also I think reject (ii), although I can think of no good reason why sensa, if they exist, should not change. As long as (iii) is open, the sensum theorist can avoid the appearance-reality problem breaking out in sensa. It is clear, however, that if (iii) is adopted it is quite misleading to say, as Prof. Broad does, that it *follows* from the sensum theory "that sensa cannot appear to have properties which they do not really have."[10] This proposition need not form part of the theory and if laid down, it is laid down quite arbitrarily in order to prevent the appearance-reality problem arising in sensa. To deal with the kind of instance in question, Prof. Broad gives the answer (iv) but it seems ill-advised, for the word *differentiation* comfortably conceals the fact that the sensum as a whole can only become more differentiated by particular spatial patches within the whole appearing different on a second occasion from how they appeared at first. It is clear that what Prof.

[7] *Ibid.*, p. 244 [p. 93, this volume. Ed.].
[8] *Ibid.*, p. 245 [p. 94, this volume. Ed.].
[9] *Mind and Its Place in Nature*, p. 189.
[10] *Scientific Thought*, p. 244 [p. 93, this volume. Ed.].

Broad wishes to maintain is that a sensum may be more than it appears to be, provided the more is not inconsistent with anything it appears to be. A simple instance will reveal the difficulty in this contention. I am waiting for a No. 3 bus and, on first glancing at a stationary bus some distance away, I think I see a number 3 on its front. On more careful inspection, however, I see that it is a number 8. It might be urged that I first of all failed to see that part of the 8 which is necessary to transform a 3 into an 8. The 8 did not appear what it was not, but it appeared less than it was. There are two ways of answering this contention: One consists in pointing out that I can just as easily mistake a 3 for an 8, in which case I see more at first than is confirmed by more careful inspection. The other, and more adequate rejoinder is to point out that in either case there was an appearance inconsistent with what careful inspection revealed. Suppose the 3 and 8 are white figures on a black background. Then in the one case something that at first seemed black, later seemed white, and in the other case, vice versa. Similarly, in the original example, if I see as pink a large number of red dots on a white background, then every red dot is appearing pink to me and so also is the interstitial white. The more that is here revealed on careful inspection does conflict with the first appearance.

There is one other point worth mentioning. Why should it be necessary to inspect a sensum carefully before one can become acquainted with it as it is? If I press one eyeball while looking at a bright light, I see queer long streaks of light running vertically through the centre of the light and varying according to the pressure on the eyeball. It is difficult to inspect anything carefully with one finger on your eyeball, but if you remove your finger, the vision disappears. Surely, it was a perfectly good sensum? Again, if looking through green glasses gives a new sensum, why not pressing your eyeball or looking out of the corner of your eye with deliberate carelessness?

The moral of this is that those who believe in sensa tell us so little about the laws of their existence that we are at liberty to make a variety of assumptions on quite funda-

mental points. For example, how do we determine the du-
ration of a sensum? If I blink my eyes while looking at a
red patch are there two sensa separated in time, or is there
only one interrupted in its career? If a change occurs in
my visual field has the sensum changed or been replaced
by another? If the latter, is there any reason why, when no
change is observed, a sensum should not be replaced by
another exactly like it? It may be said that to answer these
questions is not important. I am inclined to agree that it is
not; but the only reason I can see for this is that, sensa being wholly fictitious entities, we can attribute to them what
qualities we please.[11]

Let us consider in a more particular way the arbitrary
character of the sensum theory. Prof. Broad allows that a
sensum may move across one's visual field; but he would
not I think, allow that it can change in size or qualities.
Take the simple case where I am watching a cinema screen
on which is depicted a round red patch moving across a
background of different colour. Here, according to Prof.
Broad, is a single sensum moving across my visual field.
Supposing the round red patch remains stationary but
slowly contracts in size before finally disappearing. Here,
presumably, is a succession of sensa. Supposing, now, the
red patch moves across the screen and as it does so it di-
minishes in size, have we one or a succession of sensa? The
answer would have to be, I think: "A succession." There
would seem, then, no reason for supposing that where the
size of the moving patch is constant, there should not also
be a succession of sensa. If this is so, sensa do not move,
they merely rise up one after another in a certain spatial
order. We could equally well allow, on the other hand, that
sensa not only move but change in shape, size, colour, etc.
In fact, if the essential characteristic of a sensum is that it
is what it appears to be, then there is a very good case for
taking this view, since there certainly *appear* to be changes
in the colour and shape as well as the position of what we

---

[11] This fact is at the bottom of Mr. Ayer's contention that the
sensum theory is really only an alternative language, but we shall see
later that there is more to it than this.

experience through our senses. What is worth remarking is that there is nothing which enables us to consider one alternative nearer the truth than the other. As long as this kind of question can be decided only arbitrarily, it is clear that there is no way of determining the number of sensa. So we find them to have another peculiar property for existents; they are not numerable.

Let us consider further the notion of a sensum moving across a sense field. A sense field may appear as one single variegated sensum. If one part moves in relation to the rest, we can say (i) the whole sensum is changing, (ii) the parts of the sensum are re-arranging their relative positions, or, what Prof. Broad says, (iii) a sensum is moving across the sense field. There seems to be no good reason for adopting one explanation rather than another. Similarly, if I have a visual field, half red and half blue, I can at pleasure treat this as one sensum or as two. It is only by reference to the concrete individual reality of physical objects that I can number the appearances, distinguishing the appearance my table presents from that which my chair or my pencil presents. From a purely sensationalist point of view I am not faced with a number of sensa but with a changing variegated field of colour or, in the Kantian words, a manifold.

Before turning to consider the validity of the reasoning which is used to prove the existence of sensa, there is one other point which merits attention. One of the most serious arguments against the sensum theory is that, if it is true, it is extremely difficult to explain how from knowledge of our sensa we could come to knowledge of material things; and yet, according to Prof. Broad, "all that I ever come to know about physical objects and their qualities seems to be based upon the qualities of the sensa that I become aware of in sense-perception."[12] But an even greater difficulty faces us, viz., that of being assured that material things exist at all, i.e., relatively permanent things with certain qualities and interacting with one another. Prof. Broad says: ". . . there is nothing in my sensa to force me logi-

[12] *Scientific Thought*, p. 241 [p. 90, this volume. Ed.].

cally to the conclusion that there must be something beyond them, having the constitutive properties of physical objects. The belief that our sensa are appearances of something more permanent and complex than themselves seems to be primitive, and to arise inevitably in us with the sensing of the sensa. It is not reached by inference, and could not logically be justified by inference. On the other hand, there is no possibility of either refuting it logically, or of getting rid of it, or—so far as I can see—of co-ordinating the facts without it."[13] Prof. Luce thinks otherwise. In rejecting the existence of physical objects over and above sensa he says: "To accept both the sense-datum *and* matter is to turn the one world into two."[14]

If I believed in sensa I should be found on the side of Dr. Luce, for the difficulties of distinguishing between a primitive belief and a primitive delusion seem to me insuperable.

III

So far we have been considering the difficulties that arise from holding that sensa form a class of existents totally different from physical objects. Though the difficulties are perhaps not sufficiently serious to destroy the theory, they seem to me quite serious enough to make it desirable to look carefully into the considerations put forward for inducing belief in such entities.

These considerations seem to me to reduce to one fundamental argument, and this argument seems to me to be false, though plausible. If I am right, then the reason for believing in sensa goes.

I quoted earlier three typical arguments for the existence of sensa. I now wish to examine carefully a single argument which embodies the principle of these and other simi-

---

[13] *Ibid.*, p. 268 [p. 115, this volume. Ed.].
[14] "Immaterialism" (Annual Philosophical Lecture, British Academy, 1944), p. 6.

lar arguments. No one will deny, I think, that a situation may exist in which the following three propositions are true:

    (i) I see the rose.

    (ii) The rose appears pink to me.

    (iii) The rose is red.

The belief in sensa is reached by arguing, not unplausibly, that since what I am seeing appears pink, there exists something which *is* pink; and since the rose is red, not pink, it cannot be the rose which is pink; therefore what I am seeing is something other than the rose. Whereupon the term sensum is invented and given as a name to this existent and others like it. And so we reach the conclusion:

    (iv) I see a pink sensum.

The argument is fallacious. *That something appears pink to me is not a valid reason for concluding either that that thing is pink or that there is some other thing which is pink.* From the fact that a thing *looks* pink I can sometimes with the help of certain other propositions infer that it *is* pink or that it *is* red; I may also, with the help of certain other propositions, be able to infer that something in some other place is pink, e.g., the electric light bulb which is illuminating the rose. But I cannot infer, as is proposed, *merely from the three facts that I am seeing something, that it looks pink and that it is red, that there is a pink something where the thing appears pink to me.*

This, when we examine it, is the foundation stone on which the great edifice of the sensum theory has been raised. Is it surprising that the upper storeys present doubts and perplexities? But there is worse to come. Not only is the argument fallacious but the conclusion contradicts one of the premises, viz., (i) I see a rose. It does so because, in order that the conclusion should seem at all plausible, it has been assumed that, if I were to see a rose which actually possessed a red colour, I should see it as red, i.e., it would necessarily appear red to me. This again is an assumption in contradiction with propositions (ii) and (iii) taken together. As soon as this self-induced contradiction is discovered by the sensum theorists, repair work is put in

hand on one or other of alternative lines: (a) It is accepted
that I do not see the rose, and an account is given of the
relation in which I *do* stand to the rose and which has been
mistaken for seeing. A little reflection, of course, soon convinces those who go this way that, if this is true, it is not
only roses that are born to blush unseen, but the whole
world of material things. In this way sensa become an im-
penetrable barrier barring for ever our acquaintance
through the senses with the world of material things. This
is strong meat for any but really metaphysical natures, and
fortunately for the sensum theory there is another way of
making the necessary repairs. (b) The alternative procedure is something like this: It is certain that I do see the
rose. I have convinced myself, however, by argument that
one thing I undoubtedly see, in a plain unvarnished use of
the word *see,* is a pink rose-figured sensum. Hence the sense
in which I see the rose must be different, i.e., "seeing" is
systematically ambiguous and what exactly is meant by seeing the rose needs to be elucidated. Seeing a rose and seeing
a pink rose-figured sensum are then distinguished as quite
different ways of seeing and it is convenient to refer to seeing a sensum as "directly seeing," and seeing a rose as "seeing."[15] The analysis of seeing the rose can then be made
in terms of directly seeing a certain sort of sensum and at
the same time having perceptual assurance that . . . etc.,
the complete analysis varying from one philosopher to another.[16]

There is another way in which an attempt may be made

[15] Prof. Moore makes this use of the two terms. It is worth pointing out that in ordinary language we should be ready to say that we
were directly seeing the rose; in contrast, for example to seeing it as
reflected in a mirror or seeing it through a microscope, where the
indirectness would consist, no doubt, to our minds, in the interposition of a further medium between our eyes and the object in addition
to the usual light and air. There is still an air of paradox, consequently, about the way in which the words seeing and directly seeing
are used by sensum theorists.

[16] Philosophers tend to adopt the second alternative because it enables them to eat their cake and have it. They continue on this matter
to speak with the vulgar and think with the learned, following in this
respect the good Bishop of Clogher, the inventor of philosophical
analysis.

to justify the conclusion of the argument we have condemned as fallacious. I have argued that from the fact that something which is red appears pink, it does not follow that a pink sensum exists. It may be said that the existence of a pink sensum, while not following from the premises, is justified by a direct appeal to our sense experience. "I see it, therefore it is." The argument can be stated as follows: "I certainly see a pink something and to say that there is nothing pink is to say that I have no reason for believing in what I see now; and if I cannot believe in what I see now, how can I believe in what I see on any occasion, or any one else in what he sees on any occasion? If you deny the existence of this pink patch, you deny the existence altogether of the world revealed by the senses." The answer to this objection is simple, if we reflect, viz., "You never can believe in what you see on any occasion, it always may mislead you as to what the thing is. If you wish to state only that something appears to be so and so, this can safely be done. But this is not a statement about something made on the basis of a piece of evidence, it is a statement of the piece of evidence itself, which you already have before you without clothing it in words." Modes of appearance are clues to the nature of what exists, not existents. I submit that it is improper to ask whether the pink mode of appearing, which is how the rose appears to me, exists. You may ask whether the rose exists and whether it is red or pink; and in answering this question account must be taken of how it appears under different conditions and to different people. Although modes of appearance are not existents, they are the material and the only material on which thinking can operate to discover the nature of existing things; and it is an epistemological ideal that if we were to discover completely the nature of existing things, there would be nothing left in the modes of appearance which would not entirely harmonise with our system of knowledge and find its explanation there.

IV

On Prof. Broad's theory, sensa are entities which cannot be identified with material things or the surfaces or other parts of material things. The notion of sensum is necessary in that theory to solve the appearance-reality problem consisting in the fact that a penny, though round, may appear elliptical. The solution is "to change the subject." "What is round is the penny, what is elliptical is the sensum."[17] Having proceeded in this way, it would have been folly to get into a position in which a sensum itself might be said to appear to have a quality which in fact it did not have and thus be confronted again with the same problem. Mr. Ayer points this out.[18]

If we examine the way in which Prof. Moore and his disciples use the word sense-datum we shall see (i) that they attach a quite different meaning to the word sense-datum from that given to it by philosophers who use it in the way Prof. Broad uses sensum; (ii) that the refutation in the previous section does not apply to them; and (iii) that there is no reason, in the way they use the term, for finding any difficulty in the assertion that a sense-datum may appear to have qualities which it does not possess.

Let us consider the very careful account given by Prof. Moore of what a sense-datum is: "In order to point out to the reader what sort of things I mean by sense-data, I need only ask him to look at his own right hand. If he does this he will be able to pick out something (and unless he is seeing double, only one thing) with regard to which he will see that it is, at first sight, a natural view to take, that that thing is identical, not indeed with his whole right hand, but with that part of its surface which he is actually seeing, but will also (on a little reflection) be able to see that it is doubtful whether it can be identical with the part of the

---

[17] *Scientific Thought*, p. 245 [p. 94, this volume. Ed.].
[18] *Foundations of Empirical Knowledge*, p. 69.

surface of his hand in question. Things *of the sort* (in a certain respect) of which this thing is, which he sees in looking at his hand, and with regard to which he can understand how some philosophers should have supposed it to be part of the surface of his hand which he is seeing, while others have supposed that it can't be, are what I mean by sense-data. I therefore define the term in such a way that it is an open question whether the sense-datum which I now see in looking at my hand and which is a sense-datum of my hand, is or is not identical with that part of its surface which I am now actually seeing."[19]

This is a much quoted passage and has provoked a great deal of criticism. I wish only to make one point on it. After indicating to what we are to direct our attention Prof. Moore explains that this object of our attention, thought by some to be a part of the surface of his hand, by others not to be so, is a specimen of what he means by a sense-datum. On this definition, of course, I believe in sense-data, and so does anyone who believes that things have surfaces; and that parts of those surfaces on certain occasions appear to us. For on this statement of the theory of sense-data, the man who maintains that we see things themselves and the man who maintains that we do not see the things themselves but only some other entities which are in some way related to the things, both believe in sense-data. Instead of distinguishing between philosophers who believe in sense-data and philosophers who do not, we should have to distinguish between those who believe that "sense-datum" is just another word for a visible part of a surface, those who believe that the sense-datum, though it looks like the surface and is easily mistaken for it, is quite a different sort of thing, and those who, like Prof. Moore, are frankly puzzled as to which to think. This is very awkward; and is made more awkward by the fact that it means insisting that great numbers of philosophers, including myself, believe in sense-data, when for the purpose of distinguishing our views from those of Dr. Broad and similar views we are

[19] "The Defence of Common Sense," in *Contemporary British Philosophy*, Second Series, p. 217.

compelled to assert that we do not believe in sense-data.[20] If it is said that the term is neutral, I think the answer must be that Prof. Moore tries to use it in a neutral way but does not completely succeed. An example of the un-neutral character of the term as used by Prof. Moore is afforded by the discussion of sense-datum in "Some Judgements of Perception." He is discussing the judgement "This is an ink-stand," and says: ". . . sense-data are the sort of things *about* which such judgements as these always seem to be made—the sort of things which seem to be the real or ulti-mate subjects of all such judgements."[21] He goes on to say a little later: "If there be a thing which is this inkstand at all, it is certainly *only* known to me as *the* thing which stands in a certain relation to this sense-datum."[22] If this is meant merely to convey that the whole surface is never visible at one moment, it is obviously true. If it is meant to convey that the whole inkstand is in no way presented in perception, it seems to me erroneous, for even when I am looking at the front of it I have some kind of awareness of the back of it. Further, by walking around it I can have several different views of it, and it does not seem to me to be any one of these which is the subject of my judgement.

The subject of my judgement seems to me not to be a sense-datum, even taken as a part of the surface, but the whole inkstand, which, though not perceived in its entirety, is presented as a whole that is more than my perception reports it to be.

In replying to his critics Prof. Moore attempted to make his position clearer by the following statement: "I think I have always used, and intended to use, 'sense-datum' in such a sense that the mere fact that an object is *directly*

---

[20] As has already been pointed out, Prof. Broad uses the term "sen-sum" not "sense-datum" for his peculiar entities. So far as I can see he uses the words "sensible appearance" and not "sense-datum" as a neutral word when required. If a neutral word is necessary this is cer-tainly the nearest approach; but it seems to fall short of being really neutral, so much so that it suggests the clue to what, in my opinion, is the correct theory of perception.

[21] *Philosophical Studies*, pp. 231–2 [p. 11, this volume. Ed.].

[22] *Ibid.*, p. 234 [pp. 12–13, this volume. Ed.].

apprehended is a *sufficient* condition for saying that it is a sense-datum."[23] This statement makes clear that, as Prof. Moore uses the term *sense-datum,* it does not denote a special kind of existent but a relation which, so far as we can tell, any kind of existent might have to a perceiving mind. Whether the relation of direct apprehension is consistent with the object directly apprehended appearing to be other than it is, as Prof. Moore on other occasions holds to be possible, I cannot say but I do not think the possibility can be ruled out. It is important for the following reason: The term sense-datum, though intended to be neutral,[24] is in fact very plainly marked with the scars of combat. As a technical term, it is the index of a philosophy eager to assert that in sense experience there is an object which is given. It is an attempt both to stop the rot of Cartesian doubt and to meet the idealist contention that all perception involves inference, with its corollary that if we seek a datum in sub-perceptual sensation, we find a state where the distinction between the ego and its object vanishes. Now, if the significance of the *datum* in the term were merely to insist that in sense-experience things *appear* to us to be possessed of certain qualities, then the term would be genuinely neutral, but neither Descartes nor the Idealists would have been answered. If, on the other hand, the *datum* signifies that in sense experience I am immediately informed of the existence of certain things and of the characteristics they possess, without any possibility of being mistaken, then Descartes and the Idealists are answered, but the term is not neutral and, if our argument is correct, the implied theory is wrong.

[23] *The Philosophy of G. E. Moore,* p. 649.
[24] H. H. Price, *Perception,* p. 19. ". . . the term sense-datum is meant to be a neutral term. The use of it does not imply the acceptance of any particular theory."

V

Mr. Ayer's view[25] that the theory of sense-data is not a theory at all but simply an alternative language for speaking about such situations such as "I am perceiving a brown carpet which looks yellow to me" or "I am seeing rats which are not really there" need not detain us long. It is in sharp contrast to the use of the term sense-datum by Prof. Broad and those who follow him. The great merit of that use, we are told, is that the term sense-datum "names an element not hitherto named."[26] According to Mr. Ayer we can name everything necessary by the use of ordinary language as in the sentences quoted above. The advantage of the sense-datum language resides, as he tells us, in the fact that "it makes it possible for us to say that something real is being experienced even in cases where our perceptions are delusive."[27] This is puzzling. The sense-datum language would be a most misleading translation of our ordinary language if it resulted in our saying that the drunkard's pink rats were real, as this is precisely what the ordinary way of stating the matter denies. If what it states is that there really do appear to the drunkard to be pink rats, then it states the matter no better than ordinary language. In view of the doubt as to which, if either, of these two things it is supposed to assist us in saying, it seems to be decidedly inferior to ordinary language.

It is worth pointing out that, if you are inventing or using a technical language to speak about facts for which provision is made in the ordinary language, you are apt to be seriously misled by it unless you guide its usage carefully by constant checking with ordinary forms of expression. So far from making one's task easier, it makes it far more

---

[25] *The Foundations of Empirical Knowledge,* Ch. II.
[26] Helen M. Smith: "Is There a Problem About Sense-Data?" *Ar. Soc. Supp.* vol. XV (1936) p. 84.
[27] *The Foundations of Empirical Knowledge,* p. 69.

difficult. For that reason, in suggesting briefly an alternative to the sense-datum theory, I shall use ordinary language though, if I were more capable, I have no doubt that I could state what I have to say using the word sense-datum suitably defined.

VI

I now propose to state briefly the lines of an alternative account to the sensum theory. The account is quite simple and is implicit in the foregoing discussion. I can claim no great originality for it as it is substantially the theory put forward by Prof. Dawes Hicks[28] and called by Prof. Broad the Multiple Relation Theory of Appearance. I can claim only that I arrived at it by a somewhat different line of thought and for that reason my statement of it may have some interest. I propose to call it simply the theory of appearing. I hope to show that it is the theory implicit in common sense and that it can be defended against the more obvious objections.

We saw that the sensum theory was led into difficulties by concluding from the propositions (i) I see the rose, (ii) The rose appears pink to me, and (iii) The rose is red, to a proposition (iv) I see a pink sensum. To attain consistency it was necessary to distinguish between the meaning which the word *see* has in proposition (i) and that which it has in proposition (iv). It is obvious, however, when we reflect, that propositions such as (i) must be incomplete versions of propositions such as (ii), e.g., "I see the rose as pink" is the expanded form of the proposition (i), which says the same thing as proposition (ii), but begins with me and proceeds to the rose, instead of beginning with the rose and proceeding to me. It is evident, further, if this is so, that *see* must have the same sense but in the reverse direction, as *appears*.

[28] In his *Critical Realism*.

The account I put forward, then, is that objects themselves appear to us in sense-perception; that they in general
appear in sense-perception to have those qualities which
they in fact have; that where they appear to have qualities
which they do not in fact have, these instances are more
properly regarded as their failing in differing degrees to
appear to have the properties they do have, such failure
being accounted for by the conditions under which they are
perceived. We must be quite bold at this point and admit at
once that on this account of the matter a thing can possess
a certain quality and at the same time appear to some one
to possess another quality, which it could not actually possess in conjunction with the former quality. Let us be quite
clear about what we are saying. When I see a circular
penny as elliptical I am seeing the circular surface of the
penny, not some elliptical substitute. This circular surface,
it is true, appears elliptical to me, but that fact has no tendency to show that I am not directly aware of the circular
surface. Aeneas was none the less in the presence of his
mother Venus though she concealed from him the full
glory of her godhead.

It is clear that, on this theory, perception has a much
closer resemblance to thinking than would be allowed by
the sensum theorists. For (i) it may have a content more
or less false to the real, as thought may; and (ii) this content does not exist independent of the act of perceiving any
more than the content of a false proposition.[29] The chief
objection to this contention is stated by Prof. Broad as
follows: "It is very hard to understand how we could seem
to ourselves to *see* the property of bentness exhibited in a
concrete instance, if in fact *nothing* was present to our
minds that possessed that property."[30] I can see no great
difficulty in this, and we have seen how the attempt to escape from the imagined difficulty leads to difficulties. Four-
teen years later Prof. Broad himself was not so sure for he

[29] It is a salutary reflection in this connection that the spiritual
home of the sensum at one time opened its gates wide to an even
more peculiar entity, the proposition.

[30] *Scientific Thought*, p. 241 [p. 91, this volume. Ed.].

says: "Now one may admit that a certain particular might seem to have a characteristic which differs from and is incompatible with the characteristic which it does have. But I find it almost incredible that one particular extended patch should seem to be two particular extended patches at a distance apart from each other."[31] Prof. Price finds the same difficulty, for he says: "It is not really sense to say 'To me the candle appears double' . . . 'double' is not really a predicate at all."[32]

Seven years have passed since Prof. Broad wrote the latter of his two quoted statements so it may be that he now finds the assertion more credible. I certainly find nothing incredible in it. No doubt it is impossible for one candle to *be* two candles but there seems no reason why it should not appear to be any number of things. Finally, hallucinations and delusions need present no insuperable difficulties. There appeared to Lady Macbeth to be a dagger but there was no dagger in fact. Something appeared to be a dagger, and there are certainly problems concerning exactly what it is in such circumstances appears to be possessed of qualities which it does not possess. It is easy of course to object that an illusory dagger is not just nothing. The answer is neither "Yes, it is" nor "No, it isn't," but "An illusory dagger is a misleading expression if used to describe an element in the situation." It is misleading also in some degree to say that there exists "a dagger-like appearance," though we need not be misled by such a use of the word *appearance* if we are careful. Strictly speaking, however, there are no such things as appearances. To suppose that there are would be like supposing that because Mr. X put in an appearance, there must have been something over and above Mr. X which he was kind enough to put in. "Mr. X appeared": that is the proper mode of expression if we are to avoid difficulties.[33]

---

[31] *Mind and its Place in Nature*, p. 188.

[32] *Perception*, pp. 62-3.

[33] Cf. the judicious remark of Prof. Dawes Hicks: "When, in ordinary language, we speak of the objective constituent of a perceptual situation as being the 'appearance of' a physical object we mean not that it is the appearance which appears but that it is the physical ob-

An existent must be determinate and we saw that what are alleged to be existents and called sense-data could not meet this demand. To give rise to similar difficulties by speaking of appearances, thereby seeming to condone treating the modes in which things appear as existents, would be most inappropriate. That a thing, though wholly determinate, should fail to reveal its full determinate character to a single *coup d'oeil* is surely to be expected and our theory derives support from the fact that objects do not always appear in their fully determinate nature.

There is another point about our account of the matter. It allows that it is *possible* for certain people at certain times to become acquainted through perception with things as they are, not merely as they appear to be. This can be seen best as follows. The word *sense-datum* was substituted for the word *appearance* to emphasise that there is an indubitable element in sense experience, in contrast with the use of the term *appearance* by philosophers who denied the existence of any such given, and who used the contrast between appearance and reality to grind a metaphysical axe of their own. But, as was pointed out by Prof. Moore, the term was often used with the connotation "not a physical reality." If this connotation is accepted, it follows that, however extensive our acquaintance with sense-data, we are no whit nearer to becoming acquainted with physical objects, and it is even difficult to see how we can know *about* these latter. This is the "great barrier" objection to the theory as held by Prof. Broad and his followers. Even for those who avoid putting into the term "sense-datum" this unwarrantable connotation the term is apt to give rise to unnecessary difficulties. For example, Mr. Wisdom, more careful than most philosophers not to be misled by the term, writes: "I should agree that it is unplausible to say that, although when I see a thing in bad light my corresponding sense-datum is not identical with the observed surface of the thing, nevertheless, when the light changes,

ject which appears." (*Critical Realism*, p. 55). Even so, it is better to avoid the noun altogether, or at least always to test out the validity of its use by mentally translating into the verb.

the corresponding sense-datum which I then obtain is identical with the observed surface, I cannot say why I find this unplausible, but I do. I find such a discontinuity, such a popping in and out of the material world on so slight a provocation, most objectionable."[34] If we are content to talk in terms of appearance or, better still, of things appearing, we shall not have pseudo-problems of this kind. We need have no heart-burning about the following statement: "Although when I see a thing in bad light the surface does not appear to me in every respect as it really is, nevertheless, when the light is adequate, it does." The reason we are now talking better sense is that the language of appearance permits us to maintain (a) that a thing can not only appear what it is not, but what it is: (b) that a thing's appearing what it is not is best understood as a deviation from its appearing what it is. A terminology which purports to be neutral and yet makes these propositions sound absurd has prejudged the issue in a most unfortunate manner.[35]

On the theory outlined it is easy to explain how we can come to know about material objects for in all our perception we are perceiving material objects even though we are not always completely successful in perceiving them exactly as they are. On the sensum theory, as we have seen, it is difficult to explain why knowledge of sensa should contribute towards knowledge of material things; how we could ever have been led to the belief in material things; and, still less, how we could justify the belief.

Finally, the account of the matter I have given is, I think, remarkably close to common sense. As Prof. Broad claims that this type of theory departs as widely from common sense as the sensum theory this claim needs to be defended. He argues that, as commonly used, a statement such as "I see a table" involves the unexpressed theory that there is a situation involving two constituents, myself and the table,

---

[34] *Problems of Mind and Matter*, p. 156.

[35] In fairness to Mr. Wisdom it must be pointed out that immediately after making the statement quoted, he goes on to say something which, if I understand it rightly, is very like what I have said except that (a) he calls that which appears a sense-datum and (b) identifies it with an object's surface.

related by a relation of seeing, a relation which proceeds from me to the table. This theory, ascribed to common sense, Prof. Broad calls naïve realism.[36] Now it is only plausible to maintain that this theory is held by the ordinary man if carefully selected perceptual statements concerning objects at close range are considered. If we regard the whole range of perceptual situations the common sense belief is quite different. This belief involves that in perceptual situations objects reveal more or less of their nature to us; and common sense would find no difficulty in admitting that there are cases where very little of the nature of the object of perception is revealed. For example, statements of the following type are a commonplace: "I can just see something, but I cannot make out what it is," "I think I can see something there but I cannot be sure," "It looks like a house, but it may be just an outcrop of rock." Instances could be multiplied indefinitely. Common sense would not scruple to admit that objects do not always have the qualities which they seem to have when seen, heard, tasted, touched or smelt. It accepts without flinching that the hills which look purple in the distance are really green. It is indeed a platitude enshrined in proverbial literature that "things are seldom what they seem."

I draw attention to these elementary facts, in the first place, to point out that the only naïveté about naïve realism is that philosophers should have thought the ordinary man believed it. More important, however, is that these facts show the common sense view not to involve belief in a simple two-termed relation between me and the things I perceive, in which no possibility of illusion can arise, but a relation in which there is the possibility of the object's nature being revealed to a greater or less degree. It is true, of course, that the plain man no less than the philosopher sometimes puts as the object of *see* not the material thing but the *how it appears* as when, looking into the distance, one says "I can see a purple haze; it may be mountains or

---

[36] "Naïve Realism . . . is the explicit formulation of the belief which forms *an essential part* of the perceptual situation as such." *The Mind and Its Place in Nature*, p. 243.

cloud." No violence is done to his language if it is re-written "I see something as purple and hazy" or "There is something which appears purple and hazy." It is the lack of sufficient information to establish the nature of the object appearing which leads to the varying form of statement.

In concluding, I do not wish to suggest that no problems beset the theory of appearing. For example the two cases of a thing's appearing double and of something appearing to be where there is no such thing, present the problem: Is the apparent expanse in these cases the actual surface of any object? If so, of what object? I must, however, defer the inquiry into this and other problems to a future occasion, when I can consider the affinities of this theory with the different but closely related theory of multiple inherence and at the same time discuss some of the points in Prof. Dawes Hicks' exposition with which I am not perfectly satisfied. Here I have only been able to indicate the possibility of such an account as an appendix to my main task which has been to criticise those theories which make the notion of sense-datum fundamental in their explanations of perception.

THE THEORY OF APPEARING

RODERICK M. CHISHOLM

Philosophers who have written about perception have usually found it convenient to speak in terms of "appearances," "impressions," "phenomena," "sense-data," and the like. Many now believe, however, that by avoiding this sort of terminology we can eliminate the difficult metaphysical puzzles traditionally associated with our knowledge of the external world. They contend: (1) that we can say all we know about perception without employing this "sense-datum terminology"; (2) that the alternative terminology does not lead us to metaphysics; and, accordingly, (3) that the metaphysical problems which the consideration of perception sometimes seems to involve are really "pseudo problems," arising out of the misuse of language. In the present essay I want to show that, although (1) is true, (2) is false, and hence that (3) remains problematic.

THE SENSE-DATUM PUZZLES

What do the "sense-datum terms" refer to? Unfortunately, these terms are used in a number of different ways and few, if any, who use them succeed in conveying to others what their own particular usages happen to be. We may do well, then, to speak of a hypothetical "sense-datum philosopher" and to state his case as clearly and as fairly as possible.

The sense-datum philosopher apparently believes sense-data are entities having at least these three characteristics: (1) they may be found in any perceptual experience; (2) they are somehow essential to the perception of physical things; and (3) they are, in an important respect, independent of the physical things in the perception of which they are involved. What kind of evidence is there for assuming that such entities exist? The sense-datum philosopher would reason, I think, somewhat as follows:

"The root of the problem lies in the fact that every perceptual experience contains something that can be made to vary independently of any of the physical things being perceived. When, for example, you look at the wallpaper six feet away, you experience a fairly uniform color, but if you were to approach the wall you would find that the color you experience becomes more and more differentiated. The object you are perceiving doesn't change (we may assume), but *something* does. Or, again: if you will look at the top of the coffee table, you will find in your experience something whose geometrical shape you can change merely by walking around the table. From here you experience something diamond-shaped; if you were to stand directly above the table, you would experience something rectangular; and, in moving from here to there, you could, if you chose, note the change occurring in the experienced shapes. (There is nothing esoteric about this variation. If you were to make accurate sketches or photographs of what you see from here, and of what you see from there, you would find that the variation also occurs in *them;* the one taken from here will contain a rhomboid, the one from there a rectangle.) Similarly, merely by altering the conditions of observation in an appropriate fashion, you can vary experienced sizes, sounds, smells, and so on.

"In general, we may give the name 'sense-datum' to anything in a perceptual experience which *could* thus be varied independently of the objects being perceived. It is clear (1) that sense-data can be found in any perceptual experience, since one can alter any such experience merely by properly distorting one's perceptual apparatus or otherwise varying the conditions of observation. And (2) sense-data are *essential* to the perception of physical things: for, if the sense-data present in a perceptual experience were somehow removed and replaced by nothing else, one would not be perceiving anything at all; i.e., if everything which is capable of the sort of variation described were removed from the experience, nothing would be left of the experience. Finally, (3) sense-data are independent of the objects of perception in the sense that the sense-data and the objects are capable of the sort of independent variation described."

Once we admit that these entities referred to as "sense-data" are to be found in every perceptual experience, we are confronted with a number of perplexing questions concerning their status. In order to answer these questions, many philosophers have been led to devise intricate accounts both of the nature of the universe and of the nature of man. These questions, which we may call the *sense-datum puzzles,* may be illustrated as follows:

"Consider the various sense-data which you may experience if you examine this rectangular table top; from this corner you experience one which is diamond shaped; if you were to look straight down from the ceiling you would experience one which is rectangular; and from the roof you would experience one which is smaller than the other two. The sense-data are of different shapes and sizes; hence they cannot be identical with each other; and therefore (presumably) they cannot all be in the same place at once. Perhaps one of them is where the surface of the table is; but, if so, where are the others? Are they somewhere in the space surrounding the table? Perhaps we should say that all of them exist in the mind—or in the brain. But, in this case, what becomes of the table and how can one know anything about it? If all sense-data are thus subjective, the world must be exceedingly barren when no one is observing it. Do the sense-data come into being when we experience them, and, if they do, what kind of creation is that? Perhaps we should deny the principle that distinct things must be in different places at the same time and say that all of those sense-data are right there on the surface of the table. Or perhaps we should say that sense-data, even though some of them seem to be spatially related to each other, don't occupy places at all. . . ."

Something seems to be amiss here. These *are* metaphysical questions; the possible answers are "neutral with respect to experience." Moreover the puzzles seem to be artificial; the question "Where is the diamond-shaped sense-datum?" sounds suspiciously like the notorious pseudo problems concerning the nature of nothingness and the whereabouts of the golden mountain. And, finally, the statement "From the corner of the room the table presents a diamond-shaped sense-datum" seems to be merely a clumsy and misleading way of saying something which could have been expressed without reference to sense-data at all.

The contention to be examined, then, is that by revising the language we escape the puzzles.

THE LANGUAGE OF APPEARING

The fundamental objection to the sense-datum philosopher is that his way of discussing perception is "metaphysically charged" and needlessly so. Obviously there *is* a sense in which every perceptual experience can be made to vary independently of the physical things being perceived. But this phenomenal variability (as it might be called) can be described without referring to any "somethings" other than the physical objects which we perceive.

We don't need to say such things as "From the corner of the room, the table presents a diamond-shaped sense-datum (appearance, impression, sensation . . .)." We could say instead, "From the corner of the room, the table *appears* to be (or seems to be, or looks) diamond-shaped." So, too, with the other stock examples of the sense-datum philosophers: we can say "The stick appears bent; the railroad tracks appear to converge; the oculist's 'A' looks blurry; the train sounds fainter in the distance than it does nearby," and so on. Indeed this is the way we ordinarily *do* speak; no one tells the oculist that his "A" presents a blurry sense-datum. And with this mode of speaking we avoid the curious "somethings" which perplex the sense-datum philosopher.[1] Following Mr. Ayer, we may refer to this alternative mode of speaking as the "language of appearing," contrasting it with our preceding "sense-datum language."

It is important to note that the terms of our "language of appearing"—terms such as "appear," "look," "seem," "sound"—have a number of different senses and that only one of these senses is applicable in the present context. These are often used, not to describe phenomenal variation, but to express inclination-to-believe and to state judgments of probability. If I say "Mr. Dewey appears to have abandoned all hopes of becoming President," I mean something like "On the basis of the available evidence, it is probable that (or I am inclined to believe that) Mr. Dewey has abandoned his hopes. . . ." But when, in discussing epistemology or esthetics we employ the language of appearing and say, "The penny appears to be elliptical from this point," we *don't* mean to convey that in all probability the penny *is* elliptical or that we have any inclination to believe that it is. Mr. Broad has stated the essence of the matter:

> Appearance is not merely mistaken *judgment* about physical objects. When I judge that a penny looks elliptical I am not mistakenly ascribing elliptical shape to what is in fact round. Sensible appearances *may* lead me to make a mistaken judgment about physical objects, but they *need* not and so far as we know, commonly do not. My certainty

[1] An admirably clear statement of this point of view is to be found in G. A. Paul, "Is There a Problem about Sense-Data?" *Arist. Soc. Proc.*, suppl. vol., XV (1936), 61. For earlier versions see H. A. Prichard, *Kant's Theory of Knowledge* (1909), p. 75 ff., esp. p. 85; P. Coffey, *Epistemology or the Theory of Knowledge* (1917), I, 356–358; II, 167 ff., esp. 177; G. Dawes Hicks, *Critical Realism* (1938), p. 68 ff., esp. p. 78; and F. J. E. Woodbridge, *Nature and Mind* (1937), pp. 400–401.

that the penny looks elliptical exists comfortably alongside of my conviction that it is round. But a mistaken judgment that the penny *is* elliptical could not continue to exist after I knew that the penny was really round. The plain fact is then that "looking elliptical to me" stands for a peculiar experience, which, whatever the right analysis of it may be, is not just a mistaken judgment about the shape of the penny.[2]

It is the sense of the term "appear" (or "looks") which Mr. Broad has in mind that is intended by the phrase "language of appearing." The use of this term may be explicated in much the same way in which the sense-datum philosopher explicates the term "sense-datum," i.e., by referring to the possibility of phenomenal variation.

The sense-datum philosopher, of course, will admit that the language of appearing *can* be used in discussing these facts. But he contends that from statements in the language of appearing we can *deduce* statements in the sense-datum language. That is to say, he contends that from statements such as: (*A*) There exists something which appears diamond-shaped, we can deduce statements such as: (*S*) There exists something which *is* diamond-shaped. If he is cautious, he may grant, as Mr. Ayer does, that *S* describes exactly the same state of affairs as does *A*.[3] But he will cite the "somethings" mentioned in statements such as *S* as instances of what he means by "sense-data."

One fundamental question, then, concerns the inference from statements such as *A,* in the language of appearing, to statements such as *S,* in the sense-datum language. We may call this the *sense-datum inference.* And we may say that the *sense-datum theory* is the view which countenances this inference, whereas the *theory of appearing* is the view which does not.

Some philosophers who refuse to countenance the

[2] C. D. Broad, *Scientific Thought* (1923), pp. 236–237 [pp. 87–88, this volume. Ed.]. Broad, although he does not advocate the theory of appearing, presents an excellent account of it. Cp. Thomas Reid, *An Inquiry into the Human Mind on Principles of Common Sense* (1764), ch. vi; sec. 3.

[3] Cp. A. J. Ayer, *The Foundations of Empirical Knowledge* (1940), p. 25. Cp. pp. 55, 116–117.

sense-datum inference seem to hold that it is *invalid;* others seem to hold merely that it is *inadvisable.*[4] But in either case it is agreed that, in discussing perception, the language of appearing is preferable to the sense-datum language; that, by making the inference to sense-data, we multiply entities beyond necessity; and that, by avoiding the inference, we lose nothing but the metaphysical puzzles.

It is easy to see the *prima-facie* case for the theory of appearing. When we describe perception in terms of sense-datum we seem to have, in addition to the external objects (e.g., the table, the oculist's "A" and the train), *another* set of entities (e.g., the diamond-shaped datum, the blur, and the diminishing sound). And these other entities turn out to be extraordinarily perplexing. But when we speak in terms of appearing we have only the original external objects. Thus we avoid multiplying entities and we avoid the puzzles concerning the status and whereabouts of sense-data.

Moreover, when we describe perception in the language of appearing, without "wandering in the usages of phenomena, sense-data, impressions, and their like,"[5] we seem at the outset to preserve the convictions of the naive or nonphilosophical realist. For we can say that, when you look at the table from the corner of the room, it's the real table that you see—the table as it appears under those conditions. And we can say that when you look down the railroad tracks, or at the oculist's "A," or when you listen to the train go off into the distance, it's the real external object that you perceive—the object as it appears, in each case, under the conditions of observation. The menu may appear pink to me, with my odd glasses, and white to you; yet each of us is seeing the real menu—I am seeing it under one set of conditions and you are seeing it under another. To say that it appears pink to me and white to you is no more puzzling than to say it is north of me and south of you; in relation to me it's north and appears pink; in rela-

---

[4] Prichard, Coffey, and Dawes Hicks speak as though they believe the inference to be invalid; Paul seems to feel that it is merely inadvisable. See the works cited above.

[5] A. E. Murphy, *The Use of Reason* (1943), p. 35.

tion to you it's south and appears white. No matter how bizarre the conditions may be, if an external object appears to us at all, then clearly it is the external object that we perceive. "To be sure," writes Mr. Murphy, who is one of the most persuasive spokesmen for this way of looking at the matter, "we gain our perceptual information about such objects through such expedients as looking at them, and what we thus see of them is the way they look (appear) under the conditions in which they can be observed. But how else would a human organism see a material object?"[6] There are many philosophers, I suspect, who are content to leave the matter here.

MORE PUZZLES?

The theory of appearing, as we now have it, seems to say that appearing is relational; for instance, that "appearing pink to" designates a relation which obtains between the menu and me when I put on these odd glasses and look. Suppose, now, we ask, *"What* things may be appeared to?" The obvious answer is, of course, that the only things which may be appeared to are human beings and other organisms endowed with the appropriate sort of sense organs and nervous systems. This is certainly a sensible way to deal with the question and it is, I take it, the answer which Mr. Murphy, for instance, would be inclined to give.[7] But let us consider what follows if we answer the question this way.

If appearing is what we have said that it is, the answer would entail that where there aren't any perceiving or-

[6] A. E. Murphy, in *The Philosophy of G. E. Moore* (1942), p. 312.
[7] Murphy presents a clear statement of this view in "Dewey's Epistemology and Metaphysics," in *The Philosophy of John Dewey* (1939), pp. 219–220. Possibly some who incline toward this version of the theory of appearing might also want to add that cameras, recording machines, and other such devices can be appeared to. The sense-datum philosopher, however, is more likely to be interested in the analogies between these devices and perception.

ganisms, nothing is appeared to and hence nothing appears. When no one is looking, roses don't appear red, the menu doesn't appear pink *or* white, and, when no one is listening, the train doesn't sound any fainter when it goes off into the distance. But when we put the matter this way, this particular version of the theory of appearing becomes remarkably similar to the classical sense-datum philosophy known as "psychophysical dualism" (or at least to that version of it defended by Mr. Lovejoy in *The Revolt Against Dualism*) and seems to have just about the same merits and limitations. This type of dualism, it will be recalled, is the view which "bifurcates nature" into the world of sense-data and the world of things-in-themselves. In order to see the merits and limitations of the theory of appearing generally, it will be instructive to note the parallel between classical dualism and the version of the theory of appearing to which we seem to have been led.

According to dualism, sense-data come into existence only where there are observers who satisfy the appropriate conditions; hence, in those portions of the universe where there are no observers, or where no one is observing, there are no sense-data. According to this version of the theory of appearing, objects appear only when there are observers who satisfy the appropriate conditions; hence, in those portions of the universe where there are no observers, or where no one is observing, nothing appears.

Are unperceived roses red? According to dualism, they could be said to be red in the sense that they have powers or dispositions to contribute to the production of red sense-data for certain sorts of observers; but no red sense-datum exists out there with the roses. On this version of the theory of appearing, the roses may be said to be red in the sense that they have powers or dispositions to appear red to certain sorts of observer; but they don't appear red when no one is looking. Before anyone looks, the redness of the rose (on either view) exists as a power, possibility, or disposition. The rose is such that, if only a "normal observer" were to come into the garden, it *would* present him with a red sense-datum (or appear red for him).

When, finally, he *does* come and look, the disposition of the rose is activated and, on the one view, sense-data are *produced,* and, on the other, the roses *appear.* (Sometimes it is said, on the one view, that sense-data *emerge* and, on the other, that the roses *take on* appearances or relations of appearing.[8])

Do we perceive the real external objects? The dualist may say that we perceive them by means of their effects or "representatives" in us. But they never have such effects or representatives unless they are perceived. On this version of the theory of appearing, we perceive the external objects "the way they appear" under the conditions of observation. But they never appear that way, or any other way, unless they are perceived.

Does one theory provide us with a more "objective" account of the matter than the other does?[9] According to dualism, it is an *objective* property of the external thing to be able to produce the sense-data it does when the appropriate observers are perceiving it; but the property is *subjectively* dependent in that no sense-data can be produced unless observers are present. On the present version of the theory of appearing, it is an *objective* property of the external thing to be able to appear as it does to observers like us; but the property is *subjectively* dependent in that the object cannot appear in *any* way unless observers are present.

Do our claims to knowledge become more precarious on the one theory than on the other? On each theory we perceive the real external objects. But the dualist must decide how the sense-data which are produced in us by the ex-

[8] Murphy speaks of what external objects "take on" when we perceive them (*The Philosophy of John Dewey,* p. 220).

[9] Murphy sometimes refers to his view as "objective relativism" in order "to stress the fact that the experienced world is *at once* in some of its major features dependent on and conditioned by the special relations in which sentient (and more particularly human) organisms stand to their environment *and also* a direct presentation of that environment itself, or the order of natural events as it is under such conditions" (*ibid.,* p. 219). "Objective relativism" is here in question only to the extent that it may be correctly interpreted as a version of the theory of appearing.

ternal things aid us in knowing about the things-in-them-selves; for the sense-data come into being when we perceive and disappear when we cease to perceive. On the other view, we must decide how our being appeared to aids us in knowing about the things which thus appear; for they appear that way only when we perceive and when we cease to perceive they no longer appear at all. The dualist sometimes says that our experience of sense-data provides us with a "representative" of other parts of nature; Mr. Murphy says that our being appeared to provides us with a "fair sample" of other parts of nature.[10] To the question "How do we *know* that we have a faithful representative (or a fair sample)?" each theory may provide a similar answer.

Certainly, up to this point, the theories are remarkably similar. The classical objections to the above dualistic theses apply with equal force to our version of the theory of appearing. Whitehead and others are disturbed by the "vacuous actuality" with which unperceived objects seem to be left on the dualistic hypothesis; those who call themselves "naturalists" are sometimes disturbed by the "miracle" which is alleged to occur when sense-data "emerge"; the skeptic asks about the credentials of "representative"; and so on. The treatment of unperceived objects, on this version of the theory of appearing, is indistinguishable from that of dualism and thus they retain their qualitative vacuity; the "taking on of appearances" is as much (or as little) a "miracle" as is "emergence"; and the "fair sample" has as much (or as little) reliability as the "representative."

At one point, the parallel may seem to be strained, namely, in connection with the question "Do we perceive external objects?" For, in answer to this, the dualist some-times says that we perceive only sense-data and never external objects. Here, however, we *are* in danger of linguistic confusion. If the statement "We perceive external objects" is understood in its ordinary sense, *neither* theory entails

[10] *Ibid.*, p. 220.

anything that is inconsistent with it. If one wanted to prove that Jones, for instance, doesn't perceive external objects (in the ordinary sense of these words) one would not offer a theory about the status of sense-data; rather, one would try to show that Jones is dead, or asleep, or that his perceptual apparatus is out of order. When the dualist passes from "No sense-data exist in the external world" to "We don't perceive external objects," he may be "corrected" by reference to ordinary usage. Anyone who has doubt on *this* point may be referred to the large body of contemporary literature concerning the relation between philosophical statements and ordinary language.[11]

So far, then, the two theories are pretty much parallel. Each involves further metaphysical questions, however, and here they seem to diverge. The sense-datum philosopher is puzzled about the status of his sense-data in the physical world. He asks whether they are identical with any of the entities treated by physics; the theory of the dualist is that sense-data are "in the mind" or possibly that they are "the brain seen from its metaphysical insides." The theorist of appearing may ask, similarly, whether his relations of appearing can be identified with anything treated by physics or whether they are something which the universe somehow "takes on" when perceivers come into being. Both philosophers may also be led—I think unfortunately—to make philosophical statements about the nature of physical objects. The dualist talks about "things-in-

---

[11] Cp. N. Malcolm, "Moore and Ordinary Language," in *The Philosophy of G. E. Moore*, pp. 345–368; M. Lazerowitz, "Moore's Paradox," in *ibid.*, pp. 371–393; O. K. Bouwsma, "Des Cartes' Skepticism of the Senses," *Mind*, LIV (1945), pp. 313–322; M. Black, "Linguistic Method in Philosophy," *Phil. and Phenom. Res.*, VIII (1948), 635–649. Not all dualists, of course, have needed this enlightenment. Thus C. A. Strong, for example, held "that the sense-datum is representative, but that perception by means of the sense-datum is direct. We directly apprehend the real thing, and nothing else; its characters and also its existence" ("Is Perception Direct, or Representative?" *Mind*, XL [1931], 217). Cp. also the scholastic doctrine according to which the external object is *that which* we perceive and the "sensible species" that by *means of which* we perceive it: "Species non est *id quod* cognoscitur, sed *id quo* mens cognoscit rem" (Coffey, *op. cit.*, II, 178).

themselves" and it is easy to imagine the theorist of appearing ensnared in questions such as the following:

"Consider the statement, 'We see the rose as it appears to us.' Does this substantive phrase, 'the rose-as-it-appears-to-us,' designate a special kind of complex? If we are to continue to be sensitive to language, we should prefer to say it doesn't. Instead of saying 'We see the rose as it appears to us' we could say 'We are appeared to by the rose.'[12] This is less felicitous and possibly less pleasing to the professional naive realist; further it brings to clearer focus the problem of the *terms* of our appearing relation. Can we think of even a single respect in which they are distinguishable from the 'things-in-themselves' of the dualist? On the other hand, if we say that our substantive phrase 'the rose-as-it-appears-to-us' *does* designate a special kind of complex we are confronted with puzzles not unlike the original sense-datum puzzles. For example, what is the relation of these complexes to the rose; does the entire rose occur in them or just a part, say the surface; is the rose somehow the totality of the complexes in which it would be commonly said to occur; do these complexes, like the dualist's sense-data, exist outside of space; do they exist only when perceived? And what are the *other* terms of the appearing relation—minds, selves, brains? . . ."

As in the case of the sense-datum puzzles, something seems to be amiss. In general, such philosophical speculations about the nature of matter do not seem altogether happy. *Neither* the sense-datum philosopher nor the theorist of appearing, after all, needs to compete with physics. As we have seen, the two theories have similar consequences with respect to the nature of physical things and to the possibility of knowing them; or perhaps we should say the two theories are similarly *devoid* of such consequences. But some philosophers seem to feel that such theories, in making sense-data or appearing relations depend for their existence upon perceiving organisms, some-

---

[12] This recalls Aristotle's statement: "The activity of the sensible object and that of the percipient sense is one and the same activity" (*De Anima* II, 425 B 27).

how "impoverish" the physical world. And these philosophers may be tempted to *extend* physics and talk about the metaphysical insides of matter. Possibly they could be shown that this "impoverishment" is not as serious as they are at first led to believe. In any event, however, the problem is the same whether we choose sense-data or appearing.

But let us see whether we might be better off with some *other* version of the theory of appearing.

STILL MORE PUZZLES

From the point of view of the antimetaphysician, the other possible versions of the theory of appearing are even less hopeful than the one just considered. We need do little more than mention what the alternatives might be.

According to the version just considered, appearing is "relational" and only sentient organisms may be appeared to. Suppose, now, we deny the latter contention and say instead that *anything* may be appeared to. The redness of the rose may appear to the objects around it (and possibly to itself), and the views from mountain tops need not await the presence of living things in order to appear. This version would certainly meet some of the objections to the previous one. The uninhabited portions of the universe would have more than the "qualitative vacuity" which they possess on dualism and on our former theory; nor would there occur any "emergence" or "taking on" when sentient beings appear on the scene. But now we seem to be saying that the rose may appear red to the stone!

I suspect that by giving the theory of appearing this twist we obtain the key to significant portions of Whitehead's and Alexander's speculations. Perhaps, if we were unable to before, we can now begin to understand Whitehead's doctrine of "prehensions" according to which "all actual things are subjects, each prehending the universe from which it arises."[13] And we now have light on Alexander's thesis that "the cognitive relation" is "the simplest and most universal relation between finite things in the Universe," and that we "may ascribe 'mind' to all things alike, in various degrees."[14] Of course, if we say that the rose may appear red to the stone as well as to sentient organisms, we have to explain what it is that the sense organs and the rest of our perceptual apparatus do for us and why it is that the stone doesn't need such aids. Alexander's answer to this is that, although both the man and the stone bear a *cognitive relation* to the rose, only the man is *conscious of the rose;* Whitehead's answer is similar.[15] If we decide that the table appears to the other furniture in the room, we can ask whether it appears diamond-shaped to one piece and square to another. And so on.

If this version of the appearing seems difficult to accept, we need only turn to the various sense-datum theories in order to find suggestions for further possibilities. Recall, for example, Russell's doctrine that sense-data are constituents of the brain, or Moore's suggestion that possibly sense-data might appear to be different from what they really are. We might try saying that it is a portion of the brain that appears (and we could still say, of course, that we perceive external objects: we perceive them by being appeared to by the brain). Or, if we were really pressed, we could try saying that things might appear to appear in ways in which they don't really appear.

And if none of these possibilities gives us a satisfactory theory of appearing, there are still others. We could try saying that appearing is not relational—e.g., that the rose

---

[13] A. N. Whitehead, *Process and Reality* (1929), p. 89.

[14] S. Alexander, "The Basis of Realism," *Proceedings of the British Academy,* VI (1914), 10, 32. Cp. Francis Bacon's *Natural History:* "It is certain that all bodies whatsoever, though they have no sense, yet they have perception . . ." (quoted in Whitehead, *Science and the Modern World* [1925], p. 58). See also Locke's *Essay,* bk. IV, ch. iii, sec. 6.

[15] Whitehead believes, of course, that the relations obtain not between stones and roses but between entities of a more "concrete" sort. Thus the theory of appearing seems to lead back to something like Leibniz's monads and their conscious and unconscious perceptions.

may appear without appearing red *to* anything. In this way, we avoid the difficulties of our first theory; we don't have the cognitive stones (monads, occasions) of the second; we don't have the complications involved in saying that a brain may appear to its owner or that things may appear to appear in ways other than they really appear. But now we have a theory, which is the analogue of the theory of "unsensed sense-data," and *this* catches us in still further puzzles. Now shall we say that, when no one is around, the menu appears pink *and* white at once? We can no longer add the qualification "pink to one observer, white to another." Does "appearing pink" entail "appearing not white"? How do we answer such questions? Suppose we say that an object cannot appear pink and white at once, or clear and blurry at once, or diamond-shaped and rectangular. Consider the table in the other room; which way is *it* appearing now—diamond-shaped or rectangular, large or small, clear or blurry? How does one decide; how could one ever tell? Or perhaps we should say that the thing manifests *all* these appearances at once[16]— that at this moment the oculist's "A" appears clear, appears completely blurry, and appears in all the intervening ways; that it appears yellow (as the jaundiced man discovers); that it appears double (as one may discover by pressing the eye). . . . These, then are *puzzles of appearing* and they may be multiplied indefinitely.

SENSE-DATA AND APPEARING

Thus there are sense-datum puzzles and there are puzzles of appearing. The presumption may be that there really *is* something genuinely puzzling about perception and that we must choose, not between metaphysics and enlightenment, but between good and bad metaphysics. In the meantime, however, is there any ground for choosing be-

[16] This seems to be Coffey's version of the theory of appearing (cp. *op. cit.*, II, 175).

tween the sense-datum theory and the theory of appearing?

The two theories differ with respect to the validity of what we have called the "sense-datum inference." But otherwise they seem to be pretty nearly parallel. Given a statement in the "sense-datum language," it is an easy matter to transform it into the "language of appearing," and vice versa. Two points can be made at this stage however, which may help us to make a choice.

(1) If we want to keep our metaphysical puzzles down to a minimum (and this certainly seems to be desirable), we should prefer not to be left with the evils of *both* sense-data and appearing.[17] Now there is a significant group of experiences, other than those involved in external perception, which all of us tend to describe in the manner of the sense-datum language—namely, those experiences which involve images, after-images, dreams, hallucinations, and so on. An after-image, for instance, seems to be an entity of much the same sort as a sense-datum and it involves similar puzzles ("Is it outside of space; is it in the brain; does it come into existence when perceived; can it exist unperceived . . . ?"). If we continue to speak of such experiences in this manner, we have *one* good reason for preferring sense-data to appearing: viz., if we choose sense-data we shall have but one curious category; if we choose appearing we shall have two.

It is true that one *could* describe these experiences in the language of appearing. When I imagine a unicorn or a golden mountain, I *could* describe the experience by saying, not that I have an image of such and such a sort, but that something appears in such and such a fashion. This way of putting the matter, however, leads us at once to the peculiar problems which the theory of appearing involves. For, in this language, we speak of *something* which appears. One may now ask, "What is it that appears when I imagine a unicorn?" ("Is it a subsistent entity, or

---

[17] The sense-datum philosopher, although he countenances statements in the language of appearing, does not have to face the puzzles of appearing in addition to the sense-datum puzzles. For statements in the language of appearing are to be "analyzed" into sense-datum statements.

part of the brain, or parts of previously seen physical objects, . . . etc., etc.?") Here, perhaps, the language of appearing seems even more artificial than the language of sense-data. It is significant that no philosopher (as far as I know) has suggested that the language of appearing be applied to experiences other than those involved in external perception.[18]

(2) The objection to the validity of the sense-datum inference has something in common with the so-called "anti-rational" or "anti-intellectual" philosophies of the nineteenth and twentieth centuries. A few years ago, it will be recalled, some philosophers were saying that to "hypostatize" entities which are "finite" is to falsify reality; that these are but aspects of the Whole, to which no finite concept is adequate; and that we are not likely to advance to the Whole wandering through the mazes of tables, chairs, and railroad tracks. And others were making similar charges about the "conceptualization" of a reality which is essentially "fluid." On either objection, statements such as "Here is a table" and "There is a railroad track" are somehow illegitimate. Most of us, however, are prepared to defend the conviction that, although physical objects may never exist in isolation and although their temporal boundaries are somewhat indefinite, they are, all the same, "legitimate" subjects of discourse. Let us compare this with the conviction that there is a diamond-shaped "something" to be seen from here, a blur to be seen in the oculist's shop, and, in the case of the double images, two "somethings" to be seen and counted.[19] Possibly one will say that the entities which these terms purport to designate

---

[18] Mr. Paul, however, makes an interesting proposal. Consider the sort of situation which the sense-datum philosopher might describe as follows: "I was deceived into thinking that I saw a penny; but what I really saw was an elliptical sense-datum which was not 'of' any physical object." Paul suggests that one might do well to describe such a situation in this way: "It only seemed to me as if there was a round penny which looked [appeared] elliptical. I was really not seeing anything at all" (op. cit., p. 68). But, obviously, this kind of formulation, if taken quite literally, would give rise to still another set of problems concerning what is intended by the phrase "It only seemed to me as if. . . ."

[19] Cp. H. H. Price, Perception (1932), p. 63.

are "adverbs" of something else, as one may say that the chair is an adverb (aspect, stage) of something else, and there may even be good reason for making such assertions. But when it is objected that we cannot talk about chairs and images and sense-data, the reply must consist, essentially, of a defense of analysis and of our ability to make abstractions. Mr. Lewis has put the point emphatically: "The condemnation of abstractions is the condemnation of thought itself. Nothing that thought can ever comprise is other than some abstraction except the concrete universal; and the concrete universal is a myth."[20] The diamonds and blurs are at least as well off as the tables and chairs.

[20] C. I. Lewis, *Mind and the World Order* (1929), p. 55.

SENSATION

GILBERT RYLE

One of the things that worry me most is the notion of
sensations or sense-impressions. It seems, on the one hand,
very hard to avoid saying that hearing, seeing, and tasting
could not happen unless appropriate sense-impressions
were received; and yet also very hard to give a coherent
account of what such sense-impressions are, or how the
having of sense-impressions is connected with, say, our
hearing a conversation or our seeing a tree.

There seem to be some very good reasons for saying
that sense-impressions can occur in abnormal situations,
when no perceiving occurs. For example, after looking at
a bright light I have an after-image; or if I knock my head
I seem to see stars or lightning flashes; or when I have a
bad cold I have a singing noise in my head. One seems
bound to say that in these situations I have optical or
acoustic sensations or sense-impressions, and that it is just
in the presence of these that the similarity consists between merely having an after-image and genuinely seeing a
tree, or between merely having a singing in my head and
genuinely hearing the choir singing in the concert-hall. In
cases of genuine perception, we are inclined to say, we
both have sense-impressions, produced or stimulated in the
normal ways, and also contribute something of our own,
namely, to put it too picturesquely, the interpretation or
significance, without which we should not have perceived,
say, an oak-tree. Yet the moment we start to press this
tempting idea we are landed in familiar difficulties. Colours
as we see them and sounds as we hear them seem at once

to collapse into internal reactions or states of ourselves. The oak-tree is not really green and the tenor's voice is not literally shrill. The sense-impressions which were supposed to make perception of trees and choirs possible finish by becoming screens between ourselves and trees or choirs. The sensible qualities of things in the world cease to be qualities of those things and become, instead, momentary states of our own minds or nervous systems. They come to have the status of stomach-aches, caused, indeed, fairly indirectly by mechanical and chemical properties of external things, of the intervening medium, and of our own nervous systems, but no more to be equated with attributes of external things than my stomach-ache is an attribute of the uncooked beans which indirectly caused my stomach to ache.

There are further difficulties. First, the notion of sense-impression seems to be a technical or specialist notion. People without special theories or technical knowledge of physiology, optics, chemistry or psychology know well how to use the concepts of seeing, hearing and smelling, though not the concept of *sense-impression*. They have to be introduced to this notion by being introduced to the outlines of special theories about the physics and physiology of perception. Only after having heard a bit about the propagation of waves and the like, and then about the transmission of impulses up the nerves, and then perhaps also something about the psychology of stimuli and responses —only then can they begin to use the notion of *sense-impressions*. Consequently, in the ordinary contexts in which we talk about seeing, hearing and the rest, no mention is made of sense-impressions, any more than in ordinary contexts in which meat, vegetables, and fruit are discussed, any mention is made of calories or vitamins. As I might put it, the concept of *perception* is on a more elementary or less technical level than that of *sense-impression*. We can know all that is a part of common knowledge about seeing and hearing, without knowing anything about these impressions. But from this it follows directly that the concept of sense-impression is not any sort of component of the concept of perception, any more than the concept of *vitamin* is any sort of component of the concept of *dinner*.

Unfortunately, however, the logical situation is a confused one. For we are perfectly familiar with not one, but at least two quite different non-technical notions of *sensation*—and philosophers and psychologists have nearly always tried to equate their technical notion of *sense-impression* with one, or more often with both of these non-technical notions of *sensation*. They pass without apology from saying that without optical or auditory sense-impressions there is no seeing or hearing, to saying that seeing and hearing involve the having of sensations, as if the one assertion were a mere paraphrase of the other.

To get this point a bit clearer, let me examine in some detail the two non-technical notions of sensation.

First, there is the sense of the word 'sensation' or the word 'feeling', in which sensations or feelings are such things as pains, tickles, feelings of nausea, suffocation, thirst, and the like. A pain is what anodynes and anaesthetics exist to relieve or prevent. Sensations of this sort can be more or less acute or intense; they can be short-lived or protracted, and they are, in general, localisable in particular parts of the body. Most sensations, in this sense of the word, if not all of them, are in some degree distressing. Some philosophers, like Bishop Berkeley, have argued, quite fallaciously it seems to me, that the family which includes such things as pains, tickles and feelings of suffocation also includes such things as our sensations of temperature. When I bring my hand nearer and nearer to the fire, I begin by feeling increases in the heat, but at a certain point the heat is intense enough to hurt. Berkeley argues that therefore a feeling of warmth differs only in degree from the feeling of pain. So the feeling of warmth is a state of myself in the way in which a pain is.

But this will not do at all. For one thing, some weight must be attached to the fact that no one does suppose that painfulness characterises the fire, in the way in which they do suppose that warmth does. A child will say that the fire is so hot that it hurts his hand, and thus is already distinguishing between an effect which the fire has upon him from a property which the fire has, without which it would not hurt him. Moreover, feeling, say with one's hand, that the fire is hotter than it was, is finding the answer to a question. The owner of the hand is discriminating something, finding out a difference. In some cases he would admit to having made a mistake. He had not been careful enough. But in having a pain there is no finding anything out, no discerning of similarities or differences, no place, even, for mistakes and so no room for carefulness or lack of carefulness. Feeling, in the sense of finding out or discerning, the warmth of things is a kind of perception, and a kind at which some people, like bakers and laundry-girls, become better than other people; it is the product of an acquired skill; but feeling, in the sense of suffering pains, is not a kind of perception, and there is no question of one victim being better or worse than another at feeling toothaches. In this sense of 'feeling' or 'sensation', pains are not things the feeling of which is the product of an acquired skill. So far from the feeling of warmth being merely a lower degree of the feeling of pain, the two things are 'felt' only in quite different senses of the word. They are not even species of one genus, as perhaps seeing and tasting are species of the one genus, perception. They belong to different categories from one another. The attempt to classify felt temperatures with felt pains, and so to show that felt warmth is a state or reaction in ourselves, as pain in some way is, was a logical mistake.

We need, therefore, to distinguish the sense of 'feeling' or 'sensation' in which we call pains and tickles 'feelings' or 'sensations' from the entirely different sense in which we say that we perceive some things not by seeing, hearing, smelling, or tasting, but by feeling—the sense in which we say that a person whose feet or fingers are numb with cold has lost sensation or the power of feeling things with his fingers and toes. Let me just remind you of some of the properties of external things which are perceived by feeling, as opposed to seeing, hearing, smelling or tasting. First, to detect how hot or cold something is, we have to feel it with the hands, or lips, or tongue, or, less efficiently, with other parts of our bodies. We cannot see, hear or smell how cold things are. Next, to detect the roughness, smoothness, slipperiness or stickiness of the surfaces of things, we normally have to handle them or finger them. Next, to detect whether something is vibrating, stiff, resilient, loose in its socket and so on, we usually have to touch it, and very likely also muscularly to manipulate it. Some people are much better than others at discrimination-tasks of these kinds. Doctors can feel the pulses of patients which are too faint for you or me to detect and the trained driver can feel the car going into a skid long before the novice could have done so.

We should notice that tactual and kinaesthetic detection is unlike seeing, hearing, tasting, and smelling in one important respect. What I detect by seeing, hearing, tasting, and smelling are with extremely few exceptions, properties or features of things and happenings outside me. What I detect tactually and kinaesthetically *may* be properties or features of external though contiguous things and events; but they may be and quite often are properties or features of anatomically internal things and events. I can detect, sometimes, the beating of my own heart, the distension of my own stomach, the straining or relaxing of my own muscles, the creaking of my own joints, and the fishbone in my own throat. A doctor, I imagine, learns to detect by feeling the congestion of his own lungs.

In this sense of 'feeling', feeling is a species of perception or perceptual discrimination. We have to learn to do it; we may be better or worse than other people at doing it. There is room for care and carelessness in doing it; and there is always the possibility of making mistakes. To be able to feel things, in this sense, is to have got a certain amount of a specific skill or family of skills, just as to be able to detect and discriminate things by seeing, hearing, tasting, and smelling is to have got a certain amount of a specific skill or family of skills. In all cases alike there can be trained or untrained observers. To detect or discriminate something, whether by sight or touch, is to achieve something, namely, to find something out by the exercise of an acquired and perhaps deliberately trained skill. This shows how enormously different is the sense of the verb 'feel' when used to denote detection by touch, from the sense of the verb 'feel' when used to denote the suffering of a pain or other discomfort.

But different though these two concepts of 'feeling' or 'sensation' are, still both are quite untechnical concepts. The child has learned to use both long before he has heard of any physiological, neurological or psychological theories.

So now we can ask whether it is true that all perceiving involves the having of sensations or the feeling of anything, in either of these senses. Well, to begin with, it is perfectly clear that usually when I see, hear, taste or smell anything, or detect something by touch, I do not suffer any discomfort or pain in my eyes, ears, tongue, nose or finger tips. Seeing a tree does not hurt my eyes; and hearing a bird singing does not set up the slightest sort of tickling-feeling in my ears. Sometimes, certainly, looking at things, like the headlights of motor cars, or listening to things, like the whistle of a railway-engine a few yards away, does hurt my eyes and ears. But not only is this exceptional, but still more important, these disagreeable sensations do not help, they hinder perception. I see much better when I am not being dazzled than when I am. Sensations, in this sense, are not usually present when perception occurs; and when they are present, they tend to impair perception. They are not *sine quâ nons* of perception.

But nor is it true that when I see, hear or smell things I feel anything with my eyes, ears and nose, in the sense of detecting something tactually or kinaesthetically. When I see a green tree, I do not concomitantly detect, with my eyes, the warmth or coldness, the smoothness or roughness, the vibrations or the resilience of anything. My eyes are very inferior organs with which to detect things tactually and kinaesthetically. My ears and nose are even worse. But whether they are good or bad, when I see things with my eyes, I do not therewith have to detect something else tactually or kinaesthetically with those eyes of mine and usually I do not; and similarly with my ears and nose. With my tongue the situation is slightly different. Usually when I taste things, I do also detect with my tongue the temperature and some of the tactually and kinaesthetically discoverable properties of the food or the drink in my mouth. But even this is a case of concomitance and not dependence. I can taste the taste of onions, when there is no longer anything in my mouth with a temperature of its own or with any shape or consistency of its own. In tasting, I often do in fact, but I do not in logic have also to feel anything with my tongue, in the sense of 'feel' in which I feel the roughness of the nutshell or the smoothness of the eggshell with my fingers or, sometimes, with my tongue. My tongue is, so to speak, a double sense-organ. I can both feel things with it and taste things with it. But I can feel the shape and surfaces of things like spoons without tasting anything; and I can taste, e.g. onions or pepper without feeling anything.

So when philosophers and psychologists assert that all perceiving involves the having of sensations or the feeling of something, either they are dead wrong, or else they are using a third, quite different notion of feeling or sensation. In particular, the notion of sensing or having sense-impressions which, they assert, is a component of the notion of perceiving, must be a notion quite different both from the notion of feelings like pains and tickles, and from the notion of tactual and kinaesthetic detection or discrimination.

But at this point there arises something of a crux. When a person has a pain we think that he must, in some sense of the word, be conscious or aware of the pain; and when a person detects or discriminates something by touch, his perceiving what he perceives must also be, in some sense of the word, conscious. A person cannot require to be told by someone else that he is in pain or that he has just perceived something. Well then, what of the sense impressions which, we are told, enter into perceiving? Are we conscious of them or do we have to be told of their existence by others, or, perhaps, infer to them ourselves in accordance with some more or less technical theory of optics or neurology or psychology? It is generally maintained that our sense-impressions are certainly and necessarily things that we are conscious of and cannot be unconscious of, as we cannot, with certain reservations, be unconscious of our pains and tickles and as we cannot see, hear or taste things unconsciously. Indeed it is apt to be maintained that if sense-impressions were things of which we were unconscious, then they could not do their proper business, namely, that of providing the basic *given* elements in seeing, hearing and the rest. Well then, are we conscious of having sense-impressions? Do people ever say, whether to themselves or to anyone else, 'I am having' or 'I have just had a sense-impression of such and such a description'? Or rather, since the actual term 'sense-impression' is obviously a somewhat technical, classificatory term, do people ever say, to themselves or others, 'I am having', or 'I have just had a so and so', where the concrete filling of the vacancy 'so and so' would be something which properly fell under the technical, classificatory term 'sense-impression'? Certainly people say that they see trees or have just heard some birds singing; but these verbs of perception carry too much luggage to be what is wanted. Certainly too, people sometimes say, more non-committally, 'I see something green', or 'I have just heard a twittering noise'. But these expressions also carry too much luggage. A person who said 'I see something green' might then learn that there was a tree in front of him, and say 'Then what I saw was a green tree, though I did not at the time know that the green thing I saw was a tree'. What is wanted, apparently, is some family of expressions, in constant and familiar use by everyone, in which they report, without inference or external information, the occurrence of a conscious experience unencumbered, as yet, with any beliefs or knowledge about the existence or properties of any external object.

Sometimes it is suggested that we do report such basic experiences in such utterances as 'I seem to smell onions' or 'I thought I heard birds singing' or 'It looks as if there is a green tree over there'. In reporting mere appearances, without committing ourselves to their veracity, we are, it is suggested, reporting the having of sense-impressions without the addition of any perceptual claims about the external world. But this will not do. We use such tentative, guarded or non-committal expressions in all sorts of fields or departments, in most of which there is no question of there being any appropriate sense-impressions to isolate. I can say, after a rapid piece of calculation in my head '15 × 16 appears to make 220'; I can say, after a cursory glance 'it looks as if the river here is about twice the width of the road in front of my house'; I can say 'She appeared to be half-angry and half-amused'; and I can say 'the period of general inflation seems to be coming to an end'.

Now all these are guarded statements of what I am tempted or inclined to judge to be the case, though I do not yet commit myself to their being the case. Yet no one supposes that in saying such things I am reporting the occurrence of any sense-impressions. Statements of the form 'it looks as if'—'there seems to be'—'Apparently, . . .' are not *ex officio* dedicated to the wanted reports of the experiences alleged to be basic ingredients in sense-perception. So we cannot, unless provided with some extra restrictions which are not in fact provided, adduce idioms of these patterns as being the untutored, uninferential deliverances of our consciousness of the postulated sense-impressions. We have, in fact, no special way of reporting the occurrence of these postulated impressions; we are, therefore, without the needed marks of our being conscious of such things at all. For there is surely something absurd in maintaining that we are constantly conscious of some things in the way in which we are conscious of pains, and yet have no way of telling ourselves or other people anything whatsoever about them.

We must acknowledge, therefore, that the view of some epistemologists and psychologists that there are sense-impressions is not arrived at at all in the way in which everyone comes to know that pains and tickles occur, or in the way in which everyone comes to know that we sometimes detect things by sight, hearing, taste, and touch. The view that sense-impressions occur is arrived at as a deduction from a theory, or perhaps from two or more seemingly interlocking theories.

I want to separate out two quite different theoretical allegiances which, in their different ways, drive people to postulate sense-impressions.

(1) If a child and a man are looking at the first word of the first line of a page, the man may say that he sees the word 'Edinburgh' misprinted, where the child may not detect the misprint but say only that he sees the word 'Edinburgh'. The child's eyesight is as good as the man's, but because he is worse at spelling, he fails to see the misprint that the man sees. If now an illiterate Esquimau looks at the same part of the page, though his eyesight is excellent, he will not see a word at all, but only some black marks.

Or if a countryman and a townsman, with equally good sight, are looking at the same field, the one may say that he sees a field of young wheat, while the other may say only that he sees a field of green stuff. In these and countless other such cases, the one observer claims to discern much more than the other, though admitting that their eyesight is equally good. It is natural and tempting to say that the observer whose eyes, somehow, tell him more is putting more into his report of what he sees or that he is giving to it a fuller 'interpretation' than the other can do. He has learned more spelling or more agriculture than the other, so he includes in his report of what he sees the extra information which his previous experience and education had equipped him with. His report of what he sees is inflated with knowledge or beliefs which the other man does not possess; in short it carries a mass of ideas or thoughts, which are absent from the other observer's report of what *he* sees. In detecting a misprint or a field of young wheat he seems, therefore, to be combining the piece of seeing, which, presumably, contains only what the townsman's seeing contains, with a piece of thinking, which the townsman is unable to supply. What is more, this extra thought-luggage may be right or wrong. The countryman may have misidentified the green crop.

Now there exists a view, which is accepted almost as an axiom, that all thinking, or anyhow all thinking which is intended to result in the discovery or establishment of truths, is inferring; and therewith that all errors and mistakes issue from fallacious reasoning. Accordingly, when philosophers and psychologists consider things like the detection of misprints or the identification of the green crop with young wheat, they automatically describe the thinking-element in this detection and identification with reasoning. The question at once arises Whence then do we get the initial premises of our perceptual conclusions? On this view, the premises must be ascertained at a level prior to any thinking, and prior therefore to any exploitation of knowledge or beliefs previously acquired. There must be a totally non-cogitative acceptance of some basic premises for us to be able to move from these initial data to our correct or incorrect perceptual conclusions about misprints or young wheat. It is, I think, with this idea in mind that many thinkers use the expression 'sense-data' for the postulated sense-impressions which must be there to inaugurate our perceptual inferrings. For 'datum' ordinarily has the force of 'evidence' or 'reasons'. A datum is something that we reason from and does not itself have to be reasoned to.

This reason for postulating the existence of sense-impressions seems to me a bad reason, and bad on two scores. First, if it is not true that all thinking is inferring, then it need not be true that the thinking which enters into perceptual recognition, identification, comparison, etc., is inferring, and if it is not, then the search for its fund of premises is a search for nothing. In multiplying we think out the answers to questions, but our results are not conclusions and our mistakes are not fallacies. This thinking does not start from any data or premises; and the same might be true of the thinking that is supposed to go on in perceptual recognition, identification, etc. But second, it seems to me false or at least highly misleading to say that a man who detects a misprint or a farmer who identifies the green crop with growing wheat is necessarily *thinking* at all.

For one thing, the misprint and the nature of the crop might be discerned at sight or in a flash. As soon as his eye falls on the misprinted word, the man might start to pencil in the correction. There might be no moment, however short, in which he could be described as pondering, reflecting or putting two and two together. He might say, quite truly, that he saw the misprint the moment his eye fell on the word, and that he did not have time to think or even that he did not need to think.

To meet this sort of objection, epistemologists and psychologists sometimes say that though he does not remember doing any thinking, and though the time available for thinking seemed to be wanting, still he must have thought, and so his thinking must have been done at lightning speed—and this might be the reason why he cannot remember doing any thinking afterwards. But we should mistrust these 'musts'. Why must he have done any pondering, considering or putting two and two together? All that the argument up to date has shown is that if he had not previously learned to spell, he could not now recognise misprints at sight. But why must the exploitation of knowledge previously acquired take the form of pondering? We ponder when things are not obvious to us. But when previous training results in things being obvious at sight, which would not have been obvious without that training, why should we have to postulate a present piece of pondering to explain the immediate obviousness of the misprint? Ordinarily we account for someone needing to stop to think by showing how something was, at the start, unobvious to him. But here, apparently, the fact that the misprint is immediately obvious to him is supposed to need to be explained not just by reference to his prior education, but also by the postulation of the performance by him of a piece of thinking, with the queer property of not requiring any time for its performance.

So I maintain not only that perceptual recognition, identification, etc., need not embody any inferential thinking, but that they need not embody any thinking at all. They involve the possession and exploitation of knowledge previously acquired. But this exploitation is not thinking. So the argument for the occurrence of sense-impressions to be the data or premises for the inferential thinking embodied is doubly broken-backed.

(2) There is another theoretical allegiance which helps to drive philosophers, psychologists, physiologists, and physicists into postulating the existence of sense-impressions. This is their natural and up to a point proper allegiance to causal theories of perception. We learn from optics and acoustics about the transmission of light and sound; we learn from physiology the structure of the eye and ear; we are learning from neurophysiology about the transmission of impulses along the nerve-fibres. When we ask what makes seeing and hearing possible, and what makes them impossible or inefficient, we derive our answers, quite properly, from the relevant stretches of these scientific theories.

We trace the propagation of light from a light-giving source to the surface of a light-reflecting object and thence to the lens and the retina of the human eye; we then trace the nervous impulses set up at the retina to the right place in the brain. Some further transformation may then be supposed, such that the terminal neural impulse sets up, somehow, a psychic or mental reaction, and thus seeing takes place—or rather, since seeing a misprint requires a special education and maybe also, as is often supposed, a special act of lightning-speed thinking, we should perhaps say that the last neural impulse sets up a mental reaction which is the necessary spur or stimulus to seeing, though seeing consists not only in this stimulus but also in some part of our immediate response to it. This sort of account of perception operates naturally with the notions of propagation, transmission, impulse, stimulus and response, rather than with the notions of *data,* premises, evidence, and conclusions. Sense-impressions are now thought of not as steps in a lightning-swift argument but as links in a causal chain. They are indeed often spoken of as 'given', but they are 'given', now, in the sense in which electric shocks are given, not in the sense in which Euclid's axioms are given, i.e. are the uninferred premisses for inferred consequences. 'Given' now means 'inflicted', not, as before, 'accepted without argument'. Sense-impressions are now thought of as things impressed on us, impulses transmitted through us, not as things found by us by some sort of precogitative finding.

Now there can be no quarrelling with this sort of account, whether we are thinking of the stages covered by optics and acoustics, or whether we are thinking of the stages covered by physiology and neurophysiology. The final stage, covering a supposed jump from neural impulses in the body to mental experiences, or sense-impressions is, however, quite a different matter. It presupposes the Cartesian, body-mind view which I have found fault with at some length in my book. But, apart from this general objection, there remains the specific objection, that the existence of these sense-impressions is something postulated; they are not things which anyone reports who has not been convinced by the whole story of the chain of physical, neural and psychic impulses. Even if the Cartesian view were true, yet still we should be without the Cartesian grounds for asserting the existence of sense-impressions which we possess for pains and tickles.

What has gone wrong? It seems to me that this is what has gone wrong. The perfectly proper and necessary research into the physics of light and sound, and into the physiology of seeing and hearing came to be misrepresented as an enquiry which when completed would 'explain' seeing and hearing—explain it, that is to say, in the sense of 'explain' in which an earthquake is explained by seismological theory or diabetes is explained by a certain branch of pathology. The idea, then, is that what we need to know about seeing and hearing is the various physical and physiological conditions from modifications in which we could infer to the cessation or alteration of our seeing and hearing; in short, that our questions about perception are merely causal questions.

Now of course we have causal questions to ask about perception, and the sciences of optics and acoustics, ophthalmology and neurology have either already provided us with the answers to these causal questions, or can confidently be expected to provide them in the fairly near future. But not all our questions about perception are causal questions; and the proffering of causal answers to non-causal questions leads to inevitable dissatisfaction, which cannot be relieved by promises of yet more advanced causal answers still to be discovered.

Perceiving, as I have pointed out earlier, is exercising an acquired skill; or rather it embodies the exercise of an acquired skill. Seeing a misprint is an impossibility for someone who has not learned to spell. Now about the exercises of any acquired skills there are, of course, causal questions to be asked. If a tight-rope walker succeeds in walking along the stretched wire, we can, of course, ask and fairly easily find out the answers to all sorts of causal questions about his performance—mechanical questions about his equilibrium, physiological questions about his muscles and nerves, and pedagogic questions about the training he had received, and so on. But quite different from these causal questions are technical questions, questions, that is, about the nature of the task of tight-rope walking, about the various kinds of mistakes that are to be avoided, and the various kinds of attentiveness, courage and ingenuity which make for success—all the things which the tight-rope walker must either have been taught by his trainers or found out for himself. Lessons of this sort need not include much, if any, of the information which might be provided by the physicist, the physiologist or the psychologist. Nor does the chess player need to know anything about the physiology of his muscular system, despite the fact that he could not be good or even bad at chess if he could not move his fingers and hands where he wished.

In the same sort of way, I am arguing that some questions about perceiving, and particularly those which are of interest in epistemology, are not causal questions—though there are such questions, and many of them have been answered—but questions about, so to speak, the *crafts* or *arts* of finding things out by seeing and hearing—including questions about the nature of mistakes and failures in perception and their relations with mistakes and failures in thinking, spelling, counting, and the like.

It is not that hearing and smelling are queer happenings which are exempt from causal conditions, but that not all questions about hearing and smelling are questions about these causal conditions. Checkmating an opponent at chess is certainly a happening, and a happening conditioned by all sorts of known and unknown causes. But the chessplayer's interest is not in these causes, but in the tactics or strategy or sometimes just the luck of which the checkmating was the outcome. It is not the dull physical fact of the arrival of the Queen at a particular square, it is the fact that this arrival constituted the success or victory of the player, which is what is significant for the players and spectators of the game. Similarly, finding out something by seeing or hearing is, so to speak, a success or victory in the game of exploring the world. This seeing or hearing is of course susceptible of a complete and very complex causal explanation, given in terms of optics or acoustics, physiology, neurology and the rest; but the player's interest is not primarily in the contents of this explanation, but in the exploratory task itself and its accomplishment.

In other words, verbs like 'see' and 'hear' do not merely denote special experiences or mental happenings, with special causal antecedents; they denote achievements of tasks, or successes in undertakings. There are questions of technique to be asked about them as well as questions of causal conditioning, and questions of technique are not answerable by any multiplication of answers to questions of causal conditioning; they are questions of quite different types.

So I want to suggest that the postulation of sense-impressions as causal antecedent of seeing and hearing, only an antecedent not of a physical or physiological, but of a psychological kind arose from two sources, (1) a proper realisation of the fact that physical and physiological causal accounts of perception cannot answer technical questions about perceptual successes and failures; (2) an improper, non-realisation of the fact that what was lacking to such causal accounts was not that they needed an extra, psychological link in the causal chain; but that they were answers to causal questions and not to questions of technique. When we want to describe the differences between hearing, mishearing, and non-hearing, no discovery or postulation of causal links can give us what we want. Sense-impressions were postulated as the missing causal links which would solve a problem which was not a causal problem.

However, after all this has been said, I confess to a residual embarrassment. There is something in common between having an after-image and seeing a misprint. Both are visual affairs. How ought we to describe their affinity with one another, without falling back on to some account very much like a part of the orthodox theories of sense-impressions? To this I am stumped for an answer.

SENSE-DATA AND THE PERCEPT THEORY

Roderick Firth

During the past fifty or sixty years the traditional concept of sense-datum, which has been referred to, frequently because of epistemological or ontological considerations, by many other names ("impression", "idea", "quale", "image", "sensum", "phenomenon", etc.) has been subjected to a type of phenomenological criticism which seems to threaten the foundations of a number of contemporary philosophical systems. Considering the fact that this criticism has been ably developed, and formulated by such distinguished men as William James, Edmund Husserl, John Dewey, and the leading psychologists of the Gestalt School, it is rather surprising to discover how much of the current literature on epistemological problems is entirely unaffected by it. Such lack of concern with vital phenomenological issues may be merely a reflexion of ignorance on the part of epistemologists, but it is probably better construed as a manifestation of the widespread belief that epistemological problems, if they are truly epistemological, not only *can* but *should* be stated and solved in abstraction from all issues which might be classified as "psychological".

Although this lack of interest in the phenomenology of perception seems to be quite widespread among philosophers, there is a small but respectable group of epistemologists who have taken a very different stand. They have maintained, in effect, that the traditional epistemological and ontological distinctions between sense-data and physical objects have been so completely annihilated by the criticism of James, Husserl, Dewey, the Gestalt Psychologists, and others, that most of the epistemology of the last three centuries is now entirely outdated. Some of them have asserted, as I shall show later, that it is no longer possible even to believe that there *are* any sense-data in the traditional meaning of the term; others have said, perhaps more conservatively, that although sense-data do indeed *exist*, it is no longer possible to distinguish their epistemological status from that of physical objects. Despite such important differences of opinion concerning the precise implications of the new phenomenology of perception, however, epistemologists who belong to this second school of thought are in complete agreement that these implications (whatever they may be) are of revolutionary importance for theory of knowledge.

It may be presumptuous to attempt to reconcile two schools of thought which have existed side by side for so many years and which have so long resisted the various forces which might have been expected to increase mutual understanding and appreciation. But the attempt is surely worth the effort, and there are grounds for believing that the differences are to a large extent the result of terminological confusions. On the one hand the critics of the traditional concept of sense-datum have frequently expressed themselves in an esoteric vocabulary which is either quite misleading or quite incomprehensible to the epistemologists. Many of the latter, on the other hand, firmly convinced that the traditional phenomenology of perception is completely adequate for the formulation and solution of philosophical problems, have not taken the trouble to seek for truth in statements of their critics which they correctly recognise to be either meaningless or absurd when interpreted in terms of the traditional vocabulary of epistemology.

In view of the nature of these obstacles to mutual understanding, I shall undertake two tasks in this paper. I shall attempt in the first part to state as clearly as possible the phenomenological theory of perception which has served as a basis for most of the recent criticism of the traditional concept of sense-datum. I shall refer to this theory as the "Percept Theory of Perception" to distinguish it from the traditional "Sense-datum Theory", and I shall limit my description of it to what I take to be the bare essentials that distinguish it from the Sense-datum Theory. To overcome the linguistic obstacles I shall make an effort to describe the Percept Theory in terms of the concepts and vocabularies of contemporary epistemologists who do *not* accept it, and I shall similarly illustrate the theory, when possible, by examples drawn from the writings of these same epistemologists. I shall then attempt, in the second part of this paper, to evaluate the claims of some of the philosophers who believe that the Percept Theory is of revolutionary importance for epistemology.[1]

PART I

THE PHENOMENOLOGICAL BASIS
OF THE PERCEPT THEORY

1. THE NATURE OF SENSE-DATA

(a) *The Definition of "Sense-Datum"*

To understand the position of those who reject the Sense-datum Theory in favour of the Percept Theory, it is necessary to consider, at least briefly, the manner in which the term "sense-datum" is customarily defined. It must be recognised, first of all, that in order to define this term philosophers have always found it necessary to refer to a certain kind of *perception* or *awareness*. Sometimes, for example, sense-data are defined as the objects of *direct* perception or of *immediate* perception. Thus at the outset of Berkeley's *Three Dialogues*, Philonous defines what he

---

[1] Much of Part I and several sections of Part II are based upon the author's doctoral dissertation, Harvard University Library.

calls "sensible things" as "those only which are immediately perceived by sense".[2] Broad defines sensa as objects of which we are "directly aware" in a "perceptual situation".[3] Price defines sense-data as those things "directly present to consciousness" in perception.[4] And Moore defines sense-data as the objects of "direct apprehension", citing as an example of such apprehension the having of an after-image.[5] If, however, a philosopher wishes to speak without contradiction of *unsensed* sense-data, he may define sense-data as entities which *could be* directly or immediately observed. And if he wants to distinguish between a sense-datum and sense-*field,* he may define sense-data as the distinguishable *parts* of whatever could be observed in this manner. But in any case he makes some reference to a particular kind of observation or awareness, which he usually describes as "direct" or "immediate".

This does not mean, of course, that sense-data cannot be defined without using the *word* "observation" or the *word* "awareness"; in fact some philosophers are content to define sense-data as entities which are (or could be) *sensed,* or even as entities *given* to sense, and these definitions are merely verbal analyses of the term "sense-datum". The important point is simply that sense-data are defined not by an enumeration of their *kinds* but rather by reference to the manner in which we become *conscious* of them. We do not say that sense-data are patches of colour, rough things and smooth things, hot things and cold things, etc., for we could never be sure of exhausting the denotation of "sense-datum" in this way. Moreover, according to some theories, the surfaces of *physical objects* can likewise be described as "patches of colour", "rough", "smooth", etc., and the question whether or not

[2] Berkeley, *Three Dialogues,* in *Works,* Oxford, 1891, Vol. I, p. 381.

[3] C. D. Broad, *Scientific Thought,* p. 239, Kegan Paul, London, 1923 [p. 89, this volume. Ed.].

[4] H. H. Price, *Perception,* p. 3, McBride, New York, 1933.

[5] G. E. Moore, *Philosophical Studies,* p. 173 *et seq.*, Harcourt Brace, New York, 1922, and "A Reply to My Critics", *The Philosophy of G. E. Moore,* p. 629, Northwestern U. Press, Chicago, 1942.

some sense-data *are* surfaces of physical objects should not be prejudiced or confused by our definitions. Sense-data must be defined, therefore, by reference to the manner in which we become conscious of them: they are what we feel, sense, intuit, or immediately observe, or they are what is given to us, or what we are directly aware of, in perception. And once we understand the meaning of "sense-data" as so defined, we can presumably decide to some extent by empirical observation just what *kinds* of entities are properly called "sense-data".

(b) The Denotation of "Sense-Datum"

Nevertheless—and here we come to a matter of the greatest importance in understanding and evaluating criticisms of the Sense-datum Theory—philosophers have always found it impossible to explain the meaning of such terms as "direct awareness" and "immediate perception" without mentioning at least a few examples of the *objects* of such awareness or perception, namely, sense-data. This fact has been noticed and emphasised by Ayer and Moore. In *The Foundations of Empirical Knowledge,* Ayer points out that the terms "direct awareness" and "sense-datum" are *correlative* and that "since each of them is being used in a special, technical sense, it is not satisfactory merely to define one in terms of the other". "In order to show how one or the other of them is to be understood", therefore, it is necessary to use some other method of definition, "such as the method of giving examples".[6] Moore makes the same point. That special sense of the word "see", he says, "which is the visual variety of what Berkeley called 'direct perception' . . . can only be explained by giving examples of cases where 'see' is used in that sense".[7] It follows, therefore, that in order to understand what philosophers mean by the term "sense-datum", we must supplement our analysis of whatever explicit statements they

[6] A. J. Ayer, *The Foundations of Empirical Knowledge,* p. 61, Macmillan, New York, 1940.
[7] "A Reply to My Critics", in *Philosophy of G. E. Moore,* p. 628.

may have made on the subject, by a careful examination of the examples which they have given.

Now such an examination of the examples which contemporary philosophers have given to illustrate the meaning of the words "sense-datum" and "direct awareness", will make it quite clear that all of them who are using these words in anything like the traditional way, are in agreement on two important points. They agree, in the first place, that the sense-data directly observable by any *one* sense are quite limited in their qualities. With respect to visual perception, for example, they agree with Berkeley that it is false to say that "we immediately perceive by sight anything beside light, and colours, and figures".[8] Thus our sense-datum when we look at a dog, according to Russell, is "a canoid patch of colour".[9] And when we look at a penny stamp, according to Broad, our sensum is "a red patch of approximately square shape".[10] And when we look at an apple, according to Lewis, what is given is a "round, ruddy . . . somewhat".[11] And when we look at a tomato, according to Price, our sense-datum is "a red patch of a round and somewhat bulgy shape".[12] Thus it seems to be agreed by all these philosophers that when we gaze, for example, from a warm room at a distant, snow-capped mountain, our awareness of whiteness may properly be described as "direct", whereas our awareness of coldness may not. One of our sense-data is a white patch, shaped like a mountain peak, but our sensation of temperature, if we are aware of any at all, is one of warmth rather than coldness. In colloquial English, to be sure, we might say that the mountain "looks cold" or "appears

[8] *Principles*, in *Works*, vol. I, p. 282.

[9] Bertrand Russell, *Inquiry into Meaning and Truth*, p. 174, Norton, New York, 1940. Quine has pointed out that Russell's word "canoid" means not "dog-shaped" but "basket-shaped". (Review of Russell's *Inquiry into Meaning and Truth*, p. 30, *Journal of Symbolic Logic*, Vol. VI, no. 1.)

[10] *Scientific Thought*, p. 119.

[11] C. I. Lewis, *Mind and the World-Order*, p. 119, Scribners, New York, 1929.

[12] *Perception*, p. 3. We may overlook for the moment the disagreement among these philosophers concerning the number of spatial dimensions possessed by visual sense-data.

cold", just as we might say that it "looks white" or "appears white"; but such language is generally supposed to be unsatisfactory for theory of knowledge because it obscures the fact that the manner in which we are conscious of whiteness in such a case is very different from the manner in which we are conscious of coldness. The distinction in question is the very one that has traditionally been drawn by the use of such pairs of words as "impression" and "idea", "sensation" and "perception", "the given" and "the conceptual", "sense-datum" and "image", etc., and philosophers who use the term "direct awareness" in the traditional way must agree, therefore, that the sense-data directly observable by any one sense are quite limited in their qualities.

In the second place, all philosophers who use the term "direct awareness" in the traditional way will agree on a still more important point, *viz,* that we are never directly aware of physical objects. It may seem, on first thought, that philosophers who accept the theory of perception called "direct realism", or some other more or less sophisticated variation of naïve realism, are exceptions to this rule. Closer examination of their positions will probably show, however, that what these philosophers actually maintain is that some visual and tactual sense-data—though not, of course, data of the other senses—are literally the *surfaces* of physical objects. But these "surfaces", it should be noted, are not themselves physical objects: they are *surfaces,* and differ from physical objects in that they do not occupy a volume of space. And since these direct realists admit that it is only the *surfaces* of physical objects which we can perceive directly (*i.e.,* that our sense-data are surfaces and not physical objects) we may conclude that their theory is not distinguished by any special propositions concerning the psychology of perception.

To emphasize the fact that physical objects are not accessible to direct observation, it has long been customary among philosophers and psychologists to reserve the verb "to perceive" for those cases in which the observation in question is *not* direct. According to this convention, which

I shall adopt, the observing of physical objects is called "perceiving". Thus this second point of agreement among philosophers who use the correlative terms "sense-datum" and "direct awareness" in their traditional meanings, may be stated as follows: Physical objects are *perceived* but they are never the objects of *direct awareness*.

(c) Criticism of the Traditional Concept

Now in view of the necessity for defining the term "sense-datum" by the method of giving examples, it is clear that not only the truth but the very *meaningfulness* of the traditional Sense-datum Theory depends on the possibility of making the distinctions involved in these two points of agreement just formulated. Yet it is precisely these distinctions which have been denied by philosophers who accept the Percept Theory. They have sometimes developed their criticism in a rather haphazard manner, but I believe that their rejection of the Sense-datum Theory has always been based on objections to one or both of these two points of agreement.

The first objection consists in denying that there is any discoverable kind of observation or awareness which is present in every perception, and which takes as its objects *only* the kinds of things which have traditionally been offered as examples of sense-data. And this is not a trivial objection, for most advocates of the Percept Theory would go so far as to say that the experience of a man looking at a distant mountain from a warm room might comprise both whiteness and coldness, each in precisely the same manner, and neither in any other manner—a statement which, as I have pointed out, has been either explicitly or implicitly denied by all philosophers who use the term "sense-datum" in its traditional meaning.

The second objection to the Sense-datum Theory is one which is not entailed by the first but which many psychologists and philosophers regard as an essential part of the Percept Theory. This objection consists in maintaining that in fact *physical objects themselves* are observed as directly as patches of colour, odours, tastes, and other so-called "sense-data". The direct and immediate experience of anyone who looks at the world about him, according to this interpretation of the Percept Theory, always consists of a number of full-bodied *physical objects*. And this, of course, is flatly to deny the distinction between perception and direct awareness which is essential to the Sense-datum Theory.

Now even the first of these two objections, if valid, is sufficient to necessitate a reformulation of most of the epistemological theories in the history of modern philosophy. Just how radical that reformulation would have to be, is a question which I shall discuss later. But the second objection to the Sense-datum Theory has implications which are even more serious, especially for those theories which maintain that physical objects are all, in some more or less literal sense, "composed of" sense-data (or of possible sense-data). Not only Berkeley and other subjectivists, but many more modern philosophers including Bergson, James, Russell, the new realists, and many of the pragmatists and logical positivists, have supported the view that physical objects are knowable just because they are reducible to objects of direct awareness. But if sense-data are defined as the objects of direct awareness, and if, as some advocates of the Percept Theory have maintained, the objects of direct awareness may be *physical* objects, then physical objects are merely a subclass of sense-data. And the theory that physical objects are in some sense "composed of" sense-data is either false or tautological, of course, if it is understood that physical objects are *themselves* sense-data.

In recent years, moreover, the view that physical objects can be observed as directly as the entities which have traditionally been called "sense-data", has been used by a number of philosophers as a basis for criticizing one or more of these very epistemological positions. Wild, for example, has maintained in an article entitled "The Concept of the Given in Contemporary Philosophy", that what is actually given in perception is a "world of things".

He quotes with approval a statement of Lewis that "it is indeed the thick experience of the world of things . . . which constitutes the datum for philosophical reflexion", that "we do not see patches of colour, but trees and houses; we hear not indescribable sounds, but voices and violins". But then he goes on to criticize Lewis for abandoning this "classic view of the given" for the more restricted one of Berkeley and other modern empiricists. Modern empiricism, Wild asserts, "abandons the aim of classic philosophy to describe the *thick* experience of the world of things *as it is given*. Instead of this, it singles out a certain portion of the given as peculiarly accessible or *given* in some special sense".[13]

Reichenbach, in his *Experience and Prediction,* has also declared that physical objects are immediately given in perception and has used this as an argument against positivistic theories of "reduction". Reichenbach's position, however, is much more extreme than Wild's. According to Wild, those things that are called "sense-data" by modern epistemologists are *part* of what is given; what he objects to is the view that "the immediately given alone is given". According to Reichenbach, however, such sense-data (which he calls "impressions") are not given *at all*. "What I observe", he says, "are things, not impressions. I see tables, and houses, and thermometers, and trees, and men, and the sun, and many other things in the sphere of crude physical objects; but I have never seen my impressions of these things".[14]

Many statements of this kind have appeared in philosophical literature in recent years, and in most cases they appear to be based on the Percept Theory. The central

[13] John Wild, *Philosophy and Phenomenological Research,* pp. 70–71, September, 1940.

[14] Hans Reichenbach, *Experience and Prediction,* p. 164, U. of Chicago Press, Chicago, 1938. It is interesting to observe that in *The Unity of Science,* Kegan Paul, London, 1934, pp. 45–48, Carnap himself had questioned what Reichenbach calls the "positivistic dogma" that impressions are given. There is a view, Carnap said, that "material things are elements of the given", and although "it is not often held to-day, it is . . . more plausible than it appears and deserves more detailed investigation".

thesis of this theory now seems to be accepted by most psychologists who are interested in the phenomenology of perception, although there are, as we shall see, differences of opinion concerning the implications of the theory. The central thesis was stated by William James in his *Principles of Psychology* as concisely, I believe, as it has ever been stated. A perception, he said, "is one state of mind or nothing"; *it does not contain a sensation.*

> "We certainly ought not to say what is usually said by psychologists, and treat the perception as a sum of distinct psychic entities, the present sensation namely, *plus* a lot of images from the past, all 'integrated' together in a way impossible to describe. *The perception is one state of mind or nothing.*"[15]

We may look at a physical object in such a way, James admitted, that what we apprehend approaches "sensational nudity"; thus by turning a painting upside down, or looking at it with a purely æsthetic attitude, "we lose much of its meaning, but, to compensate for the loss, we feel more freshly the value of the mere tints and shadings, and become aware of the lack of purely sensible harmony or balance that it may show".[16] Nevertheless, the fact remains that sensations do not occur as *constituents* of perceptions, but at most only as complete and independent states of mind.

2. The Sense-datum Theory

This description of perceptual consciousness differs sharply, of course, from the traditional Sense-datum Theory, which is based on a supposed distinction between *two* constituents of perceptual consciousness: (1) direct awareness of a sense-datum and (2) mediated "perception" of a physical object. There are, however, two versions of

[15] William James, *The Principles of Psychology*, Vol. II, p. 80, Holt, New York, 1896. Italics mine except for *"plus"*.
[16] *Ibid.*, Vol. II, p. 81.

the Sense-datum Theory itself which must be distinguished in order to understand precisely what is asserted and denied by the Percept Theory: I shall refer to these two versions as the "Discursive Inference Theory" and the "Sensory Core Theory".

(a) The Discursive Inference Theory

The Discursive Inference Theory is most easily illustrated by turning to some of the great epistemological works of the British empirical school. In the *Essay concerning Human Understanding,* for example, Locke seems to maintain that perception is a discursive process which begins with awareness of a sense-datum and ends with the "idea" of a physical object. According to this analysis the perception of a physical object always involves a sensation and a *subsequent* act of judgement; every perception, therefore, includes awareness of a sense-datum as a *temporally distinct* act or state of consciousness. When we look at an alabaster globe, for example, the idea thereby imprinted on our mind is that of a flat circle. But knowing from experience that the cause of this appearance is a convex body, "judgment frames to itself the perception of a convex figure".[17] Locke admits that the transition from sense-datum to judgement "in many cases by a settled habit . . . is performed so constantly and so quick that we take that for the perception of our sensation which is an idea formed by our judgment; so that the one, *viz.* that of sensation, serves only to excite the other and is scarce taken notice of itself".[18] But he does not doubt that both the sensation and the idea of judgement always occur when we perceive a physical object and that they always occur *one after the other.*

Berkeley's analysis of perception in his *New Theory of Vision* is almost identical with Locke's. Perception is described as a process of discursive inference in which a

[17] John Locke, *An Essay Concerning Human Understanding,* Vol. I, pp. 185–186, Oxford, 1894.
[18] *Ibid.,* p. 186.

sensation "suggests" a physical object to the observer. The mind no sooner perceives a sensation, Berkeley says, ". . . but it withal perceives the different idea of distance which was wont to be connected with that sensation". Thus, "having of a long time experienced certain ideas perceivable by touch . . . to have been connected with certain ideas of sight, I do, upon perceiving these ideas of sight, forthwith conclude what tangible ideas are like to follow".[19] Berkeley recognises that there are times when "we find it difficult to discriminate between the immediate and mediate objects of sight. . . . They are, as it were, most closely twisted, blended, and incorporated together".[20] But he does not seem to doubt that in every act of perception there are really two successive events: the occurrence of a sense-datum and the occurrence of an idea which it suggests. Like Locke, in short, he maintains the Discursive Inference Theory, although frankly admitting that the successive components of perception may sometimes be hard to distinguish.

(b) The Sensory Core Theory

Almost all contemporary epistemologists who accept the Sense-datum Theory, however, have rejected the discursive inference version in favour of the Sensory Core Theory. Whereas Locke and Berkeley found it merely *difficult* to distinguish a temporally distinct state of direct awareness in every perception, most contemporary psychologists and epistemologists have found it quite *impossible*. In fact many of them have concluded that perceptual consciousness is *never* a discursive process involving a preliminary state of direct awareness. An observer might report, to be sure, that on a certain occasion he was aware of a mere noise and then subsequently judged it to be an air-raid warning; but his report would probably be more accurate if he said that he first heard (in the sense of "perceived") a siren or "some sort of whistle" and then sub-

[19] *New Theory of Vision*, in *Works*, Vol. I, p. 148.
[20] *Ibid.*, p. 151.

sequently refined his judgement. The fact that a series of perceptions may become increasingly refined or determinate, in short, does not constitute proof of the existence of separate states of direct awareness. "If the content of perception is first given and then, in a later moment interpreted", says Lewis, "we have no consciousness of such a first state of intuition unqualified by thought, though we *do* observe alteration and extension of interpretation of a given content as a psychological temporal process".[21]

The many philosophers who support the Sensory Core Theory, therefore, do so because they believe that direct awareness of a sense-datum is a constituent of perceptual consciousness even though perceptual consciousness is not a discursive process. They believe that perceptual consciousness is a twofold state consisting of (1) direct awareness of a sense-datum and (2) an element of interpretation (variously described as "belief", "acceptance", "expectation", "judgement", etc.) and they believe that these two parts exist *simultaneously*. In perceiving an apple, for example, the sense-datum—perhaps a round, red patch—is *one part* of what is before our minds; the element of interpretation which distinguishes the perception of an apple from the perception of a tomato, is the *other*. The distinctive feature of this theory, in short, is that it regards awareness of a sense-datum as literally a *part* of perceptual consciousness, but not as a part temporally distinct.

I have called this theory of perception the "Sensory Core Theory" because it asserts that there is, in some more or less literal sense, a core of sense-data in every perception. Psychologists of the Titchenerian School are sometimes said to have believed quite literally that sense-data form a core or nucleus within every perception,[22] but it is possible to accept the Sensory Core Theory, as I have defined it,

[21] *Mind and the World-Order*, p. 66.

[22] "A typical perception", Titchener said, "resolves to begin with into a number of sensations . . .—the part that we may conveniently call its core or nucleus". Around this nucleus, is the context which carries the meaning, "the fringe of related processes that gathers about the central group of sensations or images". (*A Beginner's Psychology*, pp. 114, 118, Macmillan, New York, 1922.)

without committing oneself to any such topographical analysis as Titchener's. Thus Price nowhere suggests that perceptual consciousness is strictly a nucleus of sensation surrounded by a fringe of images, but he does explicitly endorse the Sensory Core Theory. Perception involves no inference, he says, nor any discursive process whatsoever: "The two states of mind, the acquaintance with a sense-datum and the perceptual consciousness [of the object] just *arise together*."[23] Broad also accepts the Sensory Core Theory, for with certain important qualifications concerning the nature of perceptual belief, Broad is willing to say that "in a perceptual situation we are acquainted with an objective constituent which sensuously manifests certain qualities, and that this acquaintance gives rise to and *is accompanied by* a belief that the constituent is part of a larger spatio-temporal whole of a specific kind".[24] Lewis has also endorsed the Sensory Core Theory by emphasising the fact that awareness of a sense-datum does not precede but *accompanies* the other constituent of perception. "Immediate awareness", he says, "is an element *in* knowledge rather than a state of mind occurring by itself or preceding conceptual interpretation".[25] All these philosophers, and indeed the vast majority of contemporary epistemologists, believe that sense-data are distinguishable constituents of perception, and this, of course, is the view that is specifically rejected by James and other advocates of the Percept Theory.

It must be clearly understood that both the Percept Theory and the Sensory Core Theory are theories about the nature of ordinary *perceptual* states—states in which we are in some sense "conscious" of physical objects. Neither of these theories implies anything whatsoever concerning the existence of *pure* states of direct awareness—states in which we are directly aware of sense-data but *not* conscious of physical objects in the manner characteristic of ordinary

[23] *Perception*, p. 151. Italics mine.
[24] C. D. Broad, *The Mind and Its Place in Nature*, p. 153, Harcourt Brace, New York, 1929. Italics mine.
[25] *Mind and the World-Order*, p. 276.

perception. Contemporary philosophers seem to disagree about the frequency and even the possibility of such non-perceptual sensory states, but their opinions on this subject seem to be independent of their conclusions concerning the validity of the Percept Theory and the Sensory Core Theory. Lewis calls such states "states of pure esthesis", and doubts whether there are any. James says that "pure sensations", which he defines as the objects of direct acquaintance, "can only be realised in the earliest days of life. They are all but impossible to adults with memories and stores of association acquired."[26] Price believes that it is possible on rare occasions only, "in a moment of intense intellectual preoccupation", to "pass over into the state of pure sensing, where there is not even the vaguest and most inattentive acceptance of anything material at all".[27] Other philosophers, and many psychologists, however, seem to believe that pure states of sense-datum awareness are more easily obtainable, and have even said that they *must* be obtained for certain psychological and epistemological purposes.[28] Since the disagreements may be partly verbal, and since the issue is in any case not strictly relevant to an analysis of ordinary perceptual consciousness, I shall henceforth speak as though it were agreed that pure states of direct awareness *are* obtainable, but with the understanding that "pure" may be interpreted to mean "approximately pure".

3. THE PERCEPT THEORY

(a) *The Unity of Perceptual Consciousness*

The thesis that ordinary perception is, as James puts it, "one state of mind or nothing", has been systematically defended by advocates of the Percept Theory. They have tried to show that perceptual consciousness is not a two-

---

[26] *The Principles of Psychology,* Vol. II, p. 7.
[27] *Perception,* p. 165.
[28] This point is discussed more fully in Part II of this paper.

fold state by proving that all those things which are in *any* way present to consciousness in perception are present in exactly the *same* way. Or, to describe their method more precisely, they have tried to show that it is impossible to discover within perception the two types of consciousness which are essential not only for the truth but for the very meaningfulness of the Sense-datum Theory. The Gestalt psychologists, in particular, deserve credit for the patient and methodical manner in which they have presented evidence against this distinction; they have begun by showing how artificial it is and have ended by presenting arguments to destroy it completely.

The Sense-datum Theory has been made particularly vulnerable to such criticism by a shift of opinion among its supporters concerning a certain phenomenological question —the question namely, whether or not we are ever directly aware of *depth* in visual perception. There are still a few contemporary epistemologists who seem to believe, along with Locke and Berkeley, that depth is a conceptual or interpretational element in visual perception; they regularly speak of visual sense-data as "patches" of colour and describe their shapes in the language of plane geometry. But among contemporary psychologists who are investigating perceptual phenomena, there seems to be general agreement that there is no phenomenological justification for making this traditional distinction between visual depth and the other two spatial dimensions. And Price, an epistemologist whose analysis of perceptual consciousness is extremely acute, says specifically that our sense-datum when we look at a tomato has "a certain visual depth".[29]

From the point of view of those who defend the Percept Theory, the important fact about this shift of opinion within the older school of thought is not the manner in which the area of direct awareness is now delimited within perceptual consciousness. The important fact is that this shift of opinion represents a first step towards the recognition that in perception we are conscious of *many* qualities and relations which do not differ in their phenomenological status

[29] *Perception*, p. 3.

from those few which have traditionally been attributed to sense-data. Thus it is but one small step, as the Gestalt psychologists have shown, to the recognition that such qualities as simplicity, regularity, harmoniousness, clumsiness, gracefulness, and all the innumerable so-called "shape-qualities" can also have the same phenomenological status as colour and shape.[30] And it is but one small additional step from this to the recognition that the same holds true of qualities fittingly described by such adjectives as "reptilian", "feline", "ethereal", "substantial", and perhaps most of the adjectives in the dictionary. And this, of course, finally forces the admission that the qualities belonging to objects of direct awareness cannot be thought of as limited, in the manner traditionally assumed, by the use of one or another particular organ of sense. For it may sometimes, indeed, be quite correct to say that the experience of a man looking at a distant mountain from a warm room comprises both whiteness and coldness, each in precisely the same manner, and neither in any other manner.

John Dewey has discussed some of these phenomenological facts in his *Art as Experience* and has pointed out that they do not clash in any way with our knowledge of physiology. The organic processes which condition perceptual experience are not limited to processes in a particular sense-organ; the eye or the ear, as Dewey puts it, is "only the channel *through* which the total response takes place". Hence it should not be very surprising to discover that the so-called "visual qualities" do not always occupy a unique or central place in visual perception. "When we perceive, by means of the eyes as causal aids, the liquidity of water, the coldness of ice, the solidity of rocks, the bareness of trees in winter, it is certain that other qualities than those of the eye are conspicuous and controlling in perception. And it is as certain as anything can be that optical qualities do not stand by themselves with tactual and emotive qualities clinging to their skirts."[31]

[30] See W. Köhler, *Gestalt Psychology*, ch. vi, Liveright, New York, 1929.

[31] John Dewey, *Art as Experience*, pp. 122–124, Minton Balch, New York, 1934.

Dewey's primary objective in the discussion from which these sentences are quoted is to refute what I have called the *first* point of agreement among philosophers and psychologists who accept the Sense-datum Theory; his primary objective, in other words, is to show that we cannot find within ordinary perceptual consciousness a limited set of qualities having the unique phenomenological status which has been thought to distinguish the objects of direct awareness. But Dewey's description of perceptual experience also contains an implicit criticism of the *second* point of agreement among those who accept the Sense-datum Theory, and thus serves as an introduction to the final, and perhaps most important step, in the development of the Percept Theory.

(b) The Consciousness of Ostensible Physical Objects

The final step in the development of the Percept Theory consists in showing that the qualities of which we are conscious in perception are almost always presented to us, in some obvious sense, as the qualities *of physical objects*.[82] We are not conscious of liquidity, coldness, and solidity, but of the liquidity of water, the coldness of ice, and the solidity of rocks. Dewey has pointed out this phenomenological fact more explicitly in a number of other places by insisting that ordinary perceptual experience is the experience of physical nature. In *Experience and Nature,* for example, he says: "It is not experience which is experienced, but nature—stones, plants, animals, diseases, health, temperature, electricity, and so on. Things interacting in certain ways *are* experience: they are what is experienced."[33] Other philosophers and psychologists have preferred to express this fact in somewhat different terms; it is quite common, for example, to find them asserting that what is presented in perception is a "substantial whole", or a "whole physical object". Whatever the manner of expres-

---

[82] The word "physical" is not used here, of course, in any technical sense which would limit physical objects to entities like electrons and protons which constitute the special subject-matter of physics.

[33] P. 42, W. W. Norton, N.Y., 1935.

sion, however, the phenomenological fact is simply that in perception we are *conscious,* in one sense of the word, of physical objects, without at the same time being conscious, in another sense of the word, of the entities which have traditionally been called "sense-data". Perception, in short, is not a twofold state; and since we *are* conscious of physical objects we cannot possibly be conscious of sense-data in the distinctive manner required by the Sense-datum Theory.

It must not be inferred, however, that James and others who deny that perception is a twofold state would not admit that there are certain types of disposition of the perceiving organism, or possibly even certain types of conscious experience, which invariably accompany our perceptual consciousness of physical objects. Such possibilities must be considered in determining the epistemological implications of the Percept Theory and will be briefly discussed in Part II of this paper, but they are irrelevant to the central thesis of the Percept Theory. For the duality denied by those who accept this theory is a duality of what we may perhaps call the *sensuous* aspects of consciousness at the moment of ordinary perception. At that moment, they maintain, we are conscious in a certain manner of a physical object which is somehow presented to us completely clothed in sensuous qualities. These qualities are presented as qualities of the object; indeed they are in no sense abstracted or otherwise distinguished from the presented object; and they are not limited to the qualities which have traditionally been mentioned in descriptions of sense-data. And finally, according to those who accept the Percept Theory, the sensuously clothed object is the *only* sensuous content of consciousness during ordinary perception. Sense-data, of course, if they exist as the objects of *pure* states of direct awareness, may properly be described as having sensuous qualities; but sense-data do not occur as constituents of perceptual consciousness.

There is, of course, considerable room for disagreement about the proper way to express this conclusion. The traditional Sense-datum Theory is based on a supposed distinction between the direct awareness of sense-data and the mediated consciousness or "perception" of physical objects; those who reject this distinction, therefore, are rejecting not only the traditional concept of sense-datum but also the theory that ordinary perception is *mediated* in some manner or other,[34] by the presence of sense-data. Since both aspects of the traditional distinction must stand or fall together, there is no unambiguous way in which the traditional terminology can be used to express the positive conclusions of those who accept the Percept Theory. On the one hand it is probably misleading for advocates of the Percept Theory to assert bluntly, as they frequently do, that in perception we are directly aware of physical objects. For in addition to suggesting the very distinction which the Percept Theory rejects, the word "directly", when used in such a context, may have certain epistemological connotations which are not relevant to the phenomenological issue.[35] On the other hand it would create an unnecessary paradox if advocates of the Percept Theory were to assert that in ordinary perceptual experience we are not directly aware of *anything;* and this too might have confusing epistemological connotations. Consequently, even though either of these two modes of expression would be adequate if it were carefully explained, I shall avoid both of them in the following pages.

William James sometimes used the word "percept" to refer to the content of consciousness during perception; it is this fact which has made the name "Percept Theory" seem to me appropriate for the particular theory of perceptual consciousness which he himself supported. If we were to adapt this terminology to satisfy our present need we could say that according to the Percept Theory we are presented in ordinary perception not with a sense-datum but with an "object-percept" only, and we could speak more specifically, when necessary, of "cat-percepts", "mountain percepts", etc.

For the problems to be discussed in the following pages,

---

[34] The nature of this mediation is discussed in Part II of this paper.
[35] This matter is discussed at length in Part II of this paper.

however, the terminology used by Price is even more convenient. Price uses the term "ostensible material object" to refer to that part of the content of perceptual consciousness which is not a sense-datum; it is thus possible to express the fact that in perception we are conscious in a certain manner of a physical object, by saying that we are presented with an ostensible physical object. Price himself does not accept the Percept Theory, but those who do may describe their position by saying that in ordinary perception we are presented with ostensible physical objects but not with sense-data.[36] The following passage from Price, as a matter of fact, provides a fitting conclusion for this section of the discussion, for it aptly describes the unmediated character of perceptual consciousness to which supporters of the Percept Theory have tried to draw attention. That Price could write a passage like this and still accept the Sense-datum Theory, is a mystery of the kind which the next section is intended to solve:

"Somehow it is the *whole* thing, and not just a jejune extract from it, which is before the mind from the first. From the first it is the complete material thing, with back, sides, and insides as well as front, that we 'accept', that 'ostends itself' to us, and nothing less; a thing, too, persisting through time both before and after . . . and possessed of various causal characteristics. . . . Already in this single act, even in a momentary glance, we take all these elements of the object to be there, all of them; as Mr. Joseph has said in another connection, we must not suppose that because there is only a little definite before the mind, therefore there is only a definite little."[37]

4. Methodological Problems

To most philosophers and psychologists who have rejected the Sense-datum Theory as incompatible with the

[36] This terminology is not intended to commit the Percept Theory to an "act-object" analysis of sense-experience. See Author's Note at the end of this essay. [Footnote revised in 1964. Ed.]

[37] *Perception*, pp. 151–152.

real nature of perceptual consciousness, it is probably a
matter for endless amazement that there is still so much
resistance to their position. Contemporary epistemologists,
in particular, seem to be quite unaffected by criticism of
the Sense-datum Theory, although the extent of such criticism in the last fifty years has been considerable. But what
makes this resistance especially difficult to understand is
the fact that it has not usually taken the form of reasoned
argument, but of complete indifference.

If this indifference is not to be attributed to ignorance or
perversity, it is likely to suggest that there are certain fallacies or prejudices which prevent many people, and perhaps
epistemologists in particular, from examining perceptual
consciousness with complete objectivity. Köhler says that
the Sense-datum Theory (which he calls "the meaning theory") "seems to correspond to a very natural tendency in
human thinking",[38] and indeed some such explanation
seems unavoidable to those who believe, as I do, that the
Sense-datum Theory is simply not compatible with the empirical facts. In the pages immediately following, therefore,
I shall discuss a number of possible errors which might
account, at least in part, for the popularity of the Sense-
datum Theory. Such a procedure seems likely to be more
fruitful, considering the history of this issue, than further
efforts to review the phenomenological evidence for the
Percept Theory or to seek for more felicitous ways of describing perceptual consciousness.

(a) The Physiological Fallacy

It has been frequently suggested, first of all, that some
of the philosophers and psychologists who accept the Sense-
datum Theory have committed what is sometimes called
"the physiological fallacy".[39] The physiological fallacy
consists in assuming, *a priori*, some particular type of relationship between physiological facts and phenomenologi-

---

[38] *Gestalt Psychology*, p. 83.

[39] The Stimulus-error and the Constancy Hypothesis are particular
forms of this fallacy. See Köhler, *Gestalt Psychology*, pp. 90–97.

cal facts. It is empirically demonstrable, for example, that the nature of particular states of perceptual consciousness is determined partly by the direct physiological effects of the stimulus, and partly by the past experience and present interests of the perceiver. But to conclude from these facts alone that there must be at least two constituents in every state of perceptual consciousness, one of them (the sense-datum) corresponding in some simple fashion to the direct physiological effects of the stimulus, would be to commit the physiological fallacy and obscure the actual character of perceptual consciousness.

In reply to this fallacious form of argument, if made explicit, it would be sufficient to point out that the only way to decide a question of this sort is by direct inspection of perceptual consciousness itself. But Dewey and others have also shown that so far as our present knowledge of physiology is concerned, the Sense-datum Theory is not even favoured by considerations of elegance.[40]

Some philosophers have complicated the matter by actually *defining* a sense-datum as that constituent of a perception which is caused by the physical stimulus. Russell does this in his *Philosophy*, although elsewhere he accepts the conventional definition in terms of direct awareness. A sense-datum, he says in *Philosophy*, is "the core, in a perception, which is solely due to the stimulus and the sense-organ, not to past experience".[41] But even if we were to accept this definition, it would still remain an open question whether there *are* sense-data as so defined, and it is still true that this can be decided only by direct inspection of perceptual consciousness.

(b) The Sense-Datum and the Ostensible Object

It seems quite unlikely, however, that the popularity of the Sense-datum Theory among contemporary epistemologists can be accounted for as the result of the physiological fallacy. Most epistemologists are entirely too sophisticated

---

[40] See *e.g.*, *Art as Experience*, pp. 123–126.
[41] B. Russell, *Philosophy*, p. 204, Norton, New York, 1927.

to commit such a fallacy, and many of them assert specifically that the Sense-datum Theory is supported by direct inspection of perceptual consciousness. It is possible, however, that some of them have committed another error by failing to distinguish clearly between a sense-datum and the *front surface* of an ostensible physical object. This possibility deserves careful consideration, for it is not uncommon to find supporters of the Sense-datum Theory, especially in conversation about this subject, attempting to localise visual sense-data on the surfaces of ostensible objects; and they do this even though they have previously maintained that sense-data may have qualities which are quite different from the surface qualities of the ostensible physical objects which accompany them.

Now if it should turn out that what a philosopher *does* mean by a visual sense-datum is nothing more nor less than the front surface of an ostensible physical object, it would follow by definition that whenever we are visually conscious of a physical object we are conscious of a sense-datum; but in that case it would no longer be correct to say that sense-data are the objects of *direct awareness*. Direct awareness is supposed to be a distinctive mode of consciousness which, as Price puts it, is "utterly different" from our consciousness of physical objects; it "arises together with" our consciousness of physical objects and is not merely a part or aspect of it. The front surface of an ostensible physical object does, to be sure, have a special status which enables us to distinguish it as the *front* surface rather than the back; it is characteristic of our perceptual consciousness that it involves, so to speak, an intrinsic "point of view".[42] But the Sense-datum Theory could no longer be distinguished from the Percept Theory, of course, if the assertion that perceptual consciousness includes direct awareness of a sense-datum were interpreted to mean merely that perceptual consciousness involves an intrinsic point of view.

Almost all the philosophers who accept the Sense-datum Theory, moreover, have made statements which are

[42] For a careful analysis of the meaning of "point of view" *cf.* Price, *Perception,* p. 252 *et seq.*

incompatible with the proposition that visual sense-data are the front surfaces of ostensible physical objects. Thus to clarify the relationship between sense-data and the interpretational or conceptual element in perception, they say that the latter may vary with our past experience and present attitudes even though the former remain unchanged, and that the former may change even though the latter do not vary at all.[43] As naïve children, for example, our awareness of a purple sense-datum when we look at a distant mountain might be accompanied by the perception of a purple mountain, whereas an exactly similar sense-datum, occurring at a later age, might be accompanied by the perception of a green mountain. And for similar reasons the sense-data produced by tomatoes in a dark cellar might vary from light grey to dark grey with changes in the illumination, although the ostensible tomatoes might at the same time remain uniformly red. According to those who accept the Sense-datum Theory, in short, the qualities of sense-data and the qualities of ostensible physical objects can vary independently to some extent, and this implies, of course, that sense-data cannot be identified with the front surfaces of ostensible objects.

If the Sense-datum Theory were true, indeed, it would rarely, if ever, be correct to apply the same determinate adjectives both to an ostensible physical object and to the sense-datum which is presented along with it. Thus we should have to maintain that whenever we are perceiving a physical object with a surface which is ostensibly red and circular, we are also directly aware of a sense-datum which is probably elliptical in shape and which may very well be orange or purple or grey in colour. We should have to maintain, in short, that even when we look at a single physical object we are almost always conscious, though in different ways, of two colours and two shapes. To those who support the Percept Theory it seems so clear that ordinary perception is *not* characterised by any such duality, that

---

[43] Lewis, for example, says: "The same quale may be . . . the sign of different objective properties and different qualia may be the sign of the *same* objective property". *Mind and the World-Order*, p. 122.

they may perhaps be excused for suspecting that their opponents, when they actually *examine* a state of perceptual consciousness, contradict their own theory by identifying visual sense-data and the front surfaces of ostensible physical objects.

If this fallacy is committed by any of the philosophers and psychologists who accept the Sense-datum Theory, it is probably committed chiefly by those whose conception of the perceptual consciousness of physical objects is over-intellectualised. Such philosophers and psychologists are likely to conceive of perceptual consciousness as a twofold state consisting of direct awareness of a sense-datum and a *purely* intellectual or *purely* conceptual "interpretation" of this sense-datum. Our consciousness of a particular physical object in perception is consequently thought of as nothing more than a state of *belief that there exists* a physical object of a particular kind, and the special *sensuous* character of this mode of consciousness is completely overlooked.

It is easy to see that such a conception could blind one to the very phenomenological facts which would correct it, and lead to the fallacy of identifying sense-data and the front surfaces of ostensible physical objects. For even if we should decide that it is appropriate to describe our perceptual consciousness of physical objects as a kind of *belief*,[44] it is surely a very special kind of belief—the kind, namely, that is characterised by the presence of an ostensible physical object. But an ostensible physical object, as supporters of the Percept Theory have tried to point out, is presented, or appears, or "ostends itself" fully clothed in sensuous qualities. If, therefore, a philosopher or psychologist were to suppose, because he accepted *a priori* an over-intellectualised conception of perceptual consciousness, that *only* the traditional objects of direct awareness can have sensuous qualities, he could very easily fall into the error of believing that the front surface of an ostensible physical object is a sense-datum.

[44] On the suitability of this term, see Broad, *The Mind and Its Place in Nature*, p. 153 and p. 215, and Price, *Perception*, 139–142.

It is difficult to believe, however, that this error could explain the acceptance of the Sense-datum Theory by those philosophers and psychologists who show quite clearly that they are fully aware of the sensuous character of ostensible physical objects. Price, for example, has made a characteristically acute analysis of what he calls the "pseudo-intuitive" features of our perceptual consciousness of physical objects.[45] He criticizes those whom he calls "Rational Idealists" for their over-intellectualised conception of this mode of consciousness, and points out that it is actually very similar to direct awareness of sense-data. He quotes with approval Husserl's statement that the object of perception is "leibhaft gegeben", and adds that it "just comes, along with the sense-datum: it just dawns upon us, of itself".[46] In fact Price's only reason for refusing to say that our consciousness of physical objects *is* intuitive, appears to be epistemological rather than phenomenological.[47]

There is little doubt, therefore, that Price is fully aware of the sensuous character of ostensible physical objects. He seems to recognise that a ripe tomato hanging on a vine in the sun is "leibhaft gegeben" with all its sensuous qualities of redness, and smoothness, and warmth, and sweetness. Yet he would also maintain that when we look at the tomato we are ordinarily presented with *another* entity, a sense-datum, which may have qualities quite unlike those of the ostensible tomato. For those who support the Percept Theory it is difficult to see how there could be *room*, so to speak, for such conflicting sets of sensuous qualities in one and the same state of perceptual consciousness, and even Price says that in ordinary perception we "fail to distinguish" between the sense-datum and the ostensible object.[48] He does not seem to doubt, nevertheless, that there *is* a sense-datum in every perception, and a sense-datum which *can* be distinguished from the front surface of an ostensible physical object.

[45] *Perception*, pp. 150–156.
[46] *Ibid.*, p. 153.
[47] *Ibid.*, p. 156.
[48] *Ibid.*, p. 145.

(c) Explicit and Implicit Consciousness

This brings us finally to what is probably the most interesting explanation for the resistance which contemporary epistemologists have shown to the Percept Theory. For although it seems unlikely that careful phenomenologists like Price have committed either of the two fallacies so far discussed, Price's comment that in ordinary perception we "fail to distinguish" between the sense-datum and the ostensible physical object, does suggest that he, and perhaps others, are accepting a methodological presupposition which supporters of the Percept Theory would wish to reject. Our state of mind in perception, Price says, "is, as it were, a dreamy half-awake state, in which we are unaware of a difference between the sense-datum and the ostensible physical object".[49] And this naturally raises the question: How can anyone claim to *know* this particular fact about perceptual consciousness and at the same time believe that there is evidence to support the Sense-datum Theory? If it be admitted, in other words, that in perception we are *not aware* of any difference between the sense-datum and the ostensible physical object, what possible evidence could there be that both of them *are present* to consciousness during perception?[50]

The importance of this question is also indicated by certain passages in Broad's discussion of perceptual consciousness in *Scientific Thought*.[51] To illustrate what I have called "the Sensory Core Theory", Broad draws an analogy between sense-data and printed words. In reading a familiar language, he says, "what interests us as a rule is the mean-

---

[49] *Ibid.*, p. 168.

[50] This way of posing the problem avoids the difficult questions concerning the *possibility* of transcendent states of mind and unnoticed characteristics of conscious states. For three different answers to these questions, see Broad, *Scientific Thought*, pp. 244–246, Lewis, *Mind and the World-Order*, p. 64, and Ayer, *The Foundations of Empirical Knowledge*, pp. 69–72, Macmillan, New York, 1940. See also Chisholm, "The Problem of the Speckled Hen", MIND, Vol. LI, N.S. No. 204, p. 370.

[51] Pp. 247–248 [pp. 96–97, this volume. Ed.].

ing of the printed words, not the peculiarities of the print. We do not explicitly notice the latter unless there be something markedly wrong with it, such as a letter upside down. . . . In exactly the same way", he explains, "we are not as a rule interested in sensa". We ordinarily notice them only when they are queer, as when we see double, though "even in a normal case, we generally can detect the properties of sensa . . . provided that we make a special effort of attention". These statements raise the same methodological question: If it be admitted that in perception we ordinarily do not "explicitly notice" sensa, what possible evidence could there be that we are actually conscious of them?

Now it is quite possible that statements like these just quoted from Broad and Price are the results of careful phenomenology; it is possible that these philosophers can actually discover within a single perception the two levels of consciousness suggested by their statements—a level of "explicit awareness" and a level of "implicit awareness". In that case the evidence for the fact that we are implicitly aware of sense-data in perception can be obtained by *direct inspection* of perceptual consciousness, in the very same manner, indeed, in which we would proceed to obtain evidence for the fact that we do *not* "explicitly notice" such sense-data or that we "fail to distinguish" them. And in that case it might be argued that the difference between the Sense-datum Theory and the Percept Theory is little more than a difference about the meaning of such expressions as "present to consciousness"; for perhaps in the limited sense designated by the word "explicitly", most of the philosophers and psychologists who accept the Sense-datum Theory would be quite willing to admit that sense-data are *not* ordinarily present to consciousness during perception.

(d) Perceptual Reduction

Most supporters of the Percept Theory, however, have made it quite clear that their opposition to the Sense-datum Theory could not be mitigated by rephrasing the issue in terms of any such verbal distinction. They have said that direct inspection of perceptual consciousness convinces them that sense-data as traditionally described are not present *at all,* thus implying that perceptual consciousness simply does not manifest the two levels suggested by the use of such expressions as "explicitly notice". There are, to be sure, various interpretations of "explicit" and "implicit" which would make these words applicable to the content of perceptual consciousness; indeed it would be surprising if there were not in view of the complexity of perceptual phenomena. But those who support the Percept Theory seem to be unanimous in their belief that direct inspection does not reveal the presence of *sense-data,* either explicitly or implicitly, within the ordinary perceptual consciousness.

It is understandable therefore, that supporters of the Percept Theory should look elsewhere for an explanation of the fact that some philosophers and psychologists still cling to the Sense-datum Theory even though they seem to be admitting that we are not actually aware of sense-data at the moment of perception. And the explanation which naturally suggests itself is that these philosophers and psychologists would in fact admit the truth of the Percept Theory if they limited themselves to *direct inspection* of perceptual consciousness, but that they also employ *another* method, wittingly or unwittingly, in which they have greater faith.

This possibility is easily illustrated by referring to the statements I have quoted from Broad. Broad asserts, as an empirical fact, that in perception we do not explicitly notice our sense-data, just as in reading a book we do not explicitly notice the print. If this is an empirical fact, however, then Broad presumably discovered it by direct inspection of perceptual consciousness; he inspected his consciousness while reading and found that he was not explicitly noticing the print, and he inspected his consciousness during perception and found that he was not explicitly noticing sense-data. Nevertheless, Broad explains, we *can* detect the properties of the printed words by attending to the print "as in proof-reading", and we *can* similarly detect the properties of sensa by making "a special effort of attention".

Now it is clear that the special act of "attending" by means of which we explicitly notice the print and the sense-data must be at least *somewhat* different from the act of direct inspection which, Broad admits, does not reveal the presence to consciousness of either the print or the sense-data. Any other conclusion would be self-contradictory, for if the act of "attending" were *identical* with this act of direct inspection, it would obviously be impossible for anyone to discover that we do *not* explicitly notice either the print or the sense-data. And this suggests the possibility that some of the opposition to the Percept Theory can be explained on methodological grounds. It suggests that some of the contemporary philosophers and psychologists who accept the Sense-datum Theory may believe that there is a better method of discovering phenomenological facts than the method of examining the phenomena directly. A good deal has been written on this subject, but it is still interesting and important, and deserves further attention.

The method of settling phenomenological questions which has sometimes been regarded as better than the method of direct inspection, involves a unique operation which I shall call "perceptual reduction". This operation is familiar to everyone who has participated in discussions of the traditional problems of perception, because in such a context there is a certain use of the expression "really see" such that what we really see can be determined only by performing this operation, and not by direct inspection alone. Thus if I were asked simply what I *see* right now, I should probably reply: "A sheet of white paper"; but if I were asked what I *really* see, especially in the context of psychological or epistemological discussion, I should probably answer; "A patch of pale yellow". In the latter case I should assume that I was being asked to perform the operation of perceptual reduction *first* and *then* to describe my state of consciousness as revealed by direct inspection. And since this paper happens at the moment to be illuminated by artificial light, the answers to the two questions would, for physical and physiological reasons, be different.

The operation of perceptual reduction has two rather distinct effects when it is performed on a state of perceptual consciousness. The first of these two effects is to make the ostensible physical object progressively less and less determinate. If I were to perform the operation while looking at a tomato, for example, the ostensible tomato which is present to consciousness would, so to speak, become less specifically distinguished as an individual. Starting as a tomato with worm holes it might be reduced to a tomato with "some sort of holes" in it, and then to a tomato with spots on its surface, and so on. It might eventually become "some sort of globular object", or even just "some sort of physical thing".

But when this last stage is reached, or perhaps even before, there is a second effect: a radical change takes place and a *new* object of consciousness appears and grows more and more determinate. Our state of consciousness is approaching a pure state of sense-datum awareness, and this new object is therefore not an ostensible physical object at all but the kind of thing which is correctly called a sense-datum; and it is not until this second stage in the process has begun that we are able to describe what we "really see" and to report, for example, that we are presented with "a red patch of a round and somewhat bulgy shape". In fact the properties which we attribute to this new object of consciousness are usually incompatible with those which characterised the original ostensible physical object.

This description of the effects of the operation of perceptual reduction is undoubtedly over-simplified. Some psychologists and philosophers would probably insist that in the final stage, when we become aware of a sense-datum, we are also conscious of an extremely indeterminate physical object—that there are, in other words, no pure states of direct awareness. Others might maintain that the process by which the final stage is reached varies considerably from one occasion to another. But so far as the present issue is concerned, the only relevant fact is that the operation of perceptual reduction *destroys* the state of perceptual consciousness on which it is performed; it is an operation, to be precise, which has the effect of *replacing* a state of perceptual consciousness by a state in which we are aware of sense-data.

It would be difficult to exaggerate the importance of the role which has been played by the operation of perceptual reduction throughout the history of modern philosophy and modern psychology. This operation reached the height of its importance in the psychological methods of Wundt, Titchener, and their followers, who declared it to be the very essence of the experimental technique of introspective psychology. They interpreted it, however, as a procedure for *cleansing* perceptual consciousness of its nonsensory constituents. They believed, as Köhler says in criticizing them, that "as psychologists our task is to separate . . . 'meanings' from the seen material *as such,* the manifold of simple sensations". They admitted that "it may be a difficult task to effect this separation and to behold the net sensations which are the actual data"; but the ability to do so, they maintained, "is precisely the special talent which transforms the layman into a psychologist".[52]

Now whether or not it is misleading to say that the operation of perceptual reduction is a technique for "cleansing" perceptual consciousness, it is quite certain, I believe, that this operation differs from direct inspection. And it is also quite certain that it destroys the state of perceptual consciousness on which it is performed, for when we reach the final stage in which we are aware of a sense-datum, we are no longer presented with the fairly determinate ostensible physical object which originally existed. If, therefore, any of the philosophers and psychologists who accept the Sensedatum Theory have simply failed to notice the difference between direct inspection and perceptual reduction, it is fair to say that they have committed a very serious fallacy, and one which might explain the resistance which they have offered to the Percept Theory. This fallacy is one particular form of what James called the "psychological fallacy *par excellence*"—the fallacy of reading into a state of con-

[52] *Gestalt Psychology,* p. 72.

sciousness the characteristics of something (in this case *an-other* state of consciousness) which is externally related to it.[53]

(e) The Exposure Hypothesis

But perhaps there are some philosophers and psychologists who believe that perceptual reduction is a legitimate method for discovering the content of perceptual consciousness, and who are nevertheless fully aware of the difference between this method and the method of direct inspection. If they recognise this difference and the fact that the two methods yield incompatible conclusions about the nature of perceptual consciousness, and if they sincerely believe that perceptual reduction is the more trustworthy method, then it is perhaps not accurate to say that they have committed a *fallacy*. They are, however, accepting a debatable *hypothesis* which ought to be carefully formulated and examined. I shall call this hypothesis the "Exposure Hypothesis".

According to the Exposure Hypothesis, the operation of perceptual reduction does not produce a state of consciousness which is simply *other than* the original state of perception on which it is performed. It produces, on the contrary, a state of direct awareness which was contained in the original perception. To put the case very simply, indeed, we might say that according to this hypothesis the only difference between the two states is that the sense-datum of which we are aware is obscured in the earlier one by the presence of an ostensible physical object. The method of perceptual reduction, therefore, is a method designed to *expose* the sense-data which are presumed to be contained in ordinary states of perceptual consciousness. This exposure is achieved, according to the hypothesis, by destroying the consciousness of physical objects which accompanies and obscures the sense-data, so that the bare sense-data themselves become accessible to subsequent acts of direct inspection.

[53] *Principles of Psychology*, pp. 196–197.

Now to grasp the full import of the Exposure Hypothesis, it should be recognised that it grants a unique and privileged epistemological status to the particular attitude (the "reducing attitude") which we adopt in order to initiate the process of perceptual reduction. This attitude of "doubt" or "questioning" is, to be sure, an attitude of special importance to the psychologist and perhaps to the artist, but it is, on the other hand, only one among a seemingly infinite number of attitudes which we can adopt in the presence of an ostensible physical object. There are mercenary attitudes and pedagogical attitudes and martial attitudes and so on indefinitely, and each one is capable of affecting the content of perceptual consciousness; thus even though the visual stimuli are similar, for example, the qualities of a tomato as seen by a hungry child will surely be very different from the qualities of a tomato as seen by someone looking for a missile to throw at a candidate for political office. And sometimes, moreover, such changes in attitude are consciously solicited—as for example when we revisit some favourite childhood scene and try to recapture something of its former meaning. Yet it would scarcely occur to anyone to suggest that by forcing such changes of attitude we can find, in the resulting state of perceptual consciousness, the *real but previously unobservable* content of the original state. The two states would be regarded as related to one another, to be sure, by the fact that they are caused by the same external stimulus, but the one would scarcely be taken to be a *constituent* of the other.

Those who accept the Exposure Hypothesis, therefore, have singled out one particular attitude from among the multitude which we can adopt in the presence of an ostensible physical object, and have attributed to this attitude the rare epistemological power of exposing otherwise unobservable characteristics of perceptual consciousness. And there does not appear to be the slightest empirical justification for this. If the truth of the Sense-datum Theory were assumed *a priori*, and it were *also* assumed that there is *some* procedure for discovering the sense-data within ordinary perceptual consciousness, then, indeed, it might be inferred that the reducing attitude *must* have the unique epistemological power attributed to it by the Exposure Hypothesis. But in that case, of course, the Exposure Hypothesis could not in turn be used as part of an argument to support the Sense-datum Theory. Whatever the *empirically* distinguishable features of the reducing attitude may be, they do not indicate that the operation of perceptual reduction is anything more than one method among many of substituting one state of consciousness for another.

The only argument for the Exposure Hypothesis, so far as I know, which might have some appeal to an empiricist, is the argument that to deny this hypothesis is to cast suspicion on all intellectual analysis. It is possible that Price is employing this argument, for example, when he criticizes the view "that just as dissection destroys a living organism, so intellectual analysis destroys that which is analysed, and substitutes something else in its place". According to this view, he continues, "since all thought may be regarded as analysis, we are forbidden to think"[54] Lewis suggests the same argument when he writes: "The given is *in*, not before experience. But the condemnation of abstractions is the condemnation of thought itself. Nothing that thought can ever comprise is other than some abstraction which cannot exist in isolation."[55]

To infer, however, that the rejection of the Exposure Hypothesis casts suspicion on intellectual analysis, or that it implicitly denies the possibility of thought, is to overlook the very distinction which criticism of the Exposure Theory is intended to clarify—the distinction, namely, between introspective reduction and direct inspection. For there is, of course, no inconsistency at all in asserting that introspective reduction is merely a process of substitution, and at the same time maintaining that there is *another* process —i.e., direct inspection—which is quite compatible with genuine intellectual analysis and which does *not* destroy the very thing which is to be analysed. "In intellectual

[54] *Perception*, p. 15.
[55] *Mind and the World-Order*, p. 55.

analysis", says Price, "I do not *do* anything to the object before me. I *find* relations with it. I *discover* that it possesses various characteristics. . . . But those relations and characteristics were there before I discovered them. The only change that has occurred is a change in myself. I was ignorant and now I know."[56] And surely there is no reason why one who rejects the Exposure Hypothesis must deny the possibility of such a process as this.

As a matter of fact the supporters of the Percept Theory have been especially interested in *describing* the nature of perceptual consciousness, and such description requires analytical thought. The very assertion that perceptual consciousness is not a twofold state is itself the result of a kind of analytical process, and so is the more specific assertion that I am presented with an ostensible tomato clothed with certain sensuous qualities. But these assertions describe perceptual consciousness itself, as revealed by direct inspection, and not the substitute provided by the operation of perceptual reduction.

Those who accept the Sense-datum Theory have made similar distinctions in explaining their own position. They have pointed out that we cannot learn more about a particular sense-datum by changing the physical conditions of observation, for we merely frustrate ourselves if we try by such means to "get a better look" at a sense-datum. By moving our bodies, by putting on spectacles, and by turning on the light, we may indeed learn more about the stimulus-object, but if we perform these operations in order to dissect our sense-data, then indeed "we murder to dissect". And those who reject the Exposure Hypothesis are arguing analogously that we frustrate ourselves if we perform the operation of perceptual reduction in order to describe perceptual consciousness. In neither case does the argument imply that analysis is impossible.

But if the rejection of the Exposure Hypothesis does not imply the impossibility of analysis, it is difficult to see what argument could possibly be advanced to support it. Yet the hypothesis has apparently been accepted by many

[56] *Perception*, p. 15.

philosophers and psychologists in the past, and the history of the conflict between the Sense-datum Theory and the Percept Theory suggests that it will continue to be accepted for some time to come. There may, of course, be unexpressed arguments which have not been uncovered; and it is even possible that the three errors discussed in this section cannot account for more than a small part of what Köhler calls the "natural tendency" to favour the Sense-datum Theory. But if this is the case then those who support the Percept Theory will naturally hope that their opponents may soon provide them with a full explanation of the phenomenological or epistemological basis of the Sense-datum Theory.

The next and final section of this paper is devoted to an examination of some of the epistemological implications of the Percept Theory. For many philosophers it is only the possible implications of this Theory which can give importance to the phenomenological issues which we have been discussing; and it is not impossible that the revolutionary nature of some of the supposed implications of the Percept Theory can account in part for the resistance which it has encountered among epistemologists.

PART II
THE EPISTEMOLOGICAL IMPLICATIONS OF THE PERCEPT THEORY

The most revolutionary inferences which philosophers have drawn from the Percept Theory are probably those which concern the epistemological status of physical objects; we have already seen, for example, that in recent years some philosophers have used the Percept Theory as a basis for attributing to physical objects the same epistemological status that has traditionally been attributed to sense-data. But there is another possible implication of the Percept Theory which deserves prior consideration because our decision concerning its validity will necessarily influence our analysis of almost all other epistemological issues.

1. THE GIVEN AND ITS INTERPRETATION

We might wonder, specifically, whether acceptance of the Percept Theory can force us to deny completely a fact the recognition of which Lewis has called "one of the oldest and most universal of philosophic insights", the fact, namely, that "there are, in our cognitive experience, two elements: the immediate data, such as those of sense, which are presented or given to the mind, and a form, construction, or interpretation, which represents the activity of thought".[57] The distinction to which Lewis refers is, in one form or another, so fundamental to most philosophical and psychological systems, that to reject it entirely would necessitate, at the very least, a complete reformulation of these systems. And despite the phenomenological evidence for the Percept Theory, there are undoubtedly many philosophers and psychologists who would find that theory quite incredible if it could be shown to imply that the distinction between what is given, and the interpretation or construction put upon it, is entirely invalid.

But there are, I believe, three rather different senses in which this familiar distinction can be recognised even by those who accept the Percept Theory; and there is only one traditional sense in which the distinction must be denied.

(a) The Given as the Ostensible Physical Object

In the first place it must not be forgotten that the Percept Theory is a theory about perceptual *consciousness*

[57] *Mind and the World-Order*, p. 38.

and that the evidence for it is entirely phenomenological and gathered by direct inspection of many single states of perception. If, therefore, the terms "construction" and "interpretation" are defined *dispositionally*—by reference either to a tendency towards bodily behaviour of a certain kind or to a tendency to have certain kinds of conscious experience under certain conditions, or both—then the validity of the distinction between "the given" and its "interpretation" is entirely independent of, and hence compatible with, the truth of the Percept Theory. Thus for those who accept the Percept Theory the things that are given in perception would be ostensible physical objects, these being the only sensuous constituents of ordinary perceptual consciousness; and the manner in which these are interpreted would be determined by discovering the dispositions which accompany them. In many contexts, moreover (*e.g.*, in most discussions of learning) the philosophers and psychologists who have distinguished between the given and its interpretation have intended to say nothing that is incompatible with such a theory of the given; to recognise a distinction of this kind, therefore, is to admit the validity, in one historic and important sense, of what Lewis has called "one of the oldest and most universal of philosophic insights".

But that is not all that can be admitted, for it should be remembered that the Percept Theory, as I have described it, is a theory limited not only to perceptual consciousness but to the *sensuous* aspects of perceptual consciousness. It is a theory, to be more precise, about the phenomenological status of the ostensible physical object and the sensuous qualities which clothe it, and it is incompatible with the Sense-datum Theory, as we have seen, precisely because it denies the phenomenological duality of any of these sensuous qualities. If, therefore, a philosopher or psychologist happens to believe that the ostensible physical object usually does not *exhaust* the content of the consciousness during perception; if, for example, he believes that the ostensible physical object is presented together with certain bodily feelings, or with an "ostensible self"

or with an "ostensible perceiving self", or with phenomenologically irreducible "beliefs" or "judgements" or "expectations", or indeed with any other possible constituents
of consciousness whatsoever; and if, at the same time, he
does not believe that any of these constituents are sense-
data as traditionally conceived, and is therefore able consistently to admit that sensuous qualities are presented as
the qualities of the ostensible physical object and not of
any other entity; such a philosopher or psychologist, so
far as I can see, does not believe anything that is incompatible with the Percept Theory. It might consequently
be possible, by defining "interpretation" and "construction" in terms of some of these other constituents of perceptual consciousness, to give a purely phenomenological
meaning to these words so that the given (the ostensible
physical object) could be distinguished from its interpretation by direct inspection of perceptual consciousness.
Thus the historical distinction could be recognised in another sense, and a sense which would probably represent
the principal point that Lewis himself has in mind when
he says: "That present datum of experience which is
interpreted as 'activity of thought' is just as objective and
intrinsically observable a kind of datum as is the phenomenal appearance of an external object".[58] Whether or not
direct inspection of single states of perceptual consciousness *can* validate such a distinction is a difficult question,
and one which is not strictly relevant to the basic issue
under discussion; but there is nothing in the Percept
Theory to imply that it cannot.

Some of the examples which Lewis gives to illustrate the
distinction between the given and its interpretation, however, require that this distinction be recognised in another
sense, quite different from the two so far discussed; and
in this other sense the distinction is not compatible with
the Percept Theory. Lewis points out the well-known
fact that our perceptual experience varies not only with
changes in the physical conditions of observation but also

[58] *Ibid.*, p. 424.

with changes in interest, and he illustrates this by showing that the perceived qualities of a fountain pen differ for a child, a writer, and a savage. This *fact*, of course, is quite compatible with the Percept Theory, for the characteristics of ostensible physical objects do indeed vary with the attitude of the perceiver. But Lewis uses this fact to illustrate the difference between the given and its interpretation, and the distinction in this instance is drawn in a manner which is incompatible with the Percept Theory.

The distinction is drawn between a "presentation", which is supposed to be the constant and given element in the various perceptual experiences of the pen, and its "meaning" or interpretation. Speaking, for example, of the fountain pen in his hand, Lewis says: "It might happen that I remember my first experience of such a thing. If so I should find that this sort of presentation did not then mean 'fountain pen' to me."[59] But since by the expression "this sort of presentation" Lewis means a complex of qualia or sense-data[60] which are to be distinguished from the qualities of the ostensible pen, it is clear that this expression, for those who accept the Percept Theory, simply has no designatum at all within these states of perceptual consciousness. According to the Percept Theory there simply is no common core of sense-data to "mean" one thing at one time and another thing at another time. It is possible, to be sure, that the ostensible physical object presented in childhood might have had certain properties (*e.g.*, a particular shape and colour) in common with the ostensible physical object presented at the time of writing; in fact this is probably what it would ordinarily mean to say that the two presentations were "of the same sort"; but the particular distinction which Lewis has in mind, and which is essential to the Sense-datum Theory, is not one that can be defined by reference solely to the properties of the ostensible physical objects.

The problem, therefore, for those who accept the Percept Theory, is whether in rejecting this distinction between

[59] *Ibid.*, p. 49.
[60] *Ibid.*, p. 60.

the given and its interpretation they must also reject as meaningless all the epistemological and psychological principles whose formulation presupposes that the distinction is valid. In view of the historical importance of the Sense-datum Theory it is clear that this problem cannot be lightly dismissed. Whatever one may think, for example, of the ultimate value of the introspective psychology of Wundt and Titchener, it will stretch the credulity of those who are familiar with their experimental work to suggest that the principles which they formulated concerning the relationship between sensation and "meanings" are completely *meaningless*.[61] The conception of the sensory core, moreover, appears to have a certain methodological value, for differences and similarities among sensory cores have been supposed to provide psychologists with phenomenal criteria for deciding just what characteristics of perceptual consciousness can and cannot be explained by reference to physical processes in the sense-organs; it has been supposed, for example, that the fact that two perceptions have similar sensory cores guarantees that all differences between these perceptions must be explained by reference to attitudes (broadly interpreted) and the physiological conditions of attitudes. And it might not be easy, even for those psychologists who accept the Percept Theory, to dispense entirely with such methodological principles.

(b) *The Given as the Product of Perceptual Reduction*

It seems to me, however, that the solution to this problem is not so difficult as it may appear, for I believe that we can find for these particular psychological purposes, a completely satisfactory substitute for the sensory core as traditionally conceived. We can do this by applying the pragmatic maxim and asking ourselves just how psychologists have actually *decided* whether or not two perceptions are to be called "interpretations of the same sensory core".

[61] See Titchener, *A Beginner's Psychology*, ch. 1.

And if our methodological analysis in the previous section is correct, this has been decided, of course, by subjecting the two perceptions to the operation of perceptual reduction and comparing the resulting states of direct awareness. If, to use Lewis's example, two different perceptual experiences of a fountain pen are perceptually reducible to direct awareness of similar sense-data—perhaps long tapering patches of black—then it would be concluded, no matter how different the ostensible physical objects, that the two perceptions are "different interpretations of the same given". For those who accept the Percept Theory, therefore, this "method of verification" can be used to define the term "sensory core" in a way which will provide a substitute for the traditional concept. We can say that the statement "These two perceptions are different interpretations of the same sensory core", should be understood to mean: "If these two perceptions were perceptually reduced exactly similar states of direct awareness would be produced in the two cases". And to understand this second statement, of course, we do not need any concepts which are incompatible with the Percept Theory.

Ayer has called such pragmatic definitions as this "definitions in use". "We define a symbol *in use*", he says, "not by saying that it is synonymous with some other symbol, but by showing how the sentences in which it significantly occurs can be translated into equivalent sentences which contain neither the *definiendum* itself, nor any of its synonyms".[62] By means of this definition in use, then, philosophers and psychologists who accept the Percept Theory can translate into an empirical language statements about the given which would otherwise be verifiable only if the Exposure Hypothesis were valid. In preferring this definition, moreover, they do not necessarily belittle the importance for psychology of either the operation of perceptual reduction or the concept of the sensory core which is defined in terms of it. To deny the existence of the sensory core as traditionally conceived, therefore, is

[62] A. J. Ayer, *Language, Truth and Logic,* p. 68, Gollancz, 1936.

not necessarily to discredit the empirical science erected by psychologists who have assumed its existence, nor even to disparage their method.

Thanks to the definition in use, therefore, there is a third sense in which those who accept the Percept Theory may recognise what Lewis has called "one of the oldest and most universal of philosophic insights". And once a philosopher or psychologist has carefully defined "the given" in this third sense, he might, in some contexts, find it convenient to speak of the sensory core *as if* it were literally a constituent of perceptual consciousness. This policy was recommended, as a matter of fact, by Josiah Royce, who, like James, specifically rejected the Sense-datum Theory. Royce recognised the error of confusing direct inspection with any other procedure, such as perceptual reduction, in which we merely substitute a new state of consciousness for the one we are supposed to be describing; states of consciousness, he says, contain only those elements which on direct inspection they appear to contain. When we say that a mental state consists of elements which we ourselves do not distinguish in it, he says, we may be confusing the mental state with a physical object, with the brain, with the meaning of the state in a logical process, "or else, finally, we are referring to a more sophisticated state of mind which the psychologist, by his devices for analysis, has substituted for the original and naïve consciousness".[63] Nevertheless, he suggests, it may be convenient to speak of this "sophisticated state" *as if* it were part of the original and naïve consciousness. Such a linguistic device, of course, is quite compatible with the Percept Theory, and may sometimes be very useful.

[63] J. Royce, *Outlines of Psychology*, pp. 109–110, Macmillan, New York, 1903.

2. THE PHYSICAL OBJECT AND THE OSTENSIBLE PHYSICAL OBJECT

Assuming, then, that there are at least three senses in which the distinction between the given and its interpretation may be recognised by those who accept the Percept Theory, and that there is only one traditional sense in which this distinction must be denied, we are now in a position to consider some of the epistemological questions raised by the statement that *physical* objects are directly given in perception. This statement, as we have seen, has been made repeatedly in recent years by supporters of the Percept Theory, and in one natural interpretation its implications are indeed revolutionary, and probably incredible; I presume, in fact, that many epistemologists have dismissed it without further ado on the assumption that it is based on a simple confusion of physical objects with *ostensible* physical objects. But the issue is much more complex than such an explanation would suggest.

(a) The Epistemological Status of Ostensible Properties

If any of the philosophers who have said that physical objects are directly given in perception have simply failed to recognise the difference between a physical object and an *ostensible* physical object, then they have, of course, committed a fallacy of some magnitude. To demonstrate this fact with thoroughness by making an exhaustive catalogue of the common properties of physical objects, would lead us into metaphysical questions which are beyond the scope of this paper; and even an attempt at this point to find a minimum basis of agreement concerning the correct analysis of the term "physical", would distract attention from the principal issue. But anyone who accepts the Percept Theory must admit that there is at least one important fact about an *ostensible* physical object which serves to distinguish it sharply from a physical object—the fact, namely, that *some* of its properties, if not all, can be discovered by direct inspection of a single state of perceptual consciousness.[64] Whether this is taken to be an epistemological fact or an ontological fact or both, will depend on one's general theory of the mind, but it is a fact which cannot be denied by those who accept the Percept Theory without rejecting the method of direct inspection and thus the very evidence on which that theory is based.

It is equally certain, on the other hand, that whatever we may mean by "physical object", a physical object is at the very *least* a thing which transcends any one of the states which might be called a perception *of* it. This is admitted, of course, even by Berkeley and the contemporary realists who have defended various forms of epistemological monism; none of them, so far as I know, has maintained that to attribute a property to a physical object is *merely* to attribute that property to what is presented in some *one* state of perceptual consciousness. In order to confirm a statement about a physical object we may indeed require the information that can be obtained by direct inspection of a state of perception, but we also require other information—information, for example, about the relationship between this particular state of perception and other experiences, either actual or possible. And if this point is obvious to those who defend epistemological monism, it is undoubtedly still more obvious to those who accept some form of epistemological dualism. Whether, therefore, our general concept of physical object is in some sense "derived from" the presentation of ostensible physical objects in perception, or whether it is in one or another sense "a priori", the indisputable fact remains that we

---

[64] I say "some" because it is possible that a philosopher who accepts the Percept Theory might agree with Broad that things which are present to consciousness "cannot appear to have properties which they do not really have, though there is no reason why they should not have more properties than we do or can notice". *Scientific Thought*, pp. 243–244 [p. 93, this volume. Ed.].

do possess two concepts corresponding to the terms "physical object" and "ostensible physical object". And the difference between these two concepts is sufficiently proved, for present purposes, by the fact that properties of ostensible physical objects can be discovered by direct inspection of a single state of perceptual consciousness, whereas properties of physical objects cannot.

The fact that the properties of these two kinds of object are designated by the same *names,* should not be allowed to obscure this difference in the epistemological (and, for most philosophers, the ontological) status of the properties. There is, of course, some relationship between the properties of physical objects and the properties of ostensible physical objects which accounts for the fact that the word "square", for example, which designates a property of physical objects, is also used to designate a certain property of *ostensible* physical objects. Philosophers disagree, of course, about the nature of this relationship, just as they disagree about the number of words in our language which can properly be used in both the phenomenal and physical contexts. But they all agree, so far as I know, that a distinction may be made between the phenomenal use and the physical use of certain adjectives, and that this distinction reflects an important difference in the status of the designated properties.

(b) The Ostensible Physical Object and Naïve Realism

Now although it is very unlikely that a philosopher who asserts that physical or material objects are *given* in perception has committed the fallacy of confusing his concept of a physical object with his concept of an *ostensible* physical object, it is a good deal more likely that he has committed a fallacy somewhat similar to this. For he may have assumed that there is no difference at all between his own concept of an *ostensible* physical object and the *naïve* or *popular* concept of a "real" physical object. He may believe, in other words, that what the man in the street means when he says that the paving stones are grey, is precisely what he, the philosopher, would mean if he said that the *ostensible* paving stones are grey. This possibility is suggested by the frequency with which advocates of the Percept Theory describe that which is given in perception as a "naïve world", a "pre-philosophical world", a "common-sense realistic world", etc. And it might help to explain, at least in some cases, what is meant by the statement that physical objects are *given*. For if the concept of an ostensible physical object were identified with the naïve concept of a physical object, such a statement would mean simply that physical objects, in the *popular* sense of the word "physical", are the directly presented objects of consciousness in ordinary perceptual experience.

If such a statement is made by a philosopher who accepts the Percept Theory, and is intended to express one of the important implications of that theory, it cannot be lightly dismissed as true in any trivial sense. There are some possible interpretations of the word "given", of course, according to which it may be quite obviously true that physical objects, as popularly conceived, are given to the man in the street during perceptual experience. Thus it is not unlikely that there is some sense of the verb "to believe" such that the man in the street may correctly be said to *believe,* whenever he is perceptually conscious, that there exists a physical object of a certain kind; and the word "given" might accordingly be interpreted to mean "believed to exist". This cannot be the interpretation desired by supporters of the Percept Theory, however, for the Percept Theory, as we have seen, is a theory about the *sensuous* aspects of perceptual consciousness, and not about the beliefs which may accompany the presentation of an ostensible physical object. Indeed the obvious fact that the man in the street has perceptual beliefs about physical objects, is quite compatible with the rival Sense-datum Theory, whereas the statement that physical objects are *given* in perception is intended to be a criticism of that theory.

The question which now confronts us, therefore, is whether there is any reason to believe that the *sensuous* objects of perceptual consciousness (*i.e.*, ostensible physical objects) are precisely what the man in the street thinks of as "real" physical objects. It is usually true, of course, that at the moment of ordinary perception the man in the street does not *consciously judge* that the ostensible physical object is *not* a "real" physical object, but for that matter neither does the philosopher. Nor, on the other hand, is it plausible to maintain that either of them at the moment of perception, *consciously judges* that the two objects are identical. Ordinary perception is simply not reflective in a sense which would permit either of these two conscious judgements, whether or not the necessary concepts are somehow available. The fact that the philosopher possesses two distinct concepts corresponding to the terms "physical object" and "ostensible physical object", is proved by his ability to distinguish them *on reflexion;* if an advocate of the Percept Theory wishes to show, therefore, that the man in the street does *not* possess two such concepts, he must do so by proving that the man in the street *cannot* distinguish them on reflexion.

When the issue is stated in these terms, however, it becomes quite clear that however naïve the man in the street may be, his naïveté does not consist in his failure to possess *some* concept of a physical object as distinguished from an ostensible physical object. To deny this, indeed, would be to deny that he possesses any concept of "illusion", and to imply, therefore, that he is a naïve realist of a type incapable of understanding, even in some "popular" sense, what it means to say that an oar looks bent but is really straight. And perhaps it would be relevant to point out that the man in the street is usually credited with much more sophistication than this; many philosophers ranging from Berkeley to certain contemporary realists have professed to speak for him, and although they cannot all have described his views correctly in every respect, they have all agreed in constructing epistemological theories which admit the possibility of illusion. To possess the concept of illusion, however, is to recognise, at least implicitly, the very difference between a physical object and an ostensible physical object which would be most likely to impress a supporter of the Percept Theory—the difference, namely, which is reflected in the fact that the properties of physical objects, unlike those of ostensible physical objects, cannot be discovered by direct inspection of a single state of perceptual consciousness.

It would be a mistake, therefore, to say that physical objects are *given* in perception, if the purpose of this form of expression were to imply that when the man in the street says that the paving stones are grey he is talking about what the philosopher would call *ostensible* paving stones. It might seem important to point out that there is some *similarity* between an ostensible physical object and a "real" physical object as popularly conceived—that words which refer to the so-called "secondary" qualities, for example, can be used to describe both of them—but it would surely be misleading to express this fact by saying that physical objects are *given*. There seems, therefore, to be no purely *semantical* fact about the meaning of the terms "physical object" and "ostensible physical object", which could justify the statement that physical objects are given in perception. There is, however, a *phenomenological* fact which might make such a form of expression seem appropriate to some advocates of the Percept Theory. Let us consider it briefly.

(c) *The Ostensible v. the Apparently Ostensible*

This phenomenological fact is the one suggested by Dewey's statement that "it is not experience which is experienced, but nature", the fact, namely, that ostensible physical objects, as presented to us in perception, do not ordinarily *appear* ostensible. Or, to put the matter in a way which emphasises the linguistic difficulties which are always implicit in such discussions as this, ostensible physical objects are not *ostensibly ostensible*. The object of which we are conscious in perception, as Price has so aptly said, "just dawns upon us, of itself. We look and there it is."[65] Thus a tomato is perceptually presented *as* red, *as* solid, and perhaps even *as* edible, but it is not presented *as* ostensible. Nor, on the other hand, is it presented *as* non-ostensible. The terms "ostensible" and "non-ostensible" both refer to epistemological or ontological characteristics, and are properly applied to an entity, as we have seen, after considering such matters as its accessibility to direct inspection; they are *not* phenomenal qualities which ostensible physical objects wear on their faces.[66]

It is difficult to find a terminology which will keep this distinction from becoming obscured, and which will at the same time be convenient for the discussion of problems which have both phenomenological and epistemological facets. Thus although it has been convenient, and I hope not misleading, to say that we are *presented* in perception with ostensible physical objects, even such a statement is not unambiguous. In a purely phenomenological context the word "ostensible" would have to be omitted from this statement, since otherwise it could be interpreted as implying that ostensibility is one of the *presented* characteristics of the object. And questions could also be raised about the word "physical" (or any substitute such as the word "material") for this too, as we have just observed, has epistemological and ontological connotations. But the full force of the difficulty is not felt until we try to dispense with the word "physical" and say instead simply that the objects presented in perception are solid and three-dimensional, persisting through time, possessing causal characteristics, etc. For it will then become evident that each one of *these* descriptive terms also has epistemological and ontological connotations. We have already seen that such terms, when used to describe physical objects, designate properties the existence of which cannot be determined by direct inspection of a single state of percep-

<hr>

[65] *Perception*, p. 153.

[66] It might be argued that an oasis may appear ostensible to an experienced desert traveller who knows that he is experiencing a mirage. But in that case the word "ostensible" has a phenomenal significance which could be absorbed by the statement that the traveller perceives a mirage of an oasis.

tual consciousness, and we surely do not want to suggest that in perception we are presented with properties of *this* kind. The pervasiveness of this terminological difficulty, as we have also seen, is a result of the fact that in a phenomenological context most, and perhaps all, of the adjectives in our language have a meaning which they could not possibly have if they were being used to describe physical objects.

It is possible, therefore, that the philosophers who have maintained, on the basis of the Percept Theory, that physical objects are actually *given* in perception, have used this form of expression in an attempt to solve, at least partially, the terminological problem just outlined. This form of expression, as we have seen, does not by any means solve the entire problem, but it might help to emphasise the fact that the objects which are presented in perception are not presented *as* ostensible. And some advocates of the Percept Theory have thought it important to emphasise this fact because the failure of epistemologists to recognise it may have been responsible for the generation of "pseudo-problems".[67] Similarly, the statement that in perception we are "directly aware" of physical or material objects, which is often made by the same philosophers, can perhaps be accounted for as an alternative method of emphasising the same phenomenological fact. Indeed neither of these two forms of expression seems entirely inappropriate when considered in this light, although they may have been the cause, because of their traditional epistemological connotations, of more misunderstanding than they have prevented.

However this may be decided, the issues to be discussed in the following pages are primarily epistemological; and it is consequently impossible to restrict ourselves to forms of expression which would be appropriate in a purely phenomenological context. I shall continue to say, there-

---

[67] See *e.g.*, K. Duncker, "Phenomenology and Epistemology of Consciousness", *Philosophy and Phenomenological Research*, June, 1947. I believe that Duncker is clearly mistaken, however, if he intends to imply that there is no genuine problem concerning the possibility of transcending consciousness.

fore, that the objects directly presented or given in perception are *ostensible* physical objects, recognising, however, that I can say this only because I am not attempting *merely* to describe the phenomenal properties of the objects of perceptual consciousness—only, in short because I have adopted the epistemological point of view. From this point of view it is clear that physical objects, because they are things the properties of which cannot be discovered by direct inspection of a single state of perceptual consciousness, cannot reasonably be said to be "directly presented" or "given" in such a state of perceptual consciousness.

In this particular respect, of course, the distinction between an ostensible physical object and a physical object is strictly parallel to one of the most important of the traditional distinctions between a *sense-datum* and a physical object; for sense-data have traditionally been conceived as observable by direct inspection, and physical objects as knowable only through some more complex process. In fact it should now be clear that the concepts of physical object and ostensible physical object are so independent of one another, from a logical point of view, that the basic distinctions will not be affected by the outcome of the conflict between the Percept Theory and the Sense-datum Theory. The questions which remain to be answered therefore, in any attempt to evaluate the epistemological implications of the Percept Theory, are questions about the epistemological *functions* of ostensible physical objects; and the most direct way to raise these questions is to ask whether ostensible physical objects are adequate substitutes for performing the functions which sense-data have traditionally been supposed to perform in the processes by which we acquire and confirm our beliefs about the physical world.

3. EPISTEMOLOGICAL FUNCTIONS OF THE
OSTENSIBLE PHYSICAL OBJECT

(a) The Sign Function

I believe that there are two such functions, one of them perhaps more strictly psychological than epistemological. The first of these, the psychological function traditionally attributed to sense-data in the knowing process, is that of somehow *determining,* at least in part, the nature of the physical object which the perceiver in some sense "believes" to exist at the moment of perception. It is impossible to describe this function more precisely except in terms of some particular form of the Sense-datum Theory. Thus Berkeley, who accepted what I have called the "discursive inference version" of that theory, was willing to say that the sense-datum given in perceptual experience serves as a "sign" of the existence of a certain kind of physical object (for Berkeley, of course, other "ideas"). Other philosophers who have accepted the Discursive Inference Theory have said that the sense-datum "causes" us to "make a judgement about" or to "think of" a physical object. Such forms of expression are intended to imply that perceptual consciousness is discursive.

Philosophers and psychologists who accept the more common Sensory Core Theory, however, have often found it more difficult to describe the relationship between a sense-datum and perceptual beliefs. Words like "sign", "clue", and "cause", do not seem appropriate for a sensory core which is conceived as occurring simultaneously with the perceptual beliefs. "The best analogy we can offer", says Broad, ". . . is to be found in the case of reading a book. . . . If there were no print we should cognise no meaning, and if the print were different in certain specific ways we should cognise a different meaning".[68] This

[68] *Scientific Thought,* p. 66.

analogy is not very good, however, for the print on the physical page transcends the entire state of perception and might therefore be said partially to "cause" the perception, whereas awareness of the sense-datum is regarded as a *constituent* of the state, and could not be said, in the same sense, to cause the beliefs which accompany it. Perhaps those who accept the Sensory Core Theory should restrict themselves, as Broad suggests, to the statement that the sense-datum and the beliefs are functionally related in such a way that "if this sensum had different properties we should ascribe different properties to the physical object".[69] Or perhaps they might say, just a little more specifically, that sense-data and the accompanying beliefs are both caused simultaneously by certain physical events within and without the perceiving organism.

Now the Percept Theory, as we have seen, does not admit the existence in ordinary perception of a temporally distinct sensuous constituent; ostensible physical objects, therefore, cannot fulfil the function of a perceptual "sign" as conceived by Berkeley and other exponents of the Discursive Inference Theory. This is probably only a matter of academic interest to most contemporary epistemologists, however, for they have apparently rejected the Discursive Inference Theory in favour of the Sensory Core Theory. But if it is true, as those who accept this latter theory maintain, that there is *some* functional relationship between the sensuous constituents of perceptual consciousness and the beliefs which accompany them, this relationship can quite consistently be recognised by supporters of the Percept Theory. In whatever sense it is true, in other words, that consciousness of a sensuously clothed ostensible physical object is accompanied by beliefs about the existence of a real physical object of a certain kind, in that sense it is meaningful to say that the beliefs are functionally related to the characteristics of the ostensible physical

---

[69] *Ibid.*, p. 247. *Cf.* Price: The ostensible object "is forced upon me by the character of the sense-datum . . . and no other ostensible object but precisely this one could ostend itself to me here and now, the sense-datum being what it is". *Perception*, p. 148.

object. And thus we could even say, directly paraphrasing Broad's statement about sensa, that perceptual beliefs are "based upon" ostensible physical objects in such a way that if a particular ostensible physical object had different properties we should ascribe different properties to the physical object. So far as the traditional *psychological* function of sense-data is concerned, therefore, the Percept Theory gives rise to no problems which are avoided by the Sensory Core Theory; and to carry the discussion beyond this point is unnecessary for the present purpose.

(b) The Function of the Ostensible Physical Object in Confirmation

The second, and more strictly epistemological, function traditionally attributed to sense-data, is that of serving as an important part of the evidence to which we must appeal in any attempt to *justify* our beliefs about the physical world. The statements which express these beliefs, according to one of the most familiar strains of traditional empiricism, can be divided into two groups: the first includes only singular statements about physical objects or events, and the second includes all other statements about the physical world. Statements in the second group, according to this theory, can be justified only by an argument the premises of which include statements in the first group. And statements in the first group can in turn be justified ultimately only by an argument the premises of which include statements about sense-data. Thus sense-data have been regarded by many philosophers as the very foundation stones of empirical knowledge, without which a rational construction of physical science would not be even theoretically possible.

For present purposes it is unnecessary to consider the points of disagreement within this well-known school of empirical thought. There has been disagreement about the proper analysis of the statements which refer to sense-data, about the necessity for additional premises, about

the number and variety of principles of inference required
to draw conclusions about physical objects, and about the
epistemological status of such principles of inference; but
these differences may be disregarded without prejudice to
questions about the general function traditionally attributed
to sense-data. I shall say, for convenience, that all members of this empirical school believe that sense-data are
"epistemologically basic"; and the problem which immediately concerns us, therefore, is whether the Percept Theory has any implications for the theory that sense-data are
epistemologically basic. This problem is sufficiently important to deserve careful consideration even by the many
philosophers who are convinced that beliefs about physical
objects cannot be justified except in some *relative* fashion
by reference to *other* beliefs about physical objects.

Now among the singular statements which express our
beliefs about physical objects, there are some which express *perceptual* beliefs, *i.e.*, beliefs which are entertained
at a time when we are presented with an ostensible physical object, and which are, as we have said, in some sense
"based on" the ostensible physical object; such beliefs are
usually expressed by statements similar in form to the
statement "This (or that) is a tomato".

Perceptual beliefs could probably be described dispositionally by reference to tendencies towards bodily behaviour or towards conscious experiences, or both; though
perhaps, as we have already observed, some philosophers
might wish also to make some reference to *phenomenal*
events occurring simultaneously with the presentation of
the ostensible physical object.

It is convenient, in considering the epistemological implications of the Percept Theory, to begin by paying special attention to those singular statements which express
non-perceptual beliefs about physical objects but which are
commonly supposed to be justifiable by reference to *past*
perceptual experience. Thus we might consider, for example, the statement "There is a tomato behind me", with
the understanding that it expresses the present belief of

someone who has recently been presented with an ostensible tomato but who is now looking in another direction. Such beliefs, of course, constitute a considerable proportion of all our beliefs about the physical world.

Most philosophers who accept the Sense-datum Theory and who also believe that sense-data are epistemologically basic, would probably maintain that in such a case the belief expressed by the statement "There is a tomato behind me", could be justified to some extent by means of an argument based on the present memory of past sense-data. Indeed they *must* defend a position of this sort if they are to bring their theory even roughly into line with common-sense, for the fact that someone has recently had a perceptual experience of a kind that he associates with the existence of a tomato, *is* commonly regarded as epistemologically relevant to his present non-perceptual belief in the existence of a tomato. But if the Percept Theory is true, this non-perceptual belief about the tomato could almost certainly *not* be justified in this way. For assuming that the recent perception of the tomato had not been perceptually reduced for psychological or aesthetic purposes, it would simply be false to say that the observer had been aware of any sense-datum at all. The only sensuous constituent of that past perception would have been an ostensible tomato, which, as we have seen, is quite different from a sense-datum as traditionally conceived. If the present belief is to be justified by reference to *anything* that has been sensuously given, therefore, it must be justified by reference to the ostensible tomato. And it is just this phenomenal thing, indeed, that the normal observer *would* remember under such circumstances; he would remember that he had been presented with a full-bodied tomato with all its sensuous qualities of redness, smoothness, warmth, and sweetness, and not that he had been aware of a round red patch, or perhaps, depending on the lighting, a patch of some quite different colour.

The traditional analysis of justification by reference to sense-data is somewhat different, however, when the sense-data in question are conceived as *future* rather than *past* objects of direct awareness; and because of this difference it is not sufficient for those who support the Percept Theory to point out that sense-data do not occur in *ordinary* perceptual experience. According to the philosophers who believe that sense-data are epistemologically basic, the statement "There is a tomato behind me" could be justified to some extent not only by reference to past experience, but also by turning around and inspecting the new sense-datum which is thereupon presented. And in a procedure of this kind it might indeed be possible, by adopting the reducing attitude, to produce a pure state (or approximately pure state) of direct awareness. And the sense-datum which is thus presented might possibly be used as the basis of an argument to justify the original non-perceptual belief about the tomato. It would be presumptuous indeed, for those who support the Percept Theory to maintain that such a procedure is *never* followed in an attempt to justify a belief about a physical object.

It would be quite unrealistic, on the other hand, to maintain that such a procedure is *usually* or even *frequently* followed. The procedure which is usually regarded as confirming a belief about a physical object involves various operations (*e.g.*, manipulation of the object) but it does *not* involve the operation of introspective reduction. The usual procedure, as Price has aptly described it, is that of "specifying the unspecified". We look at the tomato, for example, from several points of view, turn it over in our hands, squeeze it, etc., and by these means produce a series of perceptual states. The ostensible physical object remains a tomato throughout the entire process, but the tomato becomes progressively more determinate, more specified, in each succeeding perception. And as the relatively unspecified tomato becomes more and more specified, so we at the same time become more and more convinced that our belief has been justified. There is obviously no need to refer to sense-data in describing this process, and if we were to formalise this common method of confirmation we should have to treat the series of ostensible physical objects, and not sense-data, as epistemologically basic.

There is also another fact which shows that if the Percept Theory is true, sense-data cannot be regarded as epistemologically basic without doing violence to commonsense. This is the fact that we are so often surprised, after we adopt the reducing attitude for psychological or aesthetic purposes, at the characteristics of the sense-data which are thereupon presented to us. The fact of the matter is that most of us are simply not prepared, in many cases, to predict the characteristics of the sense-data which we can produce by perceptual reduction; we are not prepared to say, for example, what the colour of our sense-datum will turn out to be if we are looking at a field of green grass on a cloudy day, or in the late afternoon when it is lighted by the rays of the setting sun. We are simply not familiar enough with the relationship between the physical stimulus and the conditions of observation on the one hand, and the sense-data which are the products of perceptual reduction on the other hand. Because of the psychological fact of object-constancy, however, the qualities of ostensible physical objects are more easily predicted; the ostensible grass, for example, is likely to be green whether the sky is clear or cloudy. However the epistemological relationship between physical objects and ostensible physical objects may be conceived, therefore, it is apparently better understood on the practical level than the relationship between physical objects and the relatively rare objects of direct awareness. This in itself seems to be a good reason for putting greater faith in a process of confirmation in which ostensible physical objects, rather than sense-data, are treated as epistemologically basic.

If the philosophers who believe that sense-data are epistemologically basic are not interested in bringing their theory into line with common practice in the justification of belief, they might still insist, to be sure, that perceptual reduction is necessary for "proper" confirmation of beliefs about the physical world. But it is difficult to see what could be said in support of such a position, unless an appeal were made to some ontological theory about the *constitution* of physical objects, in particular to a theory that physical objects are in some more or less literal sense "composed of" sense-data. Such theories, however, would lose whatever plausibility they may have if they were not themselves supported by epistemological considerations; and if the Percept Theory is true, indeed, these theories must themselves be revised if they are to retain the epistemological advantages traditionally attributed to them. To many philosophers this fact will undoubtedly seem to be one of the most important consequences of the Percept Theory, and we ought to consider it briefly before concluding our examination of the epistemological implications of the Percept Theory. Let us now do so.

4. THE PERCEPT THEORY AND
EPISTEMOLOGICAL MONISM

Epistemological monists from Berkeley to many contemporary realists have used the theory that sense-data are epistemologically basic as a premiss in their attacks on epistemological dualism. Knowledge of physical objects is possible, they have said, only if statements about physical objects can be construed, in some more or less complex manner, as statements about sense-data—or only, as some of them have preferred to say, if physical objects are somehow "composed of" sense-data. Their analysis of physical statements has not usually been based entirely on epistemological considerations, but in most cases their analysis was at least *suggested* by these considerations.

If the Percept Theory is true, however, the epistemological advantages traditionally attributed to monism can be retained only by reinterpreting statements about the physical world in terms of ostensible physical objects and events instead of sense-data. For one effect of the Percept Theory, as we have seen, is to change the denotation of the term "epistemologically basic". In whatever sense, therefore, a philosopher wishes to maintain that physical objects are "composed of" things that are epistemologically basic, in that sense he must say, if he accepts the Percept Theory, that physical objects are "composed of" ostensible physical objects. I do not propose to evaluate the results of such a reinterpretation but only to indicate what form it must take, and in particular to point out that ostensible physical objects can vary in ways that sense-data cannot, so that a new problem is uncovered as soon as we attempt such a reinterpretation.

To state this problem clearly let us say that according to the traditional forms of epistemological monism every physical object is a "family" of sense-data.[70] If we do not specify the ontological status of sense-data—whether, for example, they can exist unsensed and whether they may be "hypothetical"—this statement can be interpreted as expressing a point of agreement among epistemological monists whether they be called "idealists", "realists", or "phenomenalists". For a family of sense-data would simply be the class of all those sense-data, actual or possible, which would have to be mentioned in making a complete ontological analysis of a particular physical object.

Now according to the traditional Sense-datum Theory, as we have seen, the sense-data observable by any one sense are quite limited in their qualities; visual sense-data, for example, may vary only in shape and colour. If the shape and colour of a visual sense-datum remain unaltered throughout a given period of time, therefore, changes in the attitude of the observer during that period cannot be said to affect the sense-datum at all. In the case of ostensible physical objects, however, the case is quite different; the colour and shape of two ostensible tomatoes may be exactly similar although the ostensible tomatoes, because of changes in the attitude of the observer, are quite different in other respects. To a hungry man the tomato may be presented as warm and sweet and edible whereas to someone looking for a missile it may be presented as soft and juicy and just about as heavy as a baseball. Thus it is clear that a

[70] The term, of course, is the one used by Price for a collection of sense-data unified in a certain way. See *Perception*, p. 227.

family of ostensible physical objects is even more numerous
than a family of sense-data, and that the relations among
its members are many times more complicated. As a matter
of fact it might even be more appropriate to say that a
physical object is nothing less than a *nation* of sense-data,
the nation in its turn comprising as many families as there
are attitudes capable of affecting the content of perceptual
experience. Thus the various perspective views of a tomato
which are obtained by walking around it, could be said to
be members of one family provided that they are all determined by the same attitude. And by walking around the
tomato a second time, but with a different attitude, the observer could be said to become acquainted with members
of a second family. And so on.

A philosopher who wished to maintain such a position,
however, might not feel obliged to hold that members of
all these families must be mentioned in an ideal translation
of *every* statement about the tomato in question. He might
insist, and with considerable plausibility, that what the hungry man *means* when he uses the word "tomato" is likely
to be quite different from what the man in search of a missile means when he uses the same word, and that this difference in meaning must be reflected, in an adequate analysis,
by the choice of families to be represented in the translation. Thus there might often be cases in which the meaning
of the statement "This is a tomato", if used to express the
limited belief of a particular observer, might be adequately
translated into statements about ostensible physical objects
which belong to very few families within the nation, or perhaps to only one. This is not the place to examine such
possibilities more fully; it is sufficient for present purposes
to point out that the Percept Theory creates a new problem for the epistemological monist, but that this new problem does not appear insoluble.

5. Conclusion

We may finally conclude, therefore, that there are at least four important epistemological implications of the Percept Theory: (1) The traditional psychological distinction between the given and its meaning or interpretation, must usually be construed as a distinction between the ostensible physical object and certain accompanying events, either phenomenal or physiological or both. (2) There is one traditional meaning of "the given", however, for which there is no simple substitute in terms of the Percept Theory; for this particular meaning a more complex substitute may be provided by means of a "definition in use". (3) The denotation of the term "epistemologically basic" must be understood to be ostensible physical objects rather than those things which have traditionally been called "sense data". (4) As a result of this fact all the traditional forms of epistemological monism must be reinterpreted to make physical objects "nations" of ostensible physical objects rather than "families" of sense-data.

On the other hand the Percept Theory has no implications concerning the general epistemological or ontological status of physical objects. It does not imply that some form of epistemological monism must be correct, nor even that there is some reasonable sense in which it would be true to say, in an epistemological context, that physical objects are "directly presented" in perception. Those philosophers are mistaken, therefore, who have inferred from the Percept Theory that the traditional problems concerning the epistemology of perception are pseudo-problems, or that they must be completely recast to make them fit the phenomenological facts on which the Percept Theory is based.

The epistemological implications of the Percept Theory, we may conclude, are important but not revolutionary.

AUTHOR'S NOTE

Since this essay was written, the doctrine has become widespread among philosophers that it is a mistake (or, at the very least, misleading) to employ any form of "act-object" terminology to describe sense experience—any terminology, that is to say, in which sense experience is represented as an act of perceiving, sensing, experiencing, having, or being aware of such "objects" as appearances, images, sensa, or sense-data; and with respect to this doctrine it is of course just as wrong to say that in perception we are aware of percepts or ostensible objects as to say that we are aware of sense-data. It is important to recognize, therefore, that the phenomenological and epistemological issues discussed in this essay are entirely independent of the act-object terminology. They can be formulated in *any* terminology which allows us to describe a sensory constituent which may occur in hallucination as well as in "genuine" perception. If we agree, for example, to use the idiom "It looks as if I am seeing ——" for this purpose, the phenomenological issues discussed in Part I, Section 3 of this essay can be construed as issues concerning the types of words which may properly be inserted in the blank. It may be true, when I gaze at a snow-capped mountain, that it looks as if I am seeing a triangular patch of white. Can it also be true in this *same* purely sensory use of "looks as if" that it looks as if I am seeing a mountain capped with snow? Or, as so many philosophers have traditionally maintained, are we confusing the phenomenology of sense experience with an "interpretation" when we use words like "mountain" and "snow", and thus failing to describe our sense experience as it is really given? All the phenomenological and epistemological issues discussed in this essay may be formulated in some analogous way, using whatever idiom is approved by those who want to avoid an act-object terminology.

IS THERE A PROBLEM ABOUT
SENSE-DATA?

G. A. PAUL

The problem with which we shall be principally concerned is 'Are there such things as sense-data?' We shall
go on to consider also the questions, supposing there are
such things, whether they are private, whether they can
exist unsensed, and whether they can continue to exist
throughout a period of time or are merely momentary.

About these last problems I shall perhaps be able to say
something definite, but about the first I am unable to come
to any decision. The difficulty about it is not that there is a
problem which we can understand and to which we are unable to find the answer; the difficulty is on the contrary to
find out clearly what the problem is itself. It is the difficulty
of understanding what anyone is saying who says that there
are such things as sense-data, and is due partly to the fact
that not all the words used occur in everyday speech, a new
technical term 'sense-datum' having been brought into use.
It is not, however, due solely to the fact that a word is
being introduced which has not been used before, for there
are many cases in which this is done where there is no such
difficulty. For example the physiologists who wished to introduce the word 'fovea' to describe a certain peculiarity
of the structure of the eye can have encountered no such
difficulty. They could say that they were using 'fovea' as a
name for the slight depression in the retina diametrically
opposite to the pupil, and by dissecting eyes could point to
instances of this depression. When they had done this no
one would have any difficulty in answering the question
'Are there such things as foveas?' This is the sort of question

with which, because of its linguistic similarity, we are apt to compare our question 'Are there such things as sense-data?' and in case we should be misled by this similarity we require to point out the differences which also exist between them. Once we know that 'fovea' is being used to mean 'the slight depression in the retina diametrically opposite to the pupil' we can find the answer to Qf[1] by dissecting some eyes and finding in each case whether there is an object which answers to this description. Before we even start the experiment of dissecting we have some idea of what it will be like to find such a depression and of what it will be like to be unable to find such a depression or to find that there is no such depression.

On the other hand if we are to find whether there are such things as sense-data we need make no experiment, and no experiment of any kind will help us. Sense-data, if there are such things, are objects which, so far from needing to seek by making an experiment, we cannot help seeing every time we see anything at all. It is sometimes said that we have only to inspect what happens whenever we have any visual experience of any kind to become aware that on such occasions we always do see an object of the sort which is being called the 'sense-datum' sort. For example, it is said, you know what it is to look from an angle at the top surface of a penny lying flat on a table; in such a case the surface which you can see of the penny is round but you see it by means of an object which is not round but elliptical. A great difference becomes quickly obvious between this and the answer to Qf, where the point of asking whether there were such things as foveas was that you would know what it was like to discover a retina which lacked a depression opposite to the lens, whereas in this case you do not know what it would be like to be seeing anything whatever and not be perceiving an object of the sort in question. It then seems that either there was no point in asking Qs[2] (since you can have no idea what it would be like for the answer to be 'No') or that the point of ask-

---

[1] 'Qf' = 'the question "Are there such things as foveas?" '
[2] 'Qs' = 'the question "Are there such things as sense-data?" '

ing such a question is very different from the point of asking such a question as Qf. If this is not obvious, we can try to make it so by further consideration of the situation where you look at a penny from an angle. Sometimes in such a case it is true to say 'I see the round top surface of this penny, and I see that it is round, but it looks elliptical', and what some philosophers say is that you can become aware on inspection that it is true not only that you are seeing a round object but also that you are seeing an object which is elliptical (the elliptical object being related to the round object in a certain intimate way which we have expressed by saying that the round object is seen 'by means of it').

Some people have claimed that they are unable to find such an object, and others have claimed that they do not understand how the existence of such an object can be doubted, which drives one to ask what it would be like to be unable to find such an object and what it is like to find one. A clue is given by the fact that the claim generally made is not what would sometimes be called the 'more moderate' one that whenever we see a physical object we do in fact see a sense-datum but the 'less moderate' claim that it is logically impossible that we should see a physical object and not see a sense-datum. To call one the 'more' and the other the 'less' moderate claim is misleading, for it obscures the fact that while the 'more' moderate would be a simple empirical statement the 'less' moderate is a statement that so and so is logically impossible, i.e., in this case, a statement about the way a certain expression is to be used, viz., that 'I saw a circular penny, and I saw an elliptical object (by means of which I saw it)' is to be another way of saying 'I saw a round penny, and it looked elliptical to me'.

Is there any test which would be relevant to whether it is true that in such a case there is an object which is round and also that there is an object which is elliptical?

This brings us to the question what it means to say of a sense-datum that it is an object. To say that there are such objects as foveas is to say that in eyes there is a shallow depression opposite to the lens; to say that a fovea is an object is to say that it is a physical object or at least a depression in a physical object, that it is the sort of thing that several people can see at once, and can be pointed to by, for example, placing a probe in it. It is not in the same way clear what is meant by saying of a *sense-datum* that it is an object, for people ask about it 'is it a physical part of a physical object?', 'is it private to one percipient?', 'is it the sort of thing one can point to?' Such questions have the usual empirical look, but if we consider what facts we should consider relevant to their truth or falsity we see that they are not asking for information about 'objects' but about the uses of words, viz., 'is "observed surface" of a physical object replaceable in all sentences in which it occurs by "corresponding sense-datum"?', 'does it mean anything to say "More than one person is seeing the same sense-datum at the same time"?', 'is there anything which is (to be) called "pointing to a sense-datum"?' In saying that the word 'fovea' is to stand for a *thing* of a certain sort, meaning a *physical* thing, and at the same time *pointing* to an instance of a fovea, we say a great deal about the way the word is to be used—in fact we say all that any physiologist requires in order to be able to use the word successfully, i.e., from our pointing only to one instance of a fovea and calling it 'fovea' he knows at once what is meant by saying ever so many things about foveas, e.g., that there are and have been foveas which no one ever has or will see, that a given fovea is the same one as we examined yesterday, that it continued to exist overnight when no one was looking at it, that the person standing beside me is looking at the same fovea as I am, that it is turning a deeper yellow, and so on. This is a simple thing to point out, but it is of importance here. All that seems to happen is that someone points to an object, and says the name of the object, whereupon by watching the behaviour of the object we are enabled to make all sorts of true statements about it. Similarly it seems in telling us what sense-data are, someone refers to a situation with which we are all familiar, viz., seeing a penny obliquely, and says 'the elliptical object which is related in such and such a way to the observed surface of the penny is a sense-datum.' One is thereupon inclined to behave in the way one is justified in doing when such a thing as a fovea is pointed out to one, viz., to suppose that one knows what is to be meant by saying of such an object that, for example, objects of the same sort have existed which no one ever has or will see, that this object is the same one as I saw a short time ago, that it does or does not continue to exist when no one is looking at the penny from this angle, that it is turning a darker brown, and so on. That is, one is inclined to go on and talk as if one had just learned the name of some new kind of physical object which has just been brought to light. We know in the case of physical objects what it means to say *this object* has such and such properties', and when someone tries to point out to us an object of the sort that is to be called a 'sense-datum' we go on as if we knew in the same way what it means to say *this object* has such and such properties', 'this sense-datum has such and such properties'. But in fact the case is very different: the word 'fovea' was introduced as a name for a physical object, and we know how to use it in new cases because we know in general how words for physical objects are used in English. This statement is the crux of the present paper. There are certain general criteria which ordinarily enable us to decide whether a given physical object is the same object as we saw at a given previous time, whether it is the same object even though many of its properties are different, whether it is a different object from one we saw previously although it has very much the same properties, whether it is now changing its colour and shape, and so on. This being so, we are apt to think that all we have to do is to give a name to an object and then examine this object and watch its behaviour in order to be able to make up true statements about it in which this name occurs: we forget that the name-word is being brought into use as a member of a class of words whose use in certain contexts is already given. E.g., everyone can imagine circumstances in which it would be true to say 'He opened his eyes, saw a certain fovea, closed his eyes and did not see it for five seconds, opened them again and saw *the same fovea* again', and circumstances in which it would be false to say this (e.g. if during the five seconds someone cunningly replaced the eye-dissection he had been examining by another exactly similar). On the other hand, can anyone describe or imagine circumstances in which it would be true to say 'He saw a certain sense-datum, ceased to see it for five seconds, and then saw *the same sense-datum* again'? Would it be true to say this, for example, if it were true to say 'He saw a certain penny from a certain angle, and it looked elliptical to him, he closed his eyes and did not see it for five seconds, opened them again and saw the same penny looking exactly the same to him'? The answer is that no examination of such a situation will provide us with an answer: in the one case it seems that examination of the situation in question *will* provide an answer; in the other that it will not. It seems that in one case examination of the object in question will tell us whether it continued to exist throughout a period; but that in the other it will not. In a sense it does not do so in either case; but in the case where we introduce the word 'fovea' by pointing to one or more foveas everyone does as a matter of fact know under what conditions it is to be true to say that this is the same fovea as I saw five seconds ago, this fovea has been on this table for the last half-hour although no one has been in the room, and so on. They know this because they know under what circumstances it is true to say such things of other physical objects; but it is not *necessary* that the word 'fovea' should behave like other words for physical objects. We might, for example, say 'No fovea lasts longer than a single specious present' meaning this not as an empirical statement but as a statement of how the word fovea is to be used. We might have some good reason for adopting such a way of speaking; e.g., suppose certain minute structures in the fovea were, we discovered, annihilated and replaced every five minutes, then we might very well say 'During the last half-hour I have observed five foveas succeed one another here, each differing from the last one in respect of the minute structures (M)' or 'During the last half-hour I have observed the same fovea, the minute structures (M) in it being replaced every five minutes' and mean the same by these two statements.

The word 'sense-datum' as people have employed it does not fall into a fully-prepared scheme for its usage as a word for a physical object does, but its usage is not purely arbitrary. By this I mean that its use is connected with the use of certain words which *are* in ordinary language, e.g. 'looks', 'appears', 'appearance', and with certain uses of 'this', 'after-image', and 'image'. We shall now consider some uses of such words with which it is connected, and how it is connected with them.

We so use language that whenever it is true that I am seeing the round top surface of a penny, and know that it is round, it is true to say that the penny *looks* (e.g.) elliptical to me, in a sense in which this does not entail that I am in any way deceived about the real shape of the penny. (I shall indicate this sense by means of a suffix: 'looks*'.) The rule which has generally been adopted is that the sense-datum is correctly said to have whatever shape and colour-property the corresponding surface of the physical object looks* to me to have. E.g., suppose a red light is cast upon the penny as I view it obliquely, then if it is true that the surface which I see is round and brown, and looks* to be elliptical and red, then according to our rule it is true to say that the corresponding sense-datum *is* elliptical and red.

Those who have in practice used the word 'sense-datum' have not spoken as if what they were doing was introducing *merely* an alternative way of saying this same thing over again, but as if this new sentence which they substitute were in some way nearer to the facts. They have the idea that in some sense when a physical object looks* red to someone then something really is red, i.e., that there really are in such cases two *objects,* one which looks* red and one which *is* red, and that somehow the one which *is* red has generally been overlooked, and its existence has now for the first time been recognized. It is said that its existence cannot be doubted, for if we carefully inspect what happens when a physical object appears red to us we shall come to realize that we can see this object, and further that, while in every such case it is academically possible to doubt whether there really is a physical object which is appearing red, it is academically impossible to doubt that there is an object which *is* red. The point is that although I may have been mistaken in supposing that there was a round surface of a penny looking* elliptical to me, yet it is quite certain that there was an elliptical appearance (and that it is logically impossible that this appearance should merely have *looked* elliptical to me). I shall only point out that another way of describing the same situation is 'I thought I was seeing a round surface of a penny, which was looking elliptical to me, but in fact there was no penny there at all.' It is then asked: 'If there was no penny there at all, what was really happening? what were the elements of the situation?' and it is answered that what I was really seeing was a sense-datum which was elliptical, but was not a sense-datum 'of' a physical object (or at least not 'of' a penny). It is an equally good answer to say 'It only seemed to me as if there was a round penny which looked* elliptical. I was really not seeing anything at all.' This says just the same as the statement which contained the word 'sense-datum', and there is no question of the one saying it less or more adequately than the other.

Sometimes people explain how they are going to use 'sense-datum' by taking the case when I have an after-image with my eyes closed, in which case it is quite certain that there is no external object which is appearing, say, red. They then say that a sense-datum is any object which is seen in the sense in which the after-image is seen, and ask us to notice that whenever we see a physical object we see* an object (in this sense, which I am going to call 'see*'). It is, however, not at all clear what this means. For it is not certain that whenever I see a physical object I see any *other* object in any sense of see. What is certain is that, suppose the physical object looks* red, there is nothing to prevent me from expressing that by saying that an object which is red corresponds to the physical object, and nothing to prevent me from saying that I see* that object. Such a notation might be convenient for certain purposes, and is unlikely to mislead, because (1) it makes no sense to say of an after-image that it looks different from what it really is, and we are not tempted to say such a thing of a sense-datum, and certainly have not given any meaning to saying it of a sense-datum, and (2) it is possible, and may sometimes happen, that what we took to be an after-image turns out to be an appearance of a physical object, and vice versa. This way of talking at once suggests that there really is in such a case an object (viz., a sense-datum) about which it is doubtful whether it is an after-image, or an appearance (sense-datum) of a physical object.

My intention has not been to deny that there are sense-data, if by that is meant that (1) we can understand, to some extent at least, how people wish to use the word 'sense-datum' who have introduced it in philosophy, and that (2) sometimes statements of a certain form containing the word 'sense-datum' are true, e.g., 'I am seeing* an elliptical sense-datum "of" a round penny.' Nor do I wish to deny that the introduction of this terminology may be useful in helping to solve some philosophical problems about perception; but I do wish to deny that there is any sense in which this terminology is nearer to reality than any other which may be used to express the same facts; in particular I wish to deny that in order to give a complete and accurate account of any perceptual situation it is necessary to use a noun in the way in which 'sense-datum' is used,[3] for this leads to the notion that there are entities of a curious sort over and above physical objects which can 'have' sensible properties but cannot 'appear to have' sensible properties which they have not got.

We shall consider now certain puzzles to which the use of 'sense-datum' has given rise.

There is first the idea of the sense-datum as a sort of

---

[3] I.e., there are no facts of visual experience in order to express which it is necessary to use a noun functioning in the way 'sense-datum' does.

barrier, an entity which gets between us and the physical object. In trying to overcome the idea of its being a barrier people ask 'Is the corresponding sense-datum identical with the observed surface of the physical object?' An answer to this question is relevant to many questions commonly asked, viz., are sense-data mental or physical, are they private or public, do they exist only when someone is seeing* them or can they exist while no one is seeing* them, are they merely momentary or can they continue to exist throughout a time? In order to be able to answer 'Yes' to it philosophers have even been prepared to alter their use of 'sense-datum' so that it makes sense to say that such and such a sense-datum appears to have sensible qualities it does not in fact have'[4]; for if the answer were 'Yes', not only would the idea of a barrier be overcome, but also the second of each of these alternatives would be true, for we should say that what is a part of the surface of a physical object in this sense is physical, and we know what it is for more than one person to see the same part of the surface of a physical object, and for such a part to exist while no one is perceiving it, and for it to continue to exist throughout a period of time. The question whether a given sense-datum is identical with the corresponding surface has the air of being a question about two objects (or about one object) which is to be settled by inspecting the object or objects. Actually it is to be settled by examining not an object but our use of the two words 'sense-datum' and 'surface'; if we find some sentence which says something true about the sense-datum such that if the sentence which results from replacing the word 'sense-datum' in that sentence by the word 'surface' is either false or meaningless, that is what we shall call the sense-datum and the surface being not identical. Thus if *ex hypothesi* the corresponding surface is really round, and the sense-datum I see of it is elliptical, to say 'the sense-datum is round' is either false or nonsense; and so is 'the corresponding surface is elliptical'. This is what we call the sense-datum and the surface being not

[4] E.g. John Wisdom, *Problems of Mind and Matter*, pp. 156–7, and Ch. IX passim.

identical. Thus it is not true to say that in this case the sense-datum is physical if we mean by that that it is a part of the surface of a physical object in the sense in which the corresponding part of the surface is a part of the surface of a physical object.

It is suggested that in certain favoured cases it may yet be true that the sense-datum is identical with the corresponding surface. E.g., suppose I am looking at the penny in such a way that it looks* to me the same shape as it really is, i.e., the corresponding surface is round and the sense-datum of it is round. We have now to try and show a further difference between the way the two words behave, and at this point the most useful thing to consider is that future experience might lead us to believe that the surface in question had not been really round, whereas this same evidence would not lead us to doubt that it had looked* round to me, i.e., that the sense-datum I saw of it had been round. That is, what is evidence in such a case against the truth of 'the surface is round' is not evidence against the truth of 'the sense-datum is round'.

It is, however, not impossible to hold that in such a case it is the same object which is being called 'round', but that it is being called 'round' in two different senses, and that all that has been shown is that it is not round in one sense but may yet be round in the other.

This urges us to try to point out further differences in usage between the two words, and so we come to a problem which is thorny indeed. It is suggested that, say, a minute ago the surface, in question, of the penny was in existence but the sense-datum was not, that it only came into existence when I looked at the penny. If one takes one's cue for the use of 'sense-datum' from the use of 'looks*' this is the natural thing to say. Suppose that a minute ago the penny was in my pocket out of sight, then it is not true that 'the penny really was round and looked* ϕ to so and so', and we incline to say that if it was not looking* ϕ to anybody then there was no sense-datum of it. We ask 'How *can* there be a sense-datum which no one is seeing?' and get the answer 'A sense-datum is an object which you see.

You know that other objects which you see exist while no one is seeing them. So why should not sense-data do so likewise?' We may then say: 'Sense-data are only products, which are made by certain physical processes involved in seeing. They can have no existence apart from such processes.' To this it will perhaps be answered 'There is no reason to suppose that sense-data are manufactured by these processes. We may suppose that our sense-data exist unsensed and that all that the processes involved in seeing do is to select from among those already there.' This sort of argument arises from considering sense-data as if they were a sort of physical objects. We know what it is for physical objects, which we see, to exist during times when we are not seeing them. We often do things which we call observing that a given physical object has continued to exist unperceived throughout a given period of time; but there is nothing which we similarly call observing that a given sense-datum has continued to exist unperceived throughout a given period of time. There are certain criteria which are ordinarily used as criteria for whether a physical object has gone on existing unperceived throughout a time; but there is nothing which is a criterion of this in the case of sense-data. We may if we care introduce such criteria, i.e., we may describe what we are going to call 'observing that a sense-datum has gone on existing unperceived throughout such and such a time'; but probably we are strongly disinclined to do so, because we incline to take our use of the word 'sense-datum' from that of 'looks*', 'appears', and 'appearance'.

It does not make sense to say that a sense-datum has existed unperceived; in giving the usage of the word we have not given a use to this, but it is open to us to do so if we care.

Perhaps it will be useful here to give an example of something which similarly does not make sense, but which we require to contemplate a little before we become quite clear that it doesn't. Whether rightly or wrongly, there is attributed to the President of this session the remark: 'It is not true that I sleep *more* than other people, I only sleep *more slowly.*' It takes just a moment or two to see that sleeping is not the sort of thing that one *can* do more slowly than other people, and perhaps another moment or two to see that this means that to say that one person sleeps more slowly than another is to say something which has no meaning. The world being as it is we are not inclined to give a use to this phrase; on the other hand it is easy to describe circumstances in which we would be so inclined. Suppose, for example, that human beings were clearly divided into two kinds, those who walked and ate slowly and required a long sleep to recover from a given amount of exercise, and those who walked and ate quickly and required only a short sleep to recover from a given amount of exercise, then we should be very inclined to say that people of the first kind slept more slowly than people of the second kind.

Similarly, to say that a sense-datum has existed unperceived is to say something to which no meaning is given, but to which in certain circumstances we might be strongly inclined to give meaning. It is worth pointing out, for example, that sometimes we speak of an 'appearance' of a thing which is not an appearance to anyone. E.g., 'What a fine sunset. It must present a wonderful appearance from the top of Mochrum hill' does not imply that there is anyone there to whom it would be presented. On the other hand, we frequently use 'appearance' in a different way. E.g., suppose I look at the round surface of the penny from a certain angle, then shut my eyes or go away for five minutes, then look at it again under similar conditions from the same place, we might describe this correctly by saying that 'I saw two different appearances of it which were exactly the same in shape and colour'. We do not describe it by saying that 'I saw twice the same appearance which continued to exist during the period when I was not seeing it'. Whether we are to say that in this case I saw numerically the same sense-datum twice or that I saw two sense-data which had the same qualities is a matter of indifference, and perhaps we will never require to use 'sense-datum' in such a case and so need never make any decision on the matter. The important point is that whatever we do is not demanded by the nature of objects which we are calling 'sense-data', but that we have a choice of different notations for describing the same observations, the choice being determined only by the greater convenience of one notation, or our personal inclination, or by tossing a coin.

Whether the sense-datum in question is to be said to have existed between the times when it was observed is also, as I have tried to show, a matter for the people who wish to use the terminology to decide, should occasion arise. What is important is that whatever criteria are laid down for the existence of a sense-datum during a time when it is unobserved, to say that since these criteria are fulfilled *therefore* it is the case that there is an object exactly like a sense-datum, only that it is unobserved, is misleading. That there is such an object is not a further fact inferred from them. It is better to say that these criteria being fulfilled is what we *call* a sense-datum's existing unobserved. This is particularly important in considering theories which say that an unsensed sense-datum exists at a certain place if an observer at that place would see a sense-datum answering to the given description. We may use the fact that if an observer were to be at a given place he would see a sense-datum of a given sort as a criterion for there existing an unsensed sense-datum of that sort; but if that is all we use, the fact that an observer at that place would see such and such a sense-datum is what we *call* a sense-datum of that sort's existing at that time. This is extremely important in considering the kind of view which tries to 'mitigate the severities of phenomenalism' by saying that physical objects are groups of actual and possible (or unsensed) sense-data. The attractiveness of such a view fades when one considers what is the criterion which is being used for the existence of unsensed sense-data, and what is the relation between the criterion and the object of whose existence it is a criterion.

It is also important in considering another thing which is said, viz., that sense-data are a sort of things which only one person can ever see, i.e. that it is impossible that you should ever see my sense-data, i.e. that you should ever see a sense-datum which I see, and vice versa. People have the idea of sense-data as sort of private physical objects which each person keeps behind a high wall, and that although two people never see the same sense-datum the order in which I see my sense-data is connected in a fortunate fashion with the order in which you see yours and other people see theirs; but it is with a feeling of regret that people say 'content can't be communicated, only structure can', and it is with a feeling of discomfort that they contemplate the possibility that although when an object looks to me green, I have a green sense-datum, yet it may always be the case that when an object looks to *you* green you may have a red sense-datum, and so long as the error is systematic it is undiscoverable.

In the first place we have to consider what is meant by saying that 'content can't be communicated'. This suggests that there is some process which we can describe but can't do, viz., communicate content. It suggests that the walls between our private collections of sense-data are so high that we can't see over, but that it is not inconceivable that we should. That, however, is misleading. It makes us feel 'If only I could show you my sense-datum, we could decide whether we see the same or not'. But in fact there is nothing I can't do. I could show you all my sense-data if the words 'showing you a sense-datum of mine' had any meaning. To say that content can't be communicated is to say that 'one person has communicated the content of his sense-experiences to another' means nothing at all. To suppose otherwise is to treat sense-data as if they were a sort of physical objects, and so to assume that it makes sense to say that two people see the same sense-datum.

Ingenious circumstances have been described in which we *should* feel urged to say that one person was having another's sense-datum; but I do not propose to give such an example here. I wish to consider only two things: (1) suppose I look over your shoulder at a gas fire some feet in front of us both, and suppose that when I move my head into the position where yours is there is no difference in the way the fire looks* to me, and suppose when you move your head into the place where mine was you say that there is no difference in the way the fire looks* to you. Now suppose that we both have good eyes and have shown no signs of abnormal colour-vision. Then it is true that the gas fire looks* the same to both of us, and there is a sense in which it is true that it presents the same appearance to both of us; but do we see the same sense-datum of the fire? I.e., numerically the same sense-datum of it? Most people who have used the term 'sense-datum' would with little hesitation say that the sense-datum you see is not identical with the sense-datum I see. Why? Not because they see something about the nature of such objects which shows that they are not numerically the same, but simply because no meaning is given to 'two people are seeing the same sense-datum'.

(2) This raises the problem, what is meant by saying of *someone else* that he is seeing a sense-datum of a certain sort? When we think of such a thing we all think of a sort of inner vision inside the man's head directed on an object which we picture as a sort of screen, the whole thing being cut off from the outside world by a high barrier. We think that a man's behaving or not behaving in such and such ways is a symptom of some inner condition, viz., whether he has in fact such an object before his inner eye behind the barrier, and we regard this thing of which his behaviour is a symptom as something which we can never directly observe, but as something which might conceivably not exist even if his behaviour were exactly what it is. Such imagery is pointless. If this entity which he alone sees did not exist and his behaviour were no different from what it is, the world would appear to us to go on just the same, except that he would never really see things as they are, but only appear to. This shows that we have made a mistake about the use of such a phrase as 'other people see sense-data similar to mine'. The mistake is, as before, the one about the relation between the criterion for a thing's existence and the thing's existence. What we call someone else's seeing a sense-datum is his behaving in certain ways

in certain situations, his reacting in certain ways to certain stimuli. A man's being colour-blind is not his having pictures of *only* certain sorts in his private collection, at whose absence we can guess more or less reliably by certain tests. His being colour-blind is his behaving in certain ways. Similarly your seeing the same colour as I do on looking at a certain object, or seeing a different colour when we should expect to see the same, is not my having in my collection a differently coloured picture from what you have in yours, but my behaving in a certain way. We could easily mention tests which would ordinarily be taken as tests for deciding whether people have the same (i.e., exactly similar) sense-data under such and such conditions. (E.g., colour-choosing tests for colour-blindness.)

I do not deal with *the* problem about sense-data, which gives point to the introduction of the word at all. I mean 'How are sense-data related to physical objects?' I.e., how does our use of the word 'sense-datum' compare with our use of our words for physical objects? and does the use of the word 'sense-datum' help to free us from any of the difficulties we get into about our use of words for physical objects?

And I have not touched upon how our use of the word 'sense-datum' is related to our use of the word 'sensation'.

All I have done is to consider a number of questions about the way 'sense-datum' is brought into use, which it seems to me must be considered before anything is said about the larger problems it was introduced to deal with.

III. PHENOMENALISM AND THE CAUSAL THEORY OF PERCEPTION

TERMINATING JUDGMENTS AND OBJECTIVE BELIEFS

C. I. Lewis

1. The existence of a thing, the occurrence of an objective event, or any other objective state of affairs, is knowable only as it is verifiable or confirmable. And such objective facts can be verified, or confirmed as probable, only by presentations of sense. Thus all empirical knowledge is vested, ultimately, in the awareness of what is given and the prediction of certain passages of further experience as something which will be given or could be given. It is such predictions of possible direct experience which we have called terminating judgments; and the central importance of these for all empirical knowledge will be obvious.

The general character of terminating judgments has been indicated in discussion of the first example in the preceding chapter. They are phrased in terms of direct experience, not of the objective facts which such experience may signalize or confirm; and for this reason they are statable only in expressive language, the terms of which denote appearances as such. It may well be that no language is available to us, for such expressive use, except language which in its more usual signification would refer to objective things and states of affairs. Thus the statement "If I step forward and down, I shall come safely to rest on the step below," would, in its ordinary meaning, predict a physical event involving my body and the environment. This physical event, in case it should occur, would become an ingredient in the world's history, thereafter confirmable to the end of time. At the moment of my stepping, it would not become a complete theoretical certainty: on the contrary, it would be no more certain than the reality of the granite steps whose existence the truth of it is supposed to confirm. It is not this physical event which, in my terminating judgment, I intend to predict, but merely the passage of experience itself. And this prediction of experience is something which at the moment of stepping will become completely certain or certainly false. In making this judgment I assert nothing of objective reality but only, for example, what could still be tested if I should be a paralytic with the delusion that he still walked; and tested with positive result if that delusion were sufficiently systematic. Only by confining statements to an intent thus formulatable in expressive terms can anything be proved conclusively by single experiences: and only if *something* is conclusively true by virtue of *experience,* can any existence or fact of reality be rendered even probable. If a particular experience be delusive —that is, if the objective belief which is the interpretation put upon it be invalid—that itself, if demonstrable at all, can be demonstrated only through other *experiences.*

If it be denied that such predictions, confined to passages of experience as such, are or can be formulated—a denial which has some plausibility—still it would remain true that in such passages of experience something, whether linguistically expressible or not, becomes entirely certain; and it is only through such certainties of sense that even partial verification of objective fact can be afforded. If there be no genuinely expressive language, still there would be those direct apprehensions of sense and those terminating judgments which could only be so formulated; and any account of knowledge would need to observe them. The impossibility of their accurate expression in language would, then, merely constitute a comment upon the inessential character of language in its relation to the cognitive process; and upon the errors which lie in wait for those who substitute linguistic analysis for the examination of knowledge.

There are other questions also which the suggested manner of formulating terminating judgments will have raised in the reader's mind: why such predictions of future possible experience should require a hypothesis of action; whether if any such hypothesis is necessary there are not other conditions also; just what relation it is which is expressed by 'if-then' in such terminating judgments; and how, precisely, a terminating judgment stands related to a judgment of objective fact which it is supposed to verify or confirm. The last of these questions is the most important and the most troublesome one; and the question of other conditions than merely that supplied by a mode of action, has connection with it. We shall postpone those two until last.

The other two questions, concerning the hypothesis of action and the relation of this condition to the expected consequence, have importance for topics which lie beyond the analysis of knowledge itself. The first of them bears upon the practical significance of cognition for the guidance of action, and upon those questions of evaluation and of morals which are implicit in such practical significance. And the other, concerning the precise meaning of the kind of if-then statement which terminating judgments exemplify, has essential connection with just those metaphysical issues which were raised in the concluding section of the last chapter. In fact, it concerns precisely those fundamental questions which have been common to epistemology and metaphysics ever since the time of Hume. However, in giving attention to these two features of terminating judgments, we shall not be turning aside from our main purpose of the analysis of knowledge: the examination of them would lie directly before us in any case.

2. It has been suggested that terminating judgments are of the form "If *A* then *E*," or "*S* being given, if *A* then *E*," where '*A*' indicates some possible mode of action and '*E*' an expected empirical sequent.

The main reason why such predictions must be thus conditional, instead of categorical, is the simple one that, broadly speaking, there is nothing in the way of human experience which is predictable entirely without reference to conditions which action supplies and may alter.

It would be easy to fall into confusion here and raise a

kind of objection which would be pointless. We have all of us been brought up in the tradition of scientific or physical determinism, according to which everything which is to be is intrinsically predictable. And even though science now finds that this determinism is not, as it was previously thought to be, an indispensable presupposition of the possibility of scientific knowledge, we shall not easily be persuaded that such exceptions to categorical predictability as must now be granted are matters which affect the practicalities. It is not the subatomic phenomena, to which the physical Principle of Indetermination applies, but molar phenomena, which affect common experience and our decisions of action. Even if laws of the macroscopic are merely statistical generalizations based upon chance distributions in the realm of the microscopic, that fact could have no considerable weight for predicting matters of practical concern. Those phenomena with which empirical knowledge must mainly deal would still be categorically predictable.

These abstruse questions about physical determinism need not concern us at all. The point is that such supposedly categorical predictabilities of the physical concern objective facts, while the predictions of terminating judgments concern direct experience. The thrown ball, for example, categorically will describe a certain trajectory and fall at a certain point with a certain terminal velocity. But what *experience*, and of whom, follows from that? Certain definite experiences, supposing one places one's hands at the right point in proper position, or that one's head be in the line of flight. But the categorical predictability of the ball's behavior does not, of itself, include any categorical prediction of an experience of someone. In general, predictions of experience which might be drawn from it, are of experience conditional upon and alterable by some mode of action.

In fact the usefulness of scientific knowledge depends upon this consideration. The practical value of foreseeing what inevitably will happen, is in order to make sure that it does not happen to *us;* or that it does; according as the happening means a grievous or a gratifying experience. The use of making *categorical* prediction of *objective fact*, is in order to translate this fact into *hypothetical* predictions of *experience*, the hypothesis in question being one concerning some possible way of acting.

If it should be observed that the crux of the matter of scientific determinism is that my action as well as the objective fact is antecedently determined and intrinsically predictable, then again we can avoid this ancient and honorable problem, as one with which we have no concern. It is in fact a pseudo-problem, because it refers to a situation in which no one engaged in knowing anything which it is of any conceivable use for him to know could ever find himself. No one is ever engaged in deciding an action or an active attitude which is, for him, foreseeable. Because an act which should be foreseeable with certainty would be already decided; the question, to do or not to do, would be entirely fictitious; and the behavior, thus certainly predictable for us, would not be in any proper sense an act but something which happens to us willy-nilly. If anyone ever finds himself foreseeing an experience which is entirely inevitable—and we shall raise that question shortly—at least it will be granted that to anticipate such absolutely unavoidable experience is useless, since *ex hypothesi* nothing can be done about it.

Many things are—speaking within the limits of the practicalities—categorically predictable: the moon will be eclipsed; the day will be rainy; the course of the projectile will be thus and so. And *ipso facto,* nothing we can do will affect or alter what is thus categorically predictable. But it still remains true here that the function of our knowledge is to ameliorate our experience through guidance of our behavior. Through foreseeing rain, we may carry an umbrella and avoid finding ourselves wet and uncomfortable. The value of knowing the inevitable future fact lies precisely in the consideration that by such foreknowledge the incidence of what is predicted upon our experience may be altered by decisions open to us.

3. The point with which particularly we are concerned

here is that what is thus categorically predictable is an objective state of affairs. And it is still the case that absolute determination of such objective fact does not, in like fashion, categorically determine the *experience* of anyone; does not rule out alternatives of experience which are conditional upon some decision of action. Anything which should be categorically predictable has implications for experience: it implies, for example, all those experiences in which it could be verified or disclosed as fact. But it does not imply these experiences as categorical future fact: the predictions *of experience* into which the predictable objective fact can be translated are *hypothetical;* are contingent upon the verifier's way of acting. Certain empirical findings will be disclosed *if* he makes the appropriate tests; and presumably not otherwise. An unalterable objective fact, or an inevitable future event, does *not* imply any unalterable or unavoidable experience whatever; what it implies in terms of experience is certain eventualities contingent upon action; that *if* we behave thus and so, then inevitably, what we shall find in experience will be such and such.

There is no need to strain too far the reader's ordinary sense of objective reality, or his customary modes of formulating it. But it is necessary to draw attention to two general considerations which are of fundamental importance about our knowledge. First, that in a sense which will be obvious, a supposed objective fact, when considered apart from all disclosures in experience which bear witness to it, is in the nature of the case, lacking in human significance. The formulation of it in terms of our possible experience contains everything which could lend the notion of it significance of the sort which actually we give to it in practical life. And second, that no assigned significance in terms of experience would be genuinely practical and true to the facts of life if it were significance of an inevitable experience no action could affect. The translation of objective fact into terminating judgments, in terms of possible experience, represents its actual and vital cognitive significance. And these terminating judgments, representing the possible confirmations of objective fact, are not categorical predictions of experience but predictions of possibilities dependent for their realization upon some chosen mode of action. Only so could our knowledge of the objective fact be of any practical value or such that we should be likely to have an interest in it. Both the theoretical and the moral significance of knowledge can be justly phrased by saying that what an objective fact *means* is certain possibilities of experience which are open to realization through our action. Or if this smacks of subjectivity, then let us put it the other way about: what is signified by the possibilities of experience which we find open to our action, is the world of objective fact, whose existence and nature is in general beyond our power to affect or alter. But knowledge would not be something to be won, or valuable when obtained, if the objective fact implied categorically the experiences in which it may be verified or confirmed.

It would seem, indeed, that there is nothing in the way of experience which is predictable apart from some condition to be supplied by our active attitude. Or more precisely; no experience which, taken as a whole and in all its parts and aspects, is inevitable. What may be called inevitable experiences are not altogether such but represent some ingredient of an experience or some narrowly restricted range of alternative possibilities open to us. Some of the characteristic examples of 'experiences which are foreseeable but unavoidable', which are likely to be adduced by way of objection to this statement, are not even cases where the objective state of affairs which is categorically predictable is specific and excludes alternatives. For instance, it may be said that death is predictable with certainty; and that surely is a matter of one's further experience. But 'my death' is a highly abstract designation: the certainty of it leaves open all sorts of alternatives of time, place and manner which are still undetermined in its categorical predictability. Even when the prediction is of a highly specific state of affairs affecting us, it is still the case that the specific experience to be expected has features dependent on our decision. That the so called 'inevitable experience' is not altogether so, is evidenced by the fact that we may have a preference about anticipating or not anticipating it. Some of us wish to know just when the tooth is to be pulled; some of us definitely do not wish to know. There is still one thing we can always do about an 'inevitable experience', which is to 'be prepared for it'. 'Being prepared' somewhat alters the quality which the experience would otherwise have when it comes. And if any be inclined to set aside this kind of difference our attitude can make as trivial, we may remind him of Stoicism and the ethics of Spinoza: a whole creed of the proper way of life may be based upon this point.

Whatever may be the case about physical things and objective states of affairs, anticipatable *experience* is subject to a sort of indeterminacy principle: foreknowledge itself and our active attitude can alter the quality of it. That is one reason why the old-fashioned free-will-or-determinism controversy relates to an issue which, in terms of actual life, is mythical. There is nothing which can be anticipated which it may not be of use to know: and whatever it is of conceivable use to foresee, is such only because *something* still can be done about it; the experience with which it may affect us is still open to qualification by ourselves. Tenuous as this kind of consideration may be thought to be, still it points to a universal feature of our empirical knowledge: whatever the fact may be upon which our knowledge is directed, if we render the significance of that fact in terms of the experiences which will give evidence of it, we shall find that what thus portends is something which it is *valuable* to know because in some part or aspect it is conditional upon our decisions of action.

Admittedly some experiences—or more accurately, some generic characters of some experiences—may be predictable with practical certainty and without any possibility of avoidance. When we see the lightning, we know that we shall hear the thunder. We may tense our muscles or not; stop our ears or not; and these activities somewhat affect the quality with which what is predicted will be experienced; but the generic character of heard thunder may be unqualifiedly inevitable. Such examples are, it will be admitted, exceptional, and represent a kind of limiting case. But even here, we see that alternatives of action are not wholly eliminated; they are only severely restricted. And in that sense, what is here exemplified differs only in degree from the more general case. In fact, it may lead us precisely to the justifiable and well-considered generalization: *any* objective event which may be categorically predictable, and any objective state of affairs which may be known, will mean, when translated into terms of confirming experience, a restriction of the possibilities contingent on our action, but *never* a restriction reducing these alternatives to a single one. Even where—as in the more general case— the alternatives left open to us, in view of the objective fact in question, are too numerous to mention, still the state of affairs believed in or asserted would be reflected in the elimination of equally many *other* alternatives of experience, contingent upon chosen ways of acting, which might be open to us if this objective fact were *not* the case. That is the general nature of objective fact, when taken in terms of the experience which would verify or confirm it: it means that by nothing we can do would certain experiences be possible for us; but that there are other alternatives of experience any one of which may ensue if a suitable mode of action be adopted. That a sheet of white paper is now before me, means that in no possible way can I now proceed directly to presentation of something green and circular here in front of me, as well as meaning that certain other presentations are predictable, contingent upon appropriate decisions of action. How narrowly the alternatives of possible experience may be restricted, or how wide the range of possibilities left open, depends upon the particular objective fact or event which is in question. But in no case will it fail to eliminate certain possibilities of experience which might otherwise obtain; and in no case will it completely exclude all possibilities but one, and leave nothing whatever which is contingent upon our decision of action. It is in this fact that the universal possibility of a practical value in empirical knowledge lies: there is nothing which could be known, the knowledge of which might not enable us to avoid efforts which are fruitless, and enable us also to ameliorate our lot and improve the quality with which future experience might otherwise affect us, by choosing between alternatives of action which still are open.

This being so, it will be seen that our general formula for terminating judgments is correct on the point in question, and universally applies. The sense meaning of any verifiable statement of objective fact, is exhibitable in some set of terminating judgments each of which is hypothetical in form; it is a judgment that a certain empirical eventuation will ensue if a certain mode of action be adopted. Such judgments may be decisively verified or found false by adopting the mode of action in question and putting them to the test. And it is by such conclusive verification of terminating judgments, constituent in the meaning of it, that the objective belief—the non-terminating judgment—receives its confirmation as more or less highly probable.

4. As has been suggested, we must take this account of terminating judgments, and of their inclusion in the judgment of objective fact, as in some measure provisional until we reach the two questions which have been postponed and which are to be considered in the concluding part of this chapter. But at least we see that they will be hypothetical in form. And the general question what the if-then relation is which they assert between hypothesis and predicted consequence, is sure to be involved. It is this question of the *kind of connection* between the mode of action A and the expected experience E which is believed to hold in believing "If A then E," which will turn out upon examination to have a bearing on those issues which lie between subjectivism or phenomenalism and realism, as well as between skepticism and belief in the possibility of knowing an independently real world.

The crux of this matter lies in the question what it means for a statement of this form, "If A then E," to be true when the hypothesis 'A' is false—when the mode of action A is *not* adopted, and the test of what is believed is not made.

This is the sort of question the answer to which we know quite well so long as no one asks us for it; but when we are asked, we do not know what to say. It is indeed a matter to be determined, not by elucidation of world-shaking mysteries, but simply by careful examination of a meaning which implicitly we all intend and grasp in making assertions of this type. But to elicit that meaning is particularly troublesome. It will, unfortunately, require close attention and a somewhat involved and lengthy discussion. Also we shall find that contemporary logical studies, to which we might naturally turn for elucidation and precise formulation of the meaning of hypothetical statements, do not in fact afford the required answer. Indeed they throw no light upon it whatever, except that of eliminating various meanings of 'if-then' which might be supposed to be the one in question. What such logical studies offer us, as possible interpretations of hypothetical statements, are precisely those which are *not* possible interpretations of the intended significance of a terminating judgment or of any connection which could be asserted between a hypothesis of action and its consequence. The relation of '*A*' to '*E*' in "If *A* then *E*" is *not* justly interpreted as the relation of material implication which many current developments of logic take as fundamental; it is *not* what is called in *Principia Mathematica* a formal implication; and it is *not* a strict implication or entailment such that '*E*' is, assertedly, deducible from '*A*'. It *is* generically the same kind of relation which Hume had in mind when he spoke of 'necessary connections of matters of fact'. And Hume, as we remember, affirmed that no such relation can be established as holding: though, as we also remember, he made no doubt that it is such a relation which is *asserted* as often as any objective fact or anything going beyond presentations of sense is taken to be empirically known. And whatever objections may be raised against Hume's analysis on other points, on this point of meaning he was exactly right.

5. That the if-then relation intended in the terminating judgment "If *A* then *E*" is not a relation of the deducibility of '*E*' from '*A*'—not a strict implication or logical entail-

ment—is sufficiently evident from the consideration that this judgment itself is one of *empirical* fact and cannot be attested by mere logic. The situation which would prove it false is logically thinkable; the contrary statement, *"A but not E"* is not self-contradictory, though it is believed to be false. We must be careful here not to confuse the question precisely at issue with others which are related. As we have conceived the matter, the terminating judgment itself *is* deducible from the objective judgment in which it is a constituent: from "There is a piece of white paper before me," it is deducible that "If I turn my eyes right, this seen appearance will be displaced to the left." This relation of deducibility holds because the terminating judgment is contained in the meaning of the objective statement. But our present question does not concern this relation between the objective belief and the terminating judgment: it concerns the relation between the antecedent *'A'* and the consequent *'E'* in the terminating judgment itself. The question is not, "If it be true that a piece of white paper is before me, is it deducible that if I turn my eyes right, the seen appearance will be displaced to the left?": the question is, "What do I mean when I assert 'If I turn my eyes right, this seen appearance will be displaced to the left'?" And the present point is that I do *not* mean to assert that "The seen appearance will be displaced to the left" is *logically deducible* from the hypothesis "I turn my eyes right." I could assert that only if it were entirely unthinkable, logically, that the given presentation should be illusory, or my judgment of the objective fact subject to error. And that is not the case; nor do I take it to be so, unless unthinkingly or by some crude mistake in the analysis of empirical knowledge of objective matters of fact.

That the relation between a way of acting and the result of it, which a terminating judgment expresses, is not a relation of logical deducibility, may also be attested in another way: it is relation of a sort which could only be learned from past experience. When I see what looks like a piece of white paper, my ability to predict the experience which will result from turning my eyes is something that previous like occasions have taught me. But if '*E*' were deducible from '*A*', I should not have needed so to learn it; the truth of "If *A* then *E*" could in that case be determined without reference to any experience, merely by reflection.[1]

6. That the relation of hypothesis to consequent in a terminating judgment is not of the sort called 'material implication', will be evident by the fact that "If *A* then *E*" intends an assertion whose truth or falsity is not affected by the truth or falsity of the hypothesis '*A*'.

A material implication, "If *P* then *Q*," is commonly symbolized by '*P* ⊃ *Q*': it will be convenient to use this abbreviation. This relation '*P* ⊃ *Q*' is one which holds when and only when at least one of the two, "*P* is false" and "*Q* is true," is a true statement. Now the terminating judgment "If *A* then *E*" *does* imply that at least one of the two, "*A* is false" and "*E* is true" is or will be the case. This judgment would be taken to be proved false if '*A*' should be true (if the mode of action be adopted) and '*E*' false (the expected result fails to follow). Hence the truth of the terminating judgment "If *A* then *E*" includes and requires the truth of the material implication '*A* ⊃ *E*'. But it also intends and requires as essential something more, which the truth of '*A* ⊃ *E*' does not require. Supposing that '*A*' *is* in fact false, it still requires that if '*A*' *were* or *should be* true, '*E*'

[1] It might be objected that the sense meaning of "I turn my eyes right" includes the consequence "This seen thing is displaced to the left"; and that this is indicated by the account here given: hence that if-then propositions of the type in question will be found to state a relation of deducibility when the sense meaning of the antecedent and consequent is properly taken into account. This would be plausible if the hypothesis of action, such as "I turn my eyes right," were here a supposition of objective fact: one of the ways of confirming that my eyes turn right is this displacement of things seen to the left. But we must not confuse the *objective* statement "I turn my eyes right," with the corresponding hypothesis of a terminating judgment: in the terminating judgment, both hypothesis of action and consequent expected experience must be in expressive terms; they refer, not to objective dispositions of my body, etc., but to a direct content of felt experience. The connection between that experience, so difficult to describe, which is the expressive intent of "I turn my eyes right," and the presentation formulated as "This seen thing is displaced to the left," is a connection the reliability of which has been learned from experience and could not have been learned without it.

would be true. For instance, in believing that a piece of real paper is before me, I believe that if I turn my eyes right, the seen paper will be displaced left. But I do not now turn my eyes: I do not make this test of my objective belief. Nevertheless I believe that if I *should* turn my eyes the predicted consequence *would* follow: and *it is only because I believe the validity of such untested predictions that my belief is taken to be significant of objective fact.*

This point is verbally difficult: it takes a lot of talk to make it clear. But it is quite essential. My belief that if I should turn my eyes right (though I do not do so at present), the thing seen would be displaced to the left, is part of my belief in the objective reality of what I am looking at. I believe the terminating judgment "If A then E" to be true when I do not act in manner A, just as I believe a real thing is still there when I do not look to see. This point is fundamentally important for the distinction between 'objective reality' and 'subjective experience'. And an if-then relation of this sort, which we may express by recourse to the subjunctive mood (should — would —) *cannot* be expressed in terms of material implication. Because when the hypothesis 'A' is contrary to fact, '$A \supset E$' holds regardless of the truth or falsity of 'E', and regardless of the question whether 'E' *would be* true if 'A' *were* true.[2] For example, since I do not at present turn my eyes, it holds that "I now turn my eyes" materially implies "The thing seen is displaced." But also and for the same reason—namely, that the antecedent in the relation is false—"I turn my eyes" materially implies "The thing seen is *not* visually displaced"; and also materially implies "A loud explosion is heard," or anything else you please to mention as consequent. When 'A' is *false*, the material implication '$A \supset X$' holds, *no matter what* statement 'X' is. Thus the consequences of a

[2] The objection is possible here that when 'A' is false, and known to be false, the judgment "If A then E," if it means more than '$A \supset E$', is non-significant because untestable. This objection would beg the very point at issue; but also its invalidity may be observed from the fact that it confuses 'untestable' and 'untested': when 'A' is false, the truth of the terminating judgment "If A then E" is *untested*, but since 'A' could be or might be made true, it is not untestable.

contrary to fact statement—*in any sense in which some things are such consequences and others are not*—cannot be expressed in terms of material implication.

Let us put the matter in another way which has no reference to the particular fashion in which we have analyzed empirical objective judgments but only to the fact that a significant objective belief must be, in some sense or other, testable. Empirical test of an objective belief can only be made by setting up or seeking out the appropriate conditions and observing the result. Most frequently we make assertions of objective fact without performing those tests the results of which we should accept as verification, or partial verification, of them. In fact it is obvious that our sense of reality is a kind of continuous belief in innumerable objective facts which, at any given moment, we do not test at all. Alternatively, we may say that this belief in a real world is belief in innumerable specific consequences of innumerable possible ways of acting which, at any given moment, we find no reason to adopt. This belief in objective reality is only as strong as the correlative belief that although certain hypotheses are now false, they have certain consequences (which *would* be found true if the tests *were* made) *and not others.*

Incidentally, the alternative to this is not idealism but skepticism, just as Hume thought. A good Berkeleian believes that given presentations are 'signs of' others; and he could hardly confine such significances to those tested. The issue is not one between belief in material substance and belief in spiritual substances and modes of mind only: it is between belief in knowable reality, beyond the presentationally given (in whatever terms), and belief in none.

It is also to the point that if such tests as we make, verified or confirmed the objective facts we believe in, but only for the moment when the test is performed, we should not care to make such tests, and they would have no cognitive import. The point of such verifications is that they assure what is presently tested as something more or less to be relied upon when *not* tested. If what is proved by such trials were not proved true or rendered probable for other times and occasions than those on which the trial is made, we should have no cognitive interest in experiment, nor think it a test of anything or its result a verification of anything. If we did not believe that if something *were* tested, at times when in fact it is *not* tested, certain specifiable results *would* accrue and not others, we should not believe in objective reality or facts which obtain independently of being experienced. Where nothing specifically statable is verif*iable* though unverif*ied,* there could be no knowledge and no world of things and events which knowledge could grasp. It is no extravagance of analysis but simple fact that no conception of reality or of knowledge is possible without acknowledgment that contrary to fact hypotheses have significant consequences. And the kind of if-then relation thus believed in, is one which cannot be expressed in terms of material implication, for which any hypothesis which is false in fact has every conceivable (and inconceivable) consequence.

As has been said, this point has no dependence on our conception that the confirmation of objective beliefs is by way of terminating judgments which must be in terms of direct experience and can be formulated only in expressive language. It would hold for any plausible theory—any theory which regarded empirical knowledge as testable by experiment and observation. But if our conception of the nature of terminating judgments, and of objective judgments as being confirmed by finding these true, should be correct, then it will be obvious that the above considerations apply. The material implication '$A \supset E$' is a logically *necessary* condition of what the terminating judgment "If A then E" intends to assert: '$A \supset E$' must be true when "If A then E" is true. But it is not a logically *sufficient* condition: the meaning of the terminating judgment requires also that if 'A' be false still it holds that if 'A' were true, 'E' *would be* true, and certain other things (what is contradictory of 'E' for example) *would not* be true. This further intended meaning cannot be stated in terms of material implication, because if 'A' be false, then '$A \supset E$',

'$A \supset E$-false', '$A \supset X$' (whatever statement 'X' may be) all hold equally.

7. However, although the if-then relation of terminating judgments cannot be expressed in terms of material implication, it may be thought to be expressible in terms of another if-then relation which modern logic has made familiar; the relation called, in *Principia Mathematica*, formal implication. Before we can discuss this possibility, it will be well to explain this relation briefly; and it will be necessary to examine one question concerning the correct interpretation of it. Also the manner in which it might be supposed to apply to terminating judgments must be considered.

Formal implication is usually represented by symbolization such as '$(x) . \phi x \supset \psi x$', which may be read, "For all values of 'x', ϕx (materially) implies ψx." If the values of the variable, 'x', in 'ϕx' and 'ψx', be 'x_1', 'x_2', 'x_3', etc., then '$(x) . \phi x \supset \psi x$' will be true if and only if it is *not* the case that 'ϕx_1' is true and 'ψx_1' false, *not* the case that 'ϕx_2' is true and 'ψx_2' false, etc.; *not* the case for any (some) value of 'x', 'x_n' that 'ϕx_n' is true but 'ψx_n' is false. That is, 'ϕx' formally implies 'ψx' if and only if, whatever value of 'x', 'x_n', be chosen, 'ϕx_n' materially implies 'ψx_n', and there is no instance of 'ϕx_n' true but 'ψx_n' false.

However, this leaves it still doubtful which of two possible interpretations of expressions having the form '$(x) . \phi x \supset \psi x$' is to be taken as correct. In *Principia* and in more recent logical studies, this point has been surrounded with various complications of theory, but the question which remains over, and must remain over, after all such complications, is a simple one which admits of illustration by familiar examples, and one which cannot be avoided.[3]

---

[3] Amongst the complications of theory referred to are the questions (1) what is to be taken as a 'value of the variable' in a propositional function; whether it is the *man* John Jones or the *term* 'John Jones' which is a value of 'x' in "x lives on Main Street"; (2) whether non-existent individuals can be 'named', as contrasted with being 'described'; (3) whether when a description describes no existent, every singular statement having that description as subject-term becomes thereby false; (4) whether every statement about entities of

It means one thing to say, "Every *existent* having the property ϕ (or of which ϕ is truly predicable) has also the property ψ." And it means a different thing to say, "Every *thinkable* thing which should have the property ϕ must also have the property ψ." The second of these holds only when having the property ϕ logically entails having the property ψ; when 'ψx' is *deducible* from 'ϕx'; as, e.g., "x is an animal" is deducible from "x is a man." The first of these, however, holds not only in such cases where one property or character logically entails another but also in every case where, amongst *existent* things, one property or character is *universally accompanied* by another. Thus in the first of the above senses it would hold that "x laughs" formally implies "x is human"; that "x has horns and divided hoofs" formally implies "x chews a cud"; and (since no centaurs exist) that "x is a centaur" formally implies "x has yellow wings."

We are not, of course, concerned here with any question of the correct interpretation of *Principia Mathematica,* or the intention of its authors; nor with similar question concerning more recent developments. We need only remark the consequences, for the questions with which we *are* concerned, of taking formal implication in the one or the other of these two ways. If '$(x) . \phi x \supset \psi x$' be interpreted to mean "For all *thinkable* things, if ϕx then ψx," then the relation holds only when 'ψx' is logically deducible from 'ϕx.' The reasons why the relation between 'A' and 'E', expressed by the terminating judgment "If A then E," cannot be interpreted as a relation of logical entailment or deducibility, have already been pointed out. It is thus clear, without further discussion, that if formal implication expresses such a relation of logical entailment, then the if-then rela-

---

'higher type' can be analyzed into a statement or statements about those of the 'lowest type', 'individuals'. In my opinion, none of these questions is significant epistemologically. Any answer to (1), (2), or (3), is a verbal convention, and has no effect upon any logical or empirical fact but only on our manner of expressing these. The answer to (4) is in the affirmative; but that fact lacks the importance it might be supposed to have, since 'individuals' themselves are of different 'types'.

tion asserted in terminating judgments cannot be expressed in terms of formal implication. It is on the other interpretation only, for which '$(x) . \phi x \supset \psi x$' holds if and only if there is *no existent* having the property ϕ but lacking the property ψ, that the question whether terminating judgments are expressible in terms of formal implication, calls for further examination. We shall, accordingly, confine our further attention to this interpretation of formal implication, and speak as if it were undoubtedly the correct one.[4]

8. The reason it is plausible that terminating judgments might be expressible in terms of formal implication, is that a terminating judgment is implicitly general. The prediction "If A then E" which we make on the occasion of a given presentation S, is something we believe only because we also hold a more general belief in a connection between the mode of action A and the sequent experience E on occasions like this one. It is only as applied to this, or some other, single occasion that such prediction is decisively verifiable and has thus the character of a terminating judgment strictly so called. But for convenience we may refer to the underlying belief as the 'general form' of this terminating judgment. In order that this may be clear, let us continue with the simple example we have been using. I hold the objective belief that a real piece of paper is before me and not an illusory presentation, because of certain characters of this presentation; because this looks real and feels real. But if asked for the reasons for my belief I should have to refer to more than this single occasion in my justification. I should have to include the fact that what has looked and felt, in pertinent respects, as this does now, has turned out generally (though not universally) to be a real object of a certain kind. So far, we are concerned only with the relation between a given presentation S, and an objective belief —call it R—which is the interpretation put upon it. But in passing, we may observe that although this judgment may refer explicitly to the present occasion only, it is, by virtue

---

[4] There is, in fact, little doubt that, amongst those who grasp the distinction, this is the interpretation generally adopted—though some logicians try, with desperate ingenuity, to avoid the issue altogether.

of its ground, implicitly general. Any reason I have for making it, would apply equally to any occasion when a presentation having the pertinent characters of S should be given. That is, I believe 'R' because I judge that for *any* occasion o, if So (if S is given on occasion o), then probably Ro (probably a real thing of a certain kind is present on occasion o).

Believing 'R' (a real thing of a certain kind is before me), I make the terminating judgment "If A then E" ("If I turn my eyes the visual presentation will be displaced"). And finding this true, upon test, would constitute a further confirmation of 'R'. But again, this terminating judgment is implicitly general; it represents a confirmation taken to be possible not merely at the present instant but so long as 'R' holds true. Or more accurately; so long as 'R' holds true and the essential conditions of testing signalized by the given presentation are satisfied. That is, if I wish, as I now do, to express the terminating judgment in its general form as holding whenever the objective belief it confirms holds true, then I must reintroduce, as hypothesis, reference to some given presentation indicating applicability of the test.[5] (For example, I cannot make the suggested visual test of a real thing in the dark.) Thus what I judge is: "For every occasion o, when Ro, if So and Ao, then Eo." (On any occasion when a certain kind of real object is before me, if a presentation like this is given and I turn my eyes, this visual presentation will be displaced.) Taking the objective belief as premise, I infer the terminating judgment in the general form—as holding if and when the objective belief holds: "For every occasion o, if So and Ao then Eo."

9. We can now examine the point which is presently of interest to us; whether this terminating judgment represents an if-then relation expressible in terms of formal implication. And the question is, whether the real intent of such a judgment, "(Presuming the objective judgment which is to be confirmed) for every occasion o, if So and

---

[5] This consideration requires to be introduced here only in order to avoid gross inaccuracy. We must return to it later: for the present, it may be provisionally clear from the example.

Ao then *Eo*," will be satisfied if for every *existent or actual occasion* when *So* and *Ao* hold, *Eo* holds also. As has been said, the plausibility of this rests upon the implicitly general character of the terminating judgment, now made explicit. However, this initial plausibility disappears on further examination; and for reasons of the same sort which we have already noted in the case of material implication. A generalization whose significance is confined to *actual cases* cannot cover the intended meaning of a terminating judgment, because that meaning requires that a hypothesis should still have significant consequences (and not every conceivable consequence) when it is contrary to fact.

Here again, the point may be brought out in ways which do not depend on the conception of terminating judgments here adopted but would be pertinent to any plausible conception of empirical knowledge and the tests of it. For example, it is a practically important truth that if I should jump from a second story window I should hurt myself. As I stand before the window, the presentation given and my belief in the objective facts of gravitation lead me to make a personal prediction, "For any occasion *o*, if C. L. jumps out a window like this on occasion *o*, C. L. will be hurt on occasion *o*." Whether one takes this as an objective statement about my body and the environment, or as intended to be a terminating judgment in expressive language, and referring only to passages of immediate experience on occasions like this one, will make no essential difference to the present point. Taking this statement as a formal implication which is satisfied provided every actual occasion when C. L. jumps from a second story window is an occasion when C. L. is hurt, fails to express the important cognitive and practical intent of it. It so fails because it signifies nothing as to what *would* happen if I *should* jump, on this or any other occasion. And that significance is of the essence. As a fact, I never jump from second story windows. And that fact of itself assures the truth of the formal implication in question; because that formal implication says only, "There is no actual occasion on which C. L. jumps from a second story window and is not hurt." My significant *reason* for not jumping, which has to do with supposed consequences of the contrary-to-fact hypothesis "If I should jump," is here omitted altogether and incapable of expression in terms of such formal implication.

For the same reason—namely, that I never jump from second story windows—the following formal implications are likewise satisfied: "For every occasion *o*, 'C. L. jumps from a second story window on occasion *o*' implies 'There is an eclipse of the moon on occasion *o*' "; and "For every occasion *o*, 'C. L. jumps from a second story window on occasion *o*' implies 'After occasion *o* all rivers run uphill'." It is also a fact that I never carry a handkerchief in my sleeve. And since that is so, the formal implication likewise holds: "For every occasion *o*, 'C. L. puts a handkerchief in his sleeve on occasion *o*' implies 'C. L. is hurt on occasion *o*'." However, in the sense of 'if-then' which is pertinent to terminating judgment, or to any consequence of action derivative from objective belief, I profoundly disbelieve in practically serious consequences of carrying a handkerchief in my sleeve; and similarly disbelieve in any effect of my jumping out of windows upon eclipses of the moon or the course of rivers. The predictions which represent my knowledge of objective facts and govern my conduct are not expressible as formal implications. Attempt so to formulate them, leaves out what is precisely the kernel of the whole matter.

It might be objected that we have not, in this example, stated the cognitive and practical situation properly. The basis of my belief—it may be said—is *not* one which concerns an empty class of cases: if no one had ever jumped from a second story window, and no similar weight had dropped from a similar height with a measureable terminal velocity, I should have no ground for believing what I do. My prediction is based on a different and wider hypothesis, which is true in many instances, and has, in all observed cases, certain pertinent consequences. Furthermore, the relation between this wider hypothesis and its consequences

—it may be said—is one which *is* statable as a formal implication.

A part of this objection is correct. But the conclusion drawn concerning formal implication and this example—or any case of predicting, from our knowledge, the consequences of action—is one which does not follow and is false. It is true that the ground of my practical judgment is the conviction that if a weight of 150 pounds falls 25 feet, it will strike with sufficient force to injure a human body. And true that this conviction is based on actual instances. But precisely what makes this practical belief practical, makes it impossible to *confine the significance* of it to actual cases, and thus prevents its being accurately expressible as a formal implication. The statement, " 'x weighs 150 pounds and falls 25 feet' formally implies, 'x acquires a momentum sufficient to injure a human body upon impact'," still says nothing as to what would happen if I (weighing 150 pounds) should jump from a second story window (25 feet above the ground). What it says is only that the class of *actual* cases of 150-pound weights falling 25 feet is included in the class of actual cases in which momentum is acquired sufficient to injure a human body. No formal implication says anything about the holding of any consequence in cases in which the hypothesis is contrary to fact. Or rather; what it says in such cases is that *every* conceivable and inconceivable consequence holds, and hence none is significant. What *would* happen *if* such a weight fell such a distance, in any instance in which the weight does not in fact fall, it does not tell us; just as the formal implication, " 'x laughs' implies 'x is human'," does not tell us what would be the case if evolution had produced certain animals which do not in fact exist.

At least the objector will admit that on *this* occasion no weight of 150 pounds—whether my body or anything else—drops 25 feet. That being so, the formal implication, "If x, weighing 150 pounds, drops 25 feet, it acquires sufficient force to injure a human body" could *still* be true even if it were *false* that if I should now jump out this window I should hurt myself. This could be the case for the same reason that the formal implication, "If *x* laughs, *x* is human," is true, although "If the horse War Admiral should laugh, he would be human," is false. It is easy to suppose, by a confusion of thought, that if we should know the formal implication "In all actual cases of '*A*'-true, '*E*' is also true," we should, in knowing that, know also that *if* in any case '*A*' *should be* true, '*E*' *would be* true. But as the last example indicates, so to interpret formal implication, is simply to misunderstand what actually it asserts, and read into it something more important which no formal implication can ever state.

10. We have dwelt upon this matter at length, not from any desire to investigate logical niceties, or to insist upon verbal accuracy in interpretation, but because the issue here is a troublesome one to locate and also fundamental. No assertion of or knowledge of or belief in objective reality or fact can be understood without understanding that it has, as its practically significant and testable consequences, hypothetical propositions having the following characteristics: (1) The consequent in this hypothetical statement is not logically deducible from the antecedent. (2) Nevertheless the truth of the hypothetical statement itself—like that of one which states a relation of logical entailment or deducibility—is independent of the truth or falsity of the antecedent or hypothesis: for the if-then relation which such a hypothetical statement asserts as holding, the hypothesis has the same consequences whether it is true or false. (3) Hence this hypothetical statement may be significantly asserted when the hypothesis of it is contrary to fact and is known to be so.

Let us proceed to the kind of example which instances this issue in a form which is critical for the theory of knowledge. As long ago as Hume, it was suggested that there is no difference between the common-sense supposition of a real world (when the significance of this supposition is validly interpreted) and the summary statement that at certain times we have certain specific sense impressions. All the significance of 'order' and 'connection' of things, *so far as such orderliness of things and events is verified, or actually will be verified in future,* will be comprehended in this summary statement of actual sense-content of experience. The common-sense man regards this Humean suggestion as equivalent to the supposition that objective reality may 'go out' when unobserved but always 'come back' when observed; and considers this a kind of harmless philosophic joke. Very likely he is unable to give his instinctive repudiation of it any clear formulation. But one can be given: the difference between such fantastic subjectivism and our belief in a world which is knowable and verifiable but exists independently of being observed, is the difference between supposing on the one hand that empirical generalizations which are justified have no valid significance beyond that of formal implication, and supposing on the other hand that the verifiability of such empirical generalizations includes reference to hypothetical statements about possible experience, and that these hypothetical statements have the characteristics summarized in the preceding paragraph.

For example, I believe that there is a room next door with a desk and blackboard in it, although no one is now observing it, and although at times no one is even thinking of it. My belief in this objective reality is distinguished from the subjectivistic conception that it exists only when and as perceived, by the fact that my belief includes the following items:

(1) If at any time (while this room continues to exist), a normal observer, A. B., should put himself in position to observe this room, A. B. would have the kind of experience meant by 'observing a room with a desk and a blackboard'.

(2) "A. B. now puts himself in position to observe this room" is false: no one is now observing it.

(3) "A. B. observes a desk and blackboard" is not logically deducible from "A. B. puts himself in position to observe this room in question."

(4) It is false that "If A. B. now puts himself in position to observe this room, A. B. will see a pink elephant."

Understanding these statements in their obvious intention, the following may be noted: (1), above, is to be construed as a hypothetical statement which is general; holding for any normal observer and for any time (so long as the reality to be verified continues to exist). Statement (2) asserts that for some observer and some time, or in fact for any observer and some time (now), the antecedent in this hypothetical statement (1) is false. Statement (3), above, expresses the fact that the consequent in this hypothetical statement is not logically deducible from the antecedent or hypothesis. Statements (2) and (4) together indicate that, for the intended sense of this hypothetical assertion—of the if-then relation which it asserts—it is true for some observer and some time (A. B. now) for which its hypothesis is false; but it is *not* true that this contrary-to-fact hypothesis has any and every consequence—e.g., not true that it has the consequence "A. B. will see a pink elephant."

Taken together, these features characterize the meaning of belief in an objective reality which is verifiable but is independent of being verified or experienced. And they likewise indicate, as clearly as it seems possible to indicate it, the familiar and intended meaning of 'if-then' in statements of possible confirmations of empirical knowledge.

If this is a fair illustration of our belief in the reality of a thing when not observed, then one way of expressing such belief is in the form of a hypothetical statement about the experience of a normal observer who should act in a manner appropriate to testing what is in question under conditions permitting such test. But the meaning intended by 'if-then' in such hypothetical statements is of the essence of the matter and must be carefully regarded. It is not expressible in terms of logical deducibility nor in terms of material implication or of formal implication. An if-then relation of hypothesis to logically deducible consequence, is one which can be certified by reflection alone and does not need to be verified by experience. The if-then of material implication is such that a contrary to fact hypothesis has any and every consequence: when a thing is not being observed, the material implication, "If this thing is observed, then ——," will be true, however the blank here may be filled. And the if-then of formal implication (supposing it distinct from that of logical deducibility) is such that, in terms of it, the statement, "For any normal observer at any time, if the observer acts appropriately to verification of this thing, then a positively verifying experience results" will be satisfied if every *actually made* observation has a positive result, and without any supposition as to what *would* result in the case of confirmations not in fact attempted.[6]

This whole matter may be summarily put as follows: For any conception which takes reality to be knowable and verifiable, to believe that this or that is real means believing certain statements of the form "If such and such experiments be made, so and so will be experienced." And the further and crucial question here concerns interpretation of the if-then relation in such hypothetical statements. To take this as expressing relation of a premise to a logically deducible consequence, is out of the question: that would represent a conception difficult to identify with any historical theory, and hardly worth discussing. To take this if-then relation as one expressible in terms of material or of formal implication would be precisely equivalent to that extreme subjectivism—easily reduced to skepticism—which maintains that to be is to be perceived; which holds that there is no valid difference between the existence of

[6] This point concerns not only the issues between subjectivism and realism but also the question, now beginning to be raised, whether such metaphysical issues are meaningful. But too commonly in current discussion the genuineness of these issues is prejudiced by failure to formulate them correctly in logical terms. Perhaps it is not altogether an accident that those who repudiate metaphysics as meaningless also tend to deny any significance of hypothetical statements beyond what is expressible in terms of material or of formal implication. (There would be some exceptions to this generalization, however.) That would be a way of begging the question at issue by apparently rigorous but actually specious logical analysis. It would argue away the issue by refusing to state it; by refusing logical standing to that meaning of 'if-then' in terms of which alone the actual significance of common-sense assertions of objective belief can be expressed.

the reality believed in and the mere fact that on certain occasions certain actual perceivers actually have certain perceptions. The realistic conception that the believed-in and verifiable realities are independent of being so known or experienced, must interpret this if-then relation as one for which such hypothetical statements are true or false independently of the truth or falsity of their antecedent clauses; one for which the hypothesis has the *same* consequences whether the observation is made and the hypothesis is true, or the observation is not made and the hypothesis is contrary to fact. Thus it is a relation most clearly expressible in the form "If such and such observation *should be* made, so and so *would* be experienced."

11. This last-mentioned meaning of 'if-then', requisite to expression of any realistic conception of objective fact, is one which has no name, and one which logical analysis has largely neglected. But it is familiar to common thought and discourse. We might refer to the connections so statable as 'matter-of-fact connections' or 'natural connections' or 'real connections.' And the consequences of a hypothesis, in this sense of 'consequence', might be called its 'natural consequences' or 'real consequences'. These names would be appropriate because this sense of 'if-then' is the one connoted in any assertion of causal relationship or of connection according to natural law. It is the kind of connection we believe in when we believe that the consequences of any hypothesis are such and such because of 'the way reality is' or because the facts of nature are thus and so. It is the kind of connection which we rely upon, and implicitly assert, when we anticipate that the consequences of a certain action under certain conditions will be so and so, and cannot be otherwise. Because whoever believes in predictable consequences of action, believes that although we make our own decisions, what is to ensue once we commit ourselves is fixed and out of our hands. Only by the 'reality' of this connection, independently of the decision itself, could there be any such thing as 'foreseeable consequences' of action. Whoever contemplates a possible way of acting but discards it as unwise, believes "If I

should do so and so, the results would be such and such";
and believes this connection holds independently of the
decision itself. And whoever regrets a decision believes "If
I had done that, such and such would have come about."
And he does not believe this to be true merely because the
hypothesis is false; if he did, the regret would be spurious.

Without something determined independently of the decision to verify, there would be nothing for the verifying
experience to disclose—except itself: it would verify nothing because there would be no independent fact to be
evidenced. Whoever believes in independent reality, believes in such real connections which may be disclosed
in experience; and whoever believes in such connections,
verifiable in experience, believes in knowable but independent reality. And whoever *dis*believes in such real connections—if he is not merely confused and inconsistent—
not only disbelieves the possibility of empirical knowledge;
he disbelieves that there is anything to be so known which
it is possible to state.

As will be obvious, such connections are what Hume referred to as 'necessary connections of matters of fact'.
These are to be distinguished from 'necessary connections
of ideas'—from logical connections. A correlative point of
terminology is to be noted with respect to the frequent
phrase 'possible experience'. The verifiable import of any
matter of (objective) fact is that certain experiences are
'possible' and certain other experiences 'not possible'. But
what is in this sense 'not possible experience', may still be—
and presumably will be—entirely possible to imagine. Neither such 'possibilities' of experience nor such real ('necessary') connections are logical; determinable *a priori* by
reflection. They are discoverable only in that manner in
which empirical knowledge is acquired.[7]

---

[7] Kant also uses the word 'necessary' (*notwendig*) in this sense,
particularly in his discussion of the Analogies of Experience. And he
indicates the correlative sense of 'possible' in his discussion of the
categories of modality. He also uses the phrase 'according to a rule'
(*nach einer Regel*) as equivalent to 'necessary' in this sense. According to his conception the particular rule of connection is not necessary in the sense of *a priori*, but he believes it assured that there must

As Hume correctly maintained, the only alternative to admission that such real connections genuinely obtain, is skepticism. And that jejune character of consistent skepticism which Hume himself finally admitted, is indicated by the implication of it for action which has been remarked. Without 'necessary connections' there could be no foreseeable consequences of any active attitude; and without such determinable consequences action could not be genuine—the very idea of it would be empty. The skeptic who does not, like the ancient Cynic, refuse to turn out for a wagon, is only play-acting. Consistently he can take no active attitude; not even the attitude of not taking attitudes. And whoever can thus divest himself of his active nature—and without trying—must arouse our wonder if not excite our admiration. At least he will not take his skepticism seriously, or ask us to, since he takes *nothing* seriously.

There is, however, one fundamental difference between what we should intend by 'real connection' and what Hume meant by 'necessary connection of matters of fact'. In common with philosophers generally up to his time, Hume tends to regard the word 'knowledge' as strictly applicable only to what may be certain, and fails to give sufficient consideration to the question of probability. Hence for him the alternatives are (1) that there should be universal connections which can be established as holding between matters of fact, or (2) that no conjunction of facts can be known to be other than sheer coincidence. Without entering upon all the difficult questions which surround this matter and must be considered later, we may say at once that the idea of real connection does not require the supposition of 100 percent correlation by which, A being given, B can be predicted with certainty. It is also satisfied if the occurrence of A genuinely affects the occurrence of B: if the objective frequency of B when A is present is reliably different than when A is ab-

---

be such rules if the objective order of fact is to be distinguished from the subjective connection of mere association of ideas, and from the merely temporal order of experience as given.

sent, so that the occurrence of A is a probability-index of the occurrence of B. If such correlation can be established, then when A is given there arises a valid probability of B; e.g., if a person jumps out a second-story window he will *probably* be hurt. Such a probability-connection would be inappropriately spoken of as 'necessary', but it has the essential character mentioned above; it is significantly assertable when the hypothesis is contrary to fact and in cases where the factuality of the hypothesis is undetermined. The importance of this point concerning probability will appear shortly.

As was noted in the preceding chapter, it has often been charged by critics of pragmatism that, in identifying the meaning of empirical statements with what would verify them, one reduces the significance of objective facts believed in to a signification of experience merely; and hence that such a 'verification-theory' of meaning is really 'idealistic' or 'subjectivistic' or 'phenomenalistic'. But we now arrive at a point where the difference of this view from any subjectivistic conception can be made precise and clear.

It is here maintained that there is no significance in objective belief nor in any statement of objective fact beyond what would be expressible in terms of some theoretically possible confirmation of it. But there is in that no implication of subjectivism; it implies denial only that there is any objective thing or fact which is intrinsically unknowable—which could not be empirically evidenced to any actual or even any supposititious observer. The critic has mislocated the issue between subjectivism and the affirmation of a reality which is independent of being known, and commits an *ignoratio elenchi.*

The denial of unknowable reality does not—let us hope —imply that there is no reality which is unknown and unverified. That there can be no reality outside *actual* experience is what the subjectivist asserts. It is not here maintained, however, that reference to the totality of *actual* verifying experiences (verifications actually made or actually to be made in future) exhausts the significance of objective fact. On the contrary that is denied. As has been pointed out, an objective belief implies not only such terminating judgments as are put to the test but also assertion of those which are untested. As we have emphasized; such terminating judgments assert an if-then relation which must still hold when the hypothesis is false and the indicated verification is not made; and are thus most clearly expressible in the form "If such and such observation should be made, so and so would be observed."

It lies in the nature of the case that there must be such terminating judgments, taken to be true, which will remain untested. It is not possible to make all possible tests, for the same reasons that it is impossible to act in all possible ways or adopt all possible decisions. Our commitment to objective reality, independent of being experienced, is signalized by our commitment to terminating judgments—implicitly affirmed in affirming what implies them—which, in the case of any objective belief, remain untested; in our assertion of the observability of what is not observed; of the verifiability of what remains unverified; or possibilities of experience which never become actual.

It is by such departure from subjectivism that we find it necessary to insist that the terminating judgments, in which the verifiable meaning of objective empirical assertion is to be found, must express a real connection—independent of being found to hold by actual test—between a mode of action and a sequent eventuation of experience. The question how statements with such meaning may be assured, is the question how empirical knowledge of an objective reality is possible.

12. We may now turn to the two questions mentioned earlier but postponed. When a terminating judgment represents a possible test of an objective statement believed, finding this terminating judgment, upon trial, to be decisively true does not decisively verify the objective belief but confirms it only and shows it probable. But suppose that upon trial the terminating judgment is found false: the mode of action is adopted, but the predicted eventuation in experience fails to follow. Is the objective belief of which this is a pertinent test thereby decisively

proved false? And second: we have seen that any test of an objective statement in direct experience requires an hypothesis of action; the predicted eventuation of experience is conditional upon performance of the test. But are there not other conditions also which must be satisfied if the accrual or non-accrual of the expected empirical sequent is to have a bearing on the objective belief and constitute a test of it? These two questions are connected with one another.

We have so far spoken as if the various terminating judgments representing possible confirmations of an objective belief were simply implied in the statement of that belief; and if that should be unqualifiedly correct, then the failure of such a terminating judgment to prove true upon trial would be decisive disproof of the objective statement implying it. We noted, in passing, a doubt whether this is in fact the case, but we did not there pursue the matter.

That an objective statement is not decisively verifiable by any single test, rather naturally suggests that likewise it will not be decisively falsifiable. But that is merely an easy association of ideas and without cogency. If a statement, 'P', has numerous implications, 'Q_1', 'Q_2', 'Q_3', etc., but none of these is equivalent to 'P' itself, then the finding that any one of these implied statements, 'Q_n', is true will afford confirmation only of the truth of 'P', but finding any one of them, 'Q_n', to be false will prove decisively the falsity of 'P'. And this consideration is in point here, because no terminating judgment could be equivalent to any objective statement: if it were, then the objective statement could be proved with the same certainty which attaches to the terminating judgment when tested.

The ground, then, on which it may be doubted that objective statements are decisively falsifiable is not this one of expected symmetry in the relation to verification and to falsification. It is, rather, the direct inspection of cognitive experience itself which will suggest this doubt. For example; what I see arouses belief in a real doorknob in a certain position before me. And when I put out my hand to grasp it, the eventuation of the expected feeling of contact will constitute a confirmation of this belief as highly probable. But suppose I fail to locate and turn the knob with my hand: shall I be convinced forthwith that my belief in a doorknob where I seemed to see it is false? As a fact, no. If such failure occurs, I shall be puzzled; but perhaps as much inclined to doubt my sense of touch as my sense of sight, and rather more disposed to doubt the accuracy of my coordination than either of these. The test in question is the most usual and practical one which could readily be suggested for the belief in question, and as nearly decisive as any. And at a rough estimate, we shall think that failure of it is a somewhat less decisive proof of falsity of the belief than success would be of the truth of it. Other examples might disclose a different comparison between the degree of confirmation of the objective belief in question which positive result of putting some pertinent terminating judgment to the test would give and the assurance of its falsity which would be indicated by a negative result. And we should find many cases where decisive disproof of the terminating judgment would make us practically certain that the objective belief so tested was false. But should we find any instance in which failure would give rise to such degree of assurance that one would hazard his life and hope of future happiness on it without a second thought? That is hardly plausible: we do not feel that degree of assurance in *any* sense perception: too many other possibilities of explanation—other than truth or falsity of the objective belief—will suggest themselves, whatever the result of any single test. Off hand, one is disposed to think that if we choose the most nearly decisive of possible tests by direct experience, a positive result is about as nearly decisive of truth as a negative one will be of falsity. And we cannot well suppose that *any* test in direct experience will either prove or disprove an objective belief with absolute certainty.

This result may seem disconcerting; because it obliges a complicating qualification of the account of empirical determination of truth and falsity in general; and hence

also, of the account of the meaning of objective statements and beliefs, in that sense of meaning in which it
coincides with the criterion of applicability and truth.

Unless objective empirical statements say something
about experience, they are meaningless. We might grant
that analytic statements can have significance independently of anything which experience will test. But certainly
not empirical statements. Unless these say something
which experience will determine, directly or indirectly, they
say nothing at all. And no statement can say anything
about experience unless, by implication at least, it says
something about particular experiences, actual or possible.
But if we ask ourselves whether what we mean when we
make a statement of objective fact, is something which
any single experience can show with absolute finality to
be true or false, then candor compels us to answer in the
negative. Practical certainty; yes, in some cases: but complete theoretical certainty; no. The most that we can claim
is that for objective beliefs in general, or for most of them,
there are tests in direct experience a positive result of
which will indicate a high degree of probability, and
similarly, tests a negative result of which will indicate a
high probability of falsity. Often it will be the same test
which will answer to both these requirements: a positive
result of it will assure high probability of the belief, and a
negative result will indicate extreme improbability. Where
such is the case, we may call the test in question a *ruling
test*. But for some objective beliefs—particularly those
which are comprehensive, like a generalization of science
—some single experience might give a nearly decisive disproof, but no single test would afford an equally trustworthy confirmation. And perhaps for some objective beliefs practical certainty might be assured by some crucial
test, but no equally certain disproof could be found in any
single experience. That might be the case when satisfactory test-conditions are difficult to achieve.

13. In consequence, we shall be obliged to qualify our
previous statement of the relation between the non-terminating judgment of objective belief and any terminat-

ing judgment which constitutes a test of it. If the terminating judgment be decisively found true, then the objective belief is thereby confirmed as probable. And if the terminating judgment is found false, then the objective statement is thereby proved improbable; is disconfirmed. It is the latter consideration which obliges the qualification; the former one has all along been explicitly recognized. We can no longer say that *if* the objective belief is true, then the terminating judgment will certainly be true; we can only say it will be probable—in most cases in some high degree, perhaps amounting to practical certainty.

However, within the bounds of such a manner of approach, could we not have avoided the kind of complications which now threaten us by adopting the type of formulation which a scientific operationist would be likely to give of his scientific meanings: by saying, for example, that the concept of length or hardness is to be defined by some crucial test of it? Thus we might say "X has hardness m" means "The standard test-apparatus operated under standard conditions will make a dent of depth k in X." This provides a genuinely equivalent formulation, simply expressible and indicative of the test of truth of which we are in search. And if it be objected that there are other tests which would be pertinent and other modes of confirmation, that point too may be taken care of in such terms. The *definitive* test is as indicated; but on grounds more or less obvious, we shall recognize the fact of a high, or perhaps a 100 percent correlation between results of this test and results of others. Such other results will *confirm* hardness m; but it is the specified test which is to be accepted as the decisive proof.

As has been indicated, the trouble with this type of operationist conception is merely that it does not go far enough to reach the general and final problems of validity and truth; because the criterion as so formulated is not genuinely in terms of sense—even though it may readily suggest what further calls for formulation. It is not in terms of direct experience, as is witnessed by the fact that whether a standard apparatus in good order has been properly operated, and has penetrated the material precisely to depth k, can be and often is a question. This is a complex matter concerning which mistakes are frequently made: it pertains to objective facts offering the same general kind of problems of their assurance as does the original question about the hardness of the material tested. Hence we are called upon to say, similarly, what the test of the *test* is, and how the results reported are to be assured as trustworthy.

The physicist or biologist or psychologist may quite properly feel that he is not called upon to pursue such problems further; just as also he is not called upon for any account of the humbler and more general kind of knowledge such as one's assurance that there is a doorknob in a certain position before him. An operational definition of the usual sort meets his every requirement—so long as he does not become entangled in epistemological snarls in his own scientific methodology. (There may be something to be said on that point, but we need not pause to say it here.) But for those whose concern is with the epistemological problems, such a definition represents a starting point rather than a solution. It leaves us with three questions; What is the criterion of determination that a test apparatus is in a certain condition called 'good order'?, How are we assured that a prescribed test routine is properly carried out?, and How is the fact that the material has been penetrated to a specified depth to be assured? And from the epistemological point of view, these questions are no simpler than the original one, how we may know that the material in question has a certain degree of hardness, nor are they essentially different in kind.

For any further progress we must make connection between *any* such matter of objective fact and something directly in terms of sense, where alone we can find an *ultimate* determinant of truth or validity of an empirical belief. We can make such direct contact only in terms of what may be given in sense experience; only in terms of what appears. Sense appearances may be difficult, or even impossible, to formulate, but they are the matters of which we may be certain. And unless something is certain in terms of experience, then nothing of empirical import is even probable. Here again, we would seem not to have discarded any alternative of conception unnecessarily, but merely to have followed the compulsions of the problem and of the facts.

The complicating considerations which now confront us are two: first, that even those consequences of an objective belief which are statable in terms of the directly sense-verifiable are not such that the finding of any one of them true will prove beyond peradventure the truth of the belief, and not such that finding one of them false will be decisive proof that the belief is false. And second, that we have not yet taken account of the possible conditions, other than a condition of action, which may be essential in order that certain findings of direct experience should be pertinent to an objective belief in question.

14. Let us consider the first of these two matters. A part of the consequences of this have already been sufficiently discussed: the fact that no single terminating judgment will, upon being found true, assure the objective belief with certainty, means that objective beliefs are not decisively verifiable but confirmable only. A crucial or 'ruling' test may give assurance amounting to practical certainty, but theoretical certainty of objective fact is not attainable. And where no test can assure certainty, there is no good ground for singling out any one such possible confirmation as peculiarly exhibiting the sense significance of an objective statement: all findings which will confirm it are alike to be recognized as consequences implicit in what it means, in terms of direct experience, for that statement to be true.

It may be objected that connection between an objective statement believed and empirical findings which will confirm it should, rather, be viewed as something learned from past experience, and not as implied or contained in the objective statement itself which is believed. It is quite true, and even obvious, that without something learned from past experience no such connections as terminating judgments assert could be understood or known. We must return to that fact at a later point. But recognition of it contains nothing contrary to the conception that such connections are contained in the objective belief itself: it is *these meanings themselves* which we learn to entertain and to understand from past experience.

Such learning historically arises by association of ideas and the formation of habits. But if in any instance a belief so arising be challenged, the only justification which can be offered for it is by way of some multiplicity of inductively corroborated real connections in experience. If you move your eyes, things seen will be displaced in the field of vision—unless illusory. If you reach for what has certain recognizable but indescribable visual characters, you will feel it with your hand—if the apprehension is veridical. It is by learning such real connections in experience that we establish the actuality of things seen; learn that real objects exist having certain properties signalized by certain visual and other clues. Explicit formulation of such inductively established real connections gives us, at one and the same time, the sense meaning (experiential criteria) of our customary beliefs which we express by affirming matters of objective fact, and the basic probabilities by which an experienceable world of objects is recognized to exist.

What further remains to be weighed, is what follows from the fact that finding a predictable consequence of an objective statement to be false will disconfirm it but will not prove it certainly false. There is nothing disconcerting from the practical point of view in this discovery that objective beliefs are as difficult to disprove conclusively as they are to prove. We shall merely choose those 'ruling' tests whose results will be as nearly decisive as possible—of truth in case the result is positive, and of falsity in case they fail. The consideration which should give us pause here is the fact that we can no longer regard any terminating judgment, "When S is given, if A then E," as strictly implied by an objective statement, 'P', which is

believed. We can only say, "If P, then when presentation S is given and act A is performed, it is more or less
highly probable that E will be observed to follow." Thus
if we now ask how, precisely, the sense meaning of an
objective belief is to be understood, we find that it is to
be thought of as some set of direct empirical findings it
implies as *probable* under appropriate conditions of presentation and of action.

This does not, however, impose any difficulty, either
practical or theoretical, for the confirmation or disconfirmation of objective fact. It remains true that such confirmation or disconfirmation may be found in some certainty of sense, determined by putting some terminating
judgment to the test; and that a corresponding probability
of the belief tested may be definitely assured. For any objective statement, 'P', we shall have some set of possible
tests of it, each expressible by some terminating judgment:

If P, then when S_1 and A_1, there is a probability H
that E_1;

If P, then when S_2 and A_2, there is a probability K that
E_2;

And so on. Also there will be a probability which can be
judged that if the objective statement is false, the predicted
consequences of it will not be found when test is made:

If not-P, then when S_1 and A_1, there is a probability
M that not-E_1;

If not-P, then when S_2 and A_2, there is a probability N
that not-E_2;

And so on. Such hypothetical probabilities would have to
be adjudged directly: there are no probability-formulas
which would have much bearing upon them, and none
which would allow numerically precise estimates in the
ordinary examples of cognition where the pertinent data
hardly admit of mathematical or statistical formulation.
Further, the degree in which an objective statement is confirmed by a positive result of test, or found improbable
when the result is negative, are appropriately to be as-
sessed by a common-sense estimate of their order of
magnitude, rather than calculated out. The useful generali-

zations in this connection are merely that the degree of confirmation, when test result is positive, is the higher according as this positive result is the more *im*probable if the statement tested be *false;* and that when the test result is negative, the statement tested is the more improbable according as this negative result is the more improbable if the statement should be true. When the probability that if 'P' be false, 'E' also will be false, approximates to certainty, the assurance of 'P' itself will approximate to certainty when 'E' is found true. And when the probability of 'E' if 'P' be true, approximates to certainty, there is assurance approximating to certainty that 'P' is false when 'E' is found false.[8]

It is to be observed here that confirmation of an objec-

[8] The degree of probability established by a test is also relative to the antecedent probability of 'P'; the probability of 'P' before the test is made. The above generalizations are nevertheless unqualifiedly correct.

The truth of 'P', which is tested, is one 'cause' or explanation of 'E' when found. And we may bracket together all other possible circumstances which could explain this finding under the head 'not-P'. The principle of Inverse Probability will then apply as follows:

Let the antecedent probability of 'P' $= W$.

The antecedent probability of 'not-P' $= 1 - W$.

Let the probability of 'E' if 'P' is true $= K$.

Let the probability of 'not-E' if 'P' is false $= N$.

The probability of 'E' if 'P' is false $= 1 - N$.

Then when 'E' is found true by test, the probability of 'P' is given by

$$\frac{WK}{WK + (1 - W)\ (1 - N)}$$

This fraction will be nearer to unity according as W is nearer to unity or N is nearer to unity. Thus 'P' will be assured with a probability approximating to certainty if the probability N that 'E' will *not* be found unless 'P' is true, approximates to certainty.

The degree of disconfirmation of 'P' (the probability of 'not-P') when 'E' is found false, is given by

$$\frac{(1 - W)N}{(1 - W)N + W(1 - K)}$$

This fraction will be nearer to unity according as W, the antecedent probability of 'P', is nearer to zero, or K, the probability of "E if P" is nearer to unity. Thus the disconfirmation of 'P' when 'E' is found false, will approximate to certain falsity if the assurance of 'E' if 'P' is true, approximates to certainty.

Application of the principle of Inverse Probability here is not affected by the omission from the hypothesis above, of the conditions S and A, since when test is made these conditions are assured with certainty, and their probability-coefficients would each be unity.

tive belief, in a degree approaching certainty, is derivative from high probability that the expected test result, '*E*', will be found *false* in case the belief '*P*' is in fact not true; and not from the direct relation between '*P*' and '*E*' which would be stated by a terminating judgment of the form "If *P*, then (assuming *S* and *A*) *E*." Thus it makes no difference to the possibility of a confirmation of '*P*' approaching to certainty, that we are obliged to abandon the supposition that terminating judgments express an unqualified deducibility of the finding '*E*' from '*P*' (and '*S*' and '*A*').

There are two further facts of importance which should also be noted, about the relation between an objective belief and the test results which may serve to confirm or disconfirm it. First, that a positive result of any one such test increases the antecedent probability of a positive result of other tests not yet made; because it increases the antecedent probability of the objective belief itself, and hence increases the probability of any further consequences of it. This assures the practically important point that, even though the predictions, in terms of direct experience, which are warranted in case an objective belief is true, are not predictions with theoretical certainty but with probability only, nevertheless anything which confirms this belief adds to the assurance with which the sense-predictable consequences of it can be expected in further experience. Second, we should observe that while the objective statement believed gives only some more or less high degree of probability of any one predictable sense consequence of it, the relation of it to the whole set of such consequences, expressible by pertinent terminating judgments or to any considerable class of such consequences, will be somewhat different. If 'E_1', 'E_2', 'E_3', etc., are each such that finding it true assures some probability of '*P*', then the finding true of 'E_1' and 'E_2' and 'E_3' will quickly assure a high degree of probability, according to a principle which will be fairly obvious. This finding that *n* such consequences, each more or less improbable in case '*P*' is false, are *all* of them true, will represent a striking coincidence, highly improbable if 'P' is in fact false. The principle in question may be illustrated by the example of a number of witnesses, each of them not especially trustworthy as individual reporters, who independently tell the same circumstantial story. In case of such concurrence, one must quickly be convinced that what they tell is practically certain. In similar fashion, the probability of an objective belief, and with it of the pertinent terminating judgments as yet untested, may come to have very high probability, even on the basis of confirmations which, taken separately, might not warrant a particularly high degree of assurance.

We cannot here explain the precise meaning which should be assigned to 'probability' in the above: that must be a separate and later topic. But the appropriate sense is the same as that suggested by the commonplace expression that something is to be expected in 99 cases out of 100 (or some other fraction). And this illustration is the more apt in that the fraction mentioned is to an extent a figurative expression: no such precision as it might suggest is taken to be genuinely possible in estimating the degree of probability in question, but it is nevertheless intended as roughly accurate.

Let us apply the results of this discussion to the case of seeing the doorknob and attempting to confirm the belief thus induced by grasping. If there really is a doorknob in a certain position before me where I seem to see one, then when such visual presentation as I now have is given, if I initiate a certain not easily describable but immediately recognizable activity of grasping, a similarly indescribable but recognizable feeling of contact is to be expected in 99 cases out of 100. But if there is *no* doorknob, when such presentation is given, then in 999 cases out of 1000 if I initiate such activity the expected feeling of contact will not ensue. (Whether the probabilities are plausibly estimated here, even roughly, makes no matter for the illustration; but note that the two probabilities assigned—one for truth of the objective belief and the other if it is false—are different.) It should be remembered that while what is believed about the doorknob is stated in the language of objective fact, the content of presentation, the action adopted, and the empirical sequent, are all to be described in expressive language, as items of which we may be immediately certain. That is:

Let '*P*' = "There really is a doorknob in front of me and to the left."

Let '*S*' = "I seem to see such a doorknob."

Let '*A*' = "I seem to myself to be initiating a certain grasping motion."

Let '*E*' = "The feeling of contacting the doorknob follows." Then the two judgments made are:

(1) When *P* and *S* and *A* then, with a probability measured by 0.99, *E*.

(2) When *S* and *A* but it is false that *P* then, with a probability measured by 0.999, it will be false that *E*.

As a result of (2), if when the appearance is given and the action initiated, the expected result actually follows, then the objective belief is thereby assured with a probability which is of the same order of magnitude as 0.999. Because by the general principle of Inverse Probability, the probability of a hypothesis which is assured by finding a consequence of that hypothesis to be true, will approach to certainty when the *im*probability of that consequence if the hypothesis be *false* approaches to certainty. And by the same general principle, applied to (1) above: if the belief about the doorknob is put to the test in question and the feeling of contact with the doorknob does *not* follow, this belief will be disconfirmed, and there will be a probability having the same order of magnitude as 0.99 that it is false.

Various questions will suggest themselves here, some of them to be dealt with in the conclusion of this chapter, and others which must wait upon a more detailed discussion of probability. But provisionally; if we ask what statement of an objective belief means in terms of sense determination, the answer can now be suggested from this illustration. That there really is a doorknob where one seems to see it, means that an endless number of confirmations of this belief will be possible, one example of which would be reaching for this doorknob and finding it with one's hand as expected. It has to be recognized, however, that success of one such test will not amount to 100 percent proof of the fact believed; and that likewise a single failure will not constitute 100 percent disproof of it. If a number of tests be made by reference to such predictable sense consequences of the belief—whether repetitions of the 'same' test or tests of different such consequences—then the cumulative result of coincident success will determine a probability of the belief which will be of an even higher order of magnitude than the probability established by any single confirmation alone.[9] In this way the confirmation of the belief can, in favorable cases, approach quite close to certainty on the basis of a finite number of tests; even though theoretical certainty is not attainable. However, truth of the belief does not require unexceptionable success of attempted confirmations. (If *all* the witnesses tell exactly the same story with no discrepancy of detail, perhaps that confirmation will be 'too good to be true'.) In our attempted confirmations, we shall reasonably expect that eventually some failure may occur, even supposing the belief to be true; such exception 'having some other explanation'. For example, we sometimes fail to grasp a doorknob which really is where we seem to see it, by a failure of coordination. Consonantly, it is required for theoretical precision that the terminating judgments which are consequences of an objective fact believed, should be stated in terms of probability: if there really is a doorknob where I seem to see one, then, with a probability of about 0.99, if I try to grasp it I shall feel it with my hand.

Perhaps the question is, however, of a different sort; How do we know that the belief, or statement of it, has some certain set of terminating judgments as its consequences and not others? The only answer which can be given is that we know this in knowing what we mean by our affirmation

---

[9] For reasons which are commonplaces of induction, and could be stated in terms of principles of probability, a coincidence in the success of 'different' tests will warrant a higher degree of assurance than will be given by repetitions of the 'same' test.

of objective fact; that we must know it insofar as we know what the truth of our belief involves in any fashion in which experience can give evidence of that truth. Because such terminating judgments express the only possible determinations of objective fact which experience can afford, and hence constitute the only usable criterion of empirical objective truth. We might formulate what we mean in terms of some *decisive* test of truth, expressed in objective language, as the scientific operationist usually does. But if so, then it will be only in this same fashion of confirmation and of probability that we can assure the fact that this specified *objective* test is actually satisfied. In terms of what can be found directly in experience, and hence of that which alone is empirically determinable with certainty, confirmation only is possible for an objective belief.

15. The same considerations involved in the preceding section, have direct bearing on the other of the two questions to be investigated: Are there not other conditions of any expected result of a test of objective belief besides merely the condition of an initiation of action? And if so, must not these further conditions be introduced in the hypothesis of any terminating judgment, if it is to be fully and accurately expressed?

The example of determining hardness by use of a standard test apparatus, would make it appear that frequently there will be such further conditions of any test. And it suggests itself that in this respect that example is typical of the generality of possible confirmations of an objective belief or statement. We must assure that the apparatus is in working order; we must assure that it actually conforms to the recognized standard; we must assure that the manner of orienting the apparatus and the material is as prescribed. If these conditions be ignored, the pertinence of the result to the objective fact believed and tested, will be dubious. Thus it suggests itself that the really correct way of formulating a possible confirmation of objective fact will be such as, "If C_1 and C_2 and C_3, and A, then E"; or, combining these several conditions under one head, 'C', and putting the matter more precisely, "When S is given, if C and A, then there is a probability K that E."

However, we have seen why what 'A' and 'E' here represent must be phrased in expressive language, stating something immediately determinable as specific content of experience. Also that these same considerations compel the probability qualification of the predicted eventuality 'E'. The similar question must at once be observed as pertinent to any further condition or conditions, represented by 'C'. Are these conditions to be stated in terms of objective fact —e.g., that the apparatus actually is in good working order —or are they conditions which should be stated in terms of something which given experience itself may decisively assure? It would be the common-sense procedure, which any physicist would be pretty sure to follow, to phrase the whole matter in objective terms: the conditions, the experimental activity, and the result to be looked for, would all be expressed in terms of physical fact. He will mention separately certain safeguards to be taken in order to minimize the possibility that the test and its results may be vitiated by experimental or observational errors. But he will probably not incorporate any allowance for such possible error in the statement of the test itself. All that is perhaps as it should be. But in being so phrased in objective terms, the statement of test procedure and results will omit the questions centrally important for the epistemological problem of our possible assurance of objective physical facts. For any resolution of that kind of problem, we are obliged to inquire how, and in what measure, assurance of *any* physical fact—including not only the test performance and its physical result but also any other physical conditions of a satisfactory test—may arise from *data which can be completely assured in terms of experience.*

Observing this necessity, we see that if the test apparatus must be standard in order to make the results a genuine confirmation of physical fact; and if the apparatus must likewise be in good working condition, and so on; then the next question is: "Can we be *certain* of these test conditions?" And the answer must obviously be in the negative:

we might have reasonable assurance or even practical certainty, but the possibility of doubt could not be genuinely precluded. That being the case, the test results will have to be weighed in the light of what we *can* genuinely assure at the time of test. And this will be what we can assure by some direct observation, formulatable in terms of what can be actually given. The appropriate hypothesis of the test, as actually carried out, is *not,* then, a physical condition of the apparatus but only such assurance of this as direct observation can give.

Thus if there are conditions of objective fact for the carrying out of any test, result of which will confirm or disconfirm an objective belief, still the *determinable* conditions, which should qualify the resultant confirmation or disconfirmation, are not those of objective fact but only those which may be directly given and ascertained and which may be *indicative* of the objective and 'ideal' conditions of test. What we may fully determine, for example, is that the apparatus *appears to be* a standard test apparatus in good working order.

Furthermore, this necessity of phrasing any conditions of test in expressive terms, instead of objective terms, does not impede the possibility of any confirmation. If the degree of confirmation or disconfirmation afforded by certain observable test results, on condition of certain *physical* matters of fact, can be stated, then also it can be stated in terms of what is immediately ascertainable provided the given appearances indicate a determinable probability that these physical conditions are satisfied. If 'so far as we can see' this is a standard test apparatus in good working order, and if there is a determinable probability that if the apparatus were *not* thus satisfactory we should see some evidence of that, then there is a calculable degree of confirmation or disconfirmation on the basis of the *appearances,* if there is any statable degree of confirmation or disconfirmation on condition of the physical facts of which these appearances afford some probability. And if there are *no* appearances at the time of test which are indicative of any objective conditions essential for a test and give a certain degree of confirmation or disconfirmation, then it can never be determined that there *is* such confirmation or disconfirmation, because we should never know as even probable that a test having this result was actually carried out.

Suppose then that C be some objective matter of fact which is condition of a test, and SC be what is directly observable as evidence of C. More specifically, let us say that if SC is given, there is a probability K that C is objectively the fact. And suppose that we know

(1) If the objective belief 'P' is true, then when S is given and C is satisfied and act A is initiated, it is probable in degree M that E will be observed.

(2) If 'P' is *not* true, then when S is given and condition C is satisfied and act A is initiated, it is probable in degree N that E will *not* be observed.

Then if we substitute 'SC' for 'C' in (1) and (2), these formulations will still hold provided the probabilities, M in (1) and N in (2), be qualified by the probability K, which is that of C when SC is observed.[10] That is, (1) and (2) above, together with the consideration that when SC is observed there is a probability K that C is objectively the fact, give us the following:

(1') If the objective belief 'P' is true, then when S is given and SC is observed and act A is initiated, it is probable in degree KM that E will be observed.

(2') If 'P' is *not* true, then when S is given and SC is observed and act A is initiated, it is probable in degree KN that E will *not* be observed.

And in (1') and (2') the whole of what is to be determined, in making this single test of the truth or falsity of 'P', is stated in terms exclusively of what experience at the time of test may make completely certain.

Thus it is never necessary to include any condition of objective fact in the hypothesis of a terminating judgment, expressing the test conditions of a possible confirmation. It

[10] Because by the Multiplication Rule for probabilities, if the probability of C is K, and there is a probability M that if C then E, the probability of C and E both is KM. And when the probability coefficient of S and of A is 1, their inclusion in the hypothesis does not alter application of this rule.

would be natural to express any conditions, other than that of the test activity, in objective terms. Particularly so when we think of possible confirmations under conditions which do not presently obtain or those pertinent to tests which we have no present intention of making. But the actual cognitive validity determinable by any test cannot be so expressed. Any confirmation which actually accrues when a test is carried out, has a weight which depends, not upon the factuality of objective test conditions, of whose satisfaction we cannot be certain at the time of test, but upon our *degree of assurance* of those objective conditions which is afforded by some directly observable evidence of them. Thus those conditions which are directly pertinent to a confirmation and genuinely ascertainable are not objective facts but must be included amongst the given appearances at the time of test. They must be items of direct presentation; and we might think of them as already covered by 'S' in our paradigm, "S being given, if A then, with probability M, E."

16. However, if we thus think of the sense presentation which is condition of a confirmation as including *all* directly observable evidence which is pertinent, then it will be drawn to our attention that such presentational evidence is not confined to appearance of the thing which is object of the belief to be confirmed but will include various other circumstances of presentation. For example, in the case of seeing the doorknob and testing the belief based on it by grasping, it will not be merely the appearance of the doorknob which is a pertinent sense condition: if it is a consideration affecting the weight attaching to this confirmation that one's coordination of eye and hand should be normal, then one's feeling fit or feeling a little dizzy at the time will also be such a pertinent item of presentation. And this is in accord with our common-sense weighing of the matter in case our first attempt at grasping should fail of its expected result. How extensive and various the presentational items pertinent to a confirmation of objective fact may be, is something which will again be drawn to our attention at a later point.

Our general conclusion concerning objective beliefs and our possible knowledge of their truth will, therefore, be as follows. The theoretical as well as the practical significance of such belief is to be found in what we should accept as confirmations of it; in those testable consequences taken as implied in the belief itself. No limited number of tests would completely exhaust this significant content of any empirical objective belief. And by the same token no complete and decisive verification of them is theoretically possible, bringing our conviction to such a pitch that no conceivable further evidence could possibly weigh against it. They are never better than probable, though the degree of probability which can be assured may, in favorable cases, amount to what is commonly called practical certainty. And even where the degree of assurance validated by a single test is relatively low, the coincidence of positive results in a few such tests may quickly give rise to a very high degree of assurance. Further, there is no directly observable result of any single test which we should demand as an absolute certainty in case the belief is true, and the failure of which we should take to be disproof of the belief beyond all possible doubt. Though here again, the degree of probability that the belief is false which arises from such disconfirmation may sometimes amount to practical certainty.

This still allows, however, that the *probability* of a belief, assured by a test or tests, may be determined with finality. Because there is no requisite condition of any such test which cannot be phrased in terms of what is immediately ascertainable, and the expected result can likewise be expressed in terms of sense presentation which may be a matter of complete certainty. The fact that terminating judgments must themselves be phrased in terms of probability, has no consequence which is incompatible with that. Empirical knowledge of objective fact cannot be theoretically certain; but it can be certain that it is genuinely probable, and in auspicious cases that it is probable in high degree. There are, to be sure, further complicating considerations, not so far mentioned; in particular, the data requisite to establishment of an empirical belief as genuinely probable are more complex than is commonly recognized, and more extensive than what are usually called 'the data' in the case of such problems. Before we can come to that topic, however, we must first give attention to the more general and more fundamental question of the nature of empirical knowledge as probable, and particularly to what, precisely, it is which would be asserted in calling it probable. It is to this fundamental question that we turn in the next two chapters.

17. In view of the manner in which this chapter has been written, it will be well to append a kind of summary with special reference to logical aspects of the analysis so far. We began with a relatively simple depiction of terminating judgments, in relation to non-terminating judgments of objective fact, from which they follow, and then found it necessary to complicate this initial account. Any other manner of presentation would have run the danger of introducing so many problems at the same time that understanding of any one of them would have been prejudiced.

Let us now formulate statements made, as they would finally appear, using the example of a piece of paper before me as our paradigm. And for once let us make use of symbols, both for brevity and in order to suggest certain critical considerations of the analysis. The manner of symbolization to be adopted will not be wholly precise but will be sufficiently clear in connection with the notes to follow. Those who are interested in symbolic precision will see how that might be achieved but they will also observe that much greater complexity would be involved.

Let P = A sheet of real paper lies before me.

S_1 = A visual sheet-of-paper presentation is given.

A_1 = I move my eyes.

E_1 = A seen displacement of this presentation follows.

S_2 = I seem to feel paper with my fingers.

A_2 = I act to pick up and tear.

E_2 = A torn-paper presentation follows.

As symbolic abbreviations, let

$XY = X$ and Y.

$\sim X = $ It is false that X.

$X < Y = X$ implies Y; X has the analytic consequence Y.

$X \to Y = $ If X then in result Y.

$(h)X = $ In all probability, X.

$Xo = $ It is the case that X on occasion o.

$(o). \; Xo = $ For any occasion o, Xo.

The dot-punctuation to be used is that commonly appearing in formulas of symbolic logic. It should be understood, however, that the following are not formulas and cannot be manipulated according to the usual rules of the logical calculus. They are forms of statement which hold for the example chosen and, with certain exceptions to be mentioned, for such examples generally.

(1) $P. < \; :S_1A_1. \to .(h)E_1$

(2) $P. < \; :S_1A_2. \to .(h)E_2$

(3) $P. < \; :S_2A_1. \to .(h)E_1$

(4) $P. < \; :S_2A_2. \to .(h)E_2$

(5) $(o) \; :.Po. < \; :S_1o \; A_1o. \to .(h)E_1o$

(6) $\sim P. < \; :S_1A_1. \to .(h)\sim E_1$

(7) $PS_1A_1. < .(h)E_1$

(8) $\sim PS_1A_1. < .(h)\sim E_1$

(9) $S_1A_1E_1. < .(h)P$

(10) $S_1A_1\sim E_1. < .(h)\sim P$

(11) $S_1A_1E_1. < \; :S_2A_2. \to .(h)E_2$

NOTE 1: Let us suppose that 'S_1', or 'S_2', includes not only what it is stated above to represent but, in accordance with the discussion of 'C_1', 'C_2', 'SC', etc., in Section 15, all immediately observed conditions of whatever confirmation of 'P' is in question.

NOTE 2: It will be observed in statement (1) above that two meanings of 'if-then' are involved, symbolized respectively by '$<$' and by '$\to$'. The first of these is the relation of implication or analytic consequence which (1) asserts to hold between 'P' and '$S_1A_1. \to .(h)E_1$'. This relation, '$<$', covers not only that of any premise to a conclusion derivable from it by rules of deductive logic but also, for example, that of "T is red" to "T is colored," which cannot be certified by logical rules alone but only through knowing the meaning of 'red' and of 'colored' and understanding the relation of these two meanings to one another. Thus '$X < Y$', when true, is certifiable *a priori*, either by reference to logical rules or by reference to meanings involved or by both together. (As was made clear in Book I, whatever is certifiable by logical rules is also certifiable by reference to meanings of 'logical constants' and syntax, so that we could say more briefly that any relation '$<$' which holds is certifiable *a priori* by reference to meanings.)

The specific mode of meaning here in question is that called 'sense meaning' in Book I [of *An Analysis of Knowledge and Valuation*. Ed.]. The sense meaning of a statement consists in the experiential criteria of its application to reality. To understand what a statement means, in this mode of meaning, is to be able to recognize what would assure the truth of it. Hence the meaning of 'P' includes what would confirm it as holding; and any such confirmation is an analytic consequence of 'P'.

NOTE 3: In statement (1), 'P' is said to have the analytic consequence

$$'S_1A_1. \rightarrow . (h)E_1';$$

"When a visual sheet-of-paper presentation is given and I move my eyes, then in all probability a seen displacement of this presentation follows." Believing that a real piece of paper lies before me, I make the terminating judgment that, this presentation being given, if I move my eyes the seen displacement will supervene. And a positive result of putting this to the test will confirm my belief in the reality of the paper. But as we have observed, a negative result of the test would not decisively disprove the belief. We could not, therefore, express this analytic consequence of 'P' in the simpler form, '$S_1A_1. \rightarrow . E_1$'; and this terminating judgment does not occur unqualified in the analysis.

The relation here represented by '$\rightarrow$' depends on what we have spoken of as a 'real connection'; an inductively established correlation by virtue of which one observable item in experience is a probability-index of another. Without such real connections no belief in, or statement of, any matter of objective fact could have any content of meaning whatever. It is a relation holding by virtue of such real connection which is symbolized by '$\rightarrow$' in conjunction with the prefix '(h)'. The truth of 'P' requires that if S_1A_1, then in all probability E_1.

The reader may for a moment question whether this analytic consequence of 'P' should not be written

$$\text{'}(h)(S_1A_1.\rightarrow.E_1)\text{'};$$

"In all probability, if a sheet-of-paper presentation is given and I turn my eyes, a seen displacement will follow." But this difficulty will be removed if we observe that it arises merely from the customary but inaccurate manner of expressing hypothetical probabilities in general. When we speak of a probability, h, that if A then B, what we intend to refer to is a probability, h, of B if or when A is the case. The analytic consequence of 'P' which we wish here to express is not the probability of a relation, '$\rightarrow$', between 'S_1A_1' and 'E_1', but a *relation of probability* between them.

NOTE 4: We have suggested for '$(h)X$' the idiomatic reading, "In all probability, X," instead of "It is highly probable that X," in order to obviate in some measure a difficulty which cannot be dealt with satisfactorily in advance of the discussion of probability and the logic of probable belief. One point involved may, however, be suggested here. If, for example, one looks at the sky and predicts rain, one does not intend to assert merely that there is a probability connection between the appearance of the sky and the later occurrence of rain: that assertion would remain equally true whether in fact rain follows or not. The prediction hazarded (as probable) is that *it will rain:* an assertion which the sequel will decisively prove true or prove false. The expression "In all probability it will rain" carries some sense at least of such decisively verifiable or falsifiable prediction.

Considerations of this sort further emphasize the necessity of remarking that the terminating judgment, which expresses a prediction, does not itself occur as an unqualified constituent in the belief to be confirmed.

NOTE 5: We set down (2), (3), and (4), in addition to (1), as reminder that for a single objective belief, 'P', there may be different confirmations in which—comparing (1) with (2) or (3) with (4)—the same sense datum is cue to different tests with correspondingly different confirming results. And that—comparing (1) with (3) or (2) with (4)—different sense data may be cue to the same test and result.

It is further obvious that there may be repetition of a test: i.e., confirmations by reference to the same sense datum, test, and result on different occasions: this is indicated by the generalization of (1) in (5). Where the sense datum and the test-activity are the same, the confirming result will generally be the same. Most exceptions to this would be apparent only and due to faulty formulation of the case or failure to observe that the different confirming results have a common part which alone is essential. The infrequent real exceptions are to be explained by alternative and unobservable conditions of the test and its results; and such tests would not commonly afford a high degree of confirmation.

NOTE 6: Statement (5) expresses (1) in its general form: "For any occasion o, if 'P' holds, then if datum 'S_1' is given and test by 'A_1' is performed, result according to 'E_1' will in all probability ensue."

For (1) itself, 'S_1', 'A_1', and 'E_1' are statements, by reason of understood reference to a particular occasion: (5) expresses the fact that the given datum, the test-activity, and the confirming result on this occasion are instances, respectively, of a recognizable *kind* of datum, activity, and result, in terms of which a corresponding statement holds for *any* occasion—so long as 'P' is true. Thus in (5) 'S_1', 'A_1', and 'E_1' are allowed to represent statement functions, of which the corresponding constituents in (1) are particular values.

It may be objected that (5) is erroneously symbolized

because 'P' at least is still a statement and not a function. This would be true if 'P' should itself contain reference to a particular occasion, or occasions, on which a piece of real paper lies before me. But in that case, 'S_1', 'A_1', and 'E_1' must be restricted to the same occasion or occasions, since a test of past or future fact must in general differ from a test of present fact. We do not, for example, intend to assert, "If a piece of real paper lay before me on May 16, 1945, at 10 a.m., then on any occasion when a sheet-of-paper presentation is given and I move my eyes, a seen displacement of this presentation in all probability follows." This would be true but is not what (5) intends to assert. The probability in question would in that case be the antecedent probability of the consequent merely; truth of the hypothesis would be irrelevant; and a positive result of test would afford no confirmation of this hypothesis of a real piece of paper before me on an occasion now past. The formulation of (5) is therefore correct as given. It makes assertion concerning any occasion which is the same in 'Po', 'S_1o', 'A_1o', and 'E_1o', and no assertion concerning any occasion not implicitly referred to in some statement, 'P', which is a value of 'Po'.

Other statements on the list could be similarly generalized.

NOTE 7: The confirmation of 'P' by reference to 'S_1', 'A_1', and 'E_1', depends more directly upon (6) than upon (1); the degree of confirmation afforded by positive result of a test is relative to the *im*probability of 'E_1' in case 'P' should be false, rather than to the probability of 'E_1' when 'P' is true. (See Section 14 and footnote 8.)

It cannot be assumed that 'h' in (6) represents the *same* degree of high probability as in (1): this would seldom be the case. Where, as in our example, 'h', in (1) and (6) both, would represent a high degree of probability—whether the same or not—the test in question would be of the sort we have called a 'ruling test'.

NOTE 8: (7) follows from (1). Whether it is also equivalent to (1), depends on questions we shall not enter upon here. For example, their equivalence would require that the following also hold:

$$'S_1. < :P A_1. \rightarrow .(h)E_1',$$
$$\text{and}\quad 'S_1A_1. < :P. \rightarrow .(h)E_1'.$$

Likewise, (8) follows from (6).

NOTE 9: The most direct formulation of the confirmation of 'P' is given by (9); of the disconfirmation of 'P', by (10). As has been noted, the value of 'h' in (9) is relative to its value in (6) and in (8); and the value of 'h' in (10), to its value in (1) and in (7).

NOTE 10: We include (11) as reminder that one confirmation of an objective statement, 'P', renders probable a positive result of any further test, by establishing probability of 'P' itself. It cannot be assumed, however, that the probability of 'P' established by the finding '$S_1A_1E_1$', will be identically the probability, 'h', so established for 'E_2', according to (11). That would depend on antecedent probabilities also, and upon the relation of the tests to one another.

THE PROBLEM OF EMPIRICISM

RODERICK M. CHISHOLM

Professor C. I. Lewis, in Book II of his Carus Lectures, *An Analysis of Knowledge and Valuation,* defends the thesis that the meaning of any statement which refers to a material thing may be fully conveyed in statements which refer solely to sense-data or the sensible appearances of things. His account is perhaps the clearest and most careful defence of this empirical thesis which has yet appeared and, in consequence, it enables us to state, more clearly than has been possible before, the characteristic difficulties of empiricism.*

According to Professor Lewis, an analysis of the meaning of any ordinary thing statement, such as "This thing is red" or "That is a doorknob," will show that the statement entails an unlimited number of statements referring solely to sense-data. The sense-datum statements are "analytic consequences" of the thing statement; that this is so in any particular case "is certifiable *a priori,* either by reference to logical rules or by reference to meanings involved or by both together" (p. 249). The relation which thing statement bears to sense-datum statement is similar to that which "*T* is red" bears to "*T* is colored" (*ibid.*). Since the full meaning of any thing statement may be conveyed in the sense-datum statements which it entails, thing statements may be said to be "translatable" into sense-datum statements (p. 181).[1] The principle difficulty with this view con-

* Most of the passages referred to are reprinted in this volume in Lewis' "Terminating Judgments and Objective Beliefs." The page references are to Lewis' book. Ed.

[1] Seldom, of course, does anyone ever *formulate* any sense-datum

cerns the first step: the problem of showing that any ordinary thing statement has, as analytic consequences, statements which refer solely to sense-data.

The roots of the difficulty are the familiar facts sometimes referred to as "the relativity of sense perception." Whether a material thing will ever present, say, a red appearance or sense-datum depends partly upon the thing and partly upon the conditions under which it is observed. If one knew that the thing were red and that the lighting conditions were normal, one could predict that, to a normal observer, the thing would present a red appearance. If one knew that the lights were out, or that the observer had a certain type of color blindness, one could predict that the thing would present some other appearance. And so on, for any other thing and its possible appearances. To calculate the appearances with complete success, it is necessary to know both the thing-perceived and the (subjective and objective) observation-conditions, for it is the thing-perceived and the observation-conditions working jointly which determine what is to appear. Professor Lewis believes that "This thing is red" entails as analytic consequences an unlimited number of statements referring solely to what might appear. But the facts of "perceptual relativity" suggest that it doesn't entail *any* statement about sense-data; they suggest that a sense-datum statement is entailed only when "This thing is red" is taken in conjunction with *another* thing statement referring to observation-conditions. The translatability thesis requires that *both* observation-conditions and things-perceived be definable in terms of what might appear. But the facts of perceptual relativity indicate that it

---

statements and, as Professor Lewis admits (p. 173), it may be questioned whether the terms of ordinary language are adequate to convey judgments about sense-data. Although he finds it convenient to present his conclusions by reference to relations between *statements*, his theory does not purport to be a linguistic analysis. The problem is an epistemological one, concerning our beliefs or judgments about material things, and could be discussed without reference to statements at all. The present issues, however, may be brought into clearer focus if we follow Professor Lewis and discuss the relations between statements. It should be noted that Professor Lewis does not use the brief terms "thing statement" and "sense-datum statement."

is the joint operation of things-perceived and observation-conditions which determines what is to appear; hence the task of the empiricist would seem to be similar to that of an economist who hoped to define *both* supply and demand in terms of possible prices.

The complexity of the problem will become evident if, before turning to the details of Professor Lewis's view, we consider a simple example. Consider the thing statement

This is red   (P)

and the sense-datum statement

Redness will appear   (R).

May we say that P entails R? Possibly it will be immediately evident that no contradiction is involved in affirming P and denying R. The following considerations, however, may make the matter clearer.

Taken in conjunction with some *other* thing statement, referring to observation-conditions, P does entail R. The other statement could be

> This is observed under normal conditions; and if this is red and is observed under normal conditions, redness will appear.   (Q)

But taken in conjunction, not with Q, but with still *another* thing statement, also referring to observation-conditions, P entails not-R. This other thing statement could be

> This is observed under conditions which are normal except for the presence of blue lights; and if this is red and is observed under conditions which are normal except for the presence of blue lights, redness will not appear.   (S)

So far as ordinary usage is concerned, it is quite evident that the statement S is logically consistent with P; there is no contradiction involved in affirming one and denying the other. But the conjunction of P and S, if they are logically consistent, must entail everything that P entails and can not entail anything logically inconsistent with what P entails. If P and S entail not-R, it is impossible that P entail R. Hence

"This is red" (P) does not entail "Redness will appear" (R).

We may draw a similar conclusion with respect to any other categorical sense-datum statement R'. Although there may be a statement about observation-conditions, Q', such that "This is red" (P) and Q' entail R', there is also a statement about observation-conditions, S', such that P and S' entail not-R'. Hence P does not entail R'.

Professor Lewis admits that no thing statement, such as "This is red," entails any categorical sense-datum statement, such as "Redness will appear"; he admits further that "This is red" does not entail any sense-datum conditional, such as "If such-and-such should appear, then such-and-such would appear" (p. 237). The sort of sense-datum statement which is entailed is considerably more complicated. It is a conditional of the form: "If such-and-such a presentation (or sense-datum) should appear and such-and-such feelings of action (also sense-data) should appear, then in all probability such-and-such another sense-datum would appear" (cf. pp. 248 ff). For reasons essential to his account of knowledge and action, the antecedent of the sense-datum statement must refer both to some "sensory clue" and to a feeling of activity, and the consequent must be prefaced by some such phrase as "in all probability." These complications, however, do not affect the principle now under discussion.

We may utilize the above letters again in discussing Professor Lewis's view. One of his examples is the thing statement

There really is a doorknob in front of me and to the left.   (P)

One of the complicated sense-datum statements which are analytic consequences of this might be

If I should seem to see such a doorknob and if I should seem to myself to be initiating a certain grasping motion, then in all probability the feeling of contacting a doorknob would follow.[2]   (R)

[2] Cf. op. cit., pp. 240, 248–249. We are to suppose, of course, that the words which appear in this statement are in what Professor Lewis calls the "expressive language," referring solely to sense-data.

According to Professor Lewis, *R* is an analytic consequence of *P;* or, in other words, *P* entails *R*. But, again, if *P* entails *R*, then it is logically impossible that there be a statement *S*, consistent with *P* and such that *P* and *S* entail not-*R*. Hence, if there is such a statement *S*, *P* does not entail *R*. Is there, then, such a statement *S?*

It should be remarked that we are not asking whether there is such a statement *S* which is *true*. For Professor Lewis's theory concerns the *meaning* of thing statements, what is certifiable *a priori* by reference to logic and the meanings of terms. If there is a statement *S*, which in conjunction with *P* entails not-*R*, then, whether or not *S* is true, the theory—at least in application to this case—is mistaken.

Clearly there are many such statements *S*. One might be

> I am unable to move my limbs and my hands but am subject to delusions such that I think I'm moving them; I often seem to myself to be initiating a certain grasping motion, but, when I do, I never have the feeling of contacting anything. (*S*)

This statement in conjunction with *P* entails not-*R*. There is no reason to suppose that *S* is inconsistent with *P*. Hence it is false that *P* entails *R*. Similarly, for any other complex sense-datum statement *R'* which might be thought to be an analytic consequence of *P*, it would seem to be possible to formulate a statement *S'*, consistent with *P*, and such that P and *S'* entail not-*R'*.

Thus it remains to be seen in what sense *any* sense-datum statement can be regarded as an analytic consequence of "This thing is red" or "That is a doorknob."[3]

[3] A. J. Ayer, who also defends the translatability thesis, admits that no thing statement, such as "This thing is red," entails any particular sense-datum statement. But, he holds, the thing statement does entail numerous disjunctive "sets" of sense-data statements, "where the defining characteristic of the set is that all its members refer to sense-contents that fall within a certain specifiable range" (*Language, Truth and Logic*, 2nd edition, p. 13; cf. *Foundations of Empirical Knowledge*, pp. 240–241). E.g., each member of a set might refer to some specific shade of red, not referred to by the other members, but all of the sense-data referred to would fall within the "fairly indefinite range" of redness. The view that the thing statement entails such a set, however, is subject to the difficulties noted above in the case of

It was suggested above that statements such as "This thing is red" entail sense-datum statements only when taken in conjunction with some *other* thing statement pertaining to observation-conditions. Thus, in our earlier example, "This is red" (*P*) does entail a sense-datum statement when it is conjoined with our statement *Q:* "This is observed under normal conditions; and if this is red and is observed under normal conditions, redness will appear." Without seeking to beg any questions, we might call the latter part of *Q* a *psychophysical* statement, for it refers to sense-data which will appear under certain physical conditions. The sense-datum statement ("Redness will appear") is entailed, not by the thing statement ("This is red") but by the conjunction of: (i) the thing statement; (ii) the statement about observation-conditions ("This is observed under normal conditions"); and (iii) the psychophysical statement ("If this is red and is observed under normal conditions, redness will appear"). As we have seen, the thing statement, "This is red," if conjoined with a different statement about observation-conditions and with a different psychophysical statement, may entail a different sense-datum statement.

It could be contended that the psychophysical statement (iii) is analytic, that "If this is observed under normal conditions, redness will appear" is an analytic consequence of "This is red." This fact would be of little use to the translatability program, however. For this method of deriving sense-datum statements from "This is red" proceeds by utilizing additional thing statements ("This is observed under normal conditions," referring presumably to lighting arrangements, ocular conditions, and so on). Instead of eliminating thing statements in this manner, therefore, we would be multiplying them. And the new thing statements would present our old difficulties again.[4]

single statements; for, again, it would seem to be possible to find another thing statement which, taken in conjunction with "This thing is red," entails the contradictory of any set which Mr. Ayer might mention.

[4] Cf. H. H. Price, *Hume's Theory of the External World*, pp. 183–188.

The translatability thesis, however, does claim to provide an account of the respect in which our knowledge of things is founded in, and is verifiable and falsifiable in, sense experience. If we deny this thesis we must provide an alternative account of the manner in which such experience may be said to justify our knowledge of things.[5] This is not the place to pursue this further question in detail; but it is relevant to note that, in principle, the problem becomes similar to that of the validity of memory and that Professor Lewis's own method of treating the latter problem may in fact be applicable to both problems. The possibility of our having any knowledge at all, he believes, requires that we make two assumptions about memory: "First; whatever is remembered, whether as explicit recollection or merely in the form of our sense of the past, is *prima facie* credible because so remembered. And second; when the whole range of empirical beliefs is taken into account, all of them more or less dependent upon memorial knowledge, we find that those which are most credible can be assured by their mutual support, or . . . *congruence*" (p. 334).[6] If thing statements are not translatable into sense-datum statements, it may be that the validity of our perceptual knowledge of things requires similar assumptions. It may be that whenever the presence of a sense-datum leads one to accept a belief about a material thing (e.g., whenever, as a matter of fact, the presence of a red sense-datum leads one to accept the belief that one is observing a red thing) the belief which is thus "perceptually accepted"[7] is *prima facie* credible because it is so accepted. Indeed Mr. Price has said as much. And it may be that when the whole range of our perceptual beliefs are taken into account, all of them more or less dependent upon our perceptual acceptances, we find

[5] Similarly, we should have to reconsider the thesis, fundamental to Professor Lewis's views (as well as to Mr. Ayer's), that a synthetic statement is meaningful only to the extent to which it refers to possible experience. But it is reasonable to suppose that the acceptability of such a criterion of meaning should be secondary to considerations such as those discussed above.

[6] Cf. Bertrand Russell, *An Inquiry into Meaning and Truth*, p. 202.

[7] "Perceptual acceptance" is Mr. Price's term. Cf. *Perception*, pp. 139 ff.

that those which are most credible can be assured by their mutual support. These assumptions do not claim any faculties for man which are not involved in Professor Lewis's defence of memory.[8] Whether they will suffice for justifying perceptual knowledge, however, is a question which can be answered only on the basis of a discussion as thorough as the one which Professor Lewis devotes to memory.

[8] Such assumptions are involved in the doctrine which C. S. Peirce called "Critical Common-Sensism." Cf. *Collected Papers,* Vol. V, Book III. Certain passages in Professor Lewis's book suggest that he would not be disinclined to make similar assumptions. Cf. p. 326.

PROFESSOR CHISHOLM AND EMPIRICISM

C. I. Lewis

Professor Chisholm questions the adequacy of the account of perceptual knowledge which I have put forward, on the ground that this account is incompatible with "the familiar facts sometimes referred to as 'the relativity of sense perception.' "[1]

I have held that what the statement of a perceptually learned objective fact, such as "This (seen object) is red" or "This is square," means—in one specific, and specified, sense of the word 'meaning'—is explicable by some set of statements representing predictions of possible experience and having the form, "If S be given and act A initiated, then in all probability E will follow," where 'S', 'A', and 'E' each refers to some recognizable item of direct experience, and the colloquial phrase "in all probability" is intended to suggest a probability approximating to certainty.

Professor Chisholm's criticism is restricted to a single point. (And I wish to express my admiration for the succinctness he achieves, in discussing a complex matter, without injustice to the conception discussed.) He believes that no such prediction in terms of direct experience follows from the statement of an objective and perceptually evidenced fact without an *additional* premise or premises concerning objective conditions of the predicted experience— such as the lighting conditions in the case of "This is red," or the condition of the angle of perspective in the case of "This is square." And he believes that, because such additional premises are required, the objective statement ("This

[1] Page 348, preceding.

is red" or "This is square") can not be said to entail anything whatever in terms of direct experience.

Professor Chisholm's discussion convinces me that, in my summary,[2] I was injudicious in saying that the objective statement "entails" such predictions in terms of direct experience and calling these consequences "analytic" without making certain explanatory comments.[3] I shall attempt to make good that deficiency in concluding this note.

The more important point, however, concerns his allegation that no statement of objective fact has any consequence in terms of direct experience without further premises specifying objective conditions of the experience in question. If that objection can be sustained, then I agree with him in thinking that the type of empiricism of which my account is one variant—verification-theories and confirmation-theories of the meaning of empirical statements of objective fact—will be altogether indefensible. And the suggestion will be that some kind of coherence-theory of empirical truth should be considered instead (though Professor Chisholm does not commit himself to this suggestion).

This will be the case because, if the perceptually learned fact, "This seen object is red," has no consequence in terms of direct experience without additional premises such as "The illumination is sufficient," "The light is white and not red," "My eyes are normal," and so on for all conditions which could affect the red appearance of the thing, then obviously such further required premises will be very numerous in any given instance. Also, since these conditions will be matters of objective fact which are as difficult to assure with certainty as the statement "This object is red" itself, that statement will not be verifiable or even confirmable by anything presented or presentable in immediate experience. Only the immensely complex kind of statement, "This seen object is red, and is sufficiently illuminated with white light, and my eyes are normal, and . . .," can be subjected to any experiential test of truth: hence the sug-

[2] *An Analysis of Knowledge and Valuation*, Ch. VII, Sect. 16.
[3] The points in question are explained later in the book—Ch. X.

gestion that only a coherence-theory will be tenable and that no verification-theory or confirmation-theory can be maintained.

My own belief is that if Professor Chisholm's point can be made good, then there will be nothing left for us but skepticism; because I am convinced that any coherence-theory will have defects which are fatal.

It is important to remember here that although various relativities of the content of presentation to conditions of observation—both conditions affecting the object and conditions affecting the subject's observation of it—are commonplaces of experience, we nevertheless do obtain empirical knowledge from experiences so affected; and that what we are here discussing is no debater's point or preciosity of semantics but one of the obvious and cognitively important facts of life. When we view a square object from an angle, for example, we may see a nonrectangular appearance and not something which looks like this

□

but we may nevertheless learn from this experience that the object viewed is square. For this conclusion, we do *not* require antecedent information about our angle of vision, for the simple reason that the appearance itself evidences the angle of perspective as well as the objective shape of the thing seen. A square object seen from an angle and an object of the indicated non-rectangular shape seen from straight in front, do not appear exactly the same; we discern a directly apparent difference of the two. Otherwise, visual experience would be a wholly untrustworthy index of the objective shape of things.

The relativities of perceptual content to the conditions of observation do indeed often defeat our attempts to learn objective facts from direct experience, and are a frequent source of illusions and mistaken judgments of perception. But, in general terms, there are only three possibilities of the relation between a given appearance affected by such relativity and the objective character this appearance may lead us to ascribe to the thing observed: (1) the objective condition to which the appearance is relative will be evidenced in the character of the appearance itself, so that just this appearance is still a trustworthy index of the objective property ascribed—as in the example just discussed; or (2) the given appearance may not be discernibly different from that of some other kind of object, under conditions òther than those which actually affect this observation—so that the appearance could "deceive" us under conditions which, for all we know, may presently obtain—but because the condition which would lead to this "deception" is one which is exceptional, there is a high correlation between just this given character of the appearance and the objective property it leads us to ascribe to the thing observed; in which case it remains the fact that the given appearance is a valid *probability*-index of the objective property; or (3) on account of relativities of this kind of perception to conditions which are frequent and are not reliably reflected in any discernible difference of the given appearance, this manner of appearance is not even a probability-index of the property we ascribe to the object observed.

In case (1), such relativity is no bar to veridical judgment of the objective property ascribed on the basis of the given appearance, though superficial or careless observation might lead to error on account of this relativity. That kind of fact is a commonplace of perceptual cognition. In case (2), although the relativity in question may lead to erroneous belief in a particular instance, and this through no fault of our own, the belief induced will still be justified as *probable*, on account of the high correlation mentioned. That even the best kind of direct evidence may occasionally be affected by some unguessable condition which leads to mistaken perceptual judgment, is again a commonplace of empirical cognition. In case (3), the judgment of objective fact from the appearance given is not justified and is not knowledge, whether the guess one makes happens to be lucky or to be unlucky.

These facts I have intended to incorporate in my account. That almost any perception will be found to be an instance of case (1) in some respect, hardly affects the matter, since when one refers to what is given, this reference should be to the appearance in all its specificity and include all characteristics of the immediate experience which are pertinent to the judgment made. What is more important to observe is that perceptual knowledge of objects and states of affairs is always, in some respect or manner, an instance falling under case (2). There are all degrees of reliability of the connection between given qualia of the content of perception and objective characters of things observed which we are thus led to believe. In no case—I have supposed—is this reliability one hundred per cent and sufficient for theoretical certainty. But it is often sufficient for practical certainty; sufficient to justify our acting on the belief without hesitation. In the remaining cases—that is, where we hold the judgment as practically certain but in fact the correlation between given appearance and objective fact believed does not justify this assurance—our belief is not knowledge but an invalid perceptual judgment.

Professor Chisholm's criticism, as phrased, does not refer directly to this relation between given appearance and objective fact—though that is involved—but to the connection between statement of the objective fact and predictions of further experiences which might confirm it. Let us turn to that point, in terms of our previous example. If what I am looking at has the appearance of a square object seen from an angle, and I believe that this thing is in fact square, then innumerable possible corroborations of that belief may be suggested; e.g., that if I take three steps to the right the appearance of a square object seen from directly in front will then be presented. If I make this test, with the anticipated result, my belief will be confirmed in some measure; and if I make it with a result divergent from what I expect, it will be disconfirmed. The statement of what I believe, "This object is square," has the consequence, "If S (the now apprehended presentation) be given, and act A (three steps to the right) initiated, then in all probability E (the appearance of a square seen from directly in front) will follow."

The qualification "in all probability" is interjected here because it could happen that, although the object viewed is really square and my attempted confirmation of that fact is well judged, the test of it in this instance might give a negative result—because this particular experience is affected by some condition which I do not control and of which there is no evidence in the given presentation, S. But if this kind of untoward result should be the rule and not the exception, then my belief on the basis of this presentation or this attempted confirmation of it—one or both— would be ill-judged and not an instance of knowledge; and it would be false that the statement of objective fact, "This object is square," has this particular consequence of the form "If S and A, then in all probability E."

What I think Professor Chisholm overlooks, in his criticism, are two facts to which attention has now been drawn: first, the specificity of given appearances by which a presentation which is 'relative to' some condition of observation frequently contains a sufficient clue to this objective circumstance which affects it. Perhaps he makes use of examples in which the 'S' of my paradigm is allowed to be ambiguous or unduly circumscribed in its reference to given presentation and does not include all aspects of the experience-content which are pertinent to the prediction; or examples which are instances of observation so superficial and inattentive that judgment based on them could not properly be taken as justified. Second, he appears to overlook the importance of the probability-qualification in predictions of confirming experience. That qualification covers the point that, in cases where the given presentation is an actually justifying ground for the objective belief (and hence for prediction that further tests of it will give a positive result), it still remains true that "mistake is possible," on account of some exceptional and unguessable condition affecting a particular observation. Correlatively, one who supposes that justified perceptual judgments are instances of theoretical certainty, misreads the actual nature of empirical knowledge. Taken together, these two considerations seem to me to indicate his error in alleging that an objective statement of the kind of facts we think to learn from perception does not have as consequence any prediction of the form "If S be given and act A initiated, then in all probability experience E will follow," without additional hypotheses concerning conditions affecting the particular observation or test.

However, Professor Chisholm does well to observe that if it be supposed that a statement of objective fact 'P' ("The object viewed is square"), entails or has as analytic consequence a certain prediction of this form, "If S be given and act A initiated, then in all probability experience E will follow," then we shall encounter the seeming difficulty that some further premise, 'Q', may be such that the conjoint statement, 'P and Q,' will have as consequence a prediction which is incompatible with this consequence of 'P' alone. In our example, for instance, the additional premise, "The object seen is really behind me and I am viewing it in a mirror," would lead to the prediction that if I take three steps to the right what I shall see is my own reflection instead of any square-looking appearance. That the premise of objective fact, 'P', may have the consequence 'T' but the hypothesis 'P and Q' may have a consequence incompatible with 'T', is paradoxical; because it is a familiar rule of logic that when 'P' entails 'T', 'P and Q' (for any additional premise, 'Q') must likewise entail 'T', and can not entail anything incompatible with 'T' if 'Q' is consistent with 'P'.

What needs to be observed here—and what I omitted to mention in my summary statement of the matter—is that this familiar rule, "If 'P' entails 'T', then for any 'Q', 'P and Q' entails 'T'," can not be applied, in the manner one is likely to attempt, where 'T' is any kind of probability-statement. Probabilities are relative to the premises (factual or hypothetical) from which they are determined. And in consequence of this fact it can be—and frequently is—true that on the premise 'P' alone something, 'R', is highly probable, but on the premise 'P and Q,' 'R' is highly *im-*

probable and something else, '*S*', which is incompatible with '*R*', is highly probable. In such a case, what must be noted is that, although '*R*' and '*S*' are incompatible as unqualified statements of fact, the two statements, "On the premise '*P*' alone, '*R*' is highly probable" and "On the premise '*P* and *Q*,' '*S*' is highly probable," *can not be incompatible since both are true* and no true statement can ever be incompatible with any other which is also true. (It must also be noted that the probability-consequences themselves, " '*R*' is highly probable" and " '*S*' is highly probable," are not incompatible because, in this form, they are incompletely stated and require the preface "Relative to '*P*' " or "Relative to '*P* and *Q*' " in order to be accurate statements of fact.)

Let us take an example. "These two dice are marked in the usual manner" gives a high probability for the prediction, "In one hundred throws of these dice double-six will occur less than twenty times." But the premise, "These two dice are marked in the usual manner and are loaded to show double-six," does not justify the prediction of less than twenty double-sixes in a hundred throws, but an opposite prediction instead. And for the sake of comparison with Professor Chisholm's argument, let us also remark here that when one predicts less than twenty double-sixes in one hundred throws as a (highly probable) consequence of the premise, "These two dice are marked in the usual manner," one does *not* require the additional information, or assumption even, that the dice are honest. This prediction is justified if we *know nothing about* their being honest or loaded but only that, for properly marked dice in general, twenty double-sixes in a hundred throws is highly exceptional.

In my account of perceptual knowledge, it is *probability-*consequences of objective statements which are in question. These consequences are themselves hypothetical in form—"If *S* and *A* then *E*"—but that affects nothing here in question: in our example of the dice, for instance, we might have considered a consequence of the form, "If I throw these dice, then with a probability of 35 to 1, double-six will not appear," without otherwise affecting that illustration.

It seems to me that the plausibility of Professor Chisholm's argument depends upon overlooking the importance of the probability-qualification in the predictions of direct experience which figure in my account and the facts about probability-consequences in general which are pointed out above. When these are remembered, I think it may be evident that he adduces no consideration which is sufficient to support his critical conclusion.

In my account, objective statements of fact are said to *entail* such probability-consequences because it is consequences of this sort which are *contained in what it means* —in one sense of meaning—to assert the objective statements from which they are derivative. It is such probable eventuations of experience, as results of possible ways of acting when certain appearances present themselves, which represent what we learn when we learn objective facts; and there is no directly testable content of any belief in an objective state of affairs beyond what could be specified in such predictions.

EMPIRICAL PROPOSITIONS AND HYPOTHETICAL STATEMENTS

Isaiah Berlin

It is becoming the fashion among empiricist philosophers to assume that phenomenalism is really dead at last. Provoked into existence by non-naturalistic notions of material substance, it successfully undermined them; but it shared a sufficient number of fundamental metaphysical assumptions with its defeated rival to perish with it when the system of thought which nourished both was destroyed, in the very act of victory. A better ontology than that of Descartes or Locke, but still an ontology, it is therefore now held to be obsolete; and doubtless this is how it ought to be. But if phenomenalism is dead, the memory of it still haunts the writings of modern discussions of the nature of the external world to a surprising degree; from Eddington's notorious two desks, to the more refined and penetrating analysis of better equipped philosophical authors, it makes its presence clearly felt, usually taking the form of a sharp distinction; now between observation statements and those concerning material objects; now between two or more senses of the verb "to see"; at other times between 'basic' or 'protocol' sentences and those of ordinary speech; or between various 'modes' of speech; or between "strong" and "weak" verification. Such versions of it are almost always formally guaranteed to carry no "metaphysical" implications; nevertheless their striking resemblance to the older discredited variety is hard to overlook. Hence, an examination of its latest manifestations is not such a flogging of a dead horse as at first it may seem to be; for if it is dead, its ghost walks, and should, if possible, be laid.

Two further assumptions are made in the course of the following remarks:

(i) The argument against the phenomenalist analysis of common-sense statements leaves open the question whether the information provided by the exact sciences such as physics, can be translated without loss into phenomenalist terms. Perhaps it can; and perhaps this demonstrates something of importance; it has always been considered that the language of science could, with no alteration of its "meaning", be translated into solipsistic terms; which, however, is not held to be an argument in favour of solipsism. But if such a "translation" does not adequately render the empirical descriptions of ordinary language, this will affect the propositions of science only in so far as these claim to be an extension of ordinary language used to describe the world, and not a specialised method of referring to aspects of it for some narrower, predictive or other, purposes—a specialised use of words which may be susceptible to a phenomenalist analysis. In any case the answer to the question whether this is so is, I believe, logically independent of the rest of my argument.

(ii) Nor do I wish to deny the historical achievement of phenomenalism. Whatever its defects—and I shall wish to say that they are fatal—it has made less excusable any return to those ancient delusions which the philosophers of substance from Thales to G. F. Stout have done much to promote. But beneficent as its influence has been, it has overstayed its welcome; its continued presence does more harm than good; and the argument set out below is intended to provide additional reasons for consigning it finally to an honoured grave.

I

Many forms of modern empiricism, and in particular modern phenomenalism, rest on the view that expressions describing material objects must in principle be capable of being translated (without residue) into sets of sentences

about the data of actual or possible direct sensible acquaintance, past, present and future, on the part of real or possible observers; (sensible is here used in the widest sense
—to cover all states, activities or dispositions capable of being studied by empirical methods). Any alternative theories of how material object propositions are to be analysed
tend to be rejected out of hand by modern empiricists on
the ground that this must at some stage involve belief in
the existence of non-sensible or transcendent entities or
characteristics, and this is ruled out for the familiar reasons advanced, for example, by Berkeley, and rests on his
theory of words; according to this, no expressions purport-
ing to describe material objects can have any meaning,
let alone be true, unless all the entities or characteristics
to which they refer are either found in sensible experience
—in the sense of "sensible" defined above—or can be analysed into entities or characteristics so found. Since most
empiricists hold that any alternative analysis of material
object propositions involves the possibility of acquaintance
with non-sensible entities or characteristics—and this they
hold to be an unintelligible suggestion—phenomenalism
appears to follow automatically. Disagreement can arise
only about the adequacy of this or that suggested analysis
of how material object sentences are to be "reduced"
(without residue) to sentences describing both what the
observer does, or did, or will observe, as well as what he
would, or would have, might or might have, observed under appropriate conditions; and the provision of alternative
analyses on these lines has taxed the ingenuity of some of
the acutest philosophers of our day. But common sense
and the philosophers who are in sympathy with it, have
always felt dissatisfied. The reduction of material object
sentences into what we may, for short, call sense datum
sentences, seemed to leave something out, to substitute
something intermittent and attenuated for something solid
and continuous. To dispel this sense of discomfort, phenomenalists began to explain that it was due to a confusion: the view that they were advocating was neither a
metaphysical nor a scientific theory of what things were

made of, or how they behaved, but something less adventurous—no more than an alternative language capable of rendering all that could be described in the material object language, and recommended for its therapeutic properties as an antidote to metaphysical hankering after non-sensible substitutes. If translation into the sense datum language still seemed to leave something out—what some philosophers have called the 'irreducible categorical element' of material object propositions, this missing element was labelled emotive—a psychological residue—with no descriptive function; or else it was (with somewhat greater insight) connected with the legitimate demand for the kind and degree of vagueness, indefiniteness, and rich ambiguity of speech needed by the plain man for his normal, every day purposes. But it was claimed that at any rate the hard core of descriptive meaning could be successfully transplanted, as it were, into the new language. The phenomenalist equivalent of a material object sentence might, like a new shoe, seem uncomfortable at first, but continued use would presently dissipate this feeling. The discomfort was only "psychological", due to linguistic habits harmless in themselves, but tempting philosophers to false doctrines about both language and the world.

Common sense continued to experience a certain discomfort, but found it difficult to formulate it in words. Professor G. F. Stout[1] complained that the opaqueness—"the permanent impossibility of sensation" of material objects had been unjustifiably eliminated. Mr. W. F. R. Hardie[2] found it puzzling that 'hypothetical' causes could be said to cause 'actual' effects—but this was held, *e.g.* by Professor A. J. Ayer[3] to be mainly due to a misunderstanding of the language which phenomenalists were trying to use or "recommend". What I propose to do is to try and articulate what the main source of the discomfort felt by common sense seems to me to be, since I think that in this case the

[1] *Studies in Philosophy and Psychology,* pp. 136–37.
[2] "The Paradox of Phenomenalism", *Proceedings of the Aristotelian Society,* 1945–46.
[3] "Phenomenalism", P.A.S., 1946–47.

doctor's diagnosis too often neglects the specific nature of the patient's complaint. For it seems to me to be more than a mere source of discomfort, namely a valid and fatal objection, to the phenomenalist analysis. However, even if I am mistaken in this, the complaint itself still seems worth examining.

It may be worth adding that even if phenomenalism turns out to be unacceptable, some of the stock objections to it are not less so. For the familiar anti-phenomenalist theses are often, even when valid, formulated in such a way as to convey anxiety to salvage altogether too much from the ruins of the theory they are intended to destroy. Consider, for example, the four most familiar types of attack upon it.

(1) One of the most familiar objections urged against, for example, Berkeley, or Mill or Russell, is that when converting sentences about material objects into sentences about sense data, they fail to 'convert the observer' who 'occurs' in the protasis of the hypothetical statement, into 'sense data'—he remains irreducibly 'material'. It has indeed been suggested[4] that to 'dissolve the observer' a second proposition could be constructed, which presumably, would describe the activities of a second 'observer' who actually or potentially observes the body of the original 'observer'; this 'observer' in his turn requires a third 'observer' to observe him; and so we should get a Chinese box series of possible observers—referred to by a logically similar series of propositions, which would progressively 'reduce' or 'dissolve' the residual material object content of the original protasis. This asymptotic process of gradual whittling would tend to the ideal limit of pure phenomenalism. Then by somehow integrating the series, one might represent the material object as definable in terms of it. A criticism related to the original objection is that such ideal 'observers'

[4] This argument was first developed to the best of my belief by Professor H. H. Price. A somewhat more complicated method of the progressive "elimination" of material bodies is propounded by Mr. R. B. Braithwaite ("Propositions about Material Objects" P.A.S., 1937–38).

and their behaviour could not be properly described without perpetual reference to material objects, *e.g.* those which determine 'their' position in space, movements, etc. Each of which again, for its analysis, at every point presupposes yet other material objects, so that the attempted analysis cannot get going without breaking down at any and every point in the process. Some philosophers try to soften the force of this objection by saying that such theoretically infinite theories have pragmatic limits set by the context and the practical needs of the situation and sometimes[5] hold that sufficiently painstaking analysis (and most analysts are too lazy or bored to do the plodding required) could go a long way towards achieving pure phenomenalism. What both these kinds of objection, whether they are valid or not, suggest is that if phenomenalism fails, it very nearly achieves its result—the unresolved residue can be got down to almost vanishing point—which is perhaps as much as one can reasonably hope for.

(2) Another often heard objection is that the hypothetical propositions about the experiences of observers which are indispensable to the phenomenalist analysis, seem to involve something like the existence or reality of 'hypothetical facts' or 'hypothetical sense data', or 'unsensed sensibilia'. For otherwise, what do hypotheticals describe? Surely not nothing? And these postulated entities, unknown and unknowable to science and common sense, are, so it is urged, at least as mythological as the Lockean substratum which they were invoked to exorcise. Phenomenalism is accused of breeding new metaphysical entities—with their own pseudo-problems: but if we could only get rid of these somehow, say by an improved, non-correspondence theory of meaning, all might still be well.

(3) It has also frequently been asserted that the promised 'reduction' of common-sense language by such methods as those of Descriptions, Logical Constructions, etc., cannot in fact be performed successfully. Phenomenalists are challenged to provide an equivalent in sense datum cur-

[5] See Mr. D. G. C. Macnabb ("Phenomenalism", P.A.S. 1940–41).

rency of propositions about material objects, and when they decline to produce the precise equivalent, they are accused of uttering counterfeit cheques: and this is said to hold even more obviously of scientific entities—the promise to construct "many storied"[6] logical constructions, with sense data as foundations, and gamma particles two or three floors above—has not been kept. Phenomenalists are accused of maintaining that, although phenomenalist language might be intolerably clumsy and prolix, it could in principle always be substituted for the ellipses of common speech: that normal language has the character it has in order to serve the use that it serves; that sense datum language would doubtlessly be inconveniently precise and definite and intolerably lengthy and tedious, and would have its own unfamiliar "grammar", but that in principle the translation could be effected, although by sacrificing so much customary vagueness, ambiguity, indefiniteness, etc., as would render it useless for every day purposes. Against this, the opposition maintains that it is only necessary to try and put this programme into practice to see that it is a labour of Sisyphus and will not work: vagueness, ambiguity, etc., are inalienable properties of common-sense language; but for this, the programme could perhaps be carried out; but as it is, the claim to reduce—plausible enough *prima facie*—turns out to be hollow once the bluff is called. Yet the reason for this is still the comparatively weak one that we should lose too much in the way of nuances, range, implied meanings of words; the feeling remains that the "hard core" of meaning might still be "reduced" or translated.

(4) Finally, there are the difficulties about dealing with propositions about other minds, communication, etc., in the appropriate Humean manner, too familiar to be repeated; which theoretically leaves open the possibility of the programme advanced by Berkeley whereby phenomenalism works for material objects and breaks down only in the case of persons.

[6] See Mr. D. G. C. Macnabb (*loc. cit.*).

The above is a characteristic selection from the, by now traditional, array of anti-phenomenalist arguments. I should like to suggest that, formidable and indeed fatal as some of them may be, they are usually so formulated as to convey a misleading impression, for despite their anti-phenomenalist air they are all in effect so much concealed pro-phenomenalist propaganda. The suggestion implicit in all these criticisms is that, while the phenomenalist goal is and must be striven towards—for the alternative is a metaphysical morass—the particular avenues thus far offered by phenomenalists are unfortunately blocked by various types of logical or epistemological obstacles: in other words that some such operation is desperately needed if we are ever to eliminate unverifiable or indescribable entities, but that the techniques offered by various philosophers have all, so far, broken down. This position is not unlike the situation with regard to say Fermat's theorem: what the theorem asserts is considered as being very likely true, at any rate not demonstrably fallacious, and in any case as being the kind of assertion which should be capable of demonstration or refutation by normal mathematical techniques. Similarly all phenomenalist operations so far conducted have indeed ended in failure; but they, and only they, are the kind of processes which can, in principle, be applied. *Some* kind of phenomenalist analysis must be correct, for the only alternative is a return to Locke, or Descartes, or Kant, and that, in this enlightened age, is surely not a thinkable course.

This is the bogey used to drive philosophers back to make yet another gallant attempt to break out of the impasse—to find a 'viable' translation into the sense datum language. The impression conveyed throughout, possibly because of a faulty theory of meaning and truth, is that phenomenalism is, after all, the only possible valid view, beset though it may be by grave objections and exaggerations: the problem is one of technical skill: once it is reformulated with sufficient ingenuity the problem will be solved, or dissolved. My thesis is that phenomenalism is not even *prima facie* plausible—let alone indispensable, and minor improvements, *i.e.* tinkering, cannot make it more so. Instead, therefore, of re-examining the all too familiar current objections to phenomenalism, and the answers to them, I should like to suggest that it might be valuable to try to find out what it is that makes common sense so uncomfortable—in order to see whether this discomfort is merely "psychological", and perhaps due to the relatively accidental properties of ordinary language, or whether it is a symptom of some fatal defect in the theory.

II

What common sense, from Dr. Johnson onwards, finds paradoxical in all phenomenalist analyses, is, I believe, this: I say, "There is a brown table in the next room." This, I am told, should mean a set or range of propositions of the type, "If 'a normal observer' were to go next door and look, he would, in normal light, other normal conditions, etc., see such and such brown-coloured data, etc." I say, "But supposing no one goes next door, what have we then? Is the apodosis false? Are there no brown data and no table?" I am told, "Of course not. Nothing regarding the consequent follows from denying the antecedent. In a sense, nothing follows at all. It still remains true that *if* someone looked, etc., he *would* see brown data, etc." I accept all this and remain dissatisfied. If I believe that there was in pre-historical times a land bridge between Africa and America, then I agree—and possibly this is analytic— that if there had been an observer at that time suitably placed, he would have seen the land bridge or a portion of it. But I may wish to assert that, in fact, no such observer existed, and that the land bridge was nevertheless there, whether or not this is true. What I think common sense and Professor G. F. Stout wish to say is that the question of the existence of the land bridge, like the existence of the table next door, is one thing, and the question of the presence or absence, even hypothetically, of an observer, is another. The statement that if there had been (and there was not), any observer, he would have observed (and no one did observe), certain data, seems to them not equivalent to asserting the past existence of material objects. Categorical propositions about material objects are replaced by unfulfilled "counter-factual" hypothetical propositions about observers, and what troubles the plain man is the thought that if the hypotheticals are unfulfilled, if no observers were in fact observing, then if the phenomenalist analysis is correct, there was—in a sense datum sense— nothing at all, and, moreover, that this sense of 'existence' is basic: because the alleged material object sense in which the non-existence of actual sense data nevertheless can be 'translated into' the existence of material objects, is not a sense in which the word 'exist' is commonly understood. If he is then told that to say there was a material object— the land bridge in pre-historic times—is to say something about data there would have been if . . . he feels cheated. For these data appear to depend on the activity of observers; so that the material object becomes analysed into a series of either purely hypothetical, *i.e.* non-existent, or at best, intermittent data occurring and disappearing as the observer observes and ceases to observe. And this seems empirically a different picture of the world from that which he started by believing; and in no sense merely a description of the old picture though in different words.

I shall try to make this clearer. To analyse material objects in terms of the hypothetical data of observers is, in effect, to turn the statements about them into statements about the dispositional characteristics of observers. "The table next door exists", on this view means that you or I or X, who are in this room, are possible or potential table-data observers. This asserts the existence of a dispositional characteristic; but dispositional characteristics are so called in order to contrast them with non-dispositional characteristics, the "grammar" of which is rightly said to be different. If I ask, "Does he look much the same when he is asleep?" that is a plain, empirical question, the answer to which can be discovered by ordinary empirical means, *i.e.* by looking. But if I ask, "Is he clever even when he is asleep?" this sounds quite wrong—I am rightly told that I evidently do not understand how the word "clever" is commonly used; surely, I am told, to say that someone is clever is to say something of the following sort: that if certain sorts of questions are put to him, he will easily and correctly answer them, or that he grasps certain types of data and makes inferences from them more successfully than most people, and so on. When he is asleep, these conditions do not occur and the question is therefore inappropriate to the situation. How does all this apply to the table next door? The assertion that there is a table next door is made equivalent to what the observer would see if he looked, etc., *i.e.* a collection of hypothetical, *i.e.* dispositional-causal propositions about the observer; but when the causes do not materialise, neither, as a rule, do their effects, and when neither exists, there is a gap in the series of sense datum events. We accept this quite naturally in the case of normal dispositional characteristics: "X is irritable" is compatible with, indeed it is compatible only with, "He flies into tempers on slight provocation, or sometimes when there is no provocation at all," *i.e.* at other times there are no bursts of temper, no continuing real substratum—there does not literally exist, in the ordinary sense of "exist", something called potential irritation going on like volcanic activity underneath the surface; we do speak of unconscious or suppressed irritation, but to take this literally is to confuse words with things, to confuse the mythology of psycho-analysis with the furniture of the real world, to fall into Locke's errors. But if I say, "The table is next door (or 'the table has a back to it,' or 'the table was here two hours ago') even with no one looking," do I mean, "There are table-data whenever people look; but at other times, when no one is looking, nothing at all?" This is precisely what common sense does *not* believe to be true about tables. Common sense endows them with 'actual', *i.e.* non-dispositional characteristics in the absence of observers. The table is seen intermittently or not at all: the intermittent presence or non-existence of observers is a part of the intermittent or unrealised series of causes or conditions of its being seen; but it—the table—is assumed to have some characteristics continuously; it differs from irritability precisely in this respect—that unlike irritability it is believed to exist continuously in the literal sense when there are no intermittent data, no glances directed at the table. To analyse material object statements as statements about dispositional characteristics of observers, therefore, is to represent the material object as being, at most, an intermittent series of actual data with the gaps filled by hypothetical "non-actualised" entities, *i.e.* in the sense datum sense, by nothing at all. This, for common sense, is tantamount to destroying the continuity of the table—its history before and after it is observed, its unseen portion, its presence next door. Of course, phenomenalists stoutly and indignantly denounce this conclusion as a confusion of two senses of 'existence', a crude misunderstanding of the very notion of logical constructions. Tables, we might be answered, are logical constructions as irritability is: in both cases, the essential task is to eliminate Locke's substratum and to substitute for it a set of intermittent and hypothetical data. The unobserved table, or its unobserved back, continue to be as someone's irritability continues to be. Yet common sense does not raise difficulties of this type about the analysis of irritability; it accepts easily enough that irritability does not exist in the same sense as an actual burst of temper is said to do, that to speak of irritability is to use a kind of shorthand for a complex of causal laws and observation propositions. But when I say, "There exists a table such as you describe", am I really saying that it exists in the same sense of 'exists' as someone's irritable temper? Some characteristics of tables may, of course, genuinely be described as dispositional, *i.e.* in speaking of them, I am referring to certain causal laws and hypothetical or intermittent data— *e.g.* when I say a table is combustible or useful or expensive. But this only means something by contrast with those properties of the table which are not dispositional, and perhaps, a good many intermediate properties which we do not think of either as definitely dispositional or definitely 'actual'. The suggestion that *every* characteristic of the table is merely possible or intermittent or depends on dispositions of observers—that *everything* is dispositional, nothing actual—is exactly what common sense and Dr. Johnson revolt against, not as being untrue, but as coming close to being meaningless, and certainly as suspiciously approaching some kind of solipsism—and one not very easy to describe in empirical (or any other intelligible) language.

What common sense dislikes is precisely the crucial role played by hypotheticals in the phenomenalist analysis, and it seems to me to display a sound instinct in so doing.

For this is the central point of this entire issue: that the translation of categorical existential statements into hypotheticals (of whatever 'level'), is a dangerous operation and cannot be left to the mechanical operation of 'syntactical' rules because different types of sentence do have certain normal uses in ordinary language—at any rate in most modern European languages—which we ignore at our peril; Humpty-Dumpty's nominalism goes too far: words are sometimes masters if we are to communicate without perpetual recourse to redefinition *i.e.* if we are to communicate at all; and as we use words, categorical sentences, on the whole, tend to convey that the object referred to has occurred or is occurring or will occur in time; existed, is in existence, will exist; they have a non-descriptive, existential, ostensive element; they seem to invite us to look for the entity they purport to be about, and only when there is none such in any normal sense, *e.g.* in the case of a sentence like, "Bad temper is unattractive", do we avoid pseudo-problems by turning to the hypothetical mode of expression as the more natural, as likely to elucidate what is being asserted in words better adapted to expressing it. Existential propositions expressed categorically—in indicative sentences—tend, as it were, to "point" towards their "objects"; and demonstratives which appear in existential propositions, like, "this is", "there is", "here we have", etc., often function as substitutes for such acts of pointing to things or persons or processes. The characteristic force of

the categorical mode of expression is often exactly this—
that it acts in lieu of a gesture, of an 'act of ostension',
"Here *is* the book", I say to someone looking for it, or I
could point to it and say, "The book", and convey roughly
the same information by both methods. But hypotheticals
normally do the opposite of this. Hypotheticals, whatever
they describe or mean, whatever they entail or convey or
evince, in whatever way they are verified or fail to be verified, do *not* as a general rule directly assert that something
has been, is being, or will be occurring, or existing, or being characterised in some way: this is precisely the force
of the conditional mood, and it is realisation of this which
probably led Ramsey, for example, to assert that causal
propositions were not descriptive at all, but commands or
rules. Ramsey's analysis can easily be shown to be unsatisfactory, since it seems to rest on a fatally false view of the
nature of meaning; but the feeling which led him to so
strong a separation of general and hypothetical forms of
expression from, say, singular categorical sentences, did
not altogether lead him astray. For this gulf does divide
categoricals and hypotheticals in our normal usage:
whereas the first is normally used to describe the furniture
of the world—what is, was or will be—the second is not;
consequently, whenever a categorical (indicative) form of
expression is used, often quite idiomatically, to convey
something other than what is, or was, or will be, it is easily
and without resistance on the part of common sense, replaceable by a hypothetical (conditional) sentence—as in
the case of indicative sentences referring directly or indirectly to dispositions, or general propositions of the "all,
every, any" type. But even this is in need of a significant
qualification. If the general terms are so used as to suggest
that they possess extension of any kind, the hypothetical
form is felt to be to that extent insufficient, and categorical
expressions are required to complete the analysis. Thus,
"Anyone who was there at three o'clock saw the meteor
fall", because it is compatible with, "And no one in fact
was", can be translated into, "If anyone was there, or had
been there, etc., then he saw, or would have seen, etc.";

whereas, "He gave away his books to anyone who asked for them", is not equivalent to, "If anyone asked for, had asked for, etc., his books he was, or would have been given, etc.", but needs in addition, "and some persons did ask". It seems quite clear that in this last instance a conditional or hypothetical sentence by itself tells us nothing about what in fact happened, and an indicative or categorical one is therefore required by ordinary usage to convey "existential import"—to refer to actual events which are believed to have taken place.

All this may seem altogether too trite and obvious, but there is a corollary which is evidently less obvious, namely, that no direct translation from categoricals into hypotheticals is, as a general rule, and as our language is to-day ordinarily used, a correct analysis of, or substitute for them. And this seems to me to destroy one of the indispensable foundations of phenomenalism. For it is this sense of the illicit substitution of hypotheticals for categoricals which is responsible for the obscure feeling on the part of common sense that something—an *ersatz* entity—is being palmed off upon it by phenomenalists. Such a categorical existential material object sentence as, "The table is next door", or "There is a table next door", is used at the very least to describe something which is occurring or being characterised at the time of speaking, together (perhaps) with some sort of prediction (and what has been called retrodiction) about what has been or will be occurring or being characterised during unspecified periods of time before and after the period of speaking; and being characterised or occurring, unless the contrary is specifically stated or implied, not intermittently but continuously, and in any case not 'hypothetically'. For to say that something is occurring hypothetically is a very artificial and misleading way of saying that it is not, in the ordinary sense, occurring at all, but might or would occur if conditions were realised which in their turn may or may not be realised. Consequently, whatever common sense may mean by the sentence, "There is a table next door", it cannot accept as fully equivalent in meaning any sentence not asserting that

something is now, or has been, or will be, occurring or being characterised. It may well be that categoricals systematically entail corresponding hypotheticals (or disjunctive
sets of such)—that the proposition, "The table is next door
now" in some sense entails that if either observer A or
observer B or C, etc. were to go next door, one or other
of them could see or touch such and such data: for invisible
or intangible tables are not what we normally mean by
'table'. Likewise, it may be that hypotheticals in some cases
may be said either to entail, or else to state conditions for
the truth of, or else 'sufficiently justify' the assertion of
categoricals; in other words, that if it is true that a normal
observer (*i.e.* one free from hallucinations, etc.), sees, or
has seen, or will see, or would see, or would have seen,
certain data, under the appropriate conditions, it follows
deductively and not inductively that there is a table next
door. Something like this may be correct, and perhaps this
is all that the phenomenalist requires as against Locke's
insensible substance, or attenuated versions of it, such as
'physical occupants'.[7] For it is clear that if I am to explain
under what circumstances I *should* normally assert material
object sentences, I can do so only by invoking hypothetical
observers and their cognitive states: if I am called upon
to describe the conditions in which such and such sentences
are appropriate, then I cannot fail to make use of hypotheticals. But to describe conditions in which alone I should be
inclined to enunciate a sentence is certainly not equivalent
to giving its meaning. For my point is that the hypothetical
sense datum sentence cannot be equivalent to, or an analysis of, a material object sentence if the hypothetical (sense
datum) sentence asserts only what would be, while the
material object sentence sometimes asserts what occurs, oc-

---

[7] And this is, without doubt, the great historical service of phenomenalism—that for more than two centuries it has been pressing
home the paradoxical consequences of simultaneously holding both
that material objects, if they exist, "must" possess certain characteristics (although no one has been able to identify them at all
clearly) which cannot, in principle, be empirically observed, *and* that
these are among the characteristics with which the natural sciences
necessarily deal.

curred, or will occur in the world. Existential propositions
about material objects assert what is, was or will be, and
not what might be. Stout had every reason to be suspicious
of the description of the material world in such dubious
terms as, "The permanent possibility of sensation", because
however modified and refined, it both suggests a kind of
permanent grid-like world framework and denies it. Dr.
Johnson's well known attitude does not, after all, rest on
such a very gross misunderstanding. That is the heart of
the case against phenomenalism.

But what precisely, it may be asked, is it that such categorical existential sentences do that hypothetical ones fail
to do? Certainly I wish to avoid saying that the former
describe the facts while the latter do not, since the unhappy
term "fact" has been used in too many different senses to
be illuminating in this connexion. Nor do I wish to assert
that hypotheticals and categoricals are never interchangeable and are mutually exclusive—as if the forms of propositions could be distinguished into natural kinds corresponding to 'ontological' or Kantian categories, or 'ultimate
grooves in reality'. But I do suggest that systematic differences in verbal form are often pointers to differences
in meaning which it is important not to obscure. Hence, as
a tentative way of putting it, I submit that those categorical
propositions which we seem to be unable to 'reduce' to
other logical forms without doing apparent violence to
normal usage, tend to direct attention to—invite us to look
for—things and events in a way in which other kinds of
expressions do not. This is felt most clearly about expressions containing demonstratives like 'this', or 'that', or
'here', but applies no less to existential propositions without demonstratives which identify something in the time
series. In the case of objects with some or all of which we
claim to be acquainted by some kind of direct inspection,
this relation—which for want of a better word I propose to
call 'pointing'—can literally occur: in declaring that a particular table is here before me, a particular sound is now
growing louder, a particular doubt is now tormenting me,
I am pointing at, directing your attention to, something

with which I am directly acquainted, an event or a thing. But if I say, "The table is next door", "The cupboard has a wooden back which you cannot see", "Napoleon wore a three cornered hat", "Napoleon felt a twinge of remorse before the battle", I cannot, of course, in the literal sense be said to be acquainted with, or point at, a thing or event, for it is, in the ordinary sense of the words, not present, not here, not before me, not within my ken. And this is perhaps what lends such plausibility as it seems to have to the phenomenalist procedure of offering me hypotheticals intended both to describe unobserved characteristics and to indicate methods of observing, *i.e.* in some sense verifying them. But this will not do, for whereas the difference between categoricals and hypotheticals is one of logical form, whether syntactical or semantic, the difference between being able and not being able to observe a given object is empirical or causal. I cannot point to the table next door, or at a point beneath its surface, because it is invisible: there is the intervening wall or surface which makes this act unhelpful. In saying "There is a table next door", I am, as it were, trying to refer to the table "through the wall" or to the back or inside of the table as if it were not concealed but before me, in my sense field. If the wall becomes transparent the relevant difference between the table here, in front of me, and the further table next door disappears, for the only relevant difference between the two types of case is that I was originally in a better position in space (or time) to describe the table in front of me. There may be important semantic differences, *e.g.* in learning the use of symbols for present, as opposed to absent, entities,[8] but there is no logical difference between dividing sentences which describe things in my field of vision from those which describe things beyond the horizon.

The kind of communication which a demonstrative, categorical sentence, which purports to be true, seeks to perform in respect of unobserved objects and events, may fail to achieve its object in at least one of two ways: the entity

---

[8] I owe this point to Dr. F. Waismann.

may not exist or possess the characteristics in terms of which it is denoted; or the failure may be due to some defect in my technique—if the relevant entity is not, for whatever reason, recognised by my audience; my effort to communicate is thwarted, but only by such empirical circumstances as physical walls, or the shape of the earth, or the limitations of my senses or imagination, or the date of my birth; thwarted by that and not by something incurably hypothetical, non-existential about the sentence itself. Let me give an example: when I say that Napoleon wore a three-cornered hat, or that on the evening before the battle of Borodino he had a twinge of remorse, I do not mean (though this is not strictly relevant to the argument) that one man and one man only was called Napoleon, and who ever was so called wore a three-cornered hat, or had a twinge of remorse. Proper names are not usually mere definite descriptions. My use of the word "Napoleon" is, among other things, a substitute for a wave of the hand, an inclination of the head, etc. because I cannot point in a literal sense, if only because I was born too late; and this is ultimately an empirical obstacle like the wall of a room or the nature of light or the structure of my brain. I am inviting you to direct your attention to Napoleon or to physical or mental events in his history and there is a nondescriptive and existential force in my use of the relevant words—and in particular of proper names—because I suggest or believe or know that such events have happened—that they are part of the collection of what was and is and will be. Certain types of categorical sentences in this way direct attention to things and events which therefore are taken to exist whether or not they are observed. The fact that they are in some sense capable of being directly observed, or verified, or their existence supported by sense datum evidence, may be part of the meaning of such concepts as "thing" or "event", but it is not what is asserted when I say that they occur here or now, or have such and such characteristics; and the reason for this is that the hypotheticals which I am being offered in exchange for categoricals do not, even misleadingly and fatally, invite anyone (except it seems, some philosophers) to look for any "thing" or event in the time series. Whatever is being asserted by, "If it rains, I shall take my umbrella", or "If Hitler had not wanted it, there would have been no war", it will not be found in the inventory of events, in the historical annals of the actual world, nor am I under any impression that I am being invited to look for any such entity. (Only philosophers have gone to the length of searching for or inventing ontological 'referends' of hypothetical propositions.) Hypothetical sentences do, of course, like other empirical expressions, involve the use of words which, to have any meaning, must themselves be capable of occurring in true ostensive sentences which do in some sense 'point'—words like "rain", or "umbrella", or "Hitler", but in themselves hypotheticals do not 'point'; otherwise they would cease to be hypothetical, they would lose their conditional, non-actual-fact-asserting force.

At this point a critic might say (as Professor A. J. Ayer did say to me in discussion), something like this: "You rest your case on the generally felt distinction between what is dispositional and what is non-dispositional in the material world, and say that the latter cannot be described by hypotheticals, as the former can, without doing violence to normal usage. But this is not so. In the first place, many expressions which do not seem dispositional at first, turn out to be so on further analysis: for example, if we say that the table is heavy and six feet long, that seems at first categorical enough, but of course 'heavy' means 'if weighed according to a recognised technique, the instrument will record etc.' and 'six feet long' refers to the possible application of a ruler and so forth: these apparently categorical statements turn out, therefore, to need translation into hypotheticals to make them clear: from which it follows that the categorical form of statement by itself gives no sort of indication of how sentences mean". But this argument establishes less than it appears to do. I should not dream of maintaining that verbal or grammatical form is an infallible guide to logical form, i.e. kinds of ways in which sentences mean. Indeed, that is the whole point of exposing the

dispositional character of expressions which *prima facie*
appear non-dispositional. But because some or many categoricals are in this sense concealed hypotheticals (*i.e.* their
meaning is made clearer, or certain errors are prevented,
by the substitution of hypotheticals), because language is
flexible and the frontiers shifting and vague, it cannot follow that the distinction does not exist at all, that the frontiers are invisible—for if that were so, such words as "dispositional" and "hypothetical", (there being nothing with
which to contrast them) would not signify anything at all.
And this is not what phenomenalists or defenders of the
theory of logical constructions, if their own words are to
mean anything, want to say. At this point the critic may
say: "But this is a sheer travesty of my position. Of course
I do not wish to blur the useful distinction between hypotheticals and categoricals. What I am asserting is that all
descriptive statements can in principle be translated into
sense datum language: all material object statements will
be transposed into hypothetical statements about sense data,
and these are what they are by contrast with the only true
ultimate, irreducible categoricals, those describing someone's actual sense experiences: *e.g.* Russell's basic propositions, Carnap's protocol sentences, etc. As for your distinction between dispositional and non-dispositional
characteristics of material objects, or between hypothetical
and categorical statements as applied to material objects,
the sense datum language is perfectly well able to reproduce it in its own terminology: categorical material object
statements will be translated into hypotheticals about
sense data; hypotheticals about material objects will be
rendered by hypotheticals about hypotheticals: thus to say
that a given table looks brown is to say something about
the dispositions of certain observers; to say that it is fragile
is to say something about the dispositions of dispositions of
these same observers; the distinction is one of degree of
complexity of hypotheticals; but the whole pyramid of
them only has descriptive force if they are about—if their
ultimate subject is—the actual data of actual observers
about which all material object sentences, whether categori-

cal or hypothetical, are in the end, hypotheses or theories. For what else is there in the world but what people see and hear and imagine and do and suffer?" We are there at last: this really is what phenomenalism boils down to: that the only irreducibly categorical propositions, by contrast with which alone hypotheticals are what they are, are statements about immediate experience, capable of direct, strong, "knock-down" verification. These are basic. All else is theory and speculation about their behaviour and incidence. We have returned to the many-tiered logical constructions, with material objects and perhaps their more obvious causal properties on the floors immediately above the "basic" ground floor (or should it be basement?) and the upper levels occupied by positrons, nerve impulses, super-egos, and possibly vectors and non-Euclidean spaces and numbers too, as well as the Zeitgeist, and the British Constitution and the national character. In a sense, this position seems almost too academic in character: if phenomenalists find difficulty, in fact, in producing the sense datum equivalents of even plain categorical material object statements, their claim to produce two or more storeys of such—simple hypotheticals and over these rows of complex ones—hypotheticals about hypotheticals—seems somewhat unreal; but even if we do not press for cash in the form of basic sentences against phenomenalist cheques (as being unfair and against the spirit of the conventions in use of language) the argument still remains fallacious. For what this view comes to is that material object sentences—including existential ones—are so many general propositions or hypotheses or theories about the behaviour of sense data. And this is precisely what common sense finds so repugnant. For a general proposition or theory may be interpreted purely intensionally—*i.e.* irrespective of whether or not instances of the concepts involved in fact occur; whereas such a sentence as, "The table next door is brown" is existential and as such has extensional import, and asserts that something *is* occurring in a sense in which general or hypothetical propositions proper do not normally assert anything of this sort; if such general propositions are taken extensionally as well as intensionally, *i.e.* if general propositions about sense data are to be understood to assert more than a mere logical or causal nexus between the possible experiences of possible observers, namely, the existence or occurrence of something or other which the nexus connects, then, to perform this task, unsensed sensa or sensibilia must be introduced: and these are rightly as much taboo to phenomenalists as Lockean substances or physical occupants, and a good deal odder in character. The point is that existential material object propositions directly assert that something exists in a sense in which theories or hypotheses do not directly assert this. One can bring out this point most sharply (at the cost of some exaggeration) by asserting baldly that all theories, hypotheses, general and hypothetical propositions, etc., may be true and yet nothing exist at all; for if the protases are unfulfilled, the apodoses have no application; whereas the proposition that some existential material object propositions are true is not compatible with the proposition that nothing exists at all.[9] What this over-simple paradox serves to bring out is that the essence of hypothetical or conditional sentences is to be in a peculiar way non-committal—in the sense in which, let us say, singular (empirical) existential categoricals normally commit the speaker to something which in principle can be directly verified. Now it is notoriously impossible directly to verify unfulfilled conditionals: but all conditionals must entail at least one such unfulfilled conditional, and consequently in this respect cannot be equivalent to statements asserting only what is directly verifiable by an act of observation. Existential categoricals on the other hand, commit us because there is normally an ostensive (pointing) property about existential categorical material object propositions.[10]

[9] This is, of course, not literally true, since theories presuppose the existence of theorists with all that they need by the way of a universe in order to fix the 'grammar' of their words, but this is not part of what the theories themselves assert, nor is it logically entailed by them.

[10] It may be worth adding that such demonstratives as "there is" or "this is" are seldom employed to refer to "sense data"—for that

The same point may be brought out in yet another way. According to the phenomenalist analysis, sentences describing material objects will differ in logical type according to the presence (to my senses) or the absence of the object in question. If it is present, I am said to be acquainted with actual seen data, and my sentence is at least partially analysable into irreducibly categorical ("basic") propositions: if it is absent, it is wholly analysable into hypotheticals. But this is surely not the case: if I say that there is a brown, wooden table in this room, I can, if I like, go on to say that among the propositions which I can assert of it, some are obviously categorical, some plainly hypothetical: some perhaps of neither kind, and then it cannot make a logical difference, *i.e.* a difference of principle, whether the table is before me in the room, or hidden behind a wall: whatever is hypothetically true, *i.e.* dispositional, about the present table (or its visible portion) is doubtless equally hypothetical (dispositional) about the one next door (or its visible portion): but whatever is categorical about the first is categorical about the other—absent one—too. The actual steps which I am obliged to take in order to *verify* propositions about a given table will, of course, vary with circumstances: if the table is moved out of my den, or someone blindfolds me, I cannot do what I could have done had this not happened; but the *meaning* of the sentence which I utter, does not alter with the movements of the table or the condition of my eyes: the meaning of the sentence, "There is a brown table in my study", does not swing forwards and backwards from partially categorical to wholly hypothetical as I move around it, or saw it in half, or walk in and out of my study, or the walls of my study change from opaque to transparent and neither does it wholly consist of a cluster of hypotheticals compatible (if their antecedents are unfulfilled) with the non-existence of any experiences

---

is a term which is rarely of use in ordinary experience, and is more properly applicable to that aspect of things which concern physiologists or oculists or impressionist painters, and is useful precisely because it contrasts that which interests these specialists—purely sensuous qualities—with material objects—things—the furniture of ordinary life.

whatever. Perhaps we now see more clearly the confusion from which these odd consequences spring: namely the confounding of the meaning of what we are saying with the varying conditions under which we feel inclined to say it.

III

At this point, some uneasiness may be felt about the attribution to our language of a capacity to 'point to' objects in absence—as if the transition from pointing to objects directly perceived to this semi-metaphorical sense of pointing, may not be quite legitimate. It is here that the phenomenalist may wish to play one of his strongest cards, for one of the most tempting advantages which his theory appears to offer is that by substituting logical constructions for inferred entities, he promises to describe the world solely in terms of the so called data of immediate acquaintance. He undertakes, in effect, to describe everything by means of logical or linguistic rules, including rules for the use of conditional participles like "if" and "provided that", and otherwise confine himself solely to what we can directly and literally point to in our everyday experience. And to speak of the ostensive function of a sentence which purports to point towards, direct attention to something—the table—real enough, indeed, but not here and not now, something unobserved, *i.e.* outside the field of direct acquaintance—is this not to go beyond and against the principle of not importing unfamiliar and dubious entities, to contravene the rule of the definability ostensively of all empirical terms? Are we not introducing something not met with face to face, not directly verifiable, and consequently not directly descriptive, perhaps altogether non-empirical? And this may at first unnerve the strict empiricist; but his anxieties will be groundless. For the notion of "not here", "not observed", must in any case be introduced into language seeking to describe the world sooner or later, and how this is accomplished is a psychological rather than an epistemological question. It is one thing to admit that whatever in one's descriptive language is not governed by syntactical rules must be capable of ostensive elucidation: and a very different one to say that I may not refer to anything unless I can establish the meaning of the variables of my language in terms of what I am actually experiencing here and now; if I adopt the latter principle, I become unable to refer to the past or the future or to the experiences of others to explain "here" and "now" and "observed by me", and so on —that way lies the kind of verification theory of meaning which has more than once been shown to lead to an extravagantly solipsist analysis of the meanings of words, ending literally in nonsense. The meaning of such "basic" words as "here", "now", "observed", depend on the existence of an equally "basic" use for "not here", "not now", "not observed", in contrast with which alone the meanings of "here", "now", etc., can be established. There is no need to go on with this line of argument—such comparatively primitive notions as "not now", or "beyond the horizon", cannot be "constructed" without circularity out of sense fields occurring in "specious presents"; but without such notions classification, and therefore language, in the ordinary sense, is demonstrably impossible. Hence, this kind of objection to the possibility in principle of pointing to objects in absence cannot be considered seriously, for it rests on the assumption (ultimately perhaps traceable to Aristotle's doctrine of actual *v.* potential being) that what is not here does not exist in the same sense of 'exist' as that which is here, which rules out all possibility of descriptive symbolism. For what exists but is not here, exists and is not here, in exactly the same sense of 'exists' as what is— does exist—here. Without this, all words would lose their function of discriminating and classifying.

IV

There are two final points to be made. (1) Supposing someone were to ask, "But how can we say anything about the table apart from the hypothetical sentences describing what an observer would see if he walked round it, etc.? Is the table round or oval, dark or light brown, light or heavy? Surely the sense datum school of philosophy, if it has established nothing else, has made it clear beyond any doubt that these properties in some sense depend on the observer, his physical position, his physiological and psychological condition, etc. Surely the argument from illusion, for example, cannot be dismissed as showing nothing at all because of logical considerations of how different types of sentences are used? Does the gramophone play tunes in a desert, or to an audience which is stone deaf? How does the view advanced here differ from the most untenably naive of all forms of naive realism?" This rejoinder rests on a serious and important confusion which may in part be responsible for the desperate feeling that only phenomenalism can somehow, in the end, be true. The theories advanced by physiologists, say about the indispensability of the mechanism of the ear to the hearing of sounds are empirical theories, corroborated by observational and not linguistic tests: and to say, therefore, that the occurrence of a particular kind of hearer is to assert a causal, *i.e.* empirical, and not semantic or logical proposition. I am saying that the event described as the hearing of a sound emitted by a gramophone depends on certain necessary conditions, and amongst these the structure of the hearer's brain or ear occurs in the same sort of way as, let us say, the physical properties of the needle attached to the sound box of the gramophone. But when I analyse propositions about the meaning of sentences, I am certainly not asserting, and need not necessarily be implying, propositions stating causes or conditions of the events which they describe.

There may very well in particular cases exist a causal nexus between the person of the observer and a given material object—what this nexus is, it is the task of the natural sciences to investigate. But this causal nexus is precisely what the phenomenalist,[11] claims *not* to be discussing when he offers a reduction of categorical material object sentences to hypothetical sense datum sentences—if he were, his theory would amount to a queer kind of occasionalism, metaphysical or empirical, according to his view of connections in nature, whereby the observer who figures in the protasis of the phenomenalist hypothetical could destroy a table by averting his gaze as surely as by setting it on fire.[12] When I say that a material object exists or has certain characteristics, I am not, it seems to me, committing myself necessarily to any specific theory about the necessary or sufficient conditions of the existence or character of the object. Hence, the question of when, or for how long, the table next door is coloured brown need not in principle ever affect the answer to the question, "What do I mean when I say, 'There is a brown table next door'?" This, of course, needs qualification: the meanings of words *are* affected, and often very deeply affected, by our explicit or implicit causal beliefs, and the analysis of what is meant by an expression may very well reveal all kinds of physical or social or psychological beliefs or assumptions prevalent in a given society, a change in which could affect the meaning of words. The degree to which the dispositional characteristics of observers, treated as persons in time and space, enter into the way in which we employ material object words will vary widely: thus, it seems to me reasonably clear that when we say that there is a table next door, we are *not* implying any particular beliefs about the presence or dispositional characteristics of the normal human observer, beyond the fact that if it is a table at all, it must be not wholly invisible, intangible to him, etc.—since otherwise

[11] For example, Professor A. J. Ayer in *Arist. Soc. Proc.*, 1947.
[12] This is one of the notorious absurdities of which Berkeley is at times guilty, and on which beginners in philosophy are often taught to practise their critical powers.

it would not be what we mean by a material object. It seems a little less obvious that I can to-day say that it is coloured brown when not observed, for perhaps by now rudimentary physiological knowledge is sufficiently widespread to have imported into the notion of being coloured certain causal beliefs about the effects in the visual field of changes in our nervous system, etc. It seems very much less clear that I can say that roses smell sweet when no one smells them, or that winds howl when no one hears them, and it seems clearly eccentric to say that heard melodies are sweet, while those unheard are literally sweeter. And all this is doubtless useful in throwing light on our normal usage with regard to such words as, "smell sweet", or "howl", or "sweet melodies", some of which do, while others do not, imply the presence of persons with certain psychological, physiological, etc., attributes as observers. I am merely concerned to show that a quite sufficient number of material object sentences do *not* presuppose such dependence on the existence or behaviour of observers of this kind, that the relation of observers to material objects is more properly to be called an empirical and not a semantic question, however deeply verbal usage and empirical beliefs may be interconnected; and that consequently the view that nothing can in principle be significantly said to occur without explicit and implicit reference to observers is a major fallacy which rests on failure to distinguish between the causal propositions of natural science or common sense and propositions about meaning.

I return to my original point that phenomenalism, or at any rate the most prevalent modern form of it, seems to rest on a mistaken analysis of what normal existential material object statements state; they state that things or events existed, or exist, or will exist, or were, are, or will be, characterised by this or that characteristic; and not that something might exist or would exist, or would have existed, the truth (if not the assertion) of which is logically compatible with the non-existence of anything whatever. Even if hypothetical propositions alone describe the conditions without which we should not assert or be justified in asserting the relevant categoricals, yet the meaning of the former is not the same as the meaning of the latter. And this is so, even if we go further and hold, as some do, that the two types of proposition strictly entail one another; since whatever be the sense in which mutual entailment is regarded as tantamount to, or identical with, logical equivalence (as it is by some logicians), it is clearly not the same as the sense of identity of meaning in which two or more descriptive sentences can be said by common sense to mean the same; yet it is this last sense of "meaning the same" as between the analysans and the analysandum, and it alone, that the best known variants of modern phenomenalism seek to establish and, if the above thesis is correct, seek in vain.

THE CAUSAL THEORY

H. H. Price

In this chapter we shall return to our two main themes, namely, the relation of 'belonging to', and the nature of perceptual consciousness. We saw that the long struggle to defend Naïve Realism finally failed, despite the ingenuity of the defenders. The Naïve Realist, we may recall, maintained two theses: (1) that in the case of visual and tactual sense-data 'belonging to' means 'being part of the surface of'; (2) that perceptual consciousness is knowing that a sense-datum is part of the surface of a material thing. Both theses have turned out to be untenable. We have now to consider a radically different but equally familiar theory which maintains (1) that in the case of all sense-data (not merely visual and tactual) 'belonging to' simply means *being caused by,* so that 'M is present to my senses' will be equivalent to 'M causes a sense-datum with which I am acquainted'; (2) that perceptual consciousness is fundamentally an *inference* from effect to cause.

This theory corresponds pretty closely to the traditional doctrine of Representative Ideas, but with two differences: it is not committed to the view that sense-data are *mental,* i.e. are 'ideas' (they might be neither mental nor physical); and it is not committed to the view that visual and tactual sense-data *resemble* the material things which they belong to, though of course they might happen to do so. These differences do not seem very important. The old-fashioned Representationists when they used the term 'idea' were probably more anxious to deny, as against Naïve Realism, that sense-data are physical, than to assert that they are mental: what they wanted to assert was rather that we are immediately aware of them. And when they said that ideas 'represent' the material world, they plainly meant that the having of ideas enables us to gain *knowledge* or rational belief concerning the existence and nature of that world, and some indeed actually said that we gain it by a causal argument; they did not merely mean that the ideas happen as a matter of fact to resemble material things, as a man's shadow resembles the man.

But although the theory which we are to consider is an old one, it is by no means dead; indeed to this day it might be called the official foundation of Natural Science. The usual name for it, and the most convenient, is the *Causal Theory*. Unfortunately some writers mean by this simply the ordinary physico-physiological account of the way in which sense-data are as a matter of fact generated, by the action of other material things upon the sense-organs and nervous systems of sentient beings. That, however, is merely a *part* of Natural Science and has no claim to be the foundation of it. Like all other parts of Natural Science it is based upon observation, in this case observation of lenses, retinæ, ears, brains and the like; but it is not a theory of what observation itself is, which is the question which concerns us as philosophers. The only sort of Causal Theory which is of philosophical importance is one which discusses *this* question: and the theory that belonging to M is the same as being caused by M, and that perceptual consciousness is an inference from effect to cause, does discuss it. This, then, is what we in this book shall always mean by 'the Causal Theory'.

Before we expound the theory in detail, we must consider certain preliminary difficulties. In the first place it is obvious that we are not ordinarily conscious of making any inference at all when we see a table or a chair or a tree; and this might seem to be already a fatal objection to the theory. But several answers are offered. The theory may say, with Helmholtz and others, 'You do infer but you are not conscious[1] of inferring, because you do it so quickly and without any effort'. This will not do. If we are not con-

[1] I take it that an 'unconscious' inference means an inference which we are not conscious of.

scious of inferring, what evidence is there that we do infer at all? And if it be replied 'Of course you do, for all consciousness of matter must be inferential', we must point out that this begs the question.

A more plausible suggestion is that although we do not in fact infer the existence of the table, yet we ought to. It is said that the proposition 'This is a square table' though not *reached* by inference can only be *justified* by inference. But this, too, seems difficult. The sense-data given to us are not all square, indeed very few of them are. And yet we are convinced that the table is square. Evidently some process of correction or sifting has been going on. And this suggests that our conviction of the existence and squareness of the table may not after all require *external* justification at all. If only we would examine the sensings and acts of perceptual consciousness which immediately precede the occurrence of this conviction, might we not find that it was in some way already justified by these and needed no inference to support it? It is certain that no one except a few philosophers has ever thought that such support was needed, or offered to supply it.

This odd duality of two processes—one inevitable but irrational, the other rational but never or all but never occurring—is avoided by the third and most plausible answer to our difficulty. According to this, I have *in the past* inferred material objects from sense-data by causal arguments; in early childhood I always did so. And this has enabled me to establish the inductive generalization that wherever such and such a kind of sense-datum exists, such and such a kind of object exists too. (Indeed, the establishing of this generalization would be the chief occupation of the infant mind upon this view.) Once having established it, I proceed henceforth to apply it in a mechanical way to all my sense-data as they come along, without thinking any more about the grounds upon which it is based, and without troubling to verify it in each new case by going through the whole causal argument again. The result is that I do not now as a rule have any consciousness of the causal relation subsisting between this sense-datum and this material object. The sense-data have come to be to me *signs* of the objects, and I 'read' my sense-data much as I read a book. Still, my present power of reading the signs depends upon a long course of causal inferences in the past. And even now, it would be said, I do occasionally infer an object from my sense-data by a causal inference, e.g. when I correct an illusion, or when I consider[2] whether such and such a sense-datum is illusory or not.

Thus by this account the process is a perfectly rational one, resulting not indeed in knowledge but in rational belief. Something very like it occurs even in arithmetical and geometrical thinking. For instance, if we find a right-angled triangle we straightway take it that the square on the hypotenuse is equal to the sum of the squares on the other two sides, without going through Pythagoras's Theorem again every time. The only difference is that the major premise is here not an inductive generalization, whereas in our case it is. And this difference is not here important.

Further, we may urge that this 'mechanically' subsumptive procedure is all the more natural, the more complicated the original inferences upon which our general rule was founded. And we must now point out that in the present case they must have been very complicated indeed. No *simple* causal argument, which could be gone through again every time without trouble, will take us from a sense-datum to a material thing.

For instance, it cannot be said that the table is *the* cause of the sense-data which 'belong to' it. On the one hand, why should we go so far back? Why not say that the light rays are the cause of the sense-datum—or the retina, or the brain, or even (perhaps) the mind? All these have just as good a right to be called 'the' cause of it as the table has—that is, neither they nor the table have any right at all. But on the other hand, why not go farther back still? Why stop at the table? The electric light, the wires conveying the current, the dynamo which generates it—all these are just as necessary to the genesis of the sense-

[2] 'Considering' obviously consists of hypothetical and disjunctive reasoning, or at least contains it as an essential part.

datum as the table itself is. And we should come back at last to the prehistoric coal forests, to the sun, or even to the original nebula.

The material thing, then, is not *the* cause of the sense-datum which belongs to it. Are we to say, then, that the sense-datum belongs to the brain, the eyes, the dynamo, the sun, no less than to the table? But this would be absurd. For we have used the phrase 'belonging to' in a special meaning: a visual sense-datum *s* belongs to a material thing M when M is present to the senses of the mind which is acquainted with *s;* that is, when the plain man on sensing *s* would say 'I am seeing M'. But no one would say in the present case that he was *seeing* the sun or a dynamo, still less that he was seeing his own eye or brain. He would say he was seeing a table. It is to the table then, and to nothing else, that the sense-datum belongs. But it is causally dependent upon an indefinitely large multitude of things. How then can 'belonging to' be defined in terms of causal dependence? The Causal Theory seems to have met with disaster before it has well started. And with that, many philosophers will be tempted to leave the matter.

But I fear that we cannot rid ourselves of the theory so easily, though we may fairly complain of the lax and off-hand way in which it has often been expounded. A simple distinction between *standing* and *differential* conditions will get over the difficulty. There are certain conditions which condition *all* the sense-data of any one sense, conditions in the absence of which none of them can come into being: in the case of visual sense-data, there must be a source of light, an eye, a retina, an optic nerve, etc., and these must be in a certain state. There must also be a diaphanous medium. But these standing conditions, just because they are necessary to all the visual sense-data alike, do not wholly determine any one of them. For that, something more is wanted, a varying or differential condition which accounts for the difference between this red sense-datum and that blue one, between this square one and that elliptical one. Obviously it is absurd to identify

M with any or all of the standing conditions of *s;* but it is quite plausible to identify it with the *differential* condition of *s.* And clearly this is what the Causal Theory intends to do.

We may now sum up our discussion so far. What the Causal Theory maintains is that *given s, it is possible to infer the existence of M as s's differential condition.* On this we may note:

(1) M must be the differential condition of *s*, not just any sort of condition.

(2) Nor must it merely be so as a matter of fact. The relation of differential conditioning must be so apprehensible by us that we can pass by means of it from the apprehension of *s* to the apprehension of M.

(3) Yet this need not actually occur, and in an adult mind at least is not necessary to the *belief* in M's existence, though it is to the *knowledge* of M.

Our next task is to enquire what sort of argument it is by which (according to the Causal Theory) M can be inferred from *s* as its differential condition? One well-known account represents the argument as follows: Every event has a cause, and every sense-datum is an event. It must, then, have a cause. Its cause must either be myself or something else. But it cannot be myself, for sense-data are independent of my will. As Berkeley says: 'When I open my eyes in broad daylight it is not in my power to choose what I shall see.' Sense-data must therefore be caused by events in something other than myself.

If this is the argument, it is perfectly valueless as it stands. First, why should not sense-data be caused *by other sense-data?* We have no direct insight into causal laws. Now it seems plausible to say that sense-data are events, and there must on any view be *some* type of events 'beyond which you cannot go', events such that the causal relations subsisting between them are ultimate and cannot be explained, i.e. deduced from some combination of the causal laws governing other events. If this were not so, there would be an infinite regress, and explanation would never be possible. Why should not these events

beyond which you cannot go be simply sense-data themselves; or again certain special sorts of sense-data, say
visual and tactual ones? And until one has explored this
possibility, what right has one to go behind sense-data to
something else, whether to the mind or to a so-called external object?

Secondly, independence of my will in any case proves
nothing. For it is quite compatible with dependence on
myself, as any dream or hallucination shows. Sense-data
might well be caused by psychical processes in me
which had nothing to do with my will, and which were
even beyond the reach of introspection.

These objections are fatal to the argument as it stands.
Let us try to amend it. For 'independent of my will' let
us substitute 'independent of known psychical processes in
myself'. We can then answer the second objection. For
the example of dreams and hallucinations can now be used
on the other side. If psychologists are to be believed, a
connexion can actually be found between my dreams and
certain known states of myself: say my desires, my
memories, my interests. The same is true of hallucinations.
But is it true of ordinary sense-data? Will any introspection or any psychoanalytical technique enable us to predict what we shall see half an hour hence? 'Memory will
help.' It will, but only when the situation is familiar, and
some are not. And memory of what? Clearly only memory of past sense-data—which raises the same problem
over again. On the other hand, I see the moon rise and
the clouds come and go whether I am glad or sorry,
reminiscent or expectant. No change in any recognizable
state of myself seems to affect the differential conditions
of those sense-data, though it may well be true that the
standing conditions are partly in myself.

'But after all it is possible that there are states and processes in yourself which are beyond the reach of introspection and of psychoanalytical technique, and these may
produce your sense-data.' The reply is obvious. By what
right can any one say that they are *in myself*? If they are
independent of everything which I call myself, to say

that they are states and processes *in me* is merely playing with words: or if you will, it is splitting 'me' into two parts —one familiar part and another utterly alien part, having no connexion with the first. That second part should not be called 'me'; for it is exactly what is ordinarily called external.

We may now go back to the first objection, that sense-data may be caused by other sense-data. Here the traditional argument is not exactly in error: it has only omitted the essential point. If we were *omnisentient* beings, i.e. if we were able to sense all at once all the sense-data which can ever be sensed by every sentient human or non-human; and if this all-inclusive sensing were never interrupted by sleep or inattention: then, but only then, it would be plausible to suggest that sense-data might be caused by other sense-data, for then but not otherwise the sense-data would suffice by themselves to constitute an orderly and coherent world.

But unfortunately, though some idealist philosophers seem unaware of it, our situation is very different. Every drowsy nod, every turn of the head, every blink, would destroy the order of Nature if Nature consisted simply of *our* sense-data. Even the simplest laws, e.g. that all unsupported bodies fall, cannot be stated in terms of our sense-data alone. Those innocent persons who think that they can be, are either importing possible sense-data to supplement the actual ones, or they are tacitly assuming an omnisentient observer. I am not seeing the walls of the room below, which support this room in which I sit. Yet I do see this room, and it does not fall to the ground. The clothes in the distant back-yard hang in the air, though from here I can see no string for them to hang on. Again, when the motor-car is moving, I do not and cannot see the explosion in the cylinder. Here are effects without causes, if we insist upon stating causal laws in terms of sense-data alone. And again we have causes without effects. I drop a pencil from my window on a dark night. This should cause it to fall. But I never see it fall. No sense-datum of the required kind succeeds upon the kinaesthetic or tactual sense-datum which (upon this view) is the dropping.

It may be said that sense-data of the required kind *could* have existed in all these cases. But how do we know that they could? Either because we already know that something else exists other than sense-data, and further know the way in which that something changes, and what sort of sense-data belong to it. Or if not that, one must mean by 'causal laws' something very odd—one must mean laws connecting 'possibilities of sensation'. No doubt there are such laws. But still these possibilities are certainly not sense-data: a possibility cannot be red or round, large or small, hard or soft or smelly. But it was in terms of entities red, round, hard, soft, etc., that causal laws were to be stated, when it was said that sense-data might be caused by sense-data, and that there was no need to look for their causes in some other sphere of being, lying outside sense-data altogether.

Considerations of this kind constitute what we may call the *argument for unsensed causes:* they show that if every event has a cause and if our sense-data, or again if their comings-into-being, are events, then something else must exist besides our sense-data. This argument is the only plausible basis for the Causal Theory, though few advocates of the theory, I think, have used it. We must insist once more that it depends entirely upon the fragmentary and intermittent character of our sense-data. Thanks to this, our sense-data *taken by themselves* are chaotic and disorderly, and we have therefore to call in a new world to redress the balance of the old; or rather, to make it a world at all, instead of a chaos, we have to supplement it by something else. But were we omnisentient the argument would have no force whatever: even though our sense-data had in fact unsensed causes, we should then have had no grounds for thinking that they had. Berkeley's God has no ground for believing that Nature consists of anything but actual sense-data; but Berkeley has plenty.

But as to the *character* of this something other than

sense-data, the argument so far tells us nothing: only (as we have shown) it cannot be ourselves. So far as we have yet gone, we can only say it is something or other distinct from ourselves. We cannot even say whether it is one or many. It might quite well be a mind, so long as it is distinct from *our* minds; it might be a set of minds, or something extended in space, or none of these.

However, various lines of thought may be suggested all of which purport to answer these questions, by showing that these causes of which sense-data are the intermittent and collateral effects are *material things,* extended in space and enduring through time, and having such causal properties as Natural Science attributes to them. We may call them the *Method of Correspondence,* the *Method of Discounting,* the *Method of Sources,* the *Method of Indispensables* and the *Method of Hypothesis.*[3] These methods, with the argument for unsensed causes upon which they are all based, constitute the detailed content of the Causal Theory. We shall now examine them one by one. We hope to show that none of them, as a matter of fact, succeeds in establishing the existence of matter; and we shall then urge that all attempts to establish this by causal arguments are mistaken in principle. But we must ask the reader to be patient. We cannot reach this conclusion unless we first expound the Methods in full detail. And we shall try to make out as good a case as possible for each of them.

THE METHOD OF CORRESPONDENCE

The principle of this was adumbrated by Descartes when he laid down that there must be at least as much 'reality' in the cause as in the effect, i.e. at least as many positive attributes.[4] There must be a cause not merely for the existence of sense-data in general, but for all the par-

[3] Cf. the ethical 'methods' examined by Sidgwick.
[4] Cf. also Mr. Russell's *Analysis of Matter.*

ticular detail of all the sense-data which we actually sense. It follows that *wherever we find differences in the sense-data, there must be differences in the cause.* For instance, the data of sight differ from those of touch, and both differ from those of smell, and so on. To these differences there must *correspond* some differences in the cause or causes of the sense-data. We need not indeed suppose that to every qualitative difference in the sphere of sense-data there corresponds a *qualitative* difference in the Non-sensible. The corresponding difference might be a difference between relational characteristics. But still, it will be said, there has to be some corresponding difference or other.

But the main task of the Method is to show that there are *spatial* and *temporal* differences within the Non-sensible. If there are not, it cannot be called material (or physical) in any natural sense. To say that visual and tactual sense-data are extended (being 'extents' or 'expanses'), and that only the extended can cause the extended, would however be too simple; for visual images and the data of dreams are extended, but they are commonly held to be caused by the mind which is not. But it is claimed that there is another way of establishing the required conclusion.

Let us consider any field of view, such as the one we see at this moment. Obviously it has *parts.* Here, for instance, is a triangular white patch, there a square red one. And corresponding to each part there must be something in the Non-sensible to cause it. Again each individual patch has parts, e.g. a top half and a bottom half. Corresponding to these again there must be distinct factors in the Non-sensible. And in each of these distinct factors there must be further distinctions, corresponding to the parts of these parts, and so on.

Further, not only the diversity of the parts, but their *mode of relation* to each other must be accounted for. The parts of the sense-field are related in a three-dimensional order in the ways we call up and down, right and left, near and far. There must then be a corresponding mode of relation among the diverse factors in the Non-sensible. The diverse factors in the Non-sensible must in any case be ordered in some way. And it now turns out that their order, whatever its particular nature may be, must at any rate have three dimensions. Likewise there are relations of earlier and later between sense-data, and these relations are independent of the other three. There must then be still another mode of relation in the Non-sensible to account for this.

So far, the Method of Correspondence claims to have shown two things: (1) that there is *a plurality of factors* in the Non-sensible, (2) that they are related to each other *in an order having at least four dimensions.* (By 'having four dimensions' is meant that in this ordered manifold there are to be found four distinct and mutu-ally irreducible types of relatedness. They are mutually irreducible in this sense, that from the fact that B stands between A and C in respect of relation No. 1, you cannot infer what it stands between in respect of relations 2, 3 and 4.)

The Method now goes one step further, and claims to prove that these diverse factors have a certain *independ-ence* of each other. For we observe that one part of a sense-field can change although other parts do not: indeed this happens whenever (as we say) we see something move. Again, when we see something break (which is really a form of motion) we observe that within the sense-field one part which formerly changed as a whole has been replaced by two or more smaller parts, each of which has for the future its own separate career, and changes independently of the others. (Likewise mutual *dependence* in the sphere of sense-data signifies mutual dependence in the Non-sensible.)

And if it be objected that sense-data are not substances and therefore cannot change, the point will be re-stated as follows: During a certain period of sense-experiencing we sense not one series of sense-data, but several concur-rent series. And these series are not merely spatially sepa-rate; they are also what we may call causally separate, in that each 'goes its own way' independent of the others. From the fact that the successive members of one series A are dissimilar to one another in a certain respect (say, position in the field of view), we cannot infer that the members of a certain other series B differ from each other either in that respect, or in any respect at all—they may all be exactly alike. Thus when a man smoking a pipe sees a mouse run across the floor of his room, the successive sense-data which belong to the mouse differ from each other in colour, position and size. But the successive sense-data which belong to the table during that period do not differ from each other at all. And the smoker's kinaesthetic sense-data (the felt puffings) do indeed differ from each other in a rhythmic way, but these differences are not correlated in any discernible manner with the differences between the successive mouse-data.

To sum up: these considerations, and obviously they could be further elaborated, are supposed to prove that in the Non-sensible something (upon which the existence of our sensa depends) there is a *plurality* of factors *relatively independent* of each other, and related in an order *having at least four dimensions.* And this, it is urged, is the same as saying that the Non-sensible something is *a world of bodies in space and time,* a world which is at least as complex as common sense supposes, and may be more so.

THE METHOD OF DISCOUNTING

We have seen that each characteristic of the sense-given has its correlate in the Non-sensible; we have also seen that concomitant variation on the side of the sense-given is correlated with dependence or connexion on the side of the Non-sensible: non-concomitant variation, with independence.

We have now to apply these principles to the particular

case of the relation between somatic and non-somatic sense-data.

We have already seen that all sense-experience is somato-centric (or kinaestheto-centric): in all our sense-experience somatic and non-somatic data are present together and vary together. And we were obliged to conclude from this that the coloured surfaces we see, the pressures we feel, etc., cannot continue to exist when their somatic accompaniments are removed, e.g. when our back is turned or when we are out of the room.

But although no visual data exist when our back is turned, certain non-sensible somethings do and must, if the argument for unsensed causes be right. The question is, can we now determine the particular nature of these somethings? Obviously we must begin by inquiring into the nature of the something or somethings which are present when we *are* in the room: we can then hope to discover what difference is made to them by our removal.

It is clear that what we have called somato-centricity must have as its correlate a relation of compresence and connexion (or dependence) on the side of the Non-sensible. But we have now to observe that somato-centricity has its limits. In many respects the non-somatic data vary concomitantly with the somatic data, but not in all; in some respects the non-somatic is *independent* of the somatic.

In what respects independent? Not in respect of qualities, e.g. colour, shape, hardness, hotness; nor in respect of intensity, size or sensible position. That is why none of these, and therefore no sense-data, could be held to exist outside the somato-centric *totum*. Yet when we look at a table from various sides, push our eye out of place, drug ourselves with santonin, and in other ways change our somatic sense-data, is there not something in the visual sense-data which remains the same? Clearly there is. It is what we may vaguely call 'the general look'. All the sensible qualities alter, yet somehow this remains. It is that in virtue of which we say that it is a *table* which we are seeing throughout the process—not an elephant, or a pot of geraniums. Yet this general look which all the data have in common is not a common *quality* present in them all. There is no one shape and no one colour which qualifies them all; and there is no one size either, nor intensity nor sensible position: quite the contrary. What is common to them all is a certain *relational* characteristic: there is some one solid figure which they all resemble in greater or less degree. No one of them perhaps is exactly like any part of it: yet they all, as we say, remind us of it. This solid figure is as it were the *common theme* upon which they are diverse variations.

It is therefore natural to suppose that in the Non-sensible there are two separate factors (or sets of factors), one of which is responsible for the Common Theme, the other for the variations upon it, and for the kinaesthetic data concomitant with these. The first we will call C, the other V. When I go out of the room, what really happens (it will be said) is that C and V cease to be connected with each other, and that is why the somato-centric sense-field comes to an end. But both of them continue to exist, and in particular C does. C in fact is what is left of the table when we go out of the room.

What can we say about the characteristics of C? We cannot say directly that the figure which is the common theme is *its* figure. For the common theme is not anything existing by itself. It is not anything actual, but something imaginary or supposed, as it were an abstraction from the diversely varying visual data, which alone are actually given. But we *can* say that C has at least as many parts as the common theme has; that C's parts are arranged in an order of at least three dimensions; and that the relations which its parts have in that order are similar to the spatial relations which the common theme's parts have to one another.

This conclusion can be reached in another way. Instead of asking what on the non-somatic side remains the same in the presence of somatic variations, we can ask what differences remain in the presence of somatic sameness. Here too we are 'discounting' the somato-centric.

For instance, the size of our visual sense-data increases as we reduce the distance between them and the place where our kinaesthetic data are felt, and decreases as that distance grows larger. But if when two visual data A and B are at the *same* distance from our kinaesthetic ones there is still a difference of size between them, A being (say) twice as large as B: then *this* difference of size is not somato-centric, although differences between data at different distances are. Not that even this difference would itself subsist even if I shut my eyes or turned my back. For, after all, it is a difference between sense-data, and when the sense-data cease to exist (as they then would) it must cease too, since a relation cannot survive its terms. But it may be thought that it does directly *correspond* to some difference in the Non-sensible which would persist even if I turned my back, and would have subsisted in it even if the sense-experience by means of which I discover it had never occurred at all. And since both shape and position may be treated as functions of size, the shapes and positions of the Non-sensible somethings can also be determined in this way.

The argument will apply to change also, for change is a kind of difference. Certain changes in our visual field, for instance, are concomitant with changes in our kinaesthetic experience; but certain others are not, for they still go on even when our kinaesthetic data are kept constant. Thus as I walk things appear to move past me in the opposite direction, and the faster I walk the faster they appear to move. But even if I stand still the train appears to remove in relation to the railway embankment; there is still a *difference* between its sensible place at one moment and its sensible place at a later moment. Again, when a balloon is being blown up, my visual sense-datum grows larger and larger, even though I do not walk towards the place where it is. Such changes then correspond to some sort of systematic differences (whether to be called change or not) which would still subsist in the Non-sensible even if my sense-experience had not occurred, and are unaffected by the cessation of it.

Or if we like we may regard this as the persistence of an identity rather than the persistence of a difference. The *same* process of change continues to be observed, even though there are variations in the somatic sense-data. Thus we can make the train appear to go backwards by moving past it very quickly; but the railway embankment appears to go backwards faster, and if there is a fence beside the line, the train still passes the same number of posts in the same time. Again, we can make the balloon appear to shrink by moving backwards away from it, but the men beside it appear to shrink more quickly than it does; in relation to them, it still grows steadily larger whatever our own motion may be.

The argument will obviously apply to other illusions as well as to these simple ones. Thus if we press our eyeball out of place, everything is doubled. But a whole mass of differences, differences of size, shape, colour, position survive the doubling, and are unaffected by it. And when we displace a part of the view by means of a prism, there is again a multitude of differences which survive the displacement.

It will not apply to hallucinations, nor to such entities as *muscae volitantes,* after-images, or the spots seen in the field of view when we have a liver-attack. But that is just as it should be. What they correspond to is something in what I call my own body, or in myself, something which obviously does not form part of the object to which the data belong, and which though connected with the object while I am sensing ceases to be so connected when I am not.

The Method of Sources

Our aim as before is to discover what particular objects the Non-sensible ground of our sense-data consists of. Now what distinguishes one individual object from another? First its spatial and temporal characteristics. Secondly, its causal properties, what Locke called its *powers*. A particular object, it is suggested, is nothing else than a particular set of causal properties which, so to speak, inhabit a certain region of space during a certain period of time. We have therefore to notice just what non-sensible causal properties our sense-data give evidence of, and we must then try, as it were, to run these causal properties to earth, i.e. to discover in just what regions these properties are located.

The Method of Sources[5] purports to show that these causal properties are situated in the region where their effects (the sense-data) reach a maximum of intensity, and it regards that region as the *source* of these sense-data. This seems simple enough, but unfortunately we cannot reach this conclusion without raising and solving a number of difficulties on the way. That is why we have stated the conclusion at the beginning: otherwise the reader might lose the wood for the trees.

The first question is, why should these causal properties be anywhere at all? Not all causal properties have location in space: e.g. those which are characteristic of minds have none. Yes, but we are already supposed to know by the Method of Correspondence that the somethings upon which our sense-data depend are spatially ordered; therefore the causal properties which (on the view before us) constitute their being not only are, but are somewhere.

Now obviously we cannot directly observe these causal properties. How then are we to locate them? Clearly we can only do so by examining the corresponding effects. A cause is where it acts, i.e. where its effects are produced: for *operari sequitur esse*. This leads to the rather surprising consequence that the cause of a somato-centric field or *totum datum* is present in every part of that field; thus if the totum datum includes visual sense-data, its

[5] So far as I know, this Method was first formulated (though not under that name) by Dr. C. D. Broad. Cf. *Scientific Thought*, Chapter IX. Dr. Broad's theory, however, is not by any means a purely causal theory, and accordingly does not fall under the criticisms which we shall make below, pp. 424–433.

cause will, as it were, be spread all over the field of view. We might indeed think that we were only concerned here with the cause of a *single* sense-datum, say the visual sense-datum 'belonging to' a certain tree, and that this is confined to the place where that particular sense-datum is, though the cause of the whole visual field is spread over a large region. But this would be a mistake. For that visual sense-datum is not, so to speak, autonomous, but somato-centric; it cannot be separated from the somatic data with whose variations it varies. Moreover, the cause of this twofold effect must be spread over the whole region intervening between the two. For changes in the intervening part, e.g. those which we describe by saying that a prism or a mist has entered it, are relevant to the effect. And if the cause is situated where the effect occurs, then the cause is spread all over this region.

It might indeed be suggested, as by Professor Whitehead, that every piece of matter is everywhere: so that every differential condition of sense-experience is extended without limits. With all respect to Dr. Whitehead, this would be a disappointment. For our aim was to distinguish the situation of one differential condition from the situation of another. And if they are all everywhere, this cannot be done.

But, fortunately, although the sphere of influence, and therefore the situation, of every differential condition is extended without limit, that sphere has a centre. And the centre of A's sphere may be a long way from the centre of B's, however much the spheres themselves overlap. Moreover, it is possible to find where these centres or rather central regions are situated.

For we observe that this whole region can be divided into two parts: a *central* one where the environmental sense-data are located, and an *outer* one lying between that and the place where our somatic sense-data are felt. And we notice that what occupies the central region and what occupies the outer region are to some extent independent of each other. A change in the one is not invariably accompanied by a change in the other. Thus if a prism is introduced 'between me and the thing I am looking at', i.e. into a place intermediate between my somatic sense-datum and the central region, my visual sense-datum is altered—bent perhaps or displaced, and its edges made iridescent. Or again the sound of the thing can be altered by the introduction of a screen between myself and the thing. But if I move my point of view towards the central region, as soon as I pass the prism or the screen the alteration is undone, and I sense exactly the same sort of sense-data as I sensed from that place before. Thus it appears that the prism or the screen affects that part of the differential condition which lies on its outer side, but not the part which lies on its inner side.

On the other hand, changes sometimes occur in the central region with no corresponding change in the outer region. Thus if we come very close we can see the movement of a blade of grass in the wind, but if we stand farther off, the movement ceases to be visible: that is, the one sense-datum changes, the other does not change. It is true that we cannot observe both at once, for we cannot be in two places at once. But we notice that as soon as we come close we get a changing sense-datum, and as soon as we retire we get an unchanging one; also we can see many similar blades of grass at the same time, and while those very close to us are visibly moving, those at a distance are not. Evidently then the presence or absence of the change depends upon the centrality or non-centrality of the region.

Further, there is *never* an exact concomitance of central and non-central changes. As we move away from the centre something is always lost. There is a blurring of detail, an increasingly gross and, as it were, 'impressionistic' character about what we see. As we saw before, the differences between one sense-datum and another always grow less as we move away and increase as we approach; and this applies to difference between things successive, i.e. to change, as much as to the difference between things simultaneous.

Thus as between the central region and the outer region

there is a certain 'looseness'. And this seems to show that the differential condition is not all homogeneous, but consists of two parts, a central part and an outer part, which are to some extent independent of each other. (Or perhaps there is one part in the central region and an indefinitely large number of others surrounding it at different distances.) Thus if we are still to say that the object is spread all over its sphere of influence, at least it is not homogeneously spread. Its *distinctive* nature is fully present only in the central region, and fades gradually away as we move outwards.

But we can go further. The 'influential' character of the outer part of the sphere of influence, the power to produce in it sense-data belonging to this particular set, is *dependent* upon that which occupies the central part. If the central condition is removed or abolished, so that no sense-data of the old kind can be had in the central region, then the external condition is removed or abolished too. If the thing cannot be seen from one pace off, because some one has burnt it, it certainly cannot be seen from 50 paces off, or 500. Of course this by itself is consistent with the view that the two conditions are interdependent and stand or fall together (like the inside and outside of a door), or even that the central one depends on the outer one. But had this been so, the abolition of the outer condition would have entailed the abolition of the central condition also. And this is just what we do not find. In the dusk or on a misty day I cannot see a rock from 50 paces off, but it by no means follows that I cannot see it from one pace off. If a large obstacle is introduced between me and the central region,[6] I no longer get my visual sense-datum at all, even in broad daylight; and sounds, smells and thermal sense-data can be cut off in the same way.[7] Yet as soon as I pass the obstacle, I get my visual or other datum again, exactly as before. In all these cases the outer part of the

[6] It is strange that philosophers have not paid more attention to screens, and generally to the 'hiding' of one object by another.

[7] Why do we attribute all these differing effects to the same condition A? Presumably because they vary together.

differential condition is abolished, permanently or temporarily. But the central part is not affected in the least. It is the central condition, then, which is essential to the existence of the sense-data; without it there are no sense-data of the relevant kind at all. The outer condition is something which may or may not be added, according to circumstances; and it cannot be added at all, unless the central condition exists first. The central condition may therefore be called *the source* of all these sense-data. The central region is *the place where the material object is;* and the shape of it is the *shape of the object.*

In the same way the differential condition, for instance the differential condition A, has an auditory, an olfactory, and a thermal sphere of influence. With them, too, we can perform the same operation: in each case we reach a region of maximum intensity. In the case of smell, for instance, we reach a place where that particular smell is most intense and striking, where it most nearly monopolizes the 'field of smell' by excluding other competing smells from consciousness, and where it is most differentiated from other smells.

Now it turns out that the *same* region R is the centre of all four spheres of influence, visual, auditory, olfactory and thermal. Moreover, it is only in this region that the thing can be 'touched'. That is, tactual data coincident with the visual ones occur only when my somatic sense-data are spatially continuous with some part of this region. In particular what we may call the *obstacular* character of the thing is seated in this region. This character has two elements, corresponding to the two elements in our experience of our own movement, the visual and the kinaesthetic. My point of view can be moved up to the boundaries of the region, but not through it. And the region is also what Dr. Broad calls a 'region of discontinuity' in my kinaesthetic experience.[8] If that experience is to go on, it must undergo a more or less abrupt change at that place.

[8] *Scientific Thought*, p. 342.

Thus even if we are obliged to say that the differential condition A is in a way everywhere, we can still maintain that it has a peculiarly intimate relation with the region R. Even if it is everywhere, it is, so to speak, more at R than anywhere else. And if 'the place where A is' be taken to mean 'the place that belongs to A *as opposed to other things*', which is certainly a convenient usage, we might even say that R is *the* place of it; for the rest of its sphere of influence is shared with other things.

Further, whenever I am sensing at all, various differential conditions (usually a considerable number) are, as it were, contributing something to my *totum datum* at that moment. But the amount which any one of them contributes varies very greatly with my position. Suppose there is a field of view containing three sense-data, *a, b, c*. Let A be the differential condition of *a*. We then find that as we move our point of view towards the place where *a* is located, A's contribution steadily increases.

This increase is of three kinds: First, A contributes a larger and larger *proportion* of the total field of view and of any other concomitant sense-field that there may be; eventually perhaps the whole. Secondly, the *intensity* of its effect increases steadily; the colour grows more and more bright, and its strikingness (what Hume called its 'force and liveliness') grows greater. Thirdly, the amount of *characteristic or individuating detail* in the effect increases. Perhaps this last point needs some elucidation. Let us take the case of sight. Seen from a great distance, anything has much the same colour as anything else, a bluish purple; and within each thing the colour is pretty uniform: tree, field, or wood is just a homogeneous purplish patch. But as one comes nearer, colour differences 'come out', differences between thing and thing, and internal differences within each thing. Correspondingly differences of shape come out too, for visible shape is nothing but the boundary between two differently coloured expanses.

At last I come to a place where A's contribution reaches its maximum in these three respects. Let us call this place $p1$.

I then repeat the process from another direction. Again I can find a place where the contribution reaches a maximum: let us call it $p2$. I then do the same thing from as many other directions as possible, always operating with sense-data 'of' this object. In this way we can fix a set of places, $p1$, $p2$, $p3$ . . . each of them being a place of maximum contribution; joining these together, I find they outline a certain solid region R. This region is the *central region* of A's sphere of influence, so far as its visual effects are concerned.

Nor is it only visual experience which would lead us to that conclusion. It is true that the qualities which characterize smells and sounds are not located on surfaces, as colour is. They seem rather to permeate a volume, in the way that heat and cold do. But even if they are entirely non-spatial (as some authorities hold), this will make no difference. For sight shows us that events in non-somatic regions, e.g. the interposition of a door or other obstacle, make a difference to sounds and smells just as they do to visual data.[9] (The same applies to thermal data; but they are in any case extended in their own right.)

Clearly the method will also apply to what we may call '*horizontal*' causality as well as to the 'vertical' sort which we have been considering: i.e. to the effect of Non-sensible things on each other as well as to their production of sense-data for us to sense. For instance, there are regions occupied by gravitational and magnetic 'fields' resembling the sensational 'spheres of influence' which we have discovered.[10] We observe that any object introduced into such a region suffers a certain kind of change, say is deflected from its path; and this deflective effect is greater the nearer the object is to a certain central region, and

[9] It must also be remembered that a sound or smell is in itself incomplete, and must be taken along with the somatic sense-data with which variation it varies, and these are always extended. On the other hand, these extended elements in the total effect will be assigned to the Standing Condition. Thus so far there would be no means of localizing the Differential Condition.

[10] Cf. Mr. Russell's account of 'non-psychical analogues of perception' in his *Outline of Philosophy*.

there it reaches its maximum. There are also fields in regard to physical temperature,[11] and these, too, are spread out round a central region of maximum intensity. The wax, for instance, is observed to melt more and more quickly as it is moved towards this central region; and the nearer our piece of bread is to this region, the sooner it is toasted.

Moreover, we find that fields of several kinds have the *same* central region. And most important of all, the region which is central for horizontal causality is also central for vertical causality. Thus the source of the physical effects is the same as the source of the sense-data.

We must, however, remember that this application to horizontal causality is secondary and derivative. For before we can talk about physical fields at all, we must first have established the existence and situation of certain material things: not indeed of the things which are the centres of these fields, but of those which are affected by them, e.g. planets or pieces of wax, for fields are definable only in terms of the behaviour of the affected objects.

The Method of Indispensables

We need not say much about this. In several ways it resembles the Method of Sources. It, too, assumes that a particular thing consists of a particular set of causal properties located in a certain place. But its primary concern is with horizontal causality, not with vertical.

We get our knowledge of horizontal causality by observing that there are certain non-somato-centric[12] correlations between one sense-given change and another, e.g. between a change in one part of the visual field and a change in another part. Now if we could discover what

---

[11] We may define this for our purposes as the power of causing mercury to rise in a thermometer.

[12] Likewise non-psycho-centric. But we may leave out this complication.

is indispensable to the occurrence of such a sense-given change, we should have discovered at least a part of its cause. Further, if we could locate this indispensable, we should have discovered the shape and the position of something which is unaffected by our presence or absence, something which is neither *altered* by the Standing Condition of our sense-experience, nor *contains* it as a part; for since the correlation is non-somato-centric, what was indispensable when we were looking will remain indispensable when we are not.

Now it is quite easy to see that certain sense-given changes are *not* indispensable to the occurrence of a certain observed effect. In the case of the melting wax we can eliminate everything except (say) the stove. Moreover, most of the sense-data belonging to the stove itself can be eliminated. For instance, we see a mirror image 'of' the stove in a looking-glass, or in the polished surface of our shoe. These are not indispensable. For if the mirror is broken, and the shoe taken off, the effect still occurs exactly as before. A mirror image never *does* anything. And the distant views of the fire can also be eliminated. For if we cut them off by means of a screen put in front, we still find the effect going on when we look round the screen. Nor does the magnification of the sense-datum by means of an intervening lens increase the effect; displacement by means of an intervening prism does not reduce it. Further, certain changes in the near views, which *do* alter the effect (e.g. a slight movement of the damper), 'are not visible from a distance at all', i.e. there is no corresponding change in the distant views.

Such arguments show clearly that if any visual sense-data are indispensable it can only be those which are sensed from a minimum distance, i.e. those situated on the surface of the 'central' region, as the Method of Sources called it. And tactual sense-data also, which occur only on this surface, have the same claim to be indispensable.

But the truth is that none of our sense-data are really indispensable at all to the occurrence of the effect, not even these. For as we showed earlier in this chapter, we constantly observe effects without observing any cause for them at all; indeed, this argument from sensed effects to unsensed causes was our main ground for believing in the existence of things other than minds and sense-data. The most we can say is that there are certain privileged sense-data which come nearer to being indispensable than any others. If the material world is composed of sense-data existing in the mind of God, as some philosophers think, then it is these privileged sense-data that it must be composed of,—but they will then be not merely ours, but God's as well, and it will only be their relation to Him that will make them indispensable. Again, if we are Phenomenalists and wish to state all the laws of Nature in terms of actual and possible sense-data, then it is in terms of *these* sense-data that we must state them.

But though not even these privileged ones among our sense-data are indispensable for the occurrence of the effect, they are indispensable for something else, namely, for the prediction of it. If we wish to predict the effect, it is to tactual sense-data and to the visual sense-data of the central region, i.e. to those which are largest, most intense and display the maximum of individual detail, that we must turn. If we rely on distant or dim views, still more if we rely on sounds and smells, we shall go wrong.

Now there seems to be only one way of explaining this fact. It is true of course that we are acquainted only with the sense-data, and that these are always *inefficacious;* they are but collateral effects and all causes, vertical and horizontal, are non-sensible.[18] But it is at any rate clear that in the observation of these (in this sense) 'indispensable' sense-data, we come as near to the observation of 'horizontal' causal properties as it is possible for us to come. Otherwise, why should they be indispensable for predic-

---

[18] Cannot a sound, i.e. an auditory sense-datum, cause me to jump out of the way? But really it is the sensing which *causes* the jump. The sensing, it is true, would not have existed unless there had been a sense-datum for it to be 'directed upon': but this relation again is not a causal one.

tion? But we already know by the Method of Correspondence that there is some sort of detailed correlation between the characteristics of sense-data and the characteristics of the Non-sensible. It is therefore reasonable to conclude that these indispensable sense-data are correlated with horizontal causal properties in a more simple and direct way than other sense-data, or if we may say so, are a more direct 'expression of' their nature. (Of course all sense-data, however odd and however far from being 'indispensable' in our sense, are directly correlated with vertical causal properties, except in total hallucination. Indeed, this is an analytic proposition.)

This enables us to localize the horizontal causal properties at least approximately. We know already that the Non-sensible is spatially ordered. Therefore the causal properties which distinguish one portion of the Non-sensible from another, and so make its spatial order possible by individuating its parts, must pervade regions of space. But if so, the regions they pervade will be at least very similar to the regions occupied by the sets of indispensable sense-data, and will be related in very much the same way as these sets are related to one another.

The Method of Hypothesis

This is more modest than the others. It does not profess to argue directly from the characteristics and correlations of sense-data to the existence of a physical world having such and such particular constituents. It merely asks us to *assume* the existence of this world. And it claims that if we do, we can give a detailed explanation of our sense-data, of their existence and of the particular natures which they are observed to have: and that no other assumption that we can think of will enable us to do so.

This Method is open to serious objections. In the first place how do we come to think of this hypothesis? Do we just invent it out of the blue? And if we do, how have we been clever enough to think of just this hypothesis, with just these particular details (such complex detail too), instead of the thousand and one others which we might have thought of, most of them so much simpler? Of course we do not invent it. We have already on other grounds formed a conception of the physical world, and moreover of this particular physical world containing just this square table in front of me. And we must note that the difficulty arises not once only but many times over. We must modify our assumption to keep pace with what we call scientific discovery, or indeed with the continual growth of our own experience. Something new is always happening, and whether we like it or not we are always coming across fresh sense-data whose determinate characteristics and relations are new to us, though their generic characteristics are not.

How then do we form this conception (or assumption) —just this determinate conception, e.g. of the existence of a square table in this room (not an elephant or a round table)? The answer is clear: Either by processes described in the other Methods, or by some process which falls outside the Causal Theory altogether.

'It does not matter how we form it—instinctively if you like. That is a matter for Psychology. The point is, we have now to justify it: and this we do by finding that it alone enables us to explain our sense-data.'

But this relegation of the process to Psychology seems a little dangerous. How can we tell, until we have investigated the matter, that the process by which the conception is formed is, taken by itself, a completely non-rational one (for that is what is meant by saying 'it does not matter how it originates')? Perhaps the process is one which results not merely in the conceiving of the existence of a square table, but in the knowledge or the rational conviction of its existence. But let us leave this point for the moment, and ask how is the justification supposed to be done. Why, for instance, is this hypothesis better than Berkeley's?

The answer must of course consist in expounding just those detailed characteristics of the *explicandum* which can be accounted for on this hypothesis but not on the other. For instance, we see a certain set of coloured surfaces having various sizes and various shapes, some trapeziform, some lozenge-shaped, some square. We are told that their existence is explained by the hypothesis that there is a square-topped table which influences our sense-organs by means of rays emanating from it in all directions. But why is this a better explanation than Berkeley's? Why should the cause of the sense-data be in space at all? We can only answer by appealing to the Method of Correspondence. And granting that it is in space, why have we to assume that the most important part of it (the differential condition) is a *square* object? Why just this shape in particular out of all the shapes it might have; what in detail are the facts which can be explained by the assumption of a square object, but cannot be explained by the assumption of a round or triangular one? Just the ones on which the Method of Discounting insists: if we consider the set of sense-data, we find that a square is the common theme upon which the rest of the sensed shapes are variations. And again, they are the ones on which the Method of Sources and the Method of Indispensables insist: that these sense-data have a region of maximum intensity which is their source, which region has a square surface, and that it is the square shape and no other which we must take account of if we are predicting future sense-data in this neighbourhood, e.g. those which would occur if we took a photograph and looked at the resulting negative, or if we moved the teapot so many inches in a certain direction.

Thus as soon as we press for details it becomes obvious that the Method of Hypothesis merely repeats the other four. And the truth is, it is *not* really a hypothetical method; its so-called hypothesis is not really an assumption about whose truth we are initially open-minded, and which we invent simply with a view to explain certain puzzling facts. And the so-called justification of the hypothesis does not consist (as it should) in showing that from the assumption certain conclusions follow which are identical with the observed facts; what we really do is to argue the other way

about—from the observed facts, the characteristics and correlations of our sense-data, and the so-called assumption is
our conclusion, not our premise. Thus the attractive modesty of the Method of Hypothesis is a false modesty, a
fallacious cloak for mere plagiarism, and plagiarism at the
expense of arguments which are not hypothetical at all; the
whole method is nothing but a mystification, which reverses
the real order of our thought.

This concludes our exposition of the Causal Theory. Its
basis is clearly the fragmentariness and disconnectedness of
sense-experience; which gives occasion to the argument
from sensed effects to non-sensible causes. The Method of
Correspondence is the next step, and the other three methods are only ways of making determinate the conclusions
of this first one. We must now turn to criticism. Has the
theory succeeded in establishing its main contention that
our consciousness of material objects is inferential, and consists in arguing from sense-data to their causes?

Obviously it cannot have proved that this is our *only* way
of being conscious of material objects. The most it can
show is that it is *a* way. But we shall find that the theory
has not really established even this conclusion, that its arguments are fallacious, and that the conclusion itself is
false.

Let us begin with the Method of Correspondence, since
this is the foundation of the others. Let us grant that every
sense-datum has a cause, and that for every difference in
sense-data there must be some corresponding difference in
the Non-sensible upon which they depend. Granting this,
how much does the Method really establish?

It proves that in the Non-sensible there must be an ordered plurality of some sort; and the fact that some sense-
data are independent of others in their changes proves that
there must be some sort of independence as between the
items of this plurality. But what sort of plurality? Not necessarily, for all this Method can tell us, a plurality of mutually independent *individuals* or *things*. They might be a
number of *characteristics* of the same thing, and yet display

sufficient independence to account for the observed facts: as a man's taste in music may change without any change in his Liberalism or his liking for pork. And after all, there is no reason to think that sense-data reveal the *whole* nature of the Non-sensible. Perhaps they are correlated with only a tiny part of its total being. And if we knew more, the unity of it might seem much more striking than its diversity.

Nor does the appeal to the *spatial* characteristics of visual, tactual, and kinaesthetic data really prove that the plurality in the Non-sensible is likewise of a spatial sort. Let us take, for instance, the fact stressed in the Method of Discounting that our visual sense-data go together in sets, such that within each set there is a common theme which is variously distorted in the shapes of the several members. We can easily imagine how this could come about even if the cause or causes of these sense-data were not in space at all. Thus if I am not good at drawing and I make a number of attempts to draw a circle freehand on the blackboard, we find that none of the shapes produced is actually a circle; yet a circle may be called the common theme on which they are variations. But it does not follow that my will, which caused my hand to trace out these shapes, was circular; or that it was divided into two parts, a circular one and another which causes the distortions. What is responsible for the common theme is the *thought* of a circle, and this is not itself circular, or spatial at all. 'But is there not a visual image which is circular?' The answer is, that if I am a bad visualizer this image is every bit as inadequate as any of the shapes which I draw on the board. It is not the common theme, but one of the variations; indeed it is a whole host of them in itself, for it 'flickers' from moment to moment, changing its shape and size. Moreover, be the image as good as it will, not it but the imaging of it, the forming it and holding it before the mind, is what matters, if images come into the question at all; and the imaging is a mental act, and has no shape.

Such considerations suggest that the Causal Theory cannot even refute Berkeley. Our sense-data, including the extended ones, might all be directly produced by a spirit, provided that spirit *conceives of* a system of spatially ordered three-dimensional figures.[14] It is not necessary that the system of three-dimensional figures should actually exist: that there should *be* a world of spatially ordered solid entities. The Method of Discounting will only tell us the detail of what God thinks, and will not prove the reality of anything besides the propositions or conceptions which are before his mind.

The requirement of the *Method of Sources* can also be met by Berkeley's theory. According to Berkeley, the Method only reveals the *plan of action* which God ordinarily[15] adopts in producing our sense-data. The thought of the 'central region' is what guides God in producing sense-data. His plan is, that when He thinks of my point of view as gradually approaching nearer to a certain region R, He provides me with sense-data of gradually increasing intensity, reaching a maximum when He thinks of me as right up against it. And when He thinks of the interposition of screens or prisms between it and my point of view, He alters my sense-data, or cuts them off altogether, as the case may be. But when I by an act of will cause Him to change His thought, so that He now thinks of my point of view as situated between the screen and R, He restores the sense-data again.

Lastly, Berkeley would say that the *Method of Indispensables* only shows what thoughts God is thinking 'when there's no one about in the Quad'. The argument from the fragmentariness of sense-data to the existence of unsensed causes[16] would show that He *is* then thinking, and thinking of changes (though not changing Himself). The Method of Indispensables would tell us *what* changes (approximately) He is thinking of, and in connexion with what regions of Space He thinks of them. The changes, I sup-

[14] Cf. Mr. H. W. B. Joseph's *A Comparison of Kant's Idealism with that of Berkeley.*

[15] Not always. For God might work a miracle. And obviously the Method of Sources cannot disprove this possibility.

[16] Causes: but despite their plurality we have seen that they might be united in a single subject.

pose, are changes in the detail of His plan of action, changes in the sense-data which He *would* produce, if He had occasion to think of any one as being in the Quad.

If all this be so, the Non-sensible need be no more spatial and no more divided into a number of distinct individuals than the plot of a cinematograph play. The pictures we see on the screen are extended; but their ultimate or original cause is an act of imagination, which is not. Again the characters which we see during any one part of the performance seem to change independently of one another: the hero, the villain, the sheriff go their several ways, and each has his own history. But for all that, the act of imagination which produced the plot with all that is in it, is single.[17]

Nor is Berkeley's the only alternative which is consistent with the facts. A monadistic theory would also fit them. The monads would be ordered in an 'intelligible' non-spatial order. What sort of order? They might be ordered by means of the resemblances and differences between the sense-fields sensed by one monad and the sense-fields sensed by another. If we compared the sense-experiences of a number of different monads, and considered together all the sense-data contained in all of them, we should find that this whole aggregate of sense-data could be sorted out again into sets. Each set will be what we commonly call a set of views of the same physical object; only there will really be no object—there will be nothing but the set of views. And these sets will be just like the ones to which we apply the three Methods of Discounting, of Sources, and of Indispensables. Those monads, then, whose data belong to the same set, will be *more directly* related than those whose data belong to different ones. But these latter monads may be *indirectly* related. For instance, M2 may own sense-data which fall into the same set as M1's, and others which fall into the same set as M3's. Thus M2 and M3 will be

---

[17] We may add that even the detail of the three methods can all be copied on the screen. The sense-data can grow larger and more intense; the other side of the object can be displayed; perspectival and other distortions can occur, and so on.

indirectly related, and M2 being directly related to both may be said to be (in a non-spatial sense) 'between' them.

This really means that although (according to the theory) there really is no world of material objects—though there is not even a single space, but a plurality of spatial sense-fields, standing in no spatial relations to each other[18] —yet sense-data are ordered exactly as if there were: and by this means the several spirits which sense them are ordered too. It is true that to *discover* the order, it is necessary to *conceive* of this world of material objects, and of a single space; or at least of a unitary system of spatially related solid entities, changing in various correlated ways. The Methods still apply; and the single theme of the Method of Discounting, the central region of the Method of Sources, and the region picked out by the indispensable sense-data, are all solids of this kind. It is true also that if there is a *Monas Monadum* who creates this system of monads and by an act of harmonizing arranges the incredibly complicated correlations between the sense-data of each and the sense-data of all the rest, it too, like Berkeley's God, will have to conceive of this system of solids. But it does not follow, any more than it does on Berkeley's theory, that the system of solids *exists*. It is enough if they are conceived of.

The Causal Theory, then, will not really prove the existence of a material world, but at most, only the existence of a Non-sensible something having within it a plurality of factors.[19] For all that it can show this something may be spiritual, and it need not even possess parts. The many 'factors' might simply be many characteristics of one subject.

But will it really prove even as much as this? We shall now try to suggest that it cannot, and in doing so we shall also suggest that we have a consciousness of the material

---

[18] Just as a scene in one of my dreams stands in no spatial relation to a scene in one of yours, though both scenes are extended.

[19] It is necessary, as we have seen, to use a neutral and non-committal term.

world, but that it is not an *inferential* consciousness—neither a causal inference nor any other sort of inference.

In the first place it is obvious that none of the Methods is applicable to a single sense-datum taken by itself, but only to a *set* of sense-data. What sort of set? Not the sort of set which is *given* when a number of sense-data are presented to the mind at once, e.g. not the sort which constitutes a single field of view. A single sense-field is of no more use than a single sense-datum. How then do we come to consciousness of the required sort of set, if it is never given in sense? How, for instance, do we come to be aware of that set from which, in the Method of Discounting, the common theme is extracted? Obviously the members of it have to be picked out from a number of different sense-fields and then compared together, by what Kant calls an act of synthesis. But what kind of relation unites the set into one whole? Upon what principle, or with what question in mind, does the synthesis proceed? As we shall see later, in Chapter VIII, the guiding principle is just the thought that there is *some one solid* to which all the members of the set are related, some as constituents of it and some as distortions; the question in our mind is, what particular kind of solid is it in this particular case? Indeed, without this guiding principle not only the synthesis but the preceding picking-out of the *syntheta* from the irrelevant contexts in which they were presented would never have occurred. From the first, we are on the look out for sets of this sort: we expect to find that our sense-data 'adumbrate' solids in this way.

It follows that the Common Theme (and equally the Central Region for which the Method of Sources seeks) is not discovered by reflection on the completed set. At the beginning of the synthesis, it is already present to the mind, though in a very indeterminate form: in the process of synthesizing we determine it more and more closely; and the completion of the synthesis, whereby the whole set of data stands before the mind at once, necessarily includes the complete determination of the common theme, by their relation to which alone (in the way of being distortions or portions of it) the members are held together. Thus the Method of Discounting is simply discovering what we know already, and what we *must* know, if the set of data without which the Method cannot begin is to be present to our consciousness: either that, or it is simply another name for the process of synthesis itself—but a very perverse and misleading name.

But this is not all that we need, if we are to be conscious of those sets of sense-data upon which the Methods operate. We need the idea not merely of a solid entity, but of *Space:* the thought that every solid entity is enclosed within a wider region or 'field', in which a number of solid entities can stand related by the same sort of relations as subsist between the parts of any one of them; and that given any two solid entities, there is always a region enclosing both. If we were without this thought, how should we avoid collecting into the same set sense-data which belong to one solid and sense-data which belong to another, in cases where these solids were exactly alike in shape and size? How, for instance, can we distinguish the sense-data belonging to a lump of sugar in this room, from those belonging to a lump of sugar in that one? We can do it only because the idea of Space enables us to synthesize not merely sense-data but their *contexts,* and so to apprehend a set whose members are whole sense-fields. Thus here are two white sense-data which in themselves are so shaped that they could both be distortions of the same solid. But their contexts will not fit together as distortions of one single *set* of solids. The context of A is a distortion of one set of solids; the context of B of a different set. A then belongs to one thing, and B to another. And although these two solids with their solid neighbours turn out eventually to be united in a wider system of solids embracing both, the twoness remains.

In the Method of Sources this need for a previous *spatial synthesis* is particularly obvious. The Method requires that the observer be conscious of *moving* in a certain direction, or indeed of moving successively in a number of directions all converging on the same place. But how is he to be aware that he is moving, or if you will, that his point of view is moving?

The subject's consciousness of his own identity will not tell him this. An identical ego might conceivably sense a series of extended sense-fields standing in no spatial relation to one another—presumably this does happen in dreams and visions—and, if so, there would be no motion of himself to be aware of. (There would indeed be a point of view within or attached to each sense-field and it would be spatially related to data in its own field. But *between* these points of view there would be no spatial relations. They would just be different. We could not then speak of the *movement* of the subject's point of view, or of his movement from one point of view to another.)

Obviously the synthesis or synthetic comparison of sense-fields is the only thing that will meet the case. To be aware of my own movement, I must refer my different and successive visual data to the *same* set of spatially related solid entities. It is by reference to these solids, and to the varying distance between their surfaces and my point of view, that I fix my position at successive instants, and so know that I am moving, and in what direction. This act of *identification,* then, which is nothing but the spatial synthesis described above, is absolutely essential to the application of the Method of Sources: without this act I could never know towards what region I was moving, and even that I was moving at all. Thus in order to discover by that Method where the object A is, we must already know where objects B, C and D are, which constitute our constant 'frame of reference' for determining our own motion. This does not mean that the Method is useless, but it does mean that it is secondary; it is not our means of discovering the position and shape of *every* material object (as it professes) but only of an odd one here and there. Thus, for instance, we use it to fix the position of an invisible object by means of sound, smell, or heat; we sometimes use it to unmask a mirage; and in that modification of it which applies to horizontal causality, we use it (eked out with much 'interpolation' and analogical argument) to fix the position of a heavenly body by means of the changes which it causes in a photographic plate. Conceivably the Method of Discounting may also have this secondary and occasional use, though I have not been able to think of any instances.[20]

However this may be, so far as these two Methods profess to be *the* source of our consciousness of a determinately shaped and situated system of spatially related solid objects, they are obviously guilty of a vicious circle, and must be abandoned.

We must say the same of that consciousness of correlated sense-given changes by which causal properties are detected, and which specially concerns the Method of Indispensables. Obviously a sense-given change is some sort of *series* of sense-data. What sort of series is it, and how do we come to consciousness of it? It is not any series we please, even though temporally continuous, which will give us consciousness of causal properties in the physical world. For instance, I see a waving flag, then a tree, then a thrush in flight. Here is a series of sense-data, and there may be no temporal interval between them; but nobody would call the series a *change*. Clearly if the series is to be of the right kind, it must have some sort of *spatial* unity. Its members must all be referable as distortions or portions to some single solid entity, which retains its identity, while altering its shape or position (or qualities).[21] So much for the one sense-given change. And the same account must be given of the other, which is observed to be correlated with it. Now are not these two correlatedly-changing solid entities very much like material objects? Are they not the very objects, the position and shape of which the Method of In-

[20] Presumably because it adds so little to the results of the Spatial Synthesis, merely doing over again backwards what it has done already. And the same applies to the Method of Indispensables. But the Method of Sources, though it presupposes Spatial Synthesis, does add something. It informs us that the solid entity is a region of *maximum intensity,* and of this Spatial Synthesis, as such, says nothing.

[21] On 'standard' qualities, e.g. standard colours and scents, see Chapter VIII, pp. 209–215 [of *Perception*]. To these the qualities of sense-data are referred, as deviations from them, just as the various shapes are referred to the single solid. But we need not introduce this complication here. Obviously it does not help the three Methods.

dispensables professes to discover? Before we can begin applying it, we must already possess the knowledge which it professes to give us.

No one who studies the Causal Theory, certainly no plain man who studies it, can fail to feel that there is a certain fundamental artificiality and, as it were, incredibility about its whole procedure—and not merely about the details but about the very idea of such a theory. Why, we ask, does it invent cumbersome Methods (whether these or others) to prove something that every one has always been convinced of? For surely every one is convinced not only that there are material objects, but what shapes, sizes and positions they have. We feel, in fact, that there is no *need* for a Causal Theory; that it is all the time preaching to the converted —and as it turns out, preaching in no very convincing way. Is there anything to be said for this instinctive dissatisfaction?

I think we must admit that, historically speaking, none of us reaches the belief[22] in matter by inference, but that we all had it from the beginning; historically we all begin by *taking for granted* that visual and tactual sense-data are somehow constituents of the surfaces of material things. The Causal Theory cannot really sustain the contention that we start in infancy with a causal argument in accordance with the Four Methods; and that the argument becomes, as it were, telescoped through habit, until by the time we reach years of discretion we jump straight from the premise (the existence of such and such sense-data) to the conclusion (the existence of such and such an object). Surely as a matter of fact it is just the other way about. The jump comes first—imagine infants or cats solemnly applying the Four Methods!—and it is the causal arguments which are the product of reflection, sophistication, and sceptical disillusionment. Indeed, it *must* be the other way about. For the arguments will only prove at most the existence of *some* Non-sensible something having an ordered

[22] Perhaps we should say *not doubting* rather than *believing*.

plurality of factors: they will not prove the existence of a material world. But that we at least believe in (or rather perhaps undoubtingly accept) the existence of a material world is perfectly certain. And if we cannot reach that state of mind by inference from sense-data, and yet our sensings of sense-data occasion it (as they obviously do), we must have reached it by a jump. The state of mind may be rational or irrational; that is a point to be discussed later. But at any rate we are in it.

The Causal Theory holds that we are not entitled to consider that visual and tactual sense-data are constituents of the surfaces of material objects until we have proved that they are. But, whether we are entitled to or not, what we actually do is just the opposite: we consider them to be so until it is proved that they are not. And indeed certain privileged sense-data, as was incidentally brought out in our exposition of the three last Methods, do have a considerable claim if not to *be* constituents of the surfaces of objects, at least to be approximately coincident with them. Further, there are many others which differ so little from these privileged ones that in our ordinary practical frame of mind we easily fail to notice the difference. True, certain glaring exceptions obtrude themselves, mirror-images for instance. All men, and probably many animals, are satisfied that these are *not* constituents of the surfaces of objects. But how do they arrive at this opinion? Clearly by an argument: a material object cannot be in two places at once, but it would have to be if this were part of its surface. Thus, historically speaking, the Causal Theory has got things just the wrong way round. Historically, it is not the existence of material objects, but the existence of illusions, that we first demand proof of. (Perhaps the belief in matter could only be justified by inference; if so, it looks as if it could not be justified at all. But we are not at present discussing its justification.) Further, even when we have thus inferred that some sense-data cannot be parts of the surfaces of objects, it is a long time before we inquire into their causes. Certainly before we do we have long been familiar with all sorts of 'horizontal' causation: whereas in the Causal

Theory we begin with the discovery of 'vertical' causation, and horizontal causation is only revealed later, by the application of the Methods.

Again, historically speaking, the argument from the fragmentariness of sense-data to the existence of unsensed causes is not one that any one actually starts with. In our ordinary everyday consciousness we never doubt for a moment that the table is there when we are not looking at it, and we should never think of asking for an argument to prove this. It is the other way about. Argument is required to convince us that sense-data do *not* exist in the absence of sentients: we require none to convince us that material objects do. The fragmentary and interrupted existence of sense-data is, historically speaking, no original premise, but the conclusion of a long and elaborate argument.[23] And it is a conclusion one of whose premises, namely, that certain sense-data are *not* parts of the surfaces of the material things which they belong to, is only reached as a sort of by-product of the synthetic process whereby we assure ourselves that there *are* certain material things which *do* have surfaces of such and such sorts. These sense-data then, not being constituents of material things, need not share in that persistence and independence of sentience which are characteristic of matter. Next, considerations of continuity lead us to extend this conclusion to *all* sense-data, including normal ones. But even then, though non-material, they might still persist 'on their own'. What eventually convinces us that they do not is, I suppose, their somato-centricity. But this we notice last of all, long after we have assured ourselves of the existence of all sorts of material objects, including our own body.

Thus one of the starting-points of the Causal Theory, namely, the fragmentary and interrupted existence of sense-data, is not *historically* original at all. What of the others, that every event has a cause, and that every sense-datum is an event?

Let us first consider the conception of cause. It is surely

[23] That our *sensings* are fragmentary and intermittent is of course obvious from the first.

obvious that, historically speaking, we only reach this conception by reflecting upon the nature of certain causative substances or *things,* of whose existence, moreover, we are *already* convinced before the reflection begins. And those things are material things, including our own animate organism. We do not first have the conception of cause, and then reach the conception of matter later. On the contrary, we begin with the conception of matter, and reach the conception of cause (not without difficulty) by analysing this.

I do not indeed wish to deny that there are in some good sense 'innate ideas', that is, a power to conceive certain concepts which is not dependent upon acquaintance with instances of them, as the power to conceive redness is dependent upon acquaintance with red sense-data. On the contrary, I wish to assert that there are some innate ideas. Nor do I wish to deny, on the contrary I wish to assert, that these 'ideas' are *a priori* as well as innate, i.e. that the power to conceive these concepts is a necessary condition of the possibility of certain kinds of experience (say for making perceptual consciousness possible as distinct from mere acquaintance with sense-data). I only wish to maintain (1) that what is innate and what is *a priori* must be the whole complex notion of material thinghood, in which causality is a factor, not just the notion of cause alone; (2) that we only come to clear consciousness of such concepts as these when we have already applied them many times to acquire consciousness of entities exemplifying them: in this case, to acquire consciousness of material things.

So much for the conception of cause. But what of the proposition that every event has a cause? Is this proposition, we may ask, even true? Many people have held that some events have no causes, namely, human volitions. The most that could be maintained is that every event *in the material world* has a cause; and even this is only true of 'macroscopic' events, if the Principle of Indeterminacy be correct, not of 'microscopic' ones.

Let us now consider the application of the proposition to sense-data. Obviously if it is not applicable to them the whole Causal Theory collapses. But now in the only sense in which it could conceivably be certain that every event has a cause, the proposition is useless to the Causal Theory. For if we asserted in our minor premise that sense-data are events, we should have to mean 'are events *in the material world*'; and if so, the existence of the material world is not proved, but presupposed. But if in our major premise 'Every event has a cause' we take the term 'event' in its wider sense, and so mean only 'Everything which has a beginning has a cause', then it does not seem at all clear that the proposition is true.[24] At any rate we are much *more* sure of the existence of the material world than we are of the truth of this proposition.

[24] Cf. Kant's *Third and Fourth Antinomies.*

THE CAUSAL THEORY OF PERCEPTION

H. P. Grice

I

The Causal Theory of Perception (CTP) has for some time received comparatively little attention, mainly, I suspect, because it has been generally assumed that the theory either asserts or involves as a consequence the proposition that material objects are unobservable, and that the unacceptability of this proposition is sufficient to dispose of the theory. I am inclined to regard this attitude to the CTP as unfair or at least unduly unsympathetic and I shall attempt to outline a thesis which might not improperly be considered to be a version of the CTP, and which is, if not true, at least not too obviously false.

What is to count as holding a causal theory of perception? (1) I shall take it as being insufficient merely to believe that the perception of a material object is always to be causally explained by reference to conditions the specification of at least one of which involves a mention of the object perceived; that, for example, the perception is the terminus of a causal sequence involving at an earlier stage some event or process in the history of the perceived object. Such a belief does not seem to be philosophical in character; its object has the appearance of being a very general contingent proposition; though it is worth remarking that if the version of the CTP with which I shall be primarily concerned is correct, it (or something like it) will turn out to be a necessary rather than a contingent truth. (2) It may be held that the elucidation of the notion of perceiving a material object will include some reference to the rôle of the material object perceived in the causal ancestry of the perception (or of the sense-impression or sense-datum involved in the perception). This contention is central to what I regard as a standard version of the CTP. (3) It might be held that it is the task of the philosopher of perception not to elucidate or characterize the ordinary notion of perceiving a material object, but to provide a rational reconstruction of it, to replace it by some concept more appropriate to an ideal or scientific language: it might further be suggested that such a redefinition might be formulated in terms of the effect of the presence of an object upon the observer's sense-organ and nervous system or upon his behaviour or "behaviour-tendencies" or in terms of both of these effects. A view of this kind may perhaps deserve to be called a causal theory of perception; but I shall not be concerned with theories on these lines. (4) I shall distinguish from the adoption of a CTP the attempt to provide for a wider or narrower range of propositions ascribing properties to material objects a certain sort of causal analysis: the kind of analysis which I have in mind is that which, on *one* possible interpretation, Locke could be taken as suggesting for ascriptions of, for example, colour and temperature; he might be understood to be holding that such propositions assert that an object would, in certain standard conditions, cause an observer to have certain sorts of ideas or sense-impressions.

In Professor Price's *Perception*,[1] there appears a preliminary formulation of the CTP which would bring it under the second of the headings distinguished in the previous paragraph. The CTP is specified as maintaining (1) that in the case of all sense-data (not merely visual and tactual) "belonging to" simply means *being caused by*, so that '*M* is present to my senses' will be equivalent to '*M* causes a sense-datum with which I am acquainted'; (2) that perceptual consciousness is fundamentally an inference from effect to cause. Since it is, I think, fair to say[2] that the ex-

[1] P. 66 [p. 394, this volume. Ed.].
[2] *Cf. ibid.*, pp. 21-25.

pression "present to my senses" was introduced by Price as a special term to distinguish one of the possible senses of the verb "perceive", the first clause of the quotation above may be taken as propounding the thesis that "I am perceiving *M*" (in one sense of that expression) is to be regarded as equivalent to "I am having (or sensing) a sense-datum which is caused by *M*." (The second clause I shall for the time being ignore.) I shall proceed to consider at some length the feature which this version of the CTP shares with other non-causal theories of perception, namely, the claim that perceiving a material object involves having or sensing a sense-datum; for unless this claim can be made out the special features of the CTP become otiose.

II

The primary difficulty facing the contention that perceiving involves having or sensing a sense-datum is that of giving a satisfactory explanation of the meaning of the technical term 'sense-datum'. One familiar method of attempting this task is that of trying to prove, by means of some form of the Argument from Illusion, the existence of objects of a special sort for which the term 'sense-datum' is offered as a class-name. Another method (that adopted in a famous passage by Moore) is that of giving directions which are designed to enable one to pick out items of the kind to which the term 'sense-datum' is to be applied. The general character of the objections to each of these procedures is also familiar, and I shall, for present purposes, assume that neither procedure is satisfactory.

Various philosophers have suggested that though attempts to indicate, or demonstrate the existence of, special objects to be called sense-data have all failed, nevertheless the expression 'sense-datum' can (and should) be introduced as a technical term; its use would be explicitly defined by reference to such supposedly standard locutions as "So-and-so looks ϕ (*e.g.*, blue) to me", "It looks (feels) to me as if there were a ϕ so-and-so", "I seem to see something ϕ" and so on. Now as the objection to such proposals which I have in mind is one which might be described as an objection in principle, it is not to my present purpose to consider how in detail such an explicit definition of the notion of a sense-datum might be formulated. I should, however, remark that this programme may be by no means so easy to carry through as the casual way in which it is sometimes proposed might suggest; various expressions are candidates for the key rôle in this enterprise e.g., "looks" ("feels" etc.), "seems", "appears" and the more or less subtle differences between them would have to be investigated; and furthermore even if one has decided on a preferred candidate, not all of its uses would be suitable; if for example we decide to employ the expressions "looks" etc., are we to accept the legitimacy of the sentence "It looks indigestible to me" as providing us with a sense-datum sentence "I am having an indigestible visual sense-datum"?

A general objection to the suggested procedure might run as follows: When someone makes such a remark as "It looks red to me" a certain implication is carried, an implication which is disjunctive in form. It is implied either that the object referred to is known or believed by the speaker not to *be* red, *or* that it has been denied by someone else to be red, *or* that the speaker is doubtful whether it is red, *or* that someone else has expressed doubt whether it is red, *or* that the situation is such that though no doubt has actually been expressed and no denial has actually been made, some person or other might feel inclined towards denial or doubt if he were to address himself to the question whether the object is actually red. This may not be an absolutely exact or complete characterization of the implication, but it is perhaps good enough to be going on with. Let us refer to the condition which is fulfilled when one or other of the limbs of this disjunction is true as the *D*-or-*D* condition ('doubt or denial' condition). Now we may perhaps agree that there is liable to be something odd or even absurd about employing an

"It looks to me" locution when the appropriate *D*-or-*D* condition is fairly obviously not fulfilled; there would be something at least *prima facie* odd about my saying "That looks red to me" (not as a joke) when I am confronted by a British pillar box in normal daylight at a range of a few feet. At this point my objector advances a twofold thesis (*a*) that it is a feature of the use, perhaps of the meaning, of such locutions as "looks to me" that they should carry the implication that the *D*-or-*D* condition is fulfilled, and that if they were uttered by a speaker who did not suppose this condition was fulfilled he would be guilty of a misuse of the locutions in question (unless of course he were intending to deceive his audience into thinking that the condition was fulfilled), (*b*) that in cases where the *D*-or-*D* condition is unfulfilled the utterance employing the "looks to me" locution, so far from being uninterestingly true, is neither true nor false. Thus armed, my objector now assails the latter-day sense-datum theorist. Our every day life is populated with cases in which the sensible characteristics of the things we encounter are not the subject of any kind of doubt or controversy; consequently there will be countless situations in which the employment of the "looks to me" idiom would be out of order and neither true nor false. But the sense-datum theorist wants his sense-datum statements to be such that some one or more of them is true whenever a perceptual statement is true; for he wants to go on to give a *general* analysis of perceptual statements in terms of the notion of sense-data. But this goal must be unattainable if "looks to me" statements (and so sense-datum statements) can be truly made only in the *less* straightforward perceptual situations; and if the goal is unattainable the CTP collapses.

It is of course possible to take a different view of the linguistic phenomena outlined in my previous paragraph. One may contend that if I were to say "it looks red to me" in a situation in which the *D*-or-*D* condition is not fulfilled, what I say is (subject to certain qualifications) true, not "neuter"; while admitting that though true it might be very misleading and that its truth might be very boring and its misleadingness very important, one might still hold that its *suggestio falsi* is perfectly compatible with its literal truth. Furthermore one might argue that though perhaps someone who, without intent to deceive, employed the "it looks to me" locution when he did not suppose the *D*-or-*D* condition to be fulfilled would be guilty in some sense of a misuse of *language,* he could be said not to be guilty of a misuse of the particular locution in question; for, one might say, the implication of the fulfilment of the *D*-or-*D* condition attaches to such locutions not as a special feature of the meaning or use of these expressions, but in virtue of a general feature or principle of the use of language. The mistake of supposing the implication to constitute a "part of the meaning" of "looks to me" is somewhat similar to, though more insidious than, the mistake which would be made if one supposed that the so-called implication that one believes it to be raining was "a part of the meaning" of the expression "it is raining". The short and literally inaccurate reply to such a supposition might be that the so-called implication attaches because the expression is a propositional one, not because it is the particular propositional expression which it happens to be.

Until fairly recently it seemed to me to be very difficult indeed to find any arguments which seemed at all likely to settle the issue between these two positions. One might, for example, suggest that it is open to the champion of sense-data to lay down that the sense-datum sentence "I have a pink sense-datum" should express truth if and only if the facts are as they would have to be for it to be true, *if it were in order,* to say "Something looks pink to me", even though it may not actually be in order to say this (because the *D*-or-*D* condition is unfulfilled). But this attempt to by-pass the objector's position would be met by the reply that it begs the question; for it assumes that there is some way of specifying the facts in isolation from the implication standardly carried by such a specification; and this is precisely what the objector is denying. As a result of frustrations of this kind, I was led to suspect that neither position should be regarded as right or wrong, but that the linguistic phenomena *could* be looked at in either way, though there might be reasons for preferring to adopt one way of viewing them rather than the other; that there might be no proofs or disproofs, but only inducements. On this assumption I was inclined to rule against my objector, partly because his opponent's position was more in line with the kind of thing I was inclined to say about other linguistic phenomena which are in some degree comparable, but mainly because the objector's short way with sense-data is an even shorter way with scepticism about the material world; and I think a sceptic might complain that though his worries may well prove dissoluble he ought at least to be able to state them; if we do not allow him to state them we cannot remove the real source of his discomfort. However, I am now inclined to think that the issue is a decidable one, and that my objector's position is wrong and that of his opponent right. I shall attempt to develop a single argument (though no doubt there are others) to support this claim, and as a preliminary I shall embark on a discursus about certain aspects of the concept or concepts of implication, using some more or less well-worn examples.

III

(*Implication*)

I shall introduce four different examples and use upon them four different ideas as catalysts. All are cases in which in ordinary parlance, or at least in philosophical parlance, something might be said to be implied as distinct from being stated.

(1) "Smith has left off beating his wife", where what is implied is that Smith has been beating his wife.

(2) "She was poor but she was honest", where what is implied is (very roughly) that there is some contrast be-

tween poverty and honesty, or between her poverty and her honesty.

The first example is a stock case of what is sometimes called "presupposition" and it is often held that here the truth of what is implied is a necessary condition of the original statement's being either true or false. This might be disputed, but it is at least arguable that it is so, and its being arguable might be enough to distinguish this type of case from others. I shall however for convenience assume that the common view mentioned is correct. This consideration clearly distinguishes (1) from (2); even if the implied proposition were false, i.e. if there were no reason in the world to contrast poverty with honesty either in general or in her case, the original statement could still be false; it would be false if for example she were rich and dishonest. One might perhaps be less comfortable about assenting to its truth if the implied contrast did not in fact obtain; but the possibility of falsity is enough for the immediate purpose.

My next experiment on these examples is to ask what it is in each case which could properly be said to be the vehicle of implication (to do the implying). There are at least four candidates, not necessarily mutually exclusive. Supposing someone to have uttered one or other of my sample sentences, we may ask whether the vehicle of implication would be (a) what the speaker said (or asserted), or (b) the speaker ("did he imply that . . . .") or (c) the words the speaker used, or (d) his saying that (or again his saying that in that way); or possibly some plurality of these items. As regards (a) I think (1) and (2) differ; I think it would be correct to say in the case of (1) that what the speaker said (or asserted) implied that Smith had been beating his wife, and incorrect to say in the case of (2) that what he said (or asserted) implied that there was a contrast between *e.g.*, honesty and poverty. A test on which I would rely is the following: if accepting that the implication holds involves one in accepting an hypothetical 'if p then q' where 'p' represents the original statement and 'q' represents what is implied, then what the speaker said (or asserted) is a vehicle of implication, otherwise not. To apply this rule to the given examples, if I accepted the implication alleged to hold in the case of (1), I should feel compelled to accept the hypothetical "If Smith has left off beating his wife, then he has been beating her"; whereas if I accepted the alleged implication in the case of (2), I should not feel compelled to accept the hypothetical "If she was poor but honest, then there is some contrast between poverty and honesty, or between her poverty and her honesty." The other candidates can be dealt with more cursorily; I should be inclined to say with regard to both (1) and (2) that the speaker could be said to have implied whatever it is that is implied; that in the case of (2) it seems fairly clear that the speaker's words could be said to imply a contrast, whereas it is much less clear whether in the case of (1) the speaker's words could be said to imply that Smith had been beating his wife; and that in neither case would it be evidently appropriate to speak of his saying that, or of his saying that in that way, as implying what is implied.

The third idea with which I wish to assail my two examples is really a twin idea, that of the detachability or cancellability of the implication. (These terms will be explained.) Consider example (1): one cannot find a form of words which could be used to state or assert *just* what the sentence "Smith has left off beating his wife" might be used to assert such that when it is used the implication that Smith has been beating his wife is just absent. *Any* way of asserting what is asserted in (1) involves the implication in question. I shall express this fact by saying that in the case of (1) the implication is not *detachable* from what is asserted (or *simpliciter,* is not detachable). Furthermore, one cannot take a form of words for which both what is asserted and what is implied is the same as for (1), and *then* add a further clause withholding commitment from what would otherwise be implied, with the idea of annulling the implication without annulling the assertion. One cannot intelligibly say "Smith has left off beating his wife but I do not mean to imply that he has been beating her." I shall express this fact by saying that in the case of (1) the implication is not *cancellable* (without cancelling the assertion). If we turn to (2) we find, I think, that there is quite a strong case for saying that here the implication *is* detachable. There seems quite a good case for maintaining that if, instead of saying "She is poor but she is honest" I were to say "She is poor and she is honest", I would assert just what I would have asserted if I had used the original sentence; but there would now be no implication of a contrast between *e.g.*, poverty and honesty. But the question whether, in the case of (2), the implication is cancellable, is slightly more complex. There is a sense in which we may say that it is non-cancellable; if someone were to say "She is poor but she is honest, though of course I do not mean to imply that there is any contrast between poverty and honesty", this would seem a puzzling and eccentric thing to have said; but though we should wish to quarrel with the speaker, I do not think we should go so far as to say that his utterance was *unintelligible;* we should suppose that he had adopted a most peculiar way of conveying the news that she was poor *and* honest.

The fourth and last test that I wish to impose on my examples is to ask whether we would be inclined to regard the fact that the appropriate implication is present as being a matter of the meaning of some particular word or phrase occurring in the sentences in question. I am aware that this may not be always a very clear or easy question to answer; nevertheless I will risk the assertion that we would be fairly happy to say that, as regards (2), the fact that the implication obtains is a matter of the meaning of the word 'but'; whereas so far as (1) is concerned we should have at least some inclination to say that the presence of the implication was a matter of the meaning of some of the words in the sentence, but we should be in some difficulty when it came to specifying precisely which this word, or words are, of which this is true.

I may now deal more briefly with my remaining examples.

(3) I am reporting on a pupil at Collections. All I say is "Jones has beautiful handwriting and his English is grammatical." We might perhaps agree that there would here be a strong, even overwhelming, implication that Jones is no good at philosophy. It is plain that there is no case at all for regarding the truth of what is implied here as a pre-condition of the truth or falsity of what I have asserted; a denial of the truth of what is implied would have no bearing at all on whether what I have asserted is true or false. So (3) is much closer to (2) than (1) in this respect. Next, I (the speaker) could certainly be said to have implied that Jones is hopeless (provided that this is what I intended to get across) and my saying that (at any rate my saying *just* that and no more) is also certainly a vehicle of implication. On the other hand my words and what I say (assert) are, I think, not here vehicles of implication. (3) thus differs from both (1) and (2). The implication is cancellable but not detachable; if I add "I do not of course mean to imply that he is no good at philosophy" my whole utterance is intelligible and linguistically impeccable, even though it may be extraordinary tutorial behaviour; and I can no longer be said to have implied that he was no good, even though perhaps that is what my colleagues might conclude to be the case if I had nothing else to say. The implication is not however, detachable; any other way of making, in the same context of utterance, *just* the assertion I have made would involve the same implication. Finally, the fact that the implication holds is not a matter of any particular word or phrase within the sentence which I have uttered; so in this respect (3) is certainly different from (2) and possibly different from (1).

One obvious fact should be mentioned before I pass to the last example. This case of implication is unlike the others in that the utterance of the sentence "Jones has beautiful handwriting etc." does not *standardly* involve the implication here attributed to it; it requires a special context (that it should be uttered at Collections) to *attach* the implication to its utterance.

(4) If someone says "My wife is either in the kitchen or in the bedroom" it would normally be implied that he did not know in *which* of the two rooms she was.

This example might well be held to be very similar to the case under dispute, that of such statements as "This looks red to me", so I must be careful not to prejudge any issues to my objector's disadvantage.

I think, however, that in the case of (4) I can produce a strong argument in favour of holding that the fulfilment of the implication of the speaker's ignorance is not a precaution of the truth or falsity of the disjunctive statement. Suppose (*a*) that the speaker knows that his wife is in the kitchen, (*b*) that the house has only two rooms (and no passages etc.). Even though (*a*) is the case, the speaker can certainly say truly "My wife is in the house"; he is merely not being as informative as he could be if need arose. But the true proposition that his wife is in the house together with the true proposition that the house consists entirely of a kitchen and a bedroom, entail the proposition that his wife is either in the kitchen or in the bedroom. But if to express the proposition *p* in certain circumstances would be to speak truly, and *p*, together with another true proposition, entails *q*, then surely to express *q* in the *same* circumstances must be to speak truly. So I shall take it that the disjunctive statement in (4) does not fail to be true or false if the implied ignorance is in fact not realized. Secondly, I think it is fairly clear that in this case, as in the case of (3), we could say that the *speaker* had implied that he did not know, and also that *his saying that* (or his saying that rather than something else, *viz.*, in which room she was) implied that he did not know. Thirdly, the implication is in a sense non-detachable, in that if *in a given context* the utterance of the disjunctive sentence would involve the implication that the speaker did not know in which room his wife was, this implication would also be involved in the utterance of any other form of words which would make the same as-

sertion (*e.g.,* "The alternatives are (1) . . . . (2) . . . ."
or "One of the following things is the case: (*a*) . . . .
(*b*) . . . ."). In *another* possible sense, however, the implication could perhaps be said to be detachable; for there
will be *some* contexts of utterance in which the normal
implication will not hold; *e.g.,* the spokesman who an-
nounces, "The next conference will be either in Geneva
or in New York" perhaps does not imply that he does
not know which; for he may well be just not saying which.
This points to the fact that the implication is cancellable;
a man could say, "My wife is either in the kitchen or in
the bedroom" in circumstances in which the implication
would normally be present, and then go on, "Mind you,
I'm not saying that I don't know which"; this might be
unfriendly (and perhaps ungrammatical) but would be
perfectly intelligible. Finally, the fact that the utterance
of the disjunctive sentence normally involves the implication of the speaker's ignorance of the truth-values of the
disjuncts is, I should like to say, to be explained by reference to a general principle governing the use of language.
Exactly what this principle is I am uncertain, but a *first
shot* would be the following: "One should not make a
weaker statement rather than a stronger one unless there
is a good reason for so doing." This is certainly not an
adequate formulation but will perhaps be good enough
for my present purpose. On the assumption that such a
principle as this is of general application, one can draw
the conclusion that the utterance of a disjunctive sentence
would imply the speaker's ignorance of the truth-values
of the disjuncts, given that (*a*) the obvious reason for not
making a statement which there is some call on one to
make is that one is not in a position to make it, and given
(*b*) the logical fact that each disjunct entails the disjunctive, but not *vice versa;* which being so, the disjuncts are
stronger than the disjunctive. If the outline just given is on
the right lines, then I would wish to say, we have a reason
for refusing in the case of (4) to regard the implication of
the speaker's ignorance as being part of the meaning of
the word 'or'; someone who knows about the logical rela-

tion between a disjunction and its disjuncts, and who also knew about the alleged general principle governing discourse, could work out for himself that disjunctive utterances would involve the implication which they do in fact involve. I must insist, however, that my aim in discussing this last point has been merely to indicate the position I would wish to take up, and not to argue seriously in favour of it.

My main purpose in this sub-section has been to introduce four ideas of which I intend to make some use; and to provide some conception of the ways in which they apply or fail to apply to various types of implication. I do not claim to have presented a systematic theory of implication; that would be a very large undertaking and one for another occasion.

IV

(*The objection reconsidered*)

Let us now revert to the main topic of this section of my paper. Let us call a statement of the type expressible by such a sentence as "it looks red to me" an *L*-statement. What are we to say of the relation between an *L*-statement and the corresponding *D*-or-*D* condition, in terms of the ideas introduced in the previous sub-section? Or, rather, since this might be controversial, what would my objector think it correct to say on this subject? As I have represented his position, he is explicitly committed to holding that the fulfilment of the appropriate *D*-or-*D* condition is a necessary pre-condition of a *L*-statement's being either true or false. He is also more or less explicitly committed to holding that the implication that the *D*-or-*D* condition is fulfilled is a matter of the meaning of the word "looks" (or of the phrase "looks to me"); that, for example, someone who failed to realise that there existed this implication would *thereby* show that he did not fully understand the meaning of the expression or phrase in question. It is conceivable that this last-mentioned thesis is independent of the rest of his position, that he could if necessary abandon it without destroying the remainder of his position. I shall not, therefore, in what follows address myself directly to this point, though I have hopes that it may turn out to be *solutum ambulando*. Next, he would, I think, wish to say that the implication of the fulfilment of the *D*-or-*D* condition is neither detachable nor cancellable; but even if he should not wish to say this, he certainly *must* say it if his objection is to be of any importance. For if the implication is detachable or cancellable, all that the sense-datum theorist needs to do is to find some form of words from which the implication is detached or in which it is cancelled, and use this expression to define the notion of a sense-datum. It is not enough that *some* ways of introducing sense-data should be vulnerable to his objection; it is essential that *all* should be vulnerable. Finally, it is not obvious that he is committed either to asserting or to denying any of the possibilities as regards what may be spoken of as being the vehicle of implication, so I shall not at moment pursue this matter, though I shall suggest later that he can only maintain his position by giving what in fact is certainly a wrong answer to this question.

It is now time for the attack to begin. It seems to me that the contention that the fulfilment of the *D*-or-*D* condition is a necessary condition of the truth or falsity of an *L*-statement cannot be upheld (at any rate in its natural interpretation). For an *L*-statement can certainly be false, even if the *D*-or-*D* condition is unfulfilled. Suppose that I am confronted in normal daylight, by a perfectly normal pillar-box; suppose further that I am in the presence of a normal, unsceptical companion; both he and I know perfectly well that the pillar-box is red. However, unknown to him, I suffer chronically from Smith's Disease, attacks of which are not obvious to another party; these attacks involve, among other things perhaps, the peculiarity that at the time red things look some quite different colour to me. I know that I have this disease, and I am having (and know that I am having) an attack at the moment. In these circumstances I say, "That pillar-box looks red to me". I would suggest that here the *D*-or-*D* condition is not fulfilled; my companion would receive my remark with just that mixture of puzzlement and scorn which would please my objector; and yet when he learnt about my attack of Smith's Disease, he would certainly think that what I had said had been false.

At this point it might perhaps be suggested that though I have succeeded in producing an example of an *L*-statement which would be false, I have not succeeded in producing an example of an *L*-statement which is false when the *D*-or-*D* condition is unfulfilled; for in fact the *D*-or-*D* condition is fulfilled. For the speaker in my little story, it might be said, *has* some reason to doubt whether the pillar-box before him is red, and this is enough to ensure the fulfilment of the condition, *even though* the speaker also has information (*e.g.*, that this is the pillar-box he has seen every day for years, and that it hasn't been repainted and so on) which enables him entirely to discount this *prima facie* reason for doubt. But this will not do at all. For what is this *prima facie* reason for doubting whether the pillar-box really is red? If you like, it is that it looks blue to him. But this is an unnecessarily specific description of his reason; its looking blue to him only counts against its being really red because its looking blue is a way of failing to look red; there need be nothing specially important about its looking blue as distinct from looking any other colour, except red. So this rescue-attempt seems to involve supposing that one way of fulfilling the pre-condition of an *L*-statement's having a truth value at all, consists in its having the truth-value *F*, or at least in some state of affairs which entails that it has the truth-value *F*. But surely, that a statement should be false cannot be one way of fulfilling a pre-condition of that statement's having a truth-value; the mere fulfilment of a pre-condition of a statement's having a truth-value ought to leave it open (to be decided on other grounds) *which* truth-value it has.

Let us assume that this rear-guard action has been disposed of. Then it is tempting to argue as follows: Since

the objector can no longer maintain that fulfilment of the
D-or-*D* condition is a pre-requisite of an *L*-statement's
having a truth-value, he will have to admit that fulfilment
is *at most* a *partial truth*-condition albeit of a special kind
(*i.e.,* is *one* of the things which have to be the case if the
statement is to be true). It cannot be the *only* truth-condition, so there must be another truth-condition; indeed
we can say what this is in the light of the preceding argument; it consists in the non-fulfilment of the statement's
falsity-condition or falsity-conditions (which have just been
shown to be independent of the *D*-or-*D* condition); to
put it less opaquely, it consists in there being nothing to
make the *L*-statement false. But now, it may be thought, all
is plain sailing for the sense-datum theorist; he can simply
lay down that a sense-datum sentence is to express a truth
if and only if the second truth-condition of the corresponding *L*-statement is fulfilled, regardless of whether its first
truth condition (the *D*-or-*D* condition) is fulfilled. It will
be seen that the idea behind this argument is that, once
the objector has been made to withdraw the contention
that the fulfilment of the *D*-or-*D* condition is a condition
of an *L*-statement's having a truth-value, he can be
forced to withdraw also the contention that the implication
that the *D*-or-*D* condition is fulfilled is non-detachable;
and this destroys his position.

So far so good, perhaps, but unfortunately not yet good
enough. For the objector has a powerful-looking reply at
his disposal. He may say: "Once again you are covertly
begging the question. You are assuming, quite without justification, that because one can, in some sense, distinguish
the second truth-condition from the first, it is therefore
the case that the implication of the fulfilment of the first
(*D*-or-*D*) condition is detachable; that is, that there must
be a way of specifying the second condition which does
not carry the implication that the first condition is fulfilled.
But your argument has certainly not proved this conclusion. Consider a simple parallel: it is perfectly obvious that
objects which are not vermilion in colour may or may not
be red; so being red is not a necessary falsity-condition of

being vermilion. It is also true that being red is only a partial truth-condition of being vermilion if what this means is that to establish that something is red is not enough to establish that it is vermilion. But it does not follow (and indeed it is false) that there is any way of formulating a supplementary truth-condition for an object's being vermilion which would be free from the implication that the object in question is red. This *non sequitur* is very much the same as the one of which you are guilty; the fulfilment of the *D*-or-*D* condition may perfectly well be only a *truth*-condition of an *L*-statement, and only *one* of a pair of truth conditions at that, without its being the case that the implication of its fulfilment is detachable." He may also add the following point: "Though the contention that the fulfilment of the *D*-or-*D* condition is a pre-condition of the truth or falsity of the corresponding *L*-statement cannot be upheld under the interpretation which you have given to it, it can be upheld if it is given another not unnatural interpretation. I cannot, in view of your counter-example, maintain that for an *L*-statement to be true, or again for it to be false, the *D*-or-*D* condition must be fulfilled. But I can maintain that the *D*-or-*D* condition's fulfilment is a condition of the truth or falsity of an *L*-statement in the following sense, namely that if the *D*-or-*D* condition *is* fulfilled, then *T* and *F* are the two possibilities between which, on other grounds, the decision lies (*i.e., N* is excluded): whereas if the *D*-or-*D* condition is *not* fulfilled, then one has to decide not between these possibilities, but between the possibilities *N* and *F* (*i.e., T* is excluded)."

This onslaught can I think be met, though at the cost of some modification to the line of argument against which it was directed. I think that the following reply can be made: "There is a crucial difference between the two cases which you treat as parallel. Let us endeavour to formulate a supplementary truth condition for the form of statement '*x* is vermilion'; we might suggest the condition that *x* has the feature which differentiates vermilion things from other red things. But to suppose that *x* satisfies this condition,

but does not satisfy the first truth-condition, namely, that
x should be red, would be to commit a logical absurdity; *x*
cannot logically differ from red things which are not vermilion in *just* the way in which vermilion things differ from
red things which are not vermilion, without being red.
Consequently one cannot assert, in this case, that the second truth-condition is fulfilled without its being implied
that the first is fulfilled, nor can one go on to cancel this
implication. But in the case of an *L*-statement there is no
kind of *logical* implication between the second truth-condition and the first. For one thing, if there were such a
logical connexion, there would also have to be such a logical connexion between the *L*-statement itself and the fulfilment of the *D*-or-*D* condition; and if this were so, the
implication that the *D*-or-*D* condition is fulfilled would
have to be carried by *what was said or asserted* by the
utterance of an *L*-statement. But that this is not so can be
seen from the unacceptability of such an hypothetical as
'If this pillar-box looks red to me, then I or someone else
is, or might be, inclined to deny that it is red or to doubt
whether it is red.' For another thing, it is surely clear
that if I were now to say 'Nothing is the case which would
make it false for me to say that the palm of this hand looks
pink to me, though I do not mean to imply that I or anyone else is or might be inclined to deny that, or doubt
whether, it is pink' this would be a perfectly intelligible
remark even though it might be thought both wordy and
boring. Indeed I am prepared actually to say it. Consequently, although you may be right in claiming that it
has not been shown that the implication of the fulfilment
of the *D*-or-*D* condition is *detachable* (and indeed it may
well be non-detachable), you must be wrong in thinking
that this implication is not *cancellable*. Admittedly there
is at least one case in which an implication which is not
logical in character is at least in a sense, non-cancellable;
we found one in considering example (2) 'She was poor
but she was honest.' But if we look a little more closely we
can see that the reason why the implication here is, in a
sense, not cancellable is just that it *is* detachable (by the

use of 'and'). More fully the reason why it would be peculiar to say 'She was poor but she was honest, though I do not mean to imply that there is any contrast' is that any one who said this would have *first* gone out of his way to find a form of words which introduced the implication, and *then* would have gone to some trouble to take it out again. Why didn't he just leave it out? The upshot is, that if you say that the implication of the fulfilment of the *D*-or-*D* condition is (*a*) not logical in character and (*b*) not detachable, then you must allow that it is cancellable. And this is all that the sense-datum theorist needs." If there is an answer to this argument, I do not at present know what it is.

I will conclude by making three auxiliary points.

(1) If I am right in thinking that my objector has gone astray, then I think I can suggest a possible explanation of his coming to make his mistake. His original resistance to attempts to distinguish between the facts stated by an *L*-statement and the fulfilment of the *D*-or-*D* condition arose I think from a feeling that if the *D*-or-*D* condition were unfulfilled there would be no facts to state; and this feeling is I suspect the result of noticing the baffling character that the utterance of an *L*-statement would have in certain circumstances. But precisely *what* circumstances? I think the sort of imaginary example the objector has in mind may be the following: I and a companion are standing in front of a pillar-box in normal daylight. Each of us has every reason to suppose that the other is perfectly normal. In these circumstances he says out of the blue "This pillar-box looks red to me" and (it is assumed) I am not allowed to take this as a joke. So I am baffled. I do not know what to make of his utterance. But surely the reason why I am baffled is that I cannot see what communication-function he intends his utterance to fulfil; it has the form of an utterance designed to impart information, but what information could he possibly imagine would be imparted to me which I do not already possess. So of course this utterance is baffling. But what the objector

may not have noticed is that if in these circumstances my companion had said not "This pillar box looks red to me" but "This pillar box is red", his utterance would have been equally baffling, if not *more* baffling. My point can be stated more generally. The objector wants to attribute to *L*-statements certain special features (*e.g.*, that of being neither *T* nor *F* in certain circumstances) which distinguish them from at least some other statements. If so, he cannot derive support for his thesis from the fact that the utterance of an *L*-statement would be baffling in certain circumstances, when those circumstances are such that (*mutatis mutandis*) they would make *any statement whatever* baffling. He ought to take as his examples not *L*-statements made about objects which both speaker and audience can see perfectly clearly, but *L*-statements made about objects which the speaker can see but the audience cannot. But when the examples are thus changed, his case seems much less plausible.

(2) If I am asked to indicate what it would be *right* to say about *L*-statements and the implications involved in these utterances, I shall answer: very much the same sort of thing as I have earlier in this page suggested as regards disjunctive statements. I don't want to duplicate my earlier remarks, so I will deal with this very briefly. (i) The fulfilment of the relevant *D*-or-*D* condition is not a condition either of the truth *or* of the falsity of an *L*-statement, though if this condition is not fulfilled the utterance of the *L*-statement may well be extremely misleading (in its implication). (ii) Like my examples (3) and (4) above, we may speak either of the speaker or of his saying what he did say as vehicles of the implication; the second of these possibilities is important in that, if I am right about it, it leads to point (iii). (iii) The implication is not detachable in my official sense. For if the implication can be regarded as being carried by his saying that (rather than something else), *e.g.*, his mentioning *this* fact or putative fact rather than some other fact or putative fact, then it seems clear that any other way of stating the same fact or putative fact would involve the same implication as the original

way of stating the fact in question. (iv) Comparably with examples (3) and (4), the implication is detachable in the further possible non-official sense which I referred to earlier in connexion with (4); there will be *some* conditions of utterance in which the implication is no longer carried, *e.g.*, if I am talking to my oculist about how things look to me. (v) The implication is cancellable (I need say no more about this). (vi) As in the case of example (4), the reason why the implication is *standardly* carried is to be found in the operation of some such general principle as that giving preference to the making of a stronger rather than a weaker statement in the absence of a reason for not so doing. The implication therefore is not of a part of the meaning of the expression "looks to me". There is however here an important difference between the case of *L*-statements and that of disjunctives. A disjunctive is weaker than either of its disjuncts in a straightforward logical sense, namely, it is entailed by, but does not entail, each of its disjuncts. The statement "It looks red to me" is not, however, weaker than the statement "It is red" in just this sense; neither statement entails the other. I think that one has, nevertheless a strong inclination to regard the first of these statements as weaker than the second; but I shall not here attempt to determine in what sense of "weaker" this may be true.

(3) The issue with which I have been mainly concerned may be thought rather a fine point, but it is certainly not an isolated one. There are several philosophical theses or dicta which would I think need to be examined in order to see whether or not they are sufficiently parallel to the thesis which I have been discussing to be amenable to treatment of the same general kind. Examples which occur to me are the following: (1) You cannot see a *knife* as a knife, though you may see what is not a knife as a knife. (2) When Moore said he *knew* that the objects before him were human hands, he was guilty of misusing the word "know". (3) For an occurrence to be properly said to have a cause, it must be something abnormal or unusual. (4) For an action to be properly described as

one for which the agent is responsible, it must be the sort
of action for which people are condemned. (5) What is
actual is not also possible. (6) What is known by me to
be the case is not also believed by me to be the case. I have
no doubt that there will be other candidates besides the
six which I have mentioned. I must emphasize that I am
not saying that all these examples *are* importantly similar
to the thesis which I have been criticizing, only that, for
all I know, they *may* be. To put the matter more generally,
the position adopted by my objector seems to me to involve
a type of manoeuvre which is characteristic of more than
one contemporary mode of philosophizing. I am not con-
demning this kind of manoeuvre; I am merely suggesting that to embark on it without due caution is to risk col-
lision with the facts. Before we rush ahead to exploit
the linguistic nuances which we have detected, we should
make sure that we are reasonably clear what sort of nuances they are.

V

I hope that I may have succeeded in disposing of what
I have found to be a frequently propounded objection to
the idea of explaining the notion of a sense-datum in terms
of some member or members of the suggested family of
locutions. Further detailed work would be needed to find
the most suitable member of the family, and to select the
appropriate range of uses of the favoured member when it
is found; and, as I have indicated, neither of these tasks
may be easy. I shall, for present purposes, assume that
some range of uses of locutions of the form "It looks (feels,
etc.) to X as if" has the best chance of being found suitable. I shall furthermore assume that the safest procedure for the Causal Theorist will be to restrict the actual
occurrences of the term "sense-datum" to such classificatory labels as "sense-datum statement" or "sense-datum
sentence"; to license the introduction of a "sense-datum

terminology" to be used for the re-expression of sentences incorporating the preferred locutions seems to me both unnecessary and dangerous. I shall myself, on behalf of the CTP, often for brevity's sake talk of sense-data or sense-impressions; but I shall hope that a more rigorous, if more cumbrous, mode of expression will always be readily available. I hope that it will now be allowed that, interpreted on the lines which I have suggested, the thesis that perceiving involves having a sense-datum (involves its being the case that some sense-datum statement or other about the percipient is true) has at least a fair chance of proving acceptable.

I turn now to the special features of the CTP. The first clause of the formulation quoted above[3] from Price's *Perception* may be interpreted as representing it to be a necessary and sufficient condition of its being the case that X perceives M that X's sense-impression should be causally dependent on some state of affairs involving M. Let us first enquire whether the suggested condition is necessary. Suppose that it looks to X as if there is a clock on the shelf; what more is required for it to be true to say that X sees a clock on the shelf? There must, one might say, actually be a clock on the shelf which is in X's field of view, before X's eyes. But this does not seem to be enough. For it is logically conceivable that there should be some method by which an expert could make it look to X as if there were a clock on the shelf on occasions when the shelf was empty: there might be some apparatus by which X's cortex could be suitably stimulated, or some technique analogous to post-hypnotic suggestion. If such treatment were applied to X on an occasion when there actually was a clock on the shelf, and if X's impressions were found to continue unchanged when the clock was removed or its position altered, then I think we should be inclined to say that X did not see the clock which was before his eyes, just because we should regard the clock as playing no part in the origination of his impression. Or, to leave the realm of fantasy, it might be that it looked to me as if there were a certain sort of pillar in a certain direction at a certain distance, and there might actually be such a pillar in that place; but if, unknown to me, there were a mirror interposed between myself and the pillar, which reflected a numerically different though similar pillar, it would certainly be incorrect to say that I saw the first pillar, and correct to say that I saw the second; and it is extremely tempting to explain this linguistic fact by saying that the first pillar was, and the second was not, causally irrelevant to the way things looked to me.

There seems then a good case for allowing that the suggested condition is necessary; but as it stands it can hardly be sufficient. For in any particular perceptual situation there will be objects other than that which would ordinarily be regarded as being perceived, of which some state or mode of functioning is causally relevant to the occurrence of a particular sense-impression: this might be true of such objects as the percipient's eyes or the sun. So some restriction will have to be added to the analysis of perceiving which is under consideration. Price[4] suggested that use should be made of a distinction between "standing" and "differential" conditions: as the state of the sun and of the percipient's eyes, for example, are standing conditions in that (roughly speaking) if they were suitably altered, all the visual impressions of the percipient would be in some respect different from what they would otherwise have been; whereas the state of the perceived object is a differential condition in that a change in it would affect only some of the percipient's visual impressions, perhaps only the particular impression the causal origin of which is in question. The suggestion then is that the CTP should hold that an object is perceived if and only if some condition involving it is a differential condition of some sense-impression of the percipient. I doubt, however, whether the imposition of this restriction is adequate. Suppose that on a dark night I see, at one and the same time, a number

[4] *Op. cit.*, p. 70 [p. 398, this volume. Ed.].

of objects each of which is illuminated by a different torch; if one torch is tampered with, the effect on my visual impressions will be restricted, not general; the objects illuminated by the other torches will continue to look the same to me. Yet we do not want to be compelled to say that each torch is perceived in such a situation; concealed torches may illuminate. But this is the position into which the proposed revision of the CTP would force us.

I am inclined to think that a more promising direction for the CTP to take is to formulate the required restriction in terms of the way in which a perceived object contributes towards the occurrence of the sense-impression. A conceivable course would be to introduce into the specification of the restriction some part of the specialist's account, for example to make a reference to the transmission of light-waves to the retina; but the objection to this procedure is obvious; if we are attempting to characterize the ordinary notion of perceiving, we should not explicitly introduce material of which someone who is perfectly capable of employing the ordinary notion might be ignorant. I suggest that the best procedure for the Causal Theorist is to indicate the mode of causal connexion by examples; to say that, for an object to be perceived by X, it is sufficient that it should be causally involved in the generation of some sense-impression by X in the kind of way in which, for example, when I look at my hand in a good light, my hand is causally responsible for its looking to me as if there were a hand before me, or in which . . . (and so on), *whatever that kind of way may be;* and to be enlightened on that question one must have recourse to the specialist. I see nothing absurd in the idea that a non-specialist concept should contain, so to speak, a blank space to be filled in by the specialist; that this is so, for example, in the case of the concept of seeing is perhaps indicated by the consideration that if we were in doubt about the correctness of speaking of a certain creature with peculiar sense-organs as *seeing* objects, we might well wish to hear from a specialist a comparative account of the human eye and the relevant sense-organs of the creature in question. We do not, of course, ordinarily need the specialist's contribution; for we may be in a position to say that the same kind of mechanism is involved in a plurality of cases without being in a position to say what that mechanism is.[5]

At this point an objection must be mentioned with which I shall deal only briefly, since it involves a manoeuvre of the same general kind as that which I discussed at length earlier in this paper. The CTP as I have so expounded it, it may be said, requires that it should be linguistically correct to speak of the causes of sense-impressions which are involved in perfectly normal perceptual situations. But this is a mistake; it is quite unnatural to talk about the cause, say, of its looking to X as if there were a cat before him unless the situation is or is thought to be in some way abnormal or delusive; this being so, when a cause can, without speaking unnaturally, be assigned to an impression, it will always be something other than the presence of the perceived object. There is no natural use for such a sentence as "The presence of a cat caused it to look to X as if there were a cat before him"; yet it is absolutely essential to the CTP that there should be.

In reply to this objection I will make three points. (1) If we are to deal sympathetically with the CTP we must not restrict the Causal Theorist to the verb 'cause'; we must allow him to make use of other members of the family of causal verbs or verb-phrases if he wishes. This family includes such expressions as "accounts for", "explains", "is part of the explanation of", "is partly responsible for", and it seems quite possible that some alternative formulation of the theory would escape this objection. (2) If I regard myself as being in a position to say "There is a cat", or "I see a cat", I naturally refrain from making the weaker statement "It looks to me as if there were a cat before me", and so, *a fortiori*, I refrain from talking about the cause

[5] It might be thought that we need a further restriction, limiting the permissible degree of divergence between the way things appear to X and the way they actually are. But objects can be said to be seen even when they are looked at through rough thick glass or distorting spectacles, in spite of the fact that they may then be unrecognizable.

of its looking to me thus. But, if I was right earlier in this paper, to have made the weaker statement would have been to have said something linguistically correct and true, even if misleading; is there then any reason against supposing that it could have been linguistically correct and true, even if pointless or misleading, to have ascribed to a particular cause the state of affairs reported in the weaker statement? (3) *X* is standing in a street up which an elephant is approaching; he thinks his eyes must be deceiving him. Knowing this, I could quite naturally say to *X*, "The fact that it looks to you as if there is an elephant approaching is accounted for by the fact that an elephant is approaching, not by your having become deranged." To say the same thing to one's neighbour at the circus would surely be to say something which is true, though it might be regarded as provocative.

I have extracted from the first clause of the initial formulation of the CTP an outline of a causal analysis of perceiving which is, I hope, at least not obviously unacceptable. I have of course considered the suggested analysis only in relation to seeing; a more careful discussion would have to pay attention to non-visual perception; and even within the field of visual perception the suggested analysis might well be unsuitable for some uses of the word 'see', which would require a stronger condition than that proposed by the theory.

VI

Is the CTP, as so far expounded, open to the charge that it represents material objects as being in principle unobservable, and in consequence leads to scepticism about the material world? I have some difficulty in understanding the precise nature of the accusation, in that it is by no means obvious what, in this context, is meant by "unobservable".

(1) It would be not unnatural to take "unobservable" to

mean "incapable of being perceived". Now it may be the case that one could, without being guilty of inconsistency, combine the acceptance of the causal analysis of perceiving with the view that material objects cannot in principle be perceived, if one were prepared to maintain that it is in principle impossible for material objects to cause sense-impressions but that this impossibility has escaped the notice of common sense. This position, even if internally consistent, would seem to be open to grave objection. But even if the proposition that material objects cannot be perceived is consistent with the causal analysis of perceiving, it certainly does not appear to be a consequence of the latter; and the exposition of the CTP has so far been confined to the propounding of a causal analysis of perceiving.

(2) The critic might be equating "unobservable" with "not directly observable"; and to say that material objects are not directly observable might in turn be interpreted as saying that statements about material objects lack that immunity from factual mistake which is (or is supposed to be) possessed by at least some sense-datum statements. But if "unobservable" is thus interpreted, it seems to be *true* that material objects are unobservable, and the recognition of this truth could hardly be regarded as a matter for reproach.

(3) "Observation" may be contrasted with "inference" as a source of knowledge and so the critic's claim may be that the CTP asserts or implies that the existence of particular material objects can only be a matter of inference. But in the first place, it is not established that the acceptance of the causal analysis of perceiving commits one to the view that the existence of particular material objects is necessarily a matter of inference (though this view is explicitly asserted by the second clause of Price's initial formulation of the CTP); and secondly, many of the critics have been phenomenalists, who would themselves be prepared to allow that the existence of particular material objects is, in some sense, a matter of inference. And if the complaint is that the CTP does not represent the inference as being of the right kind, then it looks as if the critic

might in effect be complaining that the Causal Theorist is not a Phenomenalist. Apart from the fact that the criticism under discussion could now be made only by someone who not only accepted Phenomenalism but also regarded it as the only means of deliverance from scepticism, it is by no means clear that to accept a causal analysis of perceiving is to debar oneself from accepting Phenomenalism; there seems to be no patent absurdity in the idea that one could, as a first stage, offer a causal analysis of 'X perceives M', and then re-express the result in phenomenalist terms. If the CTP is to be (as it is often regarded as being) a rival to Phenomenalism, the opposition may well have to spring from the second clause of the initial formulation of the theory.

There is a further possibility of interpretation, related to the previous one. If someone has seen a speck on the horizon which is in fact a battleship, we should in some contexts be willing to say that he has seen a battleship; but we should not, I think, be willing to say that he has observed a battleship unless he has recognized what he has seen as a battleship. The criticism levelled at the CTP may then be that it asserts or entails the impossibility in principle of *knowing,* or even of being reasonably assured, that one is perceiving a particular material object, even if one is in fact perceiving it. At this point we must direct our attention to the second clause of the initial formulation of the CTP, which asserted that "perceptual consciousness is fundamentally an inference from effect to cause". I shall assume (I hope not unreasonably) that the essence of the view here being advanced is that anyone who claims to perceive a particular material object M may legitimately be asked to justify his claim; and that the only way to meet this demand, in the most fundamental type of case, is to produce an acceptable argument to the effect that the existence of M is required, or is probably required, in order that the claimant's current sense-impressions should be adequately accounted for. A detailed exposition of the CTP may supplement this clause by supplying general principles which, by assuring us of correspondences between causes and effects, are supposed to make possible the production of satisfactory arguments of the required kind.

It is clear that, if the Causal Theorist proceeds on the lines which I have just indicated, he cannot possibly be accused of having *asserted* that material objects are unobservable in the sense under consideration; for he has gone to some trouble in an attempt to show how we may be reasonably assured of the existence of particular material objects. But it may be argued that (in which is perhaps a somewhat special sense of "consequence") it is an unwanted consequence of the CTP that material objects are unobservable: for if we accept the contentions of the CTP (1) that perceiving is to be analysed in causal terms, (2) that knowledge about perceived objects depends on causal inference, and (3) that the required causal inferences will be unsound unless suitable general principles of correspondence can be provided, then we shall have to admit that knowledge about perceived objects is unobtainable: for the general principles offered, apart from being dubious both in respect of truth and in respect of status, fail to yield the conclusions for which they are designed; and more successful substitutes are not available. If this is how the criticism of the CTP is to be understood, then I shall not challenge it, though I must confess to being in some doubt whether this is what actual critics have really meant. My comment on the criticism is now that it is unsympathetic in a way that is philosophically important.

There seem to me to be two possible ways of looking at the CTP. One is to suppose an initial situation in which it is recognized that, while appearance is ultimately the only guide to reality, what appears to be the case cannot be assumed to correspond with what is the case. The problem is conceived to be that of exhibiting a legitimate method of arguing from appearance to reality. The CTP is then regarded as a complex construction designed to solve this problem; and if one part of the structure collapses, the remainder ceases to be of much interest. The second way of looking at the CTP is to think of the causal analysis of perceiving as something to be judged primarily on its intrinsic merits and not merely as a part of a solution to a prior epistemological problem, and to recognize that some version of it is quite likely to be correct; the remainder of the CTP is then regarded as consisting (1) of steps which appear to be forced upon one if one accepts the causal analysis of perceiving, and which lead to a sceptical difficulty, and (2) a not very successful attempt to meet this difficulty. This way of looking at the CTP recognizes the possibility that we are confronted with a case in which the natural dialectic elicits distressing consequences (or rather apparent consequences) from true propositions. To adopt the first attitude to the exclusion of the second is both to put on one side what may well be an acceptable bit of philosophical analysis and to neglect what might be an opportunity for deriving philosophical profit from the exposure of operations of the natural dialectic. This, I suggest, is what the critics have tended to do; though, no doubt, they might plead historical justification, in that the first way of looking at the CTP may have been that of actual Causal Theorists.

It remains for me to show that the CTP can be looked upon in the second way by exhibiting a line of argument, sceptical in character, which incorporates appropriately the elements of the CTP. I offer the following example. In the fundamental type of case, a *bona fide* claim to perceive a particular material object M is based on sense-datum statements; it is only in virtue of the occurrence of certain sense-impressions that the claimant would regard himself as entitled to assert the existence of M. Since the causal analysis of perceiving is to be accepted, the claim to perceive M involves the claim that the presence of M causally explains the occurrence of the appropriate sense-impressions. The combination of these considerations yields the conclusion that the claimant accepts the existence of M *on the grounds that* it is required for the causal explanation of certain sense-impressions; that is, the existence of M is a matter of causal inference from the occurrence of the sense-impressions. Now a model case of causal inference would be an inference from smoke to fire; the acceptability of such an inference involves the possibility of establishing a correlation between occurrences of smoke and occurrences of fire, and this is only possible because there is a way of establishing the occurrence of a fire otherwise than by a causal inference. But there is supposed to be no way of establishing the existence of particular material objects except by a causal inference from sense-impressions; so such inferences cannot be rationally justified. The specification of principles of correspondence is of course an attempt to avert this consequence by rejecting the smoke-fire model. [If this model is rejected, recourse may be had to an assimilation of material objects to such entities as electrons, the acceptability of which is regarded as being (roughly) a matter of their utility for the purposes of explanation and prediction; but this assimilation is repugnant for the reason that material objects, after having been first contrasted, as a paradigm case of uninvented entities, with the theoretical constructs or *entia rationis* of the scientist, are then treated as being themselves *entia rationis*.]

One possible reaction to this argument is, of course, "So much the worse for the causal analysis of perceiving"; but, as an alternative, the argument itself may be challenged, and I shall conclude by mentioning, without attempting to evaluate, some ways in which this might be done. (1) It may be argued that it is quite incorrect to describe many of my perceptual beliefs (*e.g.,* that there is now a table in front of me) as "inferences" of any kind, if this is to be taken to imply that it would be incumbent upon me, on demand, to justify by an argument (perhaps after acquiring further data) the contention that what appears to me to be the case actually is the case. When, in normal circumstances, it looks to me as if there were a table before me, I am entitled to say flatly that there is a table before me, and to reject any demand that I should justify my claim until specific grounds for doubting it have been indicated. It is essential to the sceptic to assume that any perceptual claim may, without preliminaries, be put on trial and that innocence, not guilt, has to be proved; but this assumption is mistaken. (2) The allegedly 'fundamental' case (which is supposed to underlie other kinds of case), in which a perceptual claim is to be establishable purely on the basis of some set of sense-datum statements, is a myth; any justification of a particular perceptual claim will rely on the truth of one or more further propositions about the material world (for example, about the percipient's body). To insist that the 'fundamental' case be selected for consideration is, in effect, to assume at the start that it is conceptually legitimate for me to treat as open to question all my beliefs about the material world at once; and the sceptic is not entitled to start with this assumption. (3) It might be questioned whether, given that I accept the existence of M on the evidence of certain sense-impressions, and given also that I think that M is causally responsible for those sense-impressions it follows that I accept the existence of M *on the grounds that* its existence is required in order to account for the sense-impressions. (4) The use made of the smoke-fire model in the sceptical argument might be criticized on two different grounds. *First,* if the first point in this paragraph is well made, there are cases in which the existence of a perceived object is not the conclusion of a causal inference, namely those in which it cannot correctly be described as a matter of inference at all. *Secondly,* the model should never have been introduced; for whereas the proposition that fires tend to cause smoke is supposedly purely contingent, this is not in general true of propositions to the effect that the presence of a material object possessing property P tends to (or will in standard circumstances) make it look to particular persons as if there were an object possessing P. It is then an objectionable feature of the sceptical argument that it first treats non-contingent connexions as if they were contingent, and then complains that such connexions cannot be established in the manner appropriate to contingent connexions. The non-contingent character of the proposition that the presence of a red (or round) object tends to make it look to particular people as if there were something red (or round) before them does not, of course, in itself preclude the particular fact that it looks to me as if there were something red before me from being explained by the presence of a particular red object; it is a non-contingent matter that corrosive substances tend to destroy surfaces to which they are applied; but it is quite legitimate to account for a particular case of surface-damage by saying that it was caused by some corrosive substance. In each case the effect might have come about in some other way.

VII

I conclude that it is not out of the question that the following version of the CTP should be acceptable: (1) It is true that X perceives M if, and only if, some present-tense sense-datum statement is true of X which reports a state of affairs for which M, in a way to be indicated by example, is causally responsible, and (2) a claim on the part of X to perceive M, if it needs to be justified at all, is justified by showing that the existence of M is required if the circumstances reported by certain true sense-datum statements, some of which may be about persons other than X, are to be causally accounted for. Whether this twofold thesis deserves to be called a Theory of Perception I shall not presume to judge; I have already suggested that the first clause neither obviously entails nor obviously conflicts with Phenomenalism; I suspect that the same may be true of the second clause. I am conscious that my version, however close to the letter, is very far from the spirit of the original theory; but to defend the spirit as well as the letter would be beyond my powers.

IV. PERCEPTION AND EMPIRICAL KNOWLEDGE

"APPEAR," "TAKE," AND "EVIDENT"

Roderick M. Chisholm

1. If a man looks toward the roof and *sees* that his cat is there, he is not likely to *say* "I take that to be a cat" or "I have adequate evidence for the proposition or hypothesis that that is a cat." But, I suggest, if he does see that his cat is there, he does take it to be his cat and he does have adequate evidence for the hypothesis that what he sees is his cat. And I would suggest, more generally, that the locution "There is something such that S *perceives that* it is *f*" may be defined as meaning: first, there is something which S takes to be *f*; secondly, S has adequate evidence for the proposition or hypothesis that the thing is *f*; and, lastly, the thing *is f*. By adding qualifications about sense organs we may formulate similar definitions of one of the more important senses of "see" and of "hear."

Such definitions will not be interesting or significant unless we can say what is meant by "take" and by "adequate evidence" without using "see," "hear," or "perceive." Let us begin, then, with the concept of *adequate evidence*.

2. "Adequate evidence" is an *epistemic* term—a term we use in appraising the epistemic, or cognitive, worth of statements, hypotheses, and beliefs. Making use of the locution, "S ought to place more confidence in *h* than in *i*," where "S" may be replaced by the name of a person and "*h*" and "*i*" by the names of propositions, beliefs, statements, or hypotheses, we may explicate some of our more important epistemic terms in the following way. "It would be *unreasonable* for S to accept *h*" means that S ought to place more confidence in *non-h* than in *h*; "*h* is *acceptable*

for S" means that it would not be unreasonable for S to accept h; "h is (epistemically) *indifferent* for S" means that both h and *non-h* are acceptable for S; and "S has *adequate evidence* for h" means that *non-h* is unreasonable for S, or, in other words, that S ought to place more confidence in h than in *non-h*. By making use of the additional locution, "S accepts h," we may define one important use of "know" and one important use of "certain." The locution "S *knows that h* is true" could be said to mean, first, that S accepts h, secondly that S has adequate evidence for h, and, thirdly, that h is true. And "S is *certain* that h is true" could be said to mean, first, that S knows that h is true, and, secondly, that there is no proposition or hypothesis i such that S ought to place more confidence in i than in h.[1]

Our present problem is this: How are we to decide which propositions are evident? Or, more exactly: By means of what principles could our subject S *apply* the locution "S has adequate evidence for h"?

In setting this problem for ourselves—the problem of "the criterion"[2]—we do not presuppose, nor should we presuppose, that there are certain principles which people actually think about, or refer to, in order to *decide* whether they have adequate evidence for their beliefs. The grammarian, similarly, may try to describe the conditions under which, say, people use the imperfect tense rather than the past perfect; but, in so doing, he does not mean to imply that, before using this tense, people think about these conditions or try to decide whether or not they apply.

It is important to note that we cannot answer our question by reference solely to the logic of induction and the theory of probability. For the principles of induction and

[1] If we wish to avoid the word "true" we may replace the locution "S accepts h" by "S accepts the hypothesis that x is f" or "S accepts the hypothesis that . . ."; then, instead of saying "h is true," we may say "x is f" or ". . . ." I have discussed the above concepts in more detail in "Epistemic Statements and the Ethics of Belief," *Philosophy and Phenomenological Research*, Vol. XVI (1956), pp. 447–460.

[2] See Sextus Empiricus, *Outlines of Pyrrhonism*, Books I and II. Cardinal Mercier described the attempts to deal with this problem as works of "criteriology"; see D. J. Mercier, *Critériologie Générale*.

probability will not tell a man which propositions are evident unless he applies them to *premises* which are evident.[3]

In the present paper, I wish to describe and to illustrate one approach to this philosophical problem.

3. I suggest that we consider the analogue of our problem in *moral philosophy*.

What do we regard as the proper way of applying our *moral* terms? To answer this question, let us ask further: How would we go about *defending* a particular application of some moral terms—say, some particular application of the term "right"?

If we say, of some particular act, that that act is *right* and if we are prepared to defend our statement, then we are prepared to appeal to some characteristic *in virtue of which* that act is right. Possibly we are prepared to show that the act is an instance of courage, or of forgiveness, or that it is motivated by a wish to decrease the amount of pain in the world. This characteristic, whatever it may be, is one such that *every* act to which it applies is an act which is right, or which "tends to be right." But it is not a characteristic which we need to describe or identify in distinctly *moral,* or *ethical,* terms. If we wish to point out that someone is motivated by the wish to decrease the amount of pain in the world, or that he is acting courageously, we can convey what we want to convey without using "right" or "good" or "ought" or any other ethical term. Let us say, following Professor Broad, that the characteristic to which we appeal is one which is "right-making."[4]

[3] Indeed, the principles of probability and induction will not tell S whether or not S has adequate evidence for a certain hypothesis h unless two epistemic conditions are fulfilled: (i) S must apply the principles to premises for which he has adequate evidence; and (ii), in so doing, S must not leave out any relevant evidence—i.e., of those hypotheses for which he has adequate evidence, his premises should include all which have a probability relation to h. Carnap refers to this second requirement, which had been formulated by Bernoulli, as the "requirement of total evidence." See Carnap's *Logical Foundations of Probability,* pp. 211 ff., 494.

[4] "Moral characteristics are always dependent upon certain other characteristics which can be described in purely neutral non-moral terms. Let us call those non-moral characteristics whose presence in anything confers rightness or goodness on it *right-making* and

There are three important points to be made about "right-making" characteristics. (1) A "right-making" characteristic is one which can be described and identified in ethically neutral language—without the use of ethical terms. (2) When we find out, or when we show, that a particular act is right, we find out, or show, that the act has some "right-making" characteristic. And (3) every act which is right is right *in virtue of* some "right-making" characteristic of the act—some characteristic such that every act which has that characteristic is right, or "tends to be right." Similar points may be made, *mutatis mutandis,* of such ethical terms as "wrong," "good," and "bad."

Among the traditional tasks of moral philosophy is that of describing characteristics which are "right-making," "wrong-making," "good-making," and the like. In listing such characteristics, the moral philosopher is not providing *definitions* of the ethical terms concerned. We may say, following one ancient usage, that he is providing *criteria* for applying these terms.

Our problem—the "problem of the criterion"—is that of finding similar criteria for applying our epistemic vocabulary.

4. Hobbes said, "The inn of evidence has no signboard." But I suggest that, whenever a man has adequate evidence for some proposition or hypothesis, he is in a state which constitutes a *mark of evidence* for that proposition or hypothesis.

What, then, would be a "mark of evidence" for a proposition or hypothesis *h?* In asking this question, we are asking: What would be a *criterion* by means of which a particular subject S might apply our locution, "S has adequate evidence for *h"?*

Just as there were three points to be made about "right-

---

wrong-making characteristics. And let us define *good-making* and *bad-making* characteristics in a similar way." C. D. Broad, "Some of the Main Problems of Ethics," *Philosophy,* Vol. 21 (1946), p. 103. Compare *Butler's Moral Philosophy,* by A. E. Duncan-Jones, Chapter Eight, Sections 1 and 2; and R. M. Hare, *The Language of Morals,* pp. 80 ff.

making" characteristics, there are three points to be made about marks of evidence—about "evidence-bearing" characteristics.

(1) A mark or criterion, for any subject S, that S has adequate evidence for a given proposition or hypothesis *h*, would be some state or condition of S which could be described without using "know," or "perceive," or "evident," or any other epistemic term. That is to say, it would be a state or condition of S which would be described in language which is "epistemically neutral."

(2) It is tempting to say that a mark for S, that S has adequate evidence for a given proposition or hypothesis *h*, would be some state or condition to which S appeals when he wishes to *show* that he has evidence for *h*—or some state or condition which he *discovers* to hold when he discovers he has adequate evidence for *h*. But the words "discover" and "show," in this present use, are themselves epistemic terms. To *discover* that some condition holds is, among other things, to acquire adequate evidence for believing that it does; and to *show* some other person that some condition holds is, among other things, to enable him to have adequate evidence for believing that it holds. If we are to formulate our second requirement in "epistemically neutral" language, I believe we must say something like this: A mark or criterion, for any subject S, that S has adequate evidence for a given proposition or hypothesis *h* would be some state or condition of S which is such that S could not make any mistake at any time about his *being* in that state or condition at that time. That is to say, S could never believe falsely at any time either that he is in that state at that time or that he is not in that state at that time.

(3) Finally, a mark or criterion, for any subject S, that S has adequate evidence for a given proposition or hypothesis *h* would be a state or condition such that, whenever S is in that state or condition, S has adequate evidence for *h*.[5]

---

[5] Cardinal Mercier formulated three requirements—those of being "internal," "objective," and "immediate"—which would be met by any adequate theory of "certitude." The first and third of his requirements, I think, may be intended to serve the purpose of the second

5. Philosophers have proposed various criteria, or marks, of evidence, but in most cases their proposals fail to meet one or more of the three conditions we have formulated.

We cannot be content to say, as apparently some philosophers would be, that a man has adequate evidence for any proposition which he *knows,* or *remembers,* or *sees,* or *perceives* to be true. For "see," "know," "remember," and "perceive," as here used, are epistemic terms—terms we have defined by means of our locution, "S ought to place more confidence in *h* than in *i.*" Such criteria, therefore, do not meet the first of our conditions.

It has been suggested that we have adequate evidence for any proposition which is accepted by "the scientists of our culture circle." It has also been suggested that we have adequate evidence for any proposition "revealed to us by God." Possibly the words "scientist" and "revealed," in these criteria, fail to conform to our first condition. In any case, both criteria fail to meet the second condition. We are all quite capable of believing falsely at any time that a given proposition is accepted by the scientists of our culture circle at that time or has been revealed to us by God at that time.

According to Descartes, we have adequate evidence for those propositions "we conceive very clearly and very distinctly." This criterion does not seem to meet our third condition. For we can conceive very clearly and very dis-

_____

one I have listed above. His second requirement serves the purpose of the third condition I have listed above. It may be interpreted as also ruling out the philosophical view that statements expressing theories of evidence are neither true nor false. Although Mercier was sensitive to the charge of circularity, he did not formulate a requirement comparable to the first one I have listed above. And the criterion of "certitude" which he proposed does not seem to meet the first of my requirements. He said that we have certitude when the subjects and predicates of our judgments *express* or *manifest* reality; but I believe that the terms "express" and "manifest," as he intended them, are epistemic terms, the meanings of which can be conveyed only by such terms as "know," "evident," or "perceive." See D. J. Mercier, *Critériologie Générale,* Eighth edition (Louvain, 1923), Sections 150–153, and *Manual of Modern Scholastic Philosophy,* Volume I, p. 369.

tinctly what is expressed by many statements we know to be false.

Are there *any* states or conditions which provide us with marks of evidence? I shall try to describe two such states.

6. The locution, "*x* appears so-and-so to S," in one of its many senses, is used to describe one mark of evidence.

Possibly the sense of "appear" I have in mind will be suggested by the following example. Let us consider the statement: "Things which are red usually appear red (look red) in ordinary light." Among the uses of "appear red" ("look red") is one such that, in that use, the statement "Things which are red usually appear red in ordinary light" is analytic. For, in this use, "appears red" may be taken to mean the same as "appears in the way that things which are red usually appear in ordinary light." But there is another use of "appears red" which is such that, in that use, the statement "Things which are red usually appear red in ordinary light" is synthetic. Using "appears red" in this second way, we could say: "There is a certain way of appearing—appearing red—which, as it happens, we have found to be the way in which red things usually appear." (The word "appear" is also intended in this second way in such statements as the following, which are to be found in the writings of empirical philosophers: "We can never know that such things as apples are red unless we first know either that they sometimes appear red or that they resemble, in important respects, things which do appear red.")

In the first of these two uses, the locution "appears so-and-so" functions essentially as a *comparative* locution. When we say of anything that it "appears so-and-so," in this sense, we mean to draw a comparison between the thing and things that *are* so-and-so. We mean to say something like this: "The thing appears the way you would normally expect things that are so-and-so to appear under conditions like these (or under conditions of such-and-such a sort)." But when we use "appears so-and-so" in the second of the two ways I have tried to describe, our statements are not in the same sense comparative statements; "*x* appears so-and-so," in this use, does not entail any such statement as "*x* appears the way things that are so-and-so might normally be expected to appear." Let us say that, in this second use, the locution "*x* appears so-and-so" is used *non-comparatively*.

According to my suggestion, then, the locution "*x* appears so-and-so to S," when used *non-comparatively*, describes a condition which provides S with a mark of evidence for the proposition that *x* appears so-and-so to S. If something appears blue to S (in the non-comparative sense of "appears blue"), then, in being thus "appeared to," S is in a state which provides him with a mark of evidence for the proposition that something appears blue to S.[6] Let us see whether this criterion of evidence fulfills our three conditions.

First, the ways of being "appeared to" in question can be described without using "know," or "perceive," or "evidence," or any other epistemic term. And since they can be described in "epistemically neutral" language, they meet the first of our conditions.

Secondly, if a subject S is "appeared to" in one of the ways in question, then, surely, he could not believe at that time that he is not being thus "appeared to." Nor could he believe that he was being thus "appeared to" at a time when he was not being thus "appeared to." Is it possible for something to appear blue to me while I believe that nothing does, or for me to believe that something appears blue to me at a time when nothing does? (If "appears blue" were meant in its comparative sense, then we should have to say that these things are quite possible. But it is here meant in its non-comparative sense.) We could say: There are ways of appearing which are such that, for any

---

[6] Strictly speaking, a mark of evidence is described, not by "*x* appears so-and-so to S," but by "S is appeared to so-and-so, i.e., in such-and-such a way." The victim of delirium tremens, who says of an hallucinatory elephant or lizard, "That appears pink," may be right in using "pink" and wrong in thinking that *something* appears pink. But he couldn't go far wrong if he said only "I'm appeared pink to"—or, in more philosophical language, "I sense pink."

subject S, whenever S is appeared to in one of those ways, it is false that S believes he is *not* being appeared to in that particular way; and whenever S is not being appeared to in one of those ways, it is false that S believes he *is* being appeared to in that particular way. Hence *appearing* may be said to satisfy the second of the conditions we have proposed for a mark of evidence.

And surely *appearing* satisfies the third of our conditions. Whenever anything appears in such-and-such a way to a subject S (or, better, whenever S is appeared to in such-and-such a way), then S has adequate evidence for the proposition that something is appearing to him (or, better, that he is being appeared to) in that particular way.

To be sure, no one is ever likely to *say* "I have adequate evidence for the proposition that something is appearing blue to me." But a man who is thus appeared to may use this proposition as a premise in the application of probability and induction. For example, if he happens to have adequate evidence for the proposition, "Most of the things that appear blue in this light are blue," if something now appears blue to him, and if he has adequate evidence for no other proposition bearing upon the probability of "This is blue," then he has adequate evidence for the proposition "This is blue." It is in this sense that he may be said to have adequate evidence for "Something appears blue to me."

7. *Empiricism,* as an epistemological thesis, may now be defined by reference to this "appearing" criterion of evidence and to the logic of probability, or confirmation.[7] According to empiricism in its most extreme form, the "appearing" criterion, when supplemented by the logic of probability, affords us our *only* criterion of evidence. If a subject S has adequate evidence for some statement *h*, then, according to this form of empiricism, either (a) *h* describes one of the ways S is being appeared to, in the non-comparative sense of "appear," or (b) *h* is a state-

---

[7] I use "empiricism" in one of its traditional senses. The word has many other meanings, of course, in recent philosophy.

ment which is probable in relation to such non-comparative appear statements.

I think that the philosophers who have accepted this empirical thesis, or some modification of it, have been influenced by certain facts concerning the way in which we defend, or try to justify, our beliefs. But I will not discuss these facts here. Rather, I will note what seems to be one of the limitations of empiricism, as defined, and I will try to formulate an alternative thesis.

The limitation of empiricism, as defined, is that it would seem to lead us to what Hume called "scepticism with regard to the senses." For it is very difficult to think of any proposition about the "external world" which is probable—more probable than not—in relation to any set of propositions about the way in which one is appeared to. That is to say, it is very difficult to think of a set of statements of this sort: one of them is a synthetic statement, attributing some property to a material thing; the others are statements of the form, "I am appeared to in such-and-such a way," where the expression "appeared to in such-and-such a way" has what I have called its non-comparative use; and, finally, the statement about the material thing is probable—more probable than not—in relation to the statements about appearing. If there are no such sets of statements and if the empirical thesis is true, then any synthetic proposition about a material thing would be one which, for each of us, is epistemically *indifferent*—no more worthy of our confidence than is its contradictory. And if all of this were true, we might well conclude, with Hume, that "it is in vain to ask, whether there be body or not?"[8]

[8] *Treatise of Human Nature,* Book I, Part IV, Section ii ("Of Scepticism with regard to the Senses"). Thomas Reid wrote as follows, with respect to the empirical thesis and its apparent sceptical consequence: "A traveler of good judgment may mistake his way, and be unawares led into a wrong track; and while the road is fair before him, he may go on without suspicion and be followed by others; but when it ends in a coal-pit, it requires no great judgment to know that he hath gone wrong, nor perhaps to find out what misled him" (*An Inquiry into the Human Mind,* Chapter One, Section 8). The empiricist may be tempted at this point to accept "phenomenalism"—the

I suggest, however, that there are other marks of evidence. One of them is described by the word "take" which occurs in our definition of "perceive." (And therefore reference to "adequate evidence" in our definition is, in a certain sense, redundant.) I shall restrict myself, in what follows, to certain comments on this additional mark of evidence.

8. What is it for a man to *take* something to have a certain characteristic—to take something to be a cat? First of all, of course, he *believes* that the thing is a cat. Secondly, the thing is appearing to him in a certain way. Thirdly, he believes (or assumes, or "takes it for granted") with respect to one of the ways he is being appeared to, that he would not now be appeared to in just that way if the thing were not a cat. (And undoubtedly he also believes, with respect to certain ways in which he might act, that if he were now to act in those ways he would be appeared to in still other catlike ways—i.e., in ways he would not be appeared to if the thing were not a cat.) And, finally, these beliefs or assumptions were not arrived at as the result of reflection, deliberation, or inference; the man didn't weigh alternatives and then *infer* that the thing was a cat.

More generally, the locution "There is something *x* such that S *takes x* to be *f*" may be said to mean this: there is something *x* such that *x* appears in some way to S; S believes that *x* is *f*; S also believes, with respect to one of the ways he is appeared to, that he would not be appeared to in that way, under the conditions which now obtain, if *x* were not *f*; and S did not arrive at these beliefs as a result of deliberation, reflection, or inference.

If a man *takes* something to be a cat, then, as I have

view that statements about material things may be translated into statements about "appearances"—in the hope that phenomenalism provides a way out of the coal-pit. But we cannot be sure that phenomenalism would provide such a way out, for no one has ever been able to make the required translations. And therefore we have no map to examine.

noted, he is not likely to *say* "I take that to be a cat." He is more likely to say "I *see* that that is a cat."[9] But the fact that he wouldn't *say* "I take that to be a cat" doesn't imply that it's false that he takes the thing to be a cat. When the King dies, his subjects do not *say* "Some public official has passed away." But the fact that they do not say it does not imply it's false that some public official has passed away.

If taking, as thus conceived, is a mark of evidence, then it must satisfy our three conditions. And I believe that it does. For (1) we have been able to say what *taking* is without using any epistemic terms; our description, or definition, does not make use of "know," "evident," "see," "perceive," or any other epistemic term. (2) No one can ever be said to believe falsely, or mistakenly, either that he is, or that he is not, taking something to be a cat. Of course a man may take something falsely to be a cat; i.e., he may *mis*take something for a cat. And a man may believe falsely today that yesterday he took something to be a cat. But no one can believe falsely now, with respect to himself, that he is now taking something to be a cat, or that he is not now taking something to be a cat. (Instead of saying "No one can believe falsely that . . . ," we may say, if we prefer, "It makes no sense to say of anyone that he believes falsely that . . .") And I suggest (3) that if a man takes something to be a cat he thereby has adequate evidence for the proposition or hypothesis that the thing *is* a cat.[10]

This theory of evidence has a kind of "internal" justification. For the hypotheses and propositions for which most of us *have* adequate evidence, if this theory is correct, indicate that most of our "takings" are true—that most of our "takings" are *perceivings*. These hypotheses and propositions indicate, as Peirce pointed out, that human beings have a tendency to make correct guesses and that

[9] If a second man is not sure that our perceiver sees that the thing is a cat, the second man will say "He *takes* it to be a cat" or—what comes to the same thing—"He *thinks he sees* that it's a cat."

[10] H. H. Price suggests a similar view in *Perception*, p. 185.

the human mind is "strongly adapted to the comprehension of the world."[11]

Some of our "takings" are false. And therefore, if what I have been saying is true, there are times when we ought to place more confidence in a false proposition than in its true contradictory. The apparent paradox involved in saying that our false "takings"—our *mis*takes—are a mark of evidence has its analogue in moral philosophy. It is difficult to avoid saying that occasionally the *right* choice— or at least the choice that is *praiseworthy*—leads to consequences which are worse than those which the *wrong*—or *blameworthy*—choice would have led to.

And theories of evidence ("So-and-so, but not such-and-such, is a mark of evidence") are, generally, very much like theories of morals ("So-and-so, but not such-and-such, is invariably *right*"). If there is any good reason to think that statements expressing theories of morals are neither true nor false, then, I feel certain, there is also a good reason to think that statements expressing theories of evidence are neither true nor false.

[11] C. S. Peirce, *Collected Papers*, 6.417.

ULTIMATE EVIDENCE

Roderick Firth

1. Chisholm's paper deals with two topics of fundamental importance for theory of knowledge. In the first
part of his paper (Sections 1 to 4), he explains what he
means by "the problem of the criterion." He maintains
that one of the tasks of the epistemologist is to find and
formulate criteria for the application of epistemic terms
such as "evidence" and "knowledge," just as the moral
philosopher must try to discover right-making characteristics, wrong-making characteristics, good-making characteristics, etc., which are criteria for the application of
ethical terms. In both cases, he asserts, (Section 3) the
problem of the criterion is to be distinguished from the
problem of analyzing concepts or providing definitions
for the terms in question: thus the definitions of epistemic
terms which Chisholm offers at the beginning of his paper,
if they are satisfactory, must not logically entail any particular answer to the issues considered in the second part
of the paper. In this second part (Sections 5 to 8) Chisholm
weighs the merits of two quite different criteria of evidence. He formulates a criterion of "appearing" which
seems to be characteristic of empiricism in one of its traditional forms, and then argues that this criterion must be
supplemented by a criterion of perceptual "taking." I think
that I disagree with Chisholm's views on each of the two
central topics of his paper; and it is possible, because of
the admirable precision and clarity with which Chisholm
has stated the issues, that I can explain the grounds of
my disagreement in a useful way. I shall be primarily

concerned to defend the traditional empiricist theory of knowledge against the charge that the empiricist criterion of evidence is inadequate; but since the case might be prejudiced against the empiricist theory by Chisholm's treatment of criteria in general, I shall first say something about this.

2. To avoid some important questions which are too general to discuss here, I shall assume with Chisholm that we can draw a meaningful distinction, at least in many cases, between the meaning or definition of a given term and those characteristics which are the non-definitive conditions for the application of that term; and, following Chisholm, I shall henceforth refer to the latter, but not to the former, as *criteria* for the application of the term. With respect to Chisholm's ethical analogy, I can agree that there are characteristics of certain actions (e.g., their tendency to promote happiness) which are, in Broad's terminology, "right-making," and which are properly described as *criteria* (at least in the absence of wrong-making characteristics) for the application of the term "right." Thus even if there is an analyzable property of rightness, as naturalistic ethicists commonly maintain, it would be a mistake to identify this property, either in whole or in part, with any of the right-making characteristics. But in the case of epistemic terms like "evidence," "perception," and "knowledge," it seems doubtful to me that the characteristics (or "marks") which Chisholm is seeking are properly described as criteria. In any event, I see no reason for thinking that the "empiricist criterion," as Chisholm describes it, is really nothing but a criterion, or that it would be so considered by most empiricists. For an empiricist might well maintain that this "empiricist criterion" actually follows from the very definition of epistemic terms and is therefore no criterion at all. A statement of the form "S perceives that x is f," when used in an epistemic sense, logically entails the statement "S has adequate evidence that x is f"; and an empiricist might maintain that this in turn *logically entails* that S has certain sense

experiences which support the statement *"x is f"* via certain principles of induction. (Let us call this, for present purposes, "the strong empiricist thesis" in contrast to the "weak empiricist thesis" which is the one formulated by Chisholm as a thesis about criteria.) The validity of this strong empiricist thesis could be tested only by logical analysis of such terms as "perceive" and "adequate evidence": it implies, if we use Chisholm's terminology of appearing to talk about sense experience, that the inductive relationship between the statement that I am being appeared to in a certain way, and the statement that I perceive something to be of such and such a kind, is an essential part of our concepts of "perception" and "adequate evidence," and must be mentioned in any satisfactory definition of these epistemic terms.

Now in view of this fact, it is a matter of crucial importance to determine the status of the definitions which Chisholm offers in the opening paragraphs of his paper. For these are proposed as definitions of epistemic terms such as "perception," "knowledge," and "adequate evidence," and yet they do *not* refer to the inductive relationship which enables us to draw inferences from sense experiences. The basic locutions, in terms of which all the epistemic terms are defined, are the locutions "S ought to place more confidence in *h* than in *i*" and "S accepts *h*"; and there seems to be no reason to suppose that either of these locutions is itself analyzable by reference to the logic of induction from sense experiences. Thus the strong empiricist thesis is ruled out *a priori* if we accept these definitions and interpret the basic locutions in anything like the ordinary way. These definitions have the effect of making epistemic statements into statements about what we ought or ought not to believe, so that anything further which an empiricist might say about the conditions of knowledge and adequate evidence, is restricted to a thesis about criteria (the weak empiricist thesis). We must ask, therefore, whether there is any good reason for accepting such an "ethical interpretation" of epistemic terms.

3. It is a familiar fact that ordinary language, in addition to typically ethical words like "ought," "wrong," and "good," which are commonly used to make statements which might be called "purely ethical," also contains a wide variety of terms which are more commonly used to make statements which are only "derivatively ethical." Most of the words which designate human virtues and vices are derivatively ethical in the sense I have in mind. Thus if we say that Socrates is courageous, our statement would normally be taken as a favorable ethical evaluation of Socrates (however we may interpret "favorable evaluation"); but it would also describe Socrates by attributing to him a trait of character (viz., courage) which is understood to be the ground of the favorable evaluation. The distinction between these two functions of the statement—the evaluative and the ground-descriptive —can be exhibited by comparing "Socrates is courageous" with an analogous statement such as "Socrates is wise," which might express an equally favorable evaluation, but which describes Socrates in a very different way. And it should also be noted that the evaluative implications of words like "courageous" and "wise" can be removed for certain purposes. In a suitable context it is possible to ask, without absurdity, whether it is in any respect good that Socrates should be courageous, and even whether courage in general is a virtue. It makes no difference whether we do or do not regard such questions as odd and uncolloquial: the significant point is that words like "courageous" do have a non-evaluative function which permits them to be used in this special way.

But so, it seems to me, do epistemic words like "adequate evidence," "perception," and "knowledge." If I assert that S has adequate evidence for *h*, my assertion might normally be understood to imply the ethical judgment that S ought to place more confidence in *h* than in non-*h* (Chisholm's definition). But surely it implies more than this: it also indicates the *ground* for saying that S ought to place more confidence in *h* than in non-*h*—the fact, namely, that S has evidence of a certain kind. The distinction between these two functions of the assertion—the ethical and the ground-descriptive—can be exhibited by showing that there are other, quite different, grounds on which we might meaningfully say that S ought to place more confidence in h than in non-h—the fact, for example, that S will be happier if he believes h, or the fact that God wants us all to believe h. In a suitable context, moreover, it is possible to use epistemic terms without their usual ethical implications. In discussing some of the doctrines of pragmatism, for example, or the roles of faith and reason in religion, it is meaningful to ask whether S ought not sometimes to believe h even though he has much stronger evidence of non-h, whether S ought not sometimes to accept on faith doctrines which he cannot be said to know, etc. These facts indicate that epistemic words, like those which designate human virtues and vices, have a ground-descriptive as well as an ethical function. And if this much is granted the strong empiricist thesis cannot be ruled out *a priori*. A philosopher who wishes to defend this thesis can admit that statements of the form "S perceives that x is f" and "S has adequate evidence for h" are normally understood to entail a judgment about what S ought to believe; but he will maintain that these epistemic statements also entail a proposition which indicates the ground of the ethical judgment. And this latter proposition, he will argue, can ultimately be analyzed only by reference to sense experience and the inductive principles which enable us to draw inferences from sense experience.

4. Let us now turn to the second part of Chisholm's paper. Even if we conclude, for the reasons I have given, that Chisholm's ethical interpretation of epistemic terms is incorrect, this second part of his paper (Section 5 to end) can still be construed as a forceful argument against the strong empiricist thesis. To do this it is only necessary to read "empiricist analysis of 'evidence'" for "empiricist criterion of evidence" in the appropriate places. Chisholm's reasons for denying that the criterion of appearing is ade-

quate would be equally good reasons for denying the strong empiricist thesis; and his reasons for preferring the criterion of perceptual taking might even be reasons for holding that the concept of "adequate evidence" cannot be analyzed except in terms of "taking." In order to evaluate these arguments, let us consider how the issues might be construed in more traditional terms, without employing the term "criterion."

Throughout the history of modern philosophy, most empiricists have maintained that our knowledge of the external world can be justified by appealing to perception, together with beliefs based on past perceptions, and that our perceptual judgments can in their turn be justified by appealing to the evidence of the senses. Thus my belief that the garden gate is ajar is justified by the fact that I see a dog digging up the peonies; and my belief that I see a *dog* (rather than a cat, for example) is justified by the character of my sense experience—by the look of the thing, or, in Chisholm's terminology, by the way I am "appeared to." But most empiricists have gone further than this: they have thought that the latter mode of justification (i.e., justification by appeal to sense experience) is evidentially ultimate. It is not, of course, the only way to justify perceptual beliefs. My belief that I see a dog is justified by the fact that I see an animal larger than a cat, that I see an animal digging in the manner characteristic of a dog, etc.; and it is facts of this sort about what I see, rather than facts about my sense experience, which I should probably mention if I were asked, "What makes you think you see a *dog?*" But regardless of what I might or might not say when questioned, it has seemed undeniable to most empiricists that the character of my sense experience provides me with evidence (and usually very good evidence) for thinking that I do (or that I do not) see such and such a thing. Thus the justification of one perceptual judgment (e.g., "I see a dog") by reference to another perceptual judgment (e.g., "I see an animal digging like a dog") is never ultimate: the latter can in turn always be supported by appealing to the evidence of the senses ("It has the look of an animal digging like a dog"). It has been generally agreed, on the other hand, that our judgments about present sense experience cannot in their turn be supported by further evidence: if I assert that something has the look of a dog to me, it does not make sense, unless the words are being used in an extraordinary way, to ask: "What reason have you for thinking that it has the look of a dog to you?" This traditional doctrine about the nature of empirical evidence, as I have so far described it, can be summed up in two propositions: (1) Sense experiences are evidence for perceptual judgments, and (2) Sense experiences are evidentially ultimate.

Now it seems to me that Chisholm does not intend to deny either of these two propositions. He specifically asserts that the fact that something appears blue to me may be evidence, under certain conditions, for the statement "This is blue" (Section 6). And the second proposition —that sense experiences are evidentially ultimate—is implied, I think, by Chisholm's stronger (and, I think, more dubious) thesis that we cannot make mistakes in judging that we are appeared to in a certain way (Section 6). Chisholm does point out, however, that sense experiences are not the *only* things which are evidentially ultimate— that perceptual takings, in particular, are ultimate in exactly the same sense. This would not be denied, to be sure, by philosophers of the empiricist tradition: they would hold, I think, that sense experiences are epistemologically ultimate because they are *experiences,* and that any experiences, whether memory experiences, feelings of emotion, or perceptual takings, are evidentially ultimate for the same reason. But Chisholm's argument does have the effect of challenging the empiricist to justify the preferred epistemological status which has traditionally been given to sense experiences as opposed to perceptual takings. Let us consider how this challenge might be met.

5. In order to do justice to the traditional empiricist theory of evidence, I think that we must consider some further facts about the evidential relationship between sense

experiences and perceptual judgments. As we commonly use the term "adequate evidence" it is quite possible for a person S to have adequate evidence for a true proposition *p* even when he does not happen to believe *p* (and, indeed, even when he believes not-*p*). We might explain S's condition in such cases by saying that he has failed to take certain evidence into account, has failed to draw rational inferences, etc. If we are to preserve this usage when speaking about the evidence for perceptual judgments, we must define our terms so that it is meaningful to make statements like the following: "S sees a dog and he has adequate evidence that he sees a dog, but he cannot decide whether he sees a dog or a cat," "S sees a dog and he has adequate evidence that he sees a dog, but he thinks he sees a cat," and "S sees a pink rat and he has adequate evidence that he sees a pink rat, but he thinks he's having an hallucination." And there is, of course, a familiar sense of "see" which does permit us to make these statements. It is not, however, the (equally important) sense of "see" which Chisholm defines in his opening paragraph, for the idiom there introduced—"S perceives (sees) that something is *f*"—entails that there is something which S takes to be *f;* and this in turn entails that there is something which S *believes* to be *f* (Section 8). If we were to talk about perception only in terms of this idiom, therefore, we should have to draw our examples of adequate evidence only from cases in which we actually believe the proposition for which the evidence is said to be adequate. And this would prejudice the issue against the traditional empiricist theory of evidence, for it would prevent us from appealing to those crucial cases in which there is no state of perceptual taking which could possibly serve as evidence for our perceptual statement.

Let us suppose, for example, that I look down from a window at dusk and see an animal in the garden, but I am in doubt whether I see a cat or a small dog. So long as I remain in a state of doubt, I can correctly be said to take something to be an animal; but I do not take something to be a cat and I do not take something to be a dog. In such a case my doubt cannot be resolved by appealing to a perceptual taking, even if we grant that perceptual takings are usually valid. The only ultimate evidence to which I can possibly appeal—assuming that I do not acquire new evidence by going down, for example, into the garden—is the evidence of my visual sense experience. Let us suppose, furthermore, that I am soon able to decide, on reflection, that the look of the thing is characteristic of a black cocker spaniel, so that I no longer have any doubt that I am seeing a dog. In such a case it would surely not be plausible to maintain that I acquired adequate evidence only when I ceased to doubt. If my visual sense experience did not change in any appreciable way, it would be true to say that I had adequate evidence for the statement "I see a dog" even when I did not think that I was seeing a dog. And this is enough to show that there are *some* cases in which sense experience provides adequate evidence for a perceptual statement and perceptual takings do not. It cannot be shown, on the other hand, by analogous methods, that there are any cases in which the contrary is true—cases in which perceptual takings provide adequate evidence for a perceptual statement and sense experience does not. The reason for this is suggested by Chisholm's definition of "S takes x to be f" (Section 8); for this definition recognizes the fact that whenever we take x to be f, we always have sense experiences which we believe to be good evidence that x is f. I think, therefore, that the epistemologist who is looking for ultimate criteria of adequate evidence for perceptual statements, or who wishes to analyze the concept of adequate evidence, is justified in concluding that sense experiences are essential and perceptual takings are not. This does not mean, of course, that perceptual takings are not good evidence for perceptual statements. They are good evidence, however, only in virtue of the truth of the general proposition that most of our "takings" are true. And this general proposition can be justified without circularity, once we admit that perceptual takings are not essential evidence in the justification of perceptual statements.

6. In conclusion I shall comment very briefly on an important methodological question which is raised by Chisholm's rejection of the traditional empiricist theory of evidence on the ground that it leads to skepticism about our knowledge of the external world (Section 7). It seems to me that the epistemologist who wants to formulate a schema for the justification of our knowledge of the external world, is faced with two quite different tasks. He must first select his premises. And in order to restrict these to a minimum, he must select them from among the statements which are evidentially ultimate: they must be statements about sense experiences, for example, and memory experiences—statements which cannot themselves be justified by inference from other statements. At this stage he can be guided only by our actual practice in justifying our beliefs, and there can be no question about the rationality of our actual practice in general. If we do in fact treat sense experiences as evidence for our perceptual statements, then they *are* evidence for our perceptual statements; and if, as I have maintained, we do not treat perceptual takings as essential to an adequate justification, then it is not necessary to include statements about perceptual takings among our premises.

Once our premises have been chosen, however, the character of the enterprise changes. It now becomes in part the purely logical task of exhibiting the principles of inference which are implicit in our treating of (say) sense experiences and memory experiences as adequate evidence; and, since the nature of these principles will depend on the meaning of the statements we are trying to justify, it becomes in part the task of choosing among rival ontological theories like phenomenalism and causal realism. It seems clear to me, however, that under no circumstances could these tasks justifiably lead us to a skeptical conclusion, for at this second stage we are merely exhibiting the logic of an evidential relationship which has already been established by the only methods possible. If we reject phenomenalism we may be surprised or shocked at the principles of inference which are needed to get

from our premises to our conclusion; but this is no
ground for skepticism, nor even, I think, for supposing
that we have started from the wrong premises. Thus it
seems to me that the principal issues which Chisholm and
I have been discussing must be settled (to use Reid's
analogy, as quoted by Chisholm) at the beginning of the
road, in full confidence that it cannot end in a coal pit.

THE PROBLEM OF PERCEPTION

A. M. QUINTON

I

The problem of perception is to give an account of the relationship of sense-experience to material objects. This relationship has traditionally been seen as logical, a matter of showing how beliefs about objects can be established or supported by what we know in immediate experience. For, it is held, only our knowledge of experience is direct, immediate, by acquaintance; what we know or claim to know about objects is indirect, derivative, by inference from what we know directly. Consequently if our beliefs about objects are to have any secure foundation, it must consist in what we know directly, by acquaintance, about sense-data. From this starting-point philosophers have gone on to present varying accounts of the type of inference involved. An extreme view is Hume's, that the passage from experiences to objects rests on 'a kind of fallacy or illusion'. Lockean causal theories assert that the connexion between experiences and objects is contingent and that knowledge of experience is good inductive evidence for beliefs, logically distinct from it about objects. The species of inference involved is transcendental hypothesis of the type to be found in scientific arguments for the existence of such unobservables as electrons or chromosomes. For phenomenalism the connexion between experiences and objects is necessary, to speak of objects is to speak in an abbreviated way about certain pervasive kinds of regularity in experience. The species of inference involved is simple inductive extrapolation. There are not two worlds, an inner and an outer, but two terminologies. The terminology of objects is used to refer to what is invariant as between the private worlds of experience.

Each view derives strength from the weaknesses of its opponent. The most emphasised weakness of phenomenalism is that, if it were true, unobserved objects would be mere possibilities and actual effects would have to arise from merely potential causes. Mill's view that objects are permanent possibilities of sensation is confronted by a fundamental and unargued incredulity. A more serious difficulty arises about the antecedents of the hypothetical statements which describe the permanent possibilities in question. For these antecedents mention objects. To assume, as phenomenalists often cheerfully do, that these references can be replaced by references to 'orienting experiences' is to beg the very question at issue. One cannot *assume* that statements about experiences are equivalent in meaning to statements about objects in order to *show* that they are. Against the causal theory it is argued that, given the sense-datum theory, it would be impossible ever to know that the logically distinct, unobservable, transcendental causes existed. For a causal inference is only legitimate if it is at least possible to obtain evidence for the existence of the cause which is independent of the events it is held to explain.

In the face of this impasse sense-datum theorists have tended to adopt a middle position of compromise. Causal theorists liken their procedure to the 'model-building' of natural scientists. The external world is a theoretical construction, fruitful and various in its predictive and explanatory consequences. Phenomenalists modify their thesis of the strict logical equivalence of statements about experiences and about objects, in view of the difficulties, in principle and practice, of translating one into the other. Both extremes are abandoned in favour of the view that it is a simple, convenient and fruitful theoretical construction. But this is rather a method of refusing to face the difficulties than of overcoming them. For what sort of theoretical construction is involved, a substantial model of the not-yet-observed like a theory of atomic structure or a mere *façon de parler* like theories of magnetic and gravitational fields?

My purpose in this paper is to overcome these difficulties by a more radical procedure, that of refuting the premise from which both problematic doctrines derive, that we are never directly aware of or acquainted with objects.

My principal target will be the conception of direct awareness or acquaintance itself. The sense-datum theory holds that corresponding to the two kinds of objects of knowledge are two kinds of knowledge—direct and indirect. Thus while no knowledge of material objects is direct, all or only knowledge of experience is direct. In more linguistic terms, while no statements about objects are basic, all or only statements about experience are basic. A piece of knowledge, then, is direct if, and only if, it can be expressed by a basic statement. But this translation is of little help since neither of the crucial terms, 'direct' and 'basic', is clearly intelligible, let alone more intelligible than the other.

Two main kinds of definition are commonly offered of these expressions, one in terms of certainty, the other in terms of inference. By the former I directly know that p (or 'p' is a basic statement) if I know for certain that p. It is held that beliefs about objects are never certain, beliefs about experience are always certain and that for any uncertain belief to be even probable something else must be certain. Consequently all beliefs about objects that are to any extent probable must be logically derived from beliefs about experience. I shall hold that all three of the premises for this conclusion are false. The incorrigibility of statements about experience has been defended, notably by Ayer, on the ground that the only mistakes to which we are liable in making such statements are 'verbal'. I shall attempt to show that this too is false. Sometimes a definition in terms of inference is preferred. I directly know that p (or 'p' is a basic statement) if I know that p without inference. It is not, of course, maintained that in coming to form a belief about an object I undertake any conscious process of reasoning. What is involved is 'implicit' inference. Nevertheless, it is held, reasons exist for beliefs about objects which it is the philosopher's business to render explicit and without reference to which no justification of these beliefs can be provided. I shall argue that there is no relevant sense of 'reason' in which a reason for them always exists.

Why should this have been thought to be so? The sense-datum theory, seemingly a variant of the empiricist principle that all our knowledge of matters of fact is based on sense-experience, tends to assume that principle's authority. But this, like other oracles, owes much of its reputation to ambiguity. It can be taken to assert three different things, two of which are uncontentious while the third deserves close inspection. First, it is an unexciting truth of physiology that sensations, physical stimulations of the sense-organs, are causally necessary conditions of our knowledge of matters of fact. Second, the establishment of any truth about objects logically requires that someone shall have seen, touched or otherwise perceived something. The chains of inference and testimony cannot hang unsupported but must terminate in observation. In this use 'sense-experience' does not mean anything so definite as 'sense-datum', it has no phenomenological flavour. Seeing a tomato is just as much an observation as seeing a round, red, shiny patch. Finally, 'based on sense-experience' can be taken to mean 'logically derived from sense-experience'. The logical derivation in question here is of statements about objects from statements about experiences. It is this third interpretation of the principle that constitutes the sense-datum theory and which I shall attempt to refute.

These definitions of 'direct' and 'basic' in terms of certainty and inference are not, however, the starting-points of sense-datum theories of perception. They are rather conclusions to the argument from illusion in terms of which the expressions 'direct' and 'basic' are normally introduced. This argument holds that objects are not always what they appear to be and that there need be no discov-

erable difference between two situations in one of which
an object is and in the other is not what it appears to be.
In consequence, all that we really know is what appears
to be the case, since, even when what appears to be the
case *is* the case, we cannot there and then tell whether it
is or not. Since we know only what appears to be the case,
the only things we really perceive are appearances. Some
philosophers have protested weakly against the later stages
of this argument. I hope to substantiate and fortify their
protest.

The mistake lies in the identification of what appears
to be the case with our sense-experience. We always know
what appears to be the case. So it is appearances, not objects, that we really perceive. But what else are these appearances but our current sense-fields, our sense-experience? The three forms of words; 'this appears to be ϕ',
'there is a ϕ appearance', 'there is a ϕ sense-datum', are held
to be equivalent in meaning. I shall argue that a statement
of what appears to be the case is rarely a description of
our sense-experience and is normally a modified, guarded
claim about what *is* the case, expressing an inclination to
believe something about objects. The ostensible firmness
and incorrigibility of these assertions is a consequence, not
of their referring to a class of private, given entities, but
rather of the modesty of the claim they make. So what
the argument from illusion establishes is not that we always infallibly know what our sense-experience is like, but
only that, whether or not we *know* what is the case, we can
always say, without much fear of contradiction, what we
are inclined to *believe* is the case. These statements do not,
then, express a special kind of direct knowledge by acquaintance nor are they premises from which statements
about objects could be inferred. For they are not claims
to knowledge at all, but more or less tentative expressions
of belief, and what is tentatively affirmed is precisely the
same as, and thus cannot be a premise for, what, in the
conclusion of the supposed inference, we claim to know
without hesitation. I shall argue, however, that we can, and
rather infrequently do, describe our experience and that

we can do this in statements containing such expressions as 'look', 'appear' and 'seem'.

The consequences of this distinction of 'appearances' from sense-data are that knowledge about experience is much less common than is widely supposed and that the greater part of our 'knowledge of appearances' is not capable of figuring as premises in inferences to beliefs about objects.

Before embarking on this another familiar argument for the sense-datum theory must be considered: what may be called the argument from scientific knowledge. There is conclusive evidence for the fact that many of our sense-experiences occur appreciably later than the events of which they give us knowledge, in particular the experiences caused by what is astronomically visible or less remotely audible. More generally, every sense-experience is at the end of a temporally extended causal chain whose first member is the supposedly perceived occurrence. Consequently, what we directly perceive, the object of acquaintance, cannot be the same as that about which we claim knowledge. But this involves no new issue of principle. It shows objects and experiences to be temporally distinct where the argument from illusion shows them to be much more generally different in character. It only shows that we do not directly perceive objects if the supposed consequence of the argument from illusion—that we perceive only our sense-experience directly—is already accepted.

The view common to all versions of the sense-datum theory that the perception of objects is really a kind of inference seems to arise from a belief that, while perception proper must be infallible, inference need not be, and thus that all mistakes are fallacies. But both perception and inference are learnt, intelligent activities which we can presumably perform with varying degrees of efficiency and success. That perception is an acquired skill has perhaps been an inducement to regard it as inference to those who suppose all intelligent activities to be species of reasoning.

Ultimately the problem of perception is that of the relation of thought or language to the world. There is a distressing correspondence with primitive cosmology. Some statements are supported by others, but what supports these others, what is tortoise to their elephant? For the whole system of knowledge cannot support itself in mid-air; it is not self-contained. There is a dilemma here. Either the ultimate support is logically related to the body of knowledge and is thus automatically brought inside the body of knowledge, since only statements can stand in logical relations, and, if so, the question of dependence on the extralinguistic world breaks out again. Or it is not and there is no answer in terms of correct inference to the request for a justification of reliance on this ultimate support.

Philosophers have sought to evade this dilemma by recourse to the Janus-faced notion of experience. The fact that we cannot, it seems, have an experience without somehow being conscious or aware of it has seemed to provide foundation-stones for the edifice of knowledge which are at once statements, capable of standing in logical relations to the rest of the structure, and parts, perhaps the sole constituents, of the extralinguistic world, self-describing entities. I shall contend that there are no such things and opt for the second horn of the dilemma which, as I hope to show, is a less painful resting-place than it might seem.

II

Our first problem is to evaluate the argument from illusion. From the unexceptionable premises that things are not always what they appear to be and that we cannot always tell, there and then, whether they are or not, it is concluded that we have direct knowledge only of appearances, never of objects. For there need be no immediately discoverable difference between two appearances of which one is in fact 'veridical' and the other 'delusive'. So what we really perceive are appearances, whether they are veridical or not depends on something that lies outside the perceptual situation. But what are these appearances that we perceive? They are, it is said, sense-data, the given, immediate experience, they are the current states of our sense-fields.

Of some uses of 'appear', 'seem', etc. it is clearly untrue to say that they figure in descriptions of experience. 'They appear to be away', said when the twice-rung doorbell of a house with drawn curtains remains unanswered, means much the same as 'they must be away' or 'they are probably away'. We are not here describing, but drawing conclusions from, what we observe. The word 'appear' serves to indicate that these conclusions are drawn with less than full confidence. There is nothing 'basic' about them.

But there is another use of 'appear' in which no reason can be given for statements containing it and which do report observations. 'It appears to be green' we might say of a distant house. If challenged we can only repeat, or perhaps correct, ourselves or protest, 'well, that is how it appears to me'. But such a statement would normally be made in answer to such questions as 'what colour is that house' and could be replaced by 'it's green, I think' or 'it's green, isn't it?' They report observations in a tentative way where we know, believe or suspect that the circumstances are unfavourable to an accurate report, that there is something wrong with or abnormal about the conditions of observation. They resemble ordinary categorical descriptions, 'that house is green', in subject-matter, but differ from them in expressing inclinations to believe rather than full beliefs.

There is a third use of 'appear', which resembles the one last mentioned, in that no reasons or evidence can be given for statements containing it, but differs from it in that certain conventional conditions of observation are supposed to obtain, whether they do or not. 'It looks to me (here, now) elliptical' we say of a plate we know to be tilted and round, supposing it to be at right angles to our line of vision. This statement answers the question 'how does it strike you, look to you, what exactly do you see?' It is replaceable by 'there is an elliptical patch in the centre of my visual field'. It is in this type of case only that the description of appearances and experience coincide.

Consider that old friend the stick half in, half out, of water. One might say of it (a) 'it is straight', (b) 'it looks bent but is really straight', (c) 'it looks bent', (d) 'it is bent'. Statement (a) is true, (b) describes the stick correctly and points out how one might be led to make a mistake about it if unaware of an abnormality (a refracting medium) in the conditions of observation, (c) gives tentative expression to the inclination mistakenly to believe (d) which is straightforwardly false. 'It looks bent' is the puzzling case. For it may be a guarded way of saying 'it is bent' (denied by 'it isn't bent') or a way of saying 'most people would be inclined to say it was bent' (denied by 'it doesn't') or a way of saying 'it looks bent to me, here, now' (which can only be denied by 'oh surely not').

So, even when not used to give tentative conclusions from evidence, the verb 'appear' and its cognates are seldom used to describe experience, but primarily to give tentative descriptions of objects. In other words, the 'appearances' that survive the argument from illusion as the proper objects of acquaintance are not ordinarily sense-experiences. These seemingly rock-bottom matters of fact are, in a way, incorrigible and, *ex hypothesi,* uninferred. But their incorrigibility is imperfect and spurious. Imperfect because both 'this is ϕ, I think' and 'this is ϕ, most people would say' can be contradicted (by 'it isn't' and 'they wouldn't') and revised accordingly. Spurious because it arises, not from their making a definite claim about something private, but from their making a weak, indefinite claim about something public. And, though uninferred, they cannot play the part of premises in inferences to categorical descriptions of objects. 'This appears to be ϕ' is no more evidence or a reason for 'this is ϕ' than are 'this may be ϕ' or 'this is probably ϕ'. All three are simply modified ways of saying 'this is ϕ', appropriate for one who is inclined, but not inclined quite confidently enough, to make the categorical statement itself.

This is not to deny that we can and do describe our experience. All I have tried to show is that we describe it very much less often than is usually supposed. Being unsure about the circumstances is a common enough occurrence. But the description of experience proper is a sophisticated procedure and one seldom called for. It is an essential accomplishment for painters, broadcasting engineers, doctors of the eye and ear, cooks and experimental psychologists. But unless we fall into their hands there is little need for us to become proficient in it. The sophistication arises with the deliberate supposition that conditions obtain which we have no reason to suppose do so in fact and perhaps every reason to suppose do not. The fact that we have laboriously to learn perspective drawing is an indication of this, as is the notorious unreliability of eye-witnesses.

That we seldom do describe our experience and then usually with difficulty does not entail that we could not set up and become proficient in the use of a private language. But it would involve a remarkable change in our attitude to the world. Normally we observe in a context of beliefs about where we are and what we are doing that the sophisticated naïveté of phenomenology would exclude. To attend to one's experience involves a radical shift in attitude, a determined effort to resist the solicitations of that submerged constellation of beliefs within which our perceptual discoveries are made.

To this extent, then, I am in sympathy with those who have argued that if the stick half in water looks bent then something really *is* bent. When I say the stick looks bent, I should discover, if I were to direct my attention to it, that my visual field contained a bent brown line. Whether it follows from this that I am in some way aware of this feature of my visual field is a question that will be answered later. But there is something to be said against this line of argument which is commonly ignored. No doubt when the stick looks bent, something else is bent. But consider these cases. I see a small glassy object in a radio shop and say 'that looks like a valve'. But in fact it is a wine-glass. For this error there is no sensory cue; it is the out-come of my general beliefs about the contents of radio shops. Again, I see what is in fact half a pair of spectacles beside a box which I mistakenly suppose to be obscuring the rest. Even when I know better, it still looks just like a pair to me but it is unlikely that my visual field contains anything corresponding to the second lens.

I have been at pains to emphasise the uncommon and sophisticated nature of the description of experience be-cause of the supposed consequence of the argument from illusion, that in every perceptual situation, even if no ob-ject is in fact perceived or if objects are misperceived, still something is perceived, our sense-experience. It would seem *prima facie* that one cannot be said to perceive some-thing unless one is in a position to describe it. But I am not in a position to describe my experience unless I am in the appropriate, sophisticated, phenomenological frame of mind.

Normally if someone says mistakenly that he sees some-thing we are not inclined to say that he really saw some-thing else. We should say of Macbeth that he thought he saw the dagger, imagined he could see it, was under the impression he could see it, but that he did not actually see it at all. In cases of illusion, as against hallucination, there will be something that really is perceived, but it will be a perfectly ordinary public object, not a private experi-ence. If I take a piece of mud on the doormat to be a letter, it will be said that what I actually saw was a piece of mud.

In general, it is not the case, when I am mistaken about what I claim to perceive, either that I am in a position to describe my experience or that I would be said really to have perceived my experience. There are reasons, never-theless, which have led philosophers to believe that I am aware of my experience, acquainted with it, in such cir-cumstances.

It is not only when in the hands of those professionally concerned with it that we attend to and describe our ex-

perience. We are sometimes forced to do so by total ignorance of the conditions of observation. Waking up in unfamiliar circumstances we may, if no other assumption
seems inviting, suppose that the conventional phenomenological conditions obtain. In exceptional circumstances of
this kind, as we come round from an anaesthetic for example, a description of our visual experience is a possible
answer to the question 'can you see anything?' But it is
worth noticing that in such cases we can also say, with
even better warrant perhaps, 'no, just a lot of yellow
streaks' instead of 'yes, a lot of yellow streaks'. Only in a
very marginal sense is a description of one's visual experience to be called 'seeing' at all.

In a way, then, we can be said sometimes to 'see' our
visual experience: when we are trying to describe it or
when we are not in a position to describe anything else.
But what of the case of a man lying in the sun on his back
with his eyes open and his mind far away? Does he see
the blue expanse with shifting white patches on it that he
could describe if he were to turn his attention to his visual
field? And what of the man who is carefully watching a
hen to discover where the gap in the hen-run is? Does
he see the green expanse of the downs beyond, that he
would in fact find occupying the greater part of his visual
field if he were to attend to it? Compare these cases with
a less problematic kind of seeing. Suppose you show me
round your garden and afterwards ask me 'did you see the
tulip tree?' If I say 'no', you may say 'you must have done,
it's right beside the summer-house I showed you'. If I still
deny seeing it, even after another look to refresh my memory, then I cannot have seen it. Yet one might be inclined
here to think that I must have seen it all the same. There
it was, ten yards away, in broad daylight, right in the middle of my field of vision. But perhaps I was concentrating
on the summer-house or thinking of something else altogether. One's visual field is in much the same case as the
tulip tree in this example. However far one's attention
may have strayed, it seems, nevertheless, that one is ines-
capably *confronted* by it. So philosophers have said that

whenever we think we see anything we really do see the contents of our visual fields. But this is an extremely hypothetical kind of seeing. All we can say is that if I had been in a different frame of mind I should have noticed the tree; I should have been able to describe the contents of my visual field.

In every perceptual situation, then, we know what appears to be the case, but this is not usually to be in a position to describe our experience. It may be true that we can be said to have sense-experiences in every perceptual situation (they are, no doubt, the *causes* of our inclinations to believe) but this is quite another matter from being aware of them, noticing them, being in a position to describe them, and nothing less than this can be involved in the claim of the sense-datum theory that it is our experience which we really perceive.

But can having experiences and being aware of them be clearly distinguished in this way? For having an experience is a mental event of the kind, it would be argued, the only direct evidence for whose existence is its presence in consciousness. One might distinguish two senses of 'awareness'. In the wider sense I am aware of any mental event that I am in any way conscious of. In the narrower sense I am only aware of what I notice or attend to, of what I am in a position to describe, of what, in fact, I have some statable knowledge of. Now it might be argued that one was aware of all experience in the wider sense and that this was sufficient reason for saying that all experience was really perceived. I do not think that this distinction can be maintained. It is not that we are really aware of a great many things which we do not notice or attend to but rather that we suppose ourselves to have a great deal of experience for whose existence we have little or no direct evidence. For ordinarily 'be aware of' and 'notice' are largely interchangeable. Both imply claims to knowledge. There are differences of nuance: to become aware of a smell of decay is to have it borne in upon one, to notice a smell of decay is to have discovered it. In implying claims to knowledge both words resemble the perceptual verbs 'see', 'hear', etc. One cannot be aware *of* something without knowing something about it, being aware *that* something is the case.

Now we are, perhaps, usually vaguely aware of the character of our experience, but far too indefinitely for the knowledge involved to support the complicated structure of beliefs that the sense-datum theory would erect on it. The faint and undetailed nature of this underlying awareness of experience is attested to by the fact that when asked to recall our experience we have more or less to reconstruct it from the objects perceived. We attend to experience often enough to know the sort of experiences normally associated with various kinds of object in various conditions. When we transfer our attention from objects to experience an enormously richer awareness of the latter is obtained. We then suppose that we were in fact having experiences of as complex and detailed a kind while attending to the objects, although we were unaware of the complexity and detail. This move is not inference supported by recollection, but a convention. It is assumed that, given unchanged objects, medium, and sense-organs, a change of attention brings about no change in the associated experiences. The idealist's problem 'does attention alter its object'? is thus a matter of convention not of fact. The convention described here lays down that it does not. By this a distinction is introduced between experiences which we have and which we are aware of. It gives a sense to the expression 'unnoticed experience'. One could equally well, if not better, opt for the other alternative and speak, not of 'unnoticed', but of 'possible' experiences, that is the experiences one would be aware of were one to adopt the phenomenological frame of mind. There is a close analogy with the problem of unsensed sense-data. Should we speak with Russell of 'sensibilia' or with Ayer of 'possible sense-data'? In each case considerations of continuity urge one convention, conceptual economy and epistemological rigour the other. In our problem continuity makes a stronger claim. For while there is a clear distinction between sensed and unsensed sense-data, there would seem to be an unbroken continuum of grades of awareness. At any rate to have an experience of which one is not aware is not so much an event as the possibility of an event, it is to be able, by appropriately directing one's attention, to become aware of an experience. The nature of these possibilities is discovered inductively. I conclude that, whether we decide to say we have experiences of which we are not aware or merely that we could have them, anything we can say about them or their possibility depends on the limited number we are aware of. It is only these, meagre or absent in most perceptual situations, which we can be said to perceive.

III

I have argued that experience cannot be the sole object of acquaintance since it is not the case that in every perceptual situation we are aware of it. If this argument is accepted it can be reinforced—if not replaced—by considering what is *meant* by saying that experience alone is the object of acquaintance. I shall first consider the view that this is so because only of experience can we have certain knowledge.

That statements about objects can never be certain (an elliptical way of saying that we can never know for certain that they are true) is sometimes affirmed on the ground that they are empirical. For it is an essential feature of empirical statements that they can be shown to be false and, it is argued, if a statement can be false there can be reasonable doubt of its truth. But if there can be reasonable doubt of its truth it cannot be certain. This argument has the notorious consequence that only necessary truths can be certain. This is not, as some have argued, merely inconvenient in assimilating one useful distinction to another, it is the outcome of a definite mistake. For it is not correct to say that a statement is certain only if there *can* be no reasonable doubt of its truth; a statement is certain, rather, if there *is* no reasonable doubt of its truth.

This familiar argument, in trying to prove that no empirical statement is certain, tries to prove too much. For, if it were correct, the supposed difference in epistemological status between objects and experiences could not consist in a difference in respect of certainty between the statements describing them. I shall consider two arguments designed to show that, in fact, there is always reasonable doubt about descriptions of objects. Both assert that descriptions of objects have implications which inevitably 'go beyond' or 'lie outside' the current observation.

The first holds that there is no limit to the set of other statements which follow from a given statement about objects. For at any time, however remote from the time to which the original statement refers, evidence will exist and could be obtained for or against it. If at any time there is no evidence, however tenuous, for or against it, it is then untestable and, therefore, without meaning. At any rate the possibility of evidence arising for any statement, however remote its reference, cannot be ruled out. So, it is argued, however much favourable evidence for the truth of a statement may have accumulated, it is always possible that all the evidence to come may point to and, in the end, enforce the opposite conclusion.

If, as I shall argue later, it is also the case that descriptions of experience can be revised, that there can be evidence for and against them distinct from the occurrence of the experience itself, then precisely the same argument can be applied to them and so no difference in epistemological status is established. In effect this argument comes to the same as the previous one; revision in the face of unfavourable evidence is as much a universal feature of empirical statements as falsifiability.

But, waiving this point for the moment, the argument is fallacious in concluding that statements with 'open consequences' are never certain. For if the statement of unfavourable evidence q is remote, in the way described, from the original statement p, then q alone will not entail the falsity of p but only in conjunction with some generalization or law of nature *r*. So *q* will only falsify or disconfirm *p* to the extent that *r* is accepted as true and applicable. It is not *p* and *q* simply that are incompatible but *p, q and r*. If *q* turns out to be true we are not therefore compelled to abandon *p*. The more remote *q* is from *p*, the more tenuous the connexion, the more we shall be inclined to abandon *r*. This critical point between abandoning *p* and abandoning *r* in face of *q* may be hard to locate, but for every statement it will exist and for every statement circumstances can be indicated in which its 'logical neighbourhood' is so densely populated with favourable evidence that no remote unfavourable evidence whatever would be taken as refuting it. So it does not follow from the fact that the set of a statement's consequences is open that there is always reasonable doubt of its truth.

The second argument about implications asserts that statements about objects are always and necessarily predictive, that they always logically imply something which the current observation is not sufficient to establish. A statement about objects always forms part of a system of beliefs of varying size, at least including assumptions about the normality—or controllable abnormality—of the conditions of observation. But this has no disastrous consequences. In the first place, no infinite regress is generated. The entailed consequences (or assumptions about the conditions of observation) are themselves statements about objects, but *their* entailed consequences (or conditions) will not all be distinct from the original statement. The implications do not fray off endlessly into the unknown, they are, rather, elements in finite, and indeed decently small, systems of mutual support. And in the second place, arising out of this, it is wrong to regard statements about objects as necessarily predictive under all circumstances. For it is perfectly possible to establish all the members of such a set of mutually supporting statements. Knowledge of the conditions of observation constitutes just such a framework which a statement about objects completes, supports and is supported by. I am not here going back on my earlier criticism of the coherence theory. These coherent sets of statements are not self-sufficient. For their members are conventionally correlated with observed situations. Loose talk about semantic or ostensive rules has ignored the indeterminacy of this correlation, the existence of slack in the application of statements about objects which the systems in which they figure take up.

In the normal course of events it is not that the entailed consequences or conditions are yet to be discovered but that they are known already. This 'systematic' character of our knowledge of objects does indeed distinguish it from our knowledge of experience, consistently with what has gone before since it is the logical correlate of the perceptual as against the phenomenological frame of mind. In the extreme, limiting case (waking up, etc.), where we have no knowledge of the conditions, all descriptions of objects are likely to be less than certain. But we are not usually in this unfortunate position and single observations can give us certain knowledge about objects.

Even if statements about objects were never certain this would not prove them to be derived from statements about experience, if being less than certain were not identified with being probable and if it were not held that nothing can be probable unless something else is certain.

The crucial error in these interconnected doctrines is the supposition that certainty and probability are exhaustive as well as mutually exclusive. Any assertion made with full confidence may be called certain but only one kind of assertion made with less than full confidence is called probable. 'It appears to be cloudy over there' is perfectly good, if weak, evidence for 'it will probably rain'. Yet the whole point of saying that it appears to be, rather than that it is, cloudy over there is to indicate lack of confidence, uncertainty. That is, a less than certain conclusion can be based on less than certain premises which are not themselves the result of inference. The word 'probably' qualifies assertions which are both tentatively advanced, held to be less than certain, and are the conclusions of inferences. This latter characteristic allows us always to challenge, to ask for the reasons for, a statement that something is probably the case and warrants the view that probability is always relative to evidence. But this evidence may itself be tentative and less than certain. To express just this 'uninferred' hesitancy is, as was shown earlier, the principal office of the words 'look', 'appear' and 'seem'. But can we describe experience in this way? The sole use we have for forms of words where these verbs are reiterated (it seems to look ϕ) is where neither verb is used to describe experience (I am inclined to think that most people would say it was ϕ). But this does not entail that phenomenological uses of these verbs cannot be tentative, that 'this looks to me, here, now, ϕ' must be certain. To modify these we use adverbial devices like 'roughly', 'more or less', 'sort of' or add the rider 'I think'. We avoid 'appear' and its kin because they suggest assignable reservations, that we realise or suspect something to be amiss with the conditions of observation or, in non-perceptual uses ('he appears to have died about 300 B.C.'), that we realise that better evidence could, in principle, be obtained. But there are no better conditions in which to describe our experiences than those in which they occur, no better evidence than that they occur. The corrigibility of a statement, in other words, does not entail that 'appear' and the rest apply to it; they apply only where assignable reservations are indicated.

Less than certain statements are not all probable; they are so only if they are the conclusions of inferences, and the premises of these inferences may be less than certain without themselves being inferred. They will be what appears to be the case if I can assign the reservations from which my tentativeness arises or what is, I think, roughly the case, if I cannot.

Finally we must consider a familiar argument against the view that all descriptions of experience are certain. A statement of fact must be expressed by a sentence containing a predicate, a general or descriptive word, and must, therefore, involve the classification of what it refers to, the discrimination of this from other things to which the predicate does not apply. Things, including experiences, do not confront us already sorted out, classified, discriminated. And like any other learnt, regular procedure classification can be carried out wrongly. The use of predicates in classifying and discriminating is essentially a matter of relating what we are describing to the things which are the standard for the application of the predicate, with which it is conventionally correlated, by which it is 'ostensively defined'.

For we can and do revise our descriptions of experience, however convinced we were of their correctness at the time we made them. Such revision could only be excluded by the presumption that recollected experiences, formerly described as ϕ, and now recalled as noticeably different from something else we want to call ϕ, must always be misrecollected. But our recollections have a credibility of their own which does not depend on what is recollected matching something which we now describe with the same predicate we applied to it. Not only can we revise past descriptions of experience, we can also be hesitant about present descriptions. Sometimes we can find no precedent for a perfectly distinct and definite but unique impression; sometimes, while inclined to give a certain description, there is some peculiarity in the situation which we cannot precisely identify and which makes us hesitate. There is a range of cases between these extremes of inadequate vocabulary and indistinct experience.

Against this view it is argued that the errors corrected by such a revision are merely *verbal*. 'All that one can properly mean . . . by saying that one doubts whether this (sense-datum) is green is that one is doubting whether "green" is the correct word to use.' (Ayer). But what else is one doubting when one doubts whether this *object* is green? There is a difference, of course, in that one can have another, better, look at the object but not at the sense-datum. But it does not follow from this that all mistakes that do not depend on unfavourable conditions of observation are not really mistakes at all. What, after all, is a 'merely verbal' error? Properly speaking, only mistaken expressions of belief due to slips of the tongue or pen or laziness and inattention. Linguistic incapacity, the source of mistaken descriptions of experience, is quite another matter. Professor Ayer has recently argued that experience is described 'not by relating it to anything else but by indicating that a certain word applies to it in virtue of a meaning-rule of the language'. The suggestion is that the application of meaning-rules is such a simple matter that it is impossible to perform it wrongly except by a slip. But meaning-rules do not have the bemusing simplicity of their 'semantic' formulation (the word 'red' applies to red things). The class of things to which a predicate applies is indeterminately bounded. Some blue things are more obviously blue than others. Again we are not equally and perfectly accomplished in the application of all predicates. We can manage 'red' and 'round' fairly well, but are less efficient with 'mauve' and 'rhomboidal'. Even if we were trained up to the highest pitch of descriptive efficiency with the predicates we do understand, it is wrong to imagine that that notoriously blunt instrument, our descriptive vocabulary, would provide a precisely appropriate caption for every situation, that it could deal exhaustively with the fecundity of experience. Behind this theory of semantic rules lurks a pair of metaphysical assumptions: that universals, in one-one correlation with predicates, are wide open to some kind of direct apprehension and that there is a decent limit to their variety. The implied analogy with the rules by means of which the truths of mathematics and logic are established is misleading. These rules are precise, definite and can be clearly stated and communicated; careful tests can be made of whether they have been employed correctly. No such laborious check of the correct employment of 'meaning-rules' is possible with the private, fluid and unstable constituents of our sense-experience.

Lack of clarity about the relation between the mere occurrence of an experience and its description has contributed to the view that we cannot, without lying or slips, misdescribe experience. Experience just happens. But being what it is we cannot help being aware of it. Yet it occurs in every perceptual situation. This confusion of the phenomenologically scrutinised with the more or less hypothetical unnoticed experience is responsible for the view that simply to have an experience is to know it for what it is. Those who have, consistently enough, denied that experience as such is properly speaking either a kind of knowledge or true or false at all, have avoided the confusion at the cost of abolishing their problem. For from mere events nothing can be logically derived; only from statements, from what can be known to be true, can other statements be inferred.

I conclude that statements about objects and about experience are sometimes certain, sometimes not. In this respect there is no sharp distinction between the two. Whether a description of objects is certain will depend largely on the circumstances in which it is given and what is known about them. Its familiarity and stability will no doubt determine whether a description of experience is certain. We can err about both from linguistic incapacity and the loose correlation of language and the world, about objects on account of unfavourable conditions of observation and about experiences (and occasionally objects) on account of their evanescence. Such difference as there is between the respective sources of error is not sufficient to substantiate a theory of acquaintance or to show one category to be logically prior to the other.

IV

Some philosophers, realising that certainty as a criterion of acquaintance or basic statements is not sufficient to distinguish objects and experience in the way the sense-datum theory requires, have proposed a different definition in terms of inference. On this view we know directly, by acquaintance, what we know without inference; basic statements are primitive, uninferred; and, while no descriptions of experience are inferred, all descriptions of objects are. The task of theory of knowledge, it is held, is to make a rational reconstruction of our knowledge of matters of fact in which the uninferred premises from which alone this knowledge can be validly derived are explicitly set out. It is agreed that we are rarely, if ever, conscious of carrying out these inferences. It is thought, nevertheless, that experiential premises must somehow 'underlie' what we believe about objects.

If this account is correct two conditions must be satisfied. Statements about experience must count as reasons or evidence for statements about objects and they must in some, no doubt rather obscure, sense be accepted by those who make statements about objects. This second, seemingly platitudinous, requirement deserves emphasis. A fact cannot be a man's reason or evidence for an assertion unless, however implicitly, he is aware of it. Someone's implicit or unconscious awareness of facts about objects can be established by observation of his behaviour. But there is no such criterion available for detecting his awareness of his experience. The view, mistaken as I have argued, that we cannot help being aware of our experience no doubt explains why it has not been thought necessary to provide any criterion for the occurrence of this supposed awareness. If my argument against the view that in every perceptual situation we are aware of our own experience is accepted, it follows that the second condition of the inference theory is unsatisfied and that the theory is mistaken. For our experiences could only be our reasons or evidence for our beliefs about objects if we were to become aware of them through adopting a completely different, phenomenological, frame of mind in our traffic with the external world. Like any other facts, facts about experience must be discovered before they can be appealed to. But even if my argument on this is not accepted, the inference theory is mistaken since the first condition mentioned is not satisfied either.

The best proof that statements about experience were

reasons or evidence for statements about objects would be that we did in fact commonly infer from the one to the other. This, however, is admittedly not the case. But, as it stands, this is of little importance. In the first place, the psychological criterion involved is exceedingly vague, seeming to do no more than mark off as cases of inference those in which a thoughtful pause supervenes between observation and announcement. Furthermore, there are many cases, unquestionably of knowledge by inference, where it is not in the least likely that any conscious process of reasoning has taken place. A girl, sitting in the drawing-room, hears the front door slam and says 'Father's home'. I hear a pattering on the roof and say 'it's raining'. I see a small pool on the kitchen floor and say 'the dog has misbehaved'. We only infer consciously in situations that are unfamiliar or complex, in the predicament of the weekend guest or the new boy on the first day of term. The detective, the busybody, the scientist are more or less professionally concerned to make the most of a small stock of data. Conscious, deliberate thinking is both exhausting and infrequent, a last resort to be appealed to only when all habitual capacities have failed. But most of our perceptual knowledge is of familiar states of affairs and acquired in familiar conditions.

That a statement is employed as a premise in a conscious process of reasoning is not the only feature of our use of that statement which shows it to count as a reason or evidence for the conclusion. More fundamental surely, is that we *give* it as our reason when challenged on the other.

Consider these five cases. I can at once reproduce the course of reasoning that led me to say that it is Mother's hat on top of the garage. This is conscious inference, where the reason given is a premise already consciously affirmed. Secondly, I can, without hesitation, answer 'by the way he sways about' when asked how I can tell someone is drunk, although I recollect no process of inferring. Thirdly, I may take some time over or require assistance in accounting for my claim that Towzer is ill by the glazed look in his eye. Fourthly, I may be unable to give any reason of my own and unwilling to accept any reason offered by another for my assertion that X dislikes Y. Yet commonly in this type of case I may be sure a reason does exist for my belief, may be extremely confident of the truth of my belief and turn out, in the end, to be quite right. Finally, consider standing in broad daylight three feet away from a large and perfectly normal chestnut cart-horse and saying 'that is a horse' or, more adventurously, 'that horse is brown'. This resembles the previous case in that one would be quite unable to give or accept any reason whatever for one's assertion. It differs from it in that one would not be in the very least abashed or apologetic about this. For, in these conditions, the challenge 'how can you tell?' is simply devoid of sense.

Still, if it were made, one might perhaps answer 'well, because it looks like a horse'. If this were intended as a description of one's experience, as interchangeable with 'there is now a shiny brown patch of a characteristic shape in the centre of my visual field', it would not be to answer the question but rather to change the subject, perhaps to offer a causal explanation of one's belief. But this interpretation proposed by the sense-datum theory, a wildly unnatural interpretation of what is, in the circumstances, a wildly unnatural remark, is surely mistaken. The statement would more naturally be intended and understood as a modification of, an infusion of tentativeness into, the original claim, expressing a lack of confidence inspired by the nagging question. As such it is not a reason. To repeat oneself in a more cautious way is not to substantiate but merely to attenuate one's original assertion. 'It looks like a horse' resembles 'it is probably a horse' or 'I think it's a horse' and not 'it has thick legs and no horns' which might be advanced to support the claim that some comparatively distant animal was a horse. For there are, of course, plenty of situations in which reasons do exist for statements about objects.

A statement cannot be inferred, then, if no reason or evidence for it exists, or, more exactly, if it does not make sense to ask for or give a reason for it. Whether or not it does make sense to ask for a reason depends on the circumstances in which the statement is made. The sentence, the form of words, 'that is a horse', may be used in an enormous variety of circumstances. In some of these it will make sense to ask 'how can you tell', in others not. The latter may be called the standard conditions of its use. It will be in such circumstances that the use of the sentence will normally be learnt. This accomplished, it will be possible to use it in an increasingly adventurous way in increasingly non-standard conditions. Connexions are established between assertions and their reasons through the discovery of a vast array of factual concomitances. That standard conditions are those in which we learn how to use a sentence helps to explain why the statements they are used to make are basic and uninferred. For in these conditions they are directly correlated with an observable situation, they are not introduced by means of other statements. (This explains 'implicit inference'. I implicitly infer, acknowledge a reason for, a statement if I was introduced to it by means of other statements but can now make it without conscious consideration of them.) For some sentences there are no standard conditions (generalizations or such implicitly general sentences as 'she is naturally shy'). With others the nature of their standard conditions may vary from person to person. A wife will be able to tell at once that her husband is depressed where others have no inkling of the fact. (A difference in capacity that leads us to speak of intuition.) Again prolonged success in a certain nonstandard use of a sentence may lead us to incorporate the conditions of this use into the standard. I say 'it is raining' when I cannot actually see the rain falling but only drops of water bouncing off the wet street. The addition of unwillingness to inability to answer the question 'how can you tell?' shows that these conditions have become standard. Standard conditions are those in which we have a right to feel certain of the truth of an assertion. The suggestion of uncertainty conveyed by the protest 'that's only an inference' would be made more obviously by the equivalent protest 'you are in no position to be sure' (*i.e.* 'these are not standard conditions'). The lawyer, who asks for a description of what one *actually* saw, devoid of inference and conjecture, is asking for a standard description, that is, a description for which the conditions one was then in were standard.

The notions of acquaintance and of the basic statements which it warrants have, therefore, a foundation in our ordinary way of thinking and speaking. The failure to locate them in their right place is due in part to the failure to distinguish between sentences and statements. For because of multiplicity of uses there are no 'basic sentences'. What we know for certain and without inference in any situation is what the circumstances we are in are the standard conditions for. This will normally be a statement about objects. But there are circumstances in which, knowing nothing about the conditions or that they are highly abnormal, we can take no description of objects as standard. In such a situation we can do no more than tentatively say what appears to be the case. If we are not prepared to do this we can, by an appropriate shift of attention, describe our experience. This last-ditch feature of statements about experience is another encouragement to the sense-datum theorist.

More important is the fact that standard conditions are not a perfect guarantee of the truth of a statement made in them. For standard conditions do not involve that all of a statement's entailed consequences have been established. The horse in the example may just possibly be a brilliantly contrived deception, a flat painted board. We could make our standard stringent enough to cater for this, by insisting on the establishment of entailed consequences, without abandoning statements about objects as basic. But it would be laborious and inconvenient to do so. The programme of convenience embodied in our actual standards is abetted by the order of nature which is uniform enough to make the risks of standard description negligible. Our standards depend on contingencies but some contingencies are highly reliable and regular. Error, as Descartes pointed out, is a product of the will rather than the understanding and arises almost entirely with nonstandard descriptions.

This minute residual imperfection is the ultimate source of the sense-datum theory. The metaphysical demand behind the theory is for an infallible basis for knowledge. So a new standard is proposed which is thought to be perfect. The justification of the new standard is that the knowledge of conditions required is always available, conditions are always standard for the description of experience. I have argued that we are not, in fact, always in standard conditions for the description of experience but rather that it is always in our power, by an appropriate shift of attention, to produce such conditions. If this is so, the sense-datum theory can be no more than the proposal of a new and exceedingly cumbrous way of thinking and speaking to be adopted from fear of a very minor risk. But whether it is true or not, whether the sense-datum theory is a proposal or, what it claims to be, an account of what actually occurs, the supposed improvement is illusory. For, in taking steps to set one exaggerated doubt at rest, it provides the opportunity for another to arise. Admittedly descriptions of experience, for which conditions are always standard, do not depend on a knowledge of conditions which may not be forthcoming. But they have weaknesses of their own. The objects we describe are largely stable and persistent; if we are unsure about them we can always look again. But experience is fleeting and momentary; to attend to it again is to make the insecure hypothesis that it has not changed. The systematic, mutually corroborative character of our beliefs about objects is not a weakness but a strength. Similarly the atomic, disconnected character of experiences, which has encouraged the view that they are self-describing entities, is a weakness. I conclude, then, that experiences are not only not in fact the basis of our empirical knowledge but that they would be inferior to the basis we have, since we are just as much open to error about them, though not entirely the same way; and we should have to revise our way of thinking and speaking completely to use them as a basis.

The relation between experiences and objects, then, neither is nor should be logical. On the contrary it is causal, a matter of psychological fact. Our beliefs about objects are based on experience in a way that requires not justification but explanation. Experiences are not *my* reasons for my beliefs about objects—to have an experience is not to know or believe anything which could be a reason in this sense—though they may be *the* reasons for my believing what I do from the point of view of the psychologist. They may, that is, be the causes of my beliefs and explain them. But they could only be my reasons for my beliefs about objects if I already knew something independently about the relations between experiences and objects.

We learn, it is said, to interpret our experiences, to give rein to Hume's principle of the imagination, to apply Kant's schematized category of substance. These forms of words at least point out that perception is an intelligent activity (not an infallible reflex), but they point it out so uncompromisingly that it is overintellectualised. Interpreting experiences suggests literary scholarship or detective work. But not all intellectual processes are types of reasoning. These phrases refer to the psychological preconditions of recognizing objects for what they are. They point out that we must learn to use the language we do use, that this is an exercise of skill not an automatism and, further, that the situations in which any one sentence may be correctly uttered are extremely various. But they do not demand and could not evoke any logical justification of our practice of thinking and speaking of a common world of objects. We cannot set out the logical relation of an assertion about objects with the experiences that occasion it, because there is no such relation. This is not to sever language from the world altogether, the sin of the coherence theory. It is simply to say that the relations that obtain within the body of our knowledge do not also connect it with what is outside.

I have considered the three principal methods of establishing the sense-datum theory: the arguments from illusion, certainty and inference. Those who hold statements about experience to be basic have misconstrued all three. Statements about experience are not known in every perceptual situation, for we cannot know what we are not aware of, they are no more certain than statements about objects and they do not differ from all statements about objects in being uninferred. Doctrines about acquaintance and basic statements are the outcome of a search for perfect standard conditions. But no standard conditions are perfect and there is no reason to say that descriptions of experience are or ought to be our standard. Our empirical knowledge already has a basis and as good a one as we can obtain. It is to be found, as we should expect, in those situations in which the use of our language is taught and learnt.

BIBLIOGRAPHY

The following are a great many of the books and article that have appeared in this century in the philosophy of percep tion. They have been selected and organized according to thei relevance to the issues discussed in this volume. The more com prehensive studies of perception—including most of the book that have appeared on the subject—are listed first, followed by a listing of works on specific topics. The following abbreviation are used: *PAS* for *Proceedings of the Aristotelian Society; AS Sup. Vol.* for *Aristotelian Society Supplementary Volume; Phil* for *Philosophical; Qtly.* for *Quarterly;* and U. P. for Universit Press.

I. COMPREHENSIVE WORKS

Armstrong, D. M. *Perception and the Physical World.* London Routledge & Kegan Paul, Ltd., 1961.

Aune, B. *Knowledge, Mind, and Nature.* New York, Randon House, 1967.

Ayer, A. J. *The Foundations of Empirical Knowledge.* London Macmillan & Co., Ltd., 1940.

———. *Language, Truth, and Logic.* London, V. Gollancz, Ltd. 1946. Second Ed., Chs. III, VII.

———. *The Problem of Knowledge.* London, Penguin Books Ltd., 1956. Ch. 3.

Broad, C. D. *The Mind and Its Place in Nature.* London K. Paul, Trench, Trubner & Co., Ltd., 1925. Ch. IV: "Sense Perception and Matter."

———. *Perception, Physics, and Reality.* Cambridge, Cambridge U. P., 1914.

Chisholm, Roderick M. *Perceiving: A Philosophical Study* Ithaca, Cornell U. P., 1957.

———. "Theory of Knowledge" in *Philosophy: The Princeton Studies: Humanistic Scholarship in America,* by R. M. Chis holm, H. Feigl, W. K. Frankena, J. Passmore, and M. Thomp son. New York, Prentice-Hall, Inc., 1964. Pp. 233–344.

Fogelin, R. *Evidence and Meaning*. London, Routledge & Kegan Paul, Ltd., 1967. Esp. Chs. III and IV.

Fritz, Charles A., Jr. *Bertrand Russell's Construction of the External World*. New York, Humanities Press, 1952.

Hamlyn, D. W. *Sensation and Perception*. London, Routledge & Kegan Paul, Ltd., 1961.

Hirst, R. J. *The Problems of Perception*. London, George Allen & Unwin, Ltd., 1959.

Lean, Martin. *Sense-Perception and Matter*. London, Routledge & Kegan Paul, Ltd., 1953.

Lewis, C. I. *An Analysis of Knowledge and Valuation*. LaSalle, Illinois, The Open Court Publishing Co., 1946.

——. *Mind and the World Order*. New York, C. Scribner's Sons, 1929.

Locke, D. *Perception and Our Knowledge of the External World*. London, George Allen & Unwin, Ltd., 1967.

Mandelbaum, Maurice. *Philosophy, Science, and Sense-Perception*. Baltimore, The Johns Hopkins Press, 1964.

Marc-Wogau, K. *Philosophical Essays*. Lund, Sweden, C. W. K. Gleerup, 1967. Part II.

Merleau-Ponty, M. *The Phenomenology of Perception*. Tr. Colin Smith. London, Routledge & Kegan Paul, Ltd., 1962.

Price, H. H. *Hume's Theory of the External World*. Oxford, The Clarendon Press, 1940.

——. *Perception*. London, Methuen & Co., Ltd., 1932.

Prichard, H. A. *Knowledge and Perception*. Oxford, The Clarendon Press, 1950.

Reichenbach, Hans. *Experience and Prediction*. Chicago, University of Chicago Press, 1938.

Russell, Bertrand. *Human Knowledge, Its Scope and Limits*. New York, Simon and Schuster, 1948. Parts III, VI.

——. *An Inquiry into Meaning and Truth*. New York, Norton and Co., 1940. Chs. VIII–XI.

——. *Our Knowledge of the External World*. London, George Allen & Unwin, Ltd., 1926. III, IV.

——. *Philosophy*. New York, Norton and Co., 1927. Part II.

——. *The Problems of Philosophy*. New York, H. Holt, 1912. Chs. I–V.

Ryle, Gilbert. *The Concept of Mind*. London, Hutchinson & Co., Ltd., 1949. Ch. VII: "Sensation and Observation."

Sellars, Wilfrid. "Empiricism and the Philosophy of Mind," in *Minnesota Studies in the Philosophy of Science*, Vol. 1, ed. Feigl and Scriven. Minneapolis, University of Minnesota Press, 1956. Reprinted in *Science, Perception, and Reality*. London, Routledge & Kegan Paul, Ltd., 1963.

Smythies, J. R. *Analysis of Perception*. London, Routledge & Kegan Paul, Ltd., 1956.

Soltis, J. *Seeing, Knowing and Believing.* London, George Allen & Unwin, Ltd., 1966.

Warnock, G. J. *Berkeley.* London, Penguin Books, Ltd., 1953.

II. Works on Specific Topics

1. *Perception, the Objects of Perception, and the Senses*

Anscombe, G. E. M. "The Intentionality of Sensation: A Grammatical Feature," in *Analytical Philosophy, Second Series,* ed. R. J. Butler. Oxford, Basil Blackwell, Ltd., 1967.

Armstrong, D. M. "Illusions of Sense," *Australasian Journal of Philosophy,* Vol. 33 (1955), pp. 88–106.

Ayer, A. J. "Perception," in *British Philosophy at the Mid-Century,* ed. C. A. Mace. George Allen & Unwin, Ltd., 1957.

Barnes, W. H. F. "On Seeing and Hearing," in *Contemporary British Philosophy,* Third Series, ed. H. D. Lewis. London, George Allen & Unwin, Ltd., 1956.

Baylis, C. A. "Professor Chisholm on Perceiving," *The Journal of Philosophy,* Vol. 56 (1959), pp. 773–91.

Chisholm, Roderick M. "Perception and Verification," *Revue International de Philosophie,* Vol. 5 (1951), pp. 251–67.

Collins, A. "The Epistemological Status of the Concept of Perception," *The Phil. Review,* Vol. 76 (1967), pp. 436–59.

Deutscher, Max. "David Armstrong and Perception," *Australasian Journal of Philosophy,* Vol. 41 (1963), pp. 80–88.

Dewey, John. "The Naturalistic Theory of Perception by the Senses," *The Journal of Philosophy,* Vol. 22 (1925), pp. 596–605.

Dretske, F. "Observational Terms," *The Phil. Review,* Vol. 74 (1965), pp. 25–42.

Duggan, T., and Taylor, R. "On Seeing Double," *Phil. Qtly.,* Vol. 8 (1958), pp. 171–74.

Firth, Roderick. "The Men Themselves; or, the Role of Causation in our Concept of Seeing," in *Studies in the Philosophy of Mind,* ed. Hector-Neri Castaneda. 1965.

Fleming, Noel. "Recognizing and Seeing As," *The Phil. Review,* Vol. 66 (1957), pp. 161–79.

Grice, H. P. "Some Remarks About the Senses," in *Analytical Philosophy,* ed. R. J. Butler. Oxford, Basil Blackwell, Ltd., 1962.

Hamlyn, D. W. *The Psychology of Perception.* London, Routledge & Kegan Paul, Ltd., 1957.

Hampshire, Stuart. "Perception and Identification," *AS Sup.* Vol. XXXV (1961), pp. 81–96.

Hanson, N. R. *Patterns of Discovery*. Cambridge, Cambridge U. P., 1958. Esp. Ch. I: "Observation."

Hardie, W. F. R. "Austin on Perception," *Philosophy*, Vol. 38 (1963), pp. 253–63.

——. "Ordinary Language and Perception," *Phil. Qtly.*, Vol. 5 (1955), pp. 97–108.

Harrod, Sir Roy. " 'Sense and Sensibilia,' " *Philosophy*, Vol. 38 (1963), pp. 227–42.

Hinton, J. M. "Perception and Identification," *The Phil. Review*, Vol. 76 (1967), pp. 421–35.

——. "Seeing and Causes," *Philosophy*, Vol. 41 (1966), pp. 348–55.

——. "Visual Experiences," *Mind*, Vol. 76 (1967), pp. 217–27.

Hirst, R. J. "Perception, Science, and Common Sense," *Mind*, Vol. 60 (1951), pp. 481–505.

King-Farlow, John. "Senses and Sensibilia," *Analysis*, Vol. 23 (1962), pp. 37–40.

Kneale, W. "Sensation and the Physical World," *Phil. Qtly.*, Vol. 1 (1951), pp. 109–26.

Locke, D. "Appearance-Determined Qualities," *Analysis*, Vol. 28 (1967), pp. 39–42.

Malcolm, Norman. "Direct Perception," in *Knowledge and Certainty*. New York, Prentice-Hall, Inc., 1963.

Mundle, C. W. K. "Common Sense vs Hirst's Theory of Perception," *PAS*, Vol. LX (1959–60), pp. 61–78.

——. "Primary and Secondary Qualities," *Analysis*, Vol. 28 (1967), pp. 33–38.

Myers, G. E. "Perception and the Sentience Hypothesis," *Mind*, Vol. 78 (1963), pp. 111–20.

Nelson, John O. "An Examination of D. M. Armstrong's Theory of Perception," *American Phil. Qtly.*, Vol. 1 (1964), pp. 154–60.

Paul, G. A. "Lenin's Theory of Perception," *Analysis*, Vol. 5 (1938), pp. 65–73. Reprinted in *Philosophy and Analysis*, ed. M. Macdonald. Oxford, Basil Blackwell, Ltd., 1954.

Price, H. H. "The Argument from Illusion," in *Contemporary British Philosophy*, Third Series, ed. H. D. Lewis. London, George Allen & Unwin, Ltd., 1956.

——. "Touch and Organic Sensation," *PAS*, Vol. XLIV (1943–44), pp. i–xxx.

Prichard, H. A. "The Apprehension of Time," in *Knowledge and Perception*. Oxford, The Clarendon Press, 1950.

——. "Perception," *ibid*.

——. "Seeing Movements," *ibid*.

Russell, Bertrand. *The Analysis of Mind*. London, George Allen & Unwin, Ltd., 1921. Chs. VII–VIII.

Ryle, Gilbert. "Perception," in *Dilemmas*, Cambridge, Cambridge U. P., 1954.

Severens, R. "Seeing," *Philosophy and Phenomenological Research*, Vol. 28 (1967), pp. 213–21.

Sibley, F. N. "Seeking, Scrutinizing, and Seeing," *Mind*, Vol. 64 (1955), pp. 455–78.

Shwayder, D. S. "The Varieties and the Objects of Visual Phenomena," *Mind*, Vol. 70 (1961), pp. 307–30.

Smart, J. J. C. "Colours," *Philosophy*, Vol. 36 (1961), pp. 121–42.

Smythies, J. R. "The Representative Theory of Perception," in *Brain and Mind*, ed. J. R. Smythies. London, Routledge & Kegan Paul, Ltd., 1965. Pp. 241–57.

Strawson, P. F. "Perception and Identification," *AS Sup. Vol.* XXXV (1961), pp. 97–120.

Swartz, R. J. "Color Concepts and Dispositions," *Synthese*, Vol. 17 (1967), pp. 202–22.

Vander Veer, G. L. "Austin on Perception," *Review of Metaphysics*, Vol. 17 (1964), pp. 557–67.

Vesey, G. N. A. "Berkeley and the Man Born Blind," *PAS*, Vol. 61 (1960–61), pp. 189–206.

White, A. R. "The Alleged Ambiguity of 'See,'" *Analysis*, Vol. 24 (1963), pp. 1–5.

Wittgenstein, Ludwig. *Philosophical Investigations*. Tr. G. E. M. Anscombe. Oxford, Basil Blackwell, Ltd., 1958. Second ed. Part II, xi.

2. *Sense-Data, Sensing, and Appearing*

Alston, W. P. "Is Sense-Datum Language Necessary?" *Philosophy of Science*, Vol. 24 (1957), pp. 41–45.

Austin, J. L. *Sense and Sensibilia*. Reconstructed from the manuscript notes by G. J. Warnock. London, Oxford U. P., 1962.

Ayer, A. J. "Has Austin Refuted the Sense-Datum Theory?" *Synthese*, Vol. 17 (1967), pp. 117–40.

———. "The Terminology of Sense-Data," *Mind*, Vol. 54 (1945), pp. 289–312. Reprinted in *Philosophical Essays*. London, Macmillan & Co., Ltd., 1954.

Bergmann, G. "Sense-Data, Linguistic Conventions, and Existence," *Philosophy of Science*, Vol. 14 (1947), pp. 152–63.

Black, Max. "The Language of Sense-Data," in *Problems of Analysis*. Ithaca, Cornell U. P., 1946.

Bouwsma, O. K. "Moore's Theory of Sense-Data," in *The Philosophy of G. E. Moore*, ed. P. A. Schilpp. Chicago, Northwestern U. P., 1942.

Britton, K. "Seeming," *AS Sup. Vol.* XXVI (1952), pp. 215–34.

Broad, C. D. "Professor Marc-Wogau's *Theorie der Sinnes-data*," *Mind,* Vol. 56 (1947), pp. 1–30, 97–131.
———. "A Reply to My Critics," in *The Philosophy of C. D. Broad,* ed. P. A. Schilpp. New York, Tudor Publishing Co., 1959. "Sense-Perception and Matter," pp. 796–812.
Bronaugh, R. N. "The Argument from the Elliptical Penny," *Phil. Qtly.,* Vol. 14 (1964), pp. 151–57.
Campbell, C. A. "Sense-Data and Judgment in Sensory Cognition," *Mind,* Vol. 56 (1947), pp. 281–316.
Chisholm, Roderick M. "The Problem of the Speckled Hen," *Mind,* Vol. 51 (1942), pp. 368–73.
Collingwood, R. G. "Sensation and Thought," *PAS,* Vol. XXIV (1923–24), pp. 55–76.
Corey, Daniel. "Are Sense-Data 'in' the Brain?" *The Journal of Philosophy,* Vol. 45 (1948), pp. 533–48.
Dore, C. "Seeming to See," *American Phil. Qtly.,* Vol. 2 (1965), pp. 312–18.
Ducasse, C. J. *Nature, Mind and Death.* LaSalle, Illinois, The Open Court Publishing Co., 1951. Chs. 13–15.
Duggan, T. "Thomas Reid's Theory of Sensation," *The Phil. Review,* Vol. 49 (1960), pp. 90–100.
Firth, Roderick. "Austin and the Argument from Illusion," *The Phil. Review,* Vol. LXXIII (1964), pp. 372–82.
Hanson, N. R. "On Having the Same Visual Experiences," *Mind,* Vol. 69 (1960), pp. 340–50.
Hare, P. and Koehl, R. "Moore and Ducasse on the Sense-Data Issue," *Philosophy and Phenomenological Research,* Vol. 28 (1968), pp. 313–31.
Hicks, G. Dawes. "The Basis of Critical Realism," in *Critical Realism,* London, Macmillan & Co., Ltd., 1938.
———. "The Nature of Sensible Appearances," *AS Sup. Vol.* VI (1926), pp. 142–61.
———. "On the Nature of Images," in *Critical Realism.*
———. "Sensible Appearances and Material Things," *ibid.*
———. "The Sensum Theory," *ibid.*
———. "Sense-Presentation and Thought," *PAS,* Vol. VI (1905–6), pp. 271–346.
Hirst, R. J. "The Difference Between Sensing and Observing," *AS Sup. Vol.* XXVIII (1954), pp. 197–218.
Lewis, D. K. "Percepts and Color Mosaics in Visual Experience," *The Phil. Review,* Vol. 75 (1966), pp. 357–68.
Lewy, C. "The Terminology of Sense-Data," *Mind,* Vol. 55 (1946), pp. 166–69.
Marc-Wogau, K. "Gilbert Ryle on Sensation," in *Philosophical Essays Dedicated to Gunnar Aspelin.* Lund, CWK Gleerup Bokförlag, 1963.

——. *Die Theorie der Sinnesdata*. Uppsala, A. B. Lundequitska Bokhandeln, 1945.

——. "On C. D. Broad's 'Theory of Sensa,'" in *The Philosophy of C. D. Broad*, ed. P. A. Schilpp. New York, Tudor Publishing Co., 1959.

Marhenke, Paul. "Moore's Analysis of Sense-Perception," in *The Philosophy of G. E. Moore*, ed. P. A. Schilpp. Chicago, Northwestern U. P., 1942.

Mates, B. "Sense-Data," *Inquiry*, Vol. 10 (1967), pp. 225–44.

Moore, G. E. *Commonplace Book 1919–1953*. London, George Allen & Unwin, Ltd., 1962. I, 25, 32, 34, 35; III, 4, 11, 13, 17–20; IV, 1, 10; V, 4, 8, 17; VII, 11; IX, 17.

——. "A Defense of Common Sense," in *Philosophical Papers*. London, George Allen & Unwin, Ltd., 1959.

——. "The Nature and Reality of the Objects of Perception," in *Philosophical Studies*. London, Routledge & Kegan Paul, Ltd., 1922.

——. "A Refutation of Idealism," *ibid*.

——. "A Reply to my Critics," in *The Philosophy of G. E. Moore*, ed. P. A. Schilpp. Chicago, Northwestern U. P., 1942.

——. "Addendum to my 'Reply,'" *ibid*.

——. "Sense-Data," in *Some Main Problems of Philosophy*. London, George Allen & Unwin, Ltd., 1953.

——. "The Status of Sense-Data," in *Philosophical Studies*.

——. "The Nature of Sensible Appearances," *AS Sup. Vol.* VI (1926), pp. 179–89.

Paul, G. A. "The Analysis of Sense-Data," *Analysis*, Vol. 3 (1935), pp. 12–20.

Price, H. H. "Appearing and Appearances," *American Phil. Qtly.*, Vol. 1 (1964), pp. 3–19.

——. Critical Notice of Ayer, *The Foundations of Empirical Knowledge*, *Mind*, Vol. 50 (1941), pp. 280–93.

——. "The Nature and Status of Sense-Data in Broad's Epistemology," in *The Philosophy of C. D. Broad*, ed. P. A. Schilpp. New York, Tudor Publishing Co., 1959.

——. "The Nature of Sensible Appearances," *AS Sup. Vol.* VI (1926), pp. 162–78.

——. "Reality and Sensible Appearance," *Mind*, Vol. 33 (1924), pp. 20–43.

——. "Seeming," *AS Sup. Vol.* XXVI (1952), pp. 215–34.

Prichard, H. A. "Appearances and Reality," *Mind*, Vol. 15 (1906), pp. 223–29.

——. *Kant's Theory of Knowledge*. London, Oxford U. P., 1909. Ch. IV.

——. "The Sense-Datum Fallacy," in *Knowledge and Perception*. Oxford, The Clarendon Press, 1950.

Quinton, A. M. "Seeming," *AS Sup. Vol.* XXVI (1952), pp. 235–52.

Russell, Bertrand. "On Scientific Method in Philosophy," in *Mysticism and Logic*. New York, Barnes and Noble, Inc., 1917.

——. "The Relation of Sense-Data to Physics," *ibid*.

——. "Reply to Criticisms," in *The Philosophy of Bertrand Russell*, ed. P. A. Schilpp. Chicago, Northwestern U. P., 1944. Pp. 700–6.

——. "The Ultimate Constituents of Matter," in *Mysticism and Logic*.

Sellars, R. W. "Sensations as Guides to Perceiving," *Mind,* Vol. 68 (1959), pp. 2–15.

Stout, G. F. "Are Presentations Mental or Physical?" *PAS,* Vol. IX (1909), pp. 226–47.

Thomas, L. E. "Looking," *Phil. Qtly.,* Vol. 7 (1957), pp. 109–15.

Vesey, G. N. A. "Berkeley and Sensations of Heat," *Phil. Review,* Vol. 69 (1960), pp. 201–10.

White, A. R. *G. E. Moore: A Critical Exposition*. Oxford, Basil Blackwell, Ltd., 1958. Ch. VIII.

Wild, John. "The Concept of the Given in Contemporary Philosophy," *Philosophy and Phenomenological Research,* Vol. 1 (1940), pp. 70–82.

Wisdom, John. *Problems of Mind and Matter*. Cambridge, Cambridge U. P., 1934. Part II.

Wittgenstein, L. "Notes for Lectures on 'Private Experience' and 'Sense-Data,'" *The Phil. Review,* Vol. 77 (1968), pp. 275–320.

Wollheim, R. "The Difference Between Sensing and Observing," *AS Sup. Vol.* XXVIII (1954), pp. 219–40.

Yolton, John W. "A Defense of Sense-Data," *Mind,* Vol. 57 (1948), pp. 1–15.

Yost, R. M., Jr. "Price on Appearing and Appearances," *The Journal of Philosophy,* Vol. 61 (1964), pp. 328–33.

3. *Phenomenalism*

Ayer, A. J. "Phenomenalism," *PAS,* Vol. 47 (1947–48). Reprinted in *Philosophical Essays*. London, Macmillan & Co., Ltd., 1954.

Barker, S. F. *Induction and Hypothesis*. Ithaca, Cornell U. P., 1957. Ch. 6.

Braithwaite, R. B. "Propositions about Material Objects," *PAS,* Vol. XXXVIII (1937–38), pp. 269–90.

Broad, C. D. "Phenomenalism," *PAS*, Vol. XV (1914–15), pp. 227–51.

Firth, Roderick. "Phenomenalism," *Proceedings of the American Philosophical Association, Eastern Division*, Vol. 1 (1952), pp. 1–20.

———. "Radical Empiricism and Perceptual Relativity," *The Phil. Review*, Vol. 59 (1950), pp. 164–83, 319–31.

Marhenke, Paul. "Phenomenalism," in *Philosophical Analysis*, ed. Max Black. Ithaca, Cornell U. P., 1950.

Hardie, W. F. R. "The Paradox of Phenomenalism," *PAS*, Vol. XLVI (1945–46), pp. 127–54.

MacNabb, D. G. C. "Phenomenalism," *PAS*, Vol. XLI (1940–41), pp. 67–90.

Sellars, Wilfrid. "Phenomenalism," in *Science, Perception, and Reality*. London, Routledge & Kegan Paul, Ltd., 1963.

Smart, J. J. C. *Philosophy and Scientific Realism*. London, Routledge & Kegan Paul, Ltd., 1963. Ch. II: "Physical Objects and Physical Theory."

Stace, W. T. "Are All Empirical Statements Merely Hypotheses?" *The Journal of Philosophy*, Vol. 44 (1947), pp. 29–38.

4. *The Causal Theory*

Aaron, R. I. "The Causal Argument for Physical Objects," *AS Sup. Vol.* XIX (1945), pp. 57–76.

Dore, Clement. "Ayer on the Causal Theory of Perception," *Mind*, Vol. 73 (1964), pp. 287–90.

Ewing, A. C. "The Causal Argument for Physical Objects," *AS Sup. Vol.* XIX (1945), pp. 32–56.

MacNabb, D. G. C. "The Causal Argument for Physical Objects," *ibid.*, pp. 77–91.

Price, H. H. "The Causal Argument for Physical Objects," *ibid.*, pp. 92–100.

Watling, J. "The Causal Theory of Perception," *Mind*, Vol. 59 (1950), pp. 539–40.

White, A. R. "The Causal Theory of Perception," *AS Sup. Vol.* XXXV (1961), pp. 153–68.

Whiteley, C. H. "The Causal Theory of Perception," *PAS*, Vol. XL (1939–40), pp. 89–102.

5. *Perception and Empirical Knowledge*

Austin, J. L. "Other Minds," *AS Sup. Vol.* XX (1946), pp. 148–87. Reprinted in *Philosophical Papers*. Oxford, The Clarendon Press, 1961.

Ayer, A. J. "Basic Propositions," in *Philosophical Analysis*, ed. Max Black. Ithaca, Cornell U. P., 1950. Reprinted in *Philosophical Essays*. London, Macmillan & Co., Ltd., 1954.

Baylis, C. A. "The Given and Perceptual Knowledge," in *Philosophical Thought in France and the United States*. Buffalo, University of Buffalo Publications in Philosophy, 1950.

Chisholm, Roderick M. "The Foundation of Empirical Statements," in *The Foundation of Statements and Decisions*, ed. K. Ajdukiewicz. Warsaw, PWN, Polish Scientific Publishers, 1965. Pp. 111–20.

———. "Russell on the Foundations of Empirical Knowledge," in *The Philosophy of Bertrand Russell*, ed. P. A. Schilpp. Chicago, Northwestern U. P., 1944.

Ewing, A. C. "Knowledge of Physical Objects," *Mind*, Vol. 52 (1943), pp. 97–121.

Firth, Roderick. "The Anatomy of Certainty," *The Phil. Review*, Vol. 76 (1967), pp. 3–27.

———. "Chisholm and the Ethics of Belief," *The Phil. Review*, Vol. 70 (1959), pp. 493–506.

———. "Coherence, Certainty, and Epistemic Priority," *The Journal of Philosophy*, Vol. 61 (1964), pp. 545–57.

Goodman, Nelson. "Sense and Certainty," *The Phil. Review*, Vol. 61 (1952), pp. 160–67.

Harman, G. "Unger on Knowledge," *The Journal of Philosophy*, Vol. 64 (1967), pp. 390–95.

Henle, Paul. "On the Certainty of Empirical Statements," *The Journal of Philosophy*, Vol. 44 (1947), pp. 625–32.

Lewis, C. I. "The Given Element in Empirical Knowledge," *The Phil. Review*, Vol. 61 (1952), pp. 168–75.

Malcolm, Norman. "Certainty and Empirical Statements," *Mind*, Vol. 51 (1942), pp. 18–46.

———. "The Verification Argument," in *Philosophical Analysis*, ed. Max Black. Ithaca, Cornell U. P., 1950. Reprinted in *Knowledge and Certainty*. New York, Prentice-Hall, Inc., 1963.

Milmed, B. K. "Lewis' Concept of Expressive Statements," *The Journal of Philosophy*, Vol. 51 (1954), pp. 201–13.

Moore, G. E. "Certainty," in *Philosophical Papers*. London, George Allen & Unwin, Ltd., 1959.

———. "Four Forms of Scepticism," *ibid*.

———. "Hume's Theory Examined," in *Some Main Problems of Philosophy*. London, George Allen & Unwin, Ltd., 1953.

———. "Material Things," *ibid*.

———. "Proof of an External World," in *Philosophical Papers*.

Quinton, A. "The Foundations of Knowledge," in *British Analytical Philosophy*, ed. B. Williams and A. Montefiore. London, Routledge & Kegan Paul, Ltd., 1966.

Reichenbach, Hans. "Are Phenomenal Reports Absolutely Certain?" *The Phil. Review*, Vol. 61 (1952), pp. 147–59.

Russell, Bertrand. "Knowledge by Acquaintance and Knowledge by Description," in *Mysticism and Logic*. New York, Barnes and Noble, Inc., 1917.

——. "On the Nature of Acquaintance," in *Logic and Knowledge*, ed. R. Marsh. London, George Allen & Unwin, Ltd., 1956.

——. "On Our Knowledge of the External World," in *Our Knowledge of the External World*. London, George Allen & Unwin, Ltd., 1926.

Thalberg, I. "Looks, Impressions, and Incorrigibility," *Philosophy and Phenomenological Research*, Vol. 25 (1965), pp. 365–74.

Unger, P. "Experience and Factual Knowledge," *The Journal of Philosophy*, Vol. 64 (1967), pp. 152–73.

Winch, P. G. "The Notion of 'Suggestion' in Thomas Reid's Theory of Perception," *Phil. Qtly.*, Vol. III (1953), pp. 327–41.

Wisdom, John. "Note on Ayer, *Language, Truth, and Logic*," in *Philosophy and Psychoanalysis*. Oxford, Basil Blackwell, Ltd., 1957.

Yolton, John W. "Broad's Views on the Nature and Existence of External Objects," in *The Philosophy of C. D. Broad*, ed. P. A. Schilpp. New York, Tudor Publishing Co., 1959.

The following bibliographical entries represent an update of works on perception, prepared for the 1976 edition.

I. Books

Ayer, A. J. *The Central Questions of Philosophy*. London, Weidenfeld and Nicolson, 1973. Chs. IV, V.

Chisholm, Roderick M. and Swartz, Robert J., Eds., *Empirical Knowledge*. Englewood Cliffs, N. J., Prentice-Hall, Inc., 1973. Chs. II, V.

Dretske, Fred I., *Seeing and Knowing*. Chicago, The University of Chicago Press, 1969.

Ginet, Carl. *Knowledge, Perception, and Memory*. Dordrecht, Holland, D. Reidel, 1975.

Hanson, Norwood Russell. *Perception and Discovery.* San Francisco, Freeman, Cooper, 1969.

Hinton, J. M. *Experiences: An Inquiry Into Some Ambiguities.* Oxford, Clarendon Press, 1973.

Pitcher, George. *A Theory of Perception.* Princeton, Princeton University Press, 1971.

Pollock, J. L. *Knowledge and Justification.* Princeton, Princeton University Press, 1975.

Ross, J. J. *The Appeal to the Given.* London, Allen & Unwin, 1970.

Sibley, F. N., Ed. *Perception.* London, Methuen, 1971.

Vesey, G. N. A. *Perception.* New York, Anchor, 1971.

II. Articles

Aquila, Richard, "Perceptions and Perceptual Judgments," in *Phil. Studies,* Vol. 28 (1975).

Borst, C. V. "Perception and Intentionality," *Mind,* Vol. 79 (1970), pp. 115-121.

Brown, Harold, "Perception and Meaning," *Studies in the Philosophy of Mind,* American Phil. Qtly. Monograph Series, No. 6 (1972), pp. 1-9.

Chisholm, Roderick M., "On the Nature of Acquaintance: A Discussion of Russell's Theory of Knowledge," in *Bertrand Russell's Philosophy,* Ed. George Nakhnikian, London, George Duckworth and Co., Ltd., 1974.

Clark, Romaine, "Sensuous Judgments," *Nous,* Vol. 7 (1973), pp. 45-55.

Cornman, J. W., "On Direct Perception," *Review of Metaphysics,* Vol. 26 (1972), pp. 38-56.

Coval, S. C. and Todd, D. D., "Adjusters and Sense-Data," *American Phil. Qtly,* Vol. 9 (1972), pp. 107-112.

Cox, J. W. Roxbee, "Distinguishing the Senses," *Mind,* Vol. 79 (1970), pp. 530-550.

Doppelt, G., "Dretske's Conception of Perception and Knowledge," *Phil. of Science,* Vol. 40 (1974), pp. 433-446.

Dretske, Fred I., "Perception from an Epistemological Point of View," *The Journal of Philosophy,* Vol. 68 (1971), pp. 584-590.

——, "Seeing and Justification," *Perception and Personal Identity,* Ed. Care and Grimm, Cleveland, Case Western University Press, 1969, pp. 42-52.

Firth, Roderick, "Sense Experience," in *Handbook of Perception,* Ed. by E. C. Carterette and M. P. Friedman, Vol. 1, Ch. 1.

French, Peter A., " 'Seeing' and 'Seeing That,' 'Observing', and 'Observing That'," in *Studies in Epistemology,* American Phil. Qtly. Monograph Series, No. 9 (1975).

Hester, Marcus, "Sensibility and Visual Acts," *American Phil. Qtly.,* Vol. 12 (1975), pp. 299-308.

Hintikka, Jaako, "The Logic of Perception," in *Perception and Personal Identity,* Ed. Care and Grimm, Cleveland, Case Western Reserve University Press, 1969, pp. 140-173.

Howell, R. "Seeing As," *Synthese,* Vol. 23 (1972), pp. 400-422.

Holman, Emmett, "Sensory Experience, Epistemic Evaluation, and Perceptual Knowledge," *Phil. Studies,* Vol. 28 (1975), pp. 173-187.

Jackson, Frank, "On the Adverbial Analysis of Visual Experience," *Metaphilosophy,* Vol. 6 (1975), pp. 127-135.

Johnson, David M., "A Formulation Model of Perceptual Knowledge," *American Phil. Qtly.,* Vol. 8 (1971), pp. 54-62.

Jones, O. R., "After Images," *American Phil. Qtly.,* Vol. 9 (1972), pp. 150-158.

Kiteley, M., "The Argument from Illusion: Object and Objections," *Mind,* Vol. 81 (1972), pp. 191-207.

Knox, John Jr., "Do Appearances Exist," in *Studies in the Theory of Knowledge,* American Phil. Qtly. Monograph Series, No. 4 (1970).

Leeds, Stephen, "Two Senses of 'Appears Red'," *Phil. Studies,* Vol. 28 (1975), pp. 199-205.

Melchert, N., "A Note on the Belief Theory of Perception," *Phil. Studies,* Vol. 24 (1971), pp. 427-429.

McKee, P. L., "A. J. Ayer on the Argument from Illusion," *Canadian Journal of Philosophy,* Vol. 3 (1974), pp. 275-280.

Parsons, Kateryn, "Mistaking Sensations," *Philosophical Review,* Vol. 79 (1970), pp. 201-213.

Pastin, Mark, "C. I. Lewis' Radical Foundationalism," *Nous,* Vol. 9 (1975), pp. 407-420.

Pickering, F. R., "A Refutation of an Objection to the Causal Theory of Perception," *Analysis,* Vol. 34 (1974), pp. 129-132.

Pollock, John, "Perceptual Knowledge," *Phil. Review,* Vol. 80 (1972), pp. 287-319.

———, "The Structure of Epistemic Justification," *Studies in the Theory of Knowledge,* American Phil. Qtly. Monograph Series, No. 4 (1970).

Rogers, G. A. J., "The Veil of Perception," *Mind,* Vol. 84 (1975), pp. 210-224.

Self, D. J., "Sense Data and the Argument from Illusion," *Dialogue,* Vol. 16 (1974), pp. 53-56.

Sellars, Wilfrid, "Giveness and Explanatory Coherence," *The Journal of Philosophy,* Vol. 70 (1973), pp. 612-624.

———, "The Adverbial Theory of the Objects of Sensation," *Metaphilosophy,* Vol. 6 (1975), pp. 144-160.

Slimis, E., "Normal Conditions and Perceivers," *Studies in Epistemology,* American Phil. Qtly. Monograph Series, No. 9 (1975).

Stainsby, H. V., "Austin on Ryle on Seeing and 'Seeing'," *Mind,* Vol. 82 (1973), p. 608.

———, "Sight and Sense-Data," *Mind,* Vol. 79 (1970), pp. 170-187.

Swartz, Robert, "Seeing and Substitutivity," *The Journal of Philosophy,* Vol. 70 (1972), pp. 526-536.

Thalberg, Irving, "Ingredients of Perception," *Analysis,* Vol. 33 (1973), pp. 145-155.

Warnock, G. J., "Seeing and Knowing," *Mind,* Vol. 79 (1970), pp. 281-287.

DATE DUE
